I0223049

# UNIVERSAL IDEOLOGY: THE THOUGHT OF P. R. SARKAR

## Other Books by Chuck and Tom Paprocki

History, Ideology and Revolution:  A Trilogy

Book One:  The Untold Story of Western
Civilization

Volume One:  The Age of Mothers - The
Matriarchy
Volume Two: The Age of Warriors
Volume Three: The Age of Intellectual Priests
Volume Four:  The Age of Merchant Capitalists
Volume Five: Pax Americana

Book Two: Universal Ideology: The Thought
of P. R. Sarkar

Book Three: Nuclear Revolution: A Clarion Call

# UNIVERSAL IDEOLOGY: THE THOUGHT OF P. R. SARKAR

Chuck and Tom Paprocki

Inner World Publications
San German, Puerto Rico
www.innerworldpublications.com

Copyright 2019 by Chuck & Tom Paprocki

All rights reserved under International and
Pan-American Copyright Conventions

Published in the United States by
Inner World Publications
P.O. Box 1613, San German, Puerto Rico, 00683

Library of Congress Control Number: 2020939987
ISBN: 9781881717805

Cover Design:  Tom Paprocki

All rights reserved. This book, or parts thereof, may
not be reproduced in any form or by any means, electronic
or mechanical, including photocopying, recording, or by
any information storage or retrieval system, without the
permission of the publisher except for brief quotations.

Cover Photo:  Prabhat Rainjan Sarkar was born in
India on May 21, 1921. He became a spiritual master in the
Tantrik Yoga tradition of Lord Shiva and Lord Krishna.
He was also a philosopher, author, poet, composer, lin-
guist, and scientist. Unconvinced that the current religious and political ideologies governing human thought
were capable of uniting humanity to resolve our common
social and environment problems, he propounded a universal ideology, which he called Neo-Humanism that
blends spiritual science and social science. To propagate
his ideas he founded Ananda Marga in 1955 whose mission is "self-realization and service to all." P. R Sarkar
denounced capitalism and communism, contending that
materialism keeps human beings from recognizing their
highest potential. As a political revolutionary, he spoke
openly about the corruption in the Indian government
and paid the price of a freedom fighter.

# Dedication

To The Memory of Prabhat Rainjan Sarkar,
our spiritual guide

# Contents

# Chapter Two: Human Nature                          92

# Chapter Three:  Spirituality                           139

# Chapter Five: The Economics of Progressive Socialism                  280

# Introduction

*Light and darkness cannot co-exist. Similarly, devotion or love for God cannot co-exist with hatred, vanity, jealousy, tendency to harm others, divisiveness and any kind of dogma. The true seekers of self-realization or God-realization must not forget or overlook this truth even for a single day, even for a single moment. P. R. Sarkar*

IDEOLOGIES, AS WE DISCOVERED in Book One, *The Untold Story of Western Civilization*, derive from the fundamental need of human beings to understand how the world came into existence and what our purpose is in its flow. Such worldviews usually include ideas about God, nature, human beings, and society. Beneath the daily scenes of our lives, we have always striven to know more about the context of our personal and collective existence. The same perennial questions are asked by each succeeding generation. How did this world come into being? What is the nature of this world? Who made this world? How did humans come to be? What does God want from us? What is the right way to live in this world? These fundamental questions have prompted innumerable stories throughout time, as each tribe or people have developed their own explanations of the meaning of life. In ancient history, these stories were called myths. In the Middle Ages they were called religion. In the modern world, they are called science or philosophy. They are all ideologies.

In the time of pre-history and ancient history, every tribe developed its own creation myth. These myths generally led to the assumption that the world was made and controlled by an all-powerful being, a goddess or god. For example, a Slovenia myth holds that:

God Created the World with his eyes. At the beginning, there was nothing but God, and God slept. His repose lasted for all eternity. But he was destined to wake up. When he woke from sleep he looked around, and every look produced a star. Surprised, God set on a journey to see what his eyes had created.[1]

From the creation myth of the aborigines of Australia:

Now a long, long time ago of course, in the beginning, when there was no people, no trees, no plants whatever on this land, "Guthi-guthi," the spirit of our ancestral being, he lived up in the sky. So he came down and he wanted to create the special land for people and animals and birds to live in. So Guthi-guthi came down and he went on creating the land for the people—after he'd set the borders in place and the sacred sights, the birthing places of all the Dreamings, where all our Dreamings were to come out of.[2]

From the Comanche in southwest United States:

One day the Great Spirit collected swirls of dust from the four directions in order to create the Comanche people. These people formed from the earth had the strength of mighty storms. Unfortunately, a shape-shifting demon was also created and began to torment the people. The Great Spirit cast the demon into a bottomless pit. To seek revenge the demon took refuge in the fangs and stingers of poisonous creatures and continues to harm people every chance it gets.[3]

Everywhere people told themselves stories of how the world came to be. Even though we look at these stories as myths, they hold sentimental power for the people who believe in them. Today Christians and Jews still take the creation myth of Adam, Eve, and the serpent to be true. This myth served to explain to the Jews and Christians their relation to

God and the cause of suffering in the world. Unfortunately, the myth of Adam and Eve has been used by men to dominate and persecute women throughout the entire history of Western Civilization. This is the power of myths and how they can supersede rational thought.

In the evolution of human society, the rich and powerful have always developed stories to justify their dominance over people. This is true of the warriors-kings in ancient history, the intellectual-priests in the Middle Ages, and the merchants-capitalists in modern history. The ideology of the warrior age was "might makes right."[4] And it was later amplified to become the "divine right of kings."[5] The warrior ideology was buttressed by the worship of war gods to whom the warriors prayed for victory. The ideology of the warrior-kings did not have to be particularly sophisticated because they controlled the masses by brute force, not by the persuasion of ideas. Even so, the people were led to believe that the kings held power by virtue of their closeness to a divinity. This was the dominant reality during the days of ancient history.

As people became more sophisticated, so did their stories. Competing religious sects began to create complex myths to justify the superiority of their god and to rationalize their priest class' dominance of others. Distinct priest classes put themselves in charge of maintaining the temples of their imagined deities and in so doing embellished their stories of the gods. In time, they positioned themselves as the interpreters of the will of the gods and thereby gained control over the minds of the people. In this way, ever more complex religious ideologies developed over time. As they became institutionalized, these myths turned into dogmas, which are supposed irrefutable truths that no one could challenge under penalty of torture, death, and eternal damnation. Dogmas have always set up boundaries in the minds of men and women as to what constitutes reality and, in doing so, have constricted and stultified the expansion of human knowledge and spiritual growth. In Western civilization, as Jewish, Christian, and Islamic religions evolved, each created their own dogmas to explain reality and what God wanted from people. In this way, the priests came to supplant the warriors as the ruling authorities.

During the Middle Ages in Europe, when the Catholic Church dominated society, the priests continued to weave their complex system of myths based on their religious dogmas. The dogmas were rife with supernatural occurrences to awe and frighten the people. Whatever the Church said was taken to be the ultimate truth. Church dogmas were transcribed into laws and anyone who spoke against these dogmas faced torture or death.

The Church dogmas went so far as to claim the right of priests to control one's soul. To disobey the commandments of the church, they claimed, resulted in eternal damnation. Such powerful dogmas cowed the people and ensured the reign of the priest class. If someone disobeyed the will of the priests, who, according to their own pronouncements, spoke for God, he or she would face eternal torture in the afterlife. During the Middle Ages, such torture also applied to this life as well.

Typical Church dogmas consist of the myths of heaven and hell, the use of indulgences (i.e., paying money to get your sins forgiven), praying for favors, creating the need for an intercessor between you and God (i.e. confessing your sins to a priest[6]), the worship of mythical gods, the suppression of women, the myth that ours is the true religion chosen by God, the myth that if you die in battle fighting for your religion or your country you will go to heaven. These and many more fabrications keep people in thrall to a priest class.

In the West, after the revolution against Catholicism, the Christian Protestants used Calvinist dogmas to justify the rule of the capitalists, asserting that they were the chosen "elite" who ruled in accordance with God's will. In the Middle East, the Islamic fundamentalists use dogma to build their armies and kill non-believers. In the Far East, the Hindu priests use dogmas to keep the people locked in an immutable caste system. All religions, insofar as they are creations of male priest classes, suppress women. None of this is to say that God, the Divine Consciousness, does not exist. It is only to point out how religions manipulate the idea of God for their own group or individual self-aggrandizement.

Dogmas prevent the evolution of human consciousness. They have no relation to rationality, logic, or reason and depend upon blind faith and fear to ensure compliance. Dogmas are used to create an inferiority complex among the "sinners" and a superiority complex among the "true believers." In time, these dogmas, based upon nonsensical myths, stories, and twisted logic became encoded in the sentiments of a people.

During the Enlightenment period, after a hundred years of religious wars between the Catholic Church and the Protestant revolutionaries, secular philosophies emerged. Some of these ideologies, like those of Hegel and Kant, were based upon the primacy of philosophical ideas (idealism). Others, like those of Bacon, Hobbes, and Locke, were based on the primacy of matter (materialism). The split in the worldviews of these secular "free-thinkers" created the divide between philosophy and science that we know today.

With the rise of capitalism in modern society, a new ideology emerged to justify the merchant class's rise to power in modern society. Their ideology became known as classical liberalism. In order for the merchants to come into power, they had to free themselves from the dogmas and laws of the church-state. In place of Church dogmas and aristocratic rule, they advocated personal liberty, limited government, private property rights, and *laissez-faire economics.*[7] In time, their myths became more sophisticated; adding new tenets and principles, and these changes eventually gave rise to the split between contemporary left-wing and right-wing ideologies. Conservatives today generally support the privileges of the individual over the needs of the general population. The liberals and democratic socialists generally support social welfare as a balance to the capitalist class's continued exploitation. Both the left and the right support capitalist ideology, which is based on the dogma of the supremacy of *self-interest* and the right of the strong to exploit people, places, and things for their own self-aggrandizement.[8] In this brief look at the evolution of ideologies, we have mentioned three distinct types of ideologies, dogma-centered, self-centered, and matter-centered.

But things, obviously, are more complicated than this simple narrative on how ideologies emerged. In reviewing western history in *The Untold Story of Western Civilization*, we have learned that creation stories did not remain isolated. Rather, in the clash and cohesion between different people, ideologies often merged, and whether they were imposed by the strong on the weak or were accepted because they were superior, human society grew incrementally more sophisticated and universal in scope. This is not to suggest that the evolution of different peoples has been uniform. As we continue our historic march through different ideologies, our understanding of God, nature, and ourselves continues to grow.

The clash of different ideologies causes our minds to work harder and our consciousness to expand. Each worldview has brought something to the table. Magical thinking (prehistory and matriarchal), religious thinking, and scientific thinking have all added depth and coherence to our conception of God, ourselves, and the universe. Science, while still limited in scope, as was any preceding ideology, is nonetheless based on reason and demands proof of one's belief beyond superstition, dogma, or blind faith.

## The Need for a Universal Ideology to Serve the Common Good

The main problem with ideologies based on dogma, self-centeredness, and materialism is that they have all ignored the spiritual dimension of our humanity. As such, they are unable to provide a rationale for human unity. Rather, current social thought keeps us helplessly grabbing at the bars of our psycho-physical prison cells, cursing and shoving each other out of fear and anger as the fire in the prison continues to grow. Current ideologies have reached an evolutionary dead end. They no longer serve human interest. As the world slips into social and environmental crises, we urgently need a new way of looking at reality. While we do not want to throw the baby out with the bath water, we need a worldview that can integrate the best of current ideologies for the benefit of all. We need a unifying idea that addresses our physical, mental, and spiritual nature, our individual and collective nature, as well as our relation with other species and the universe. In short, we need an idea big enough to encompass the common good.

Today, people may disagree on a hundred points, but one thing that everyone agrees on, if not logically, at least emotionally, is that Western Civilization is in a state of decline and given our increased financial and environmental vulnerabilities, we may be moving closer to civilizational collapse. Yet, we find ourselves grossly hindered in our efforts to create an alternative course of action because we lack a comprehensive ideology that could motivate us as a human race to move in unison to address our common welfare. We remain lost in divisive nationalistic and religious sentiments, unable to act for our common survival and common good. Without a universal ideology, we continue to move closer to the brink of catastrophe and away from our dream of a benevolent future for our children.

## The Limits of Current Mainstream Ideologies

### Organized Religions

While organized religions claim to be spiritual organizations, they are mainly political organizations that use spirituality as a justification for their existence. For the most part, religions are built on myths and stories, dogmas, censures, and rituals. Conversely, spirituality consists of two simple acts, love of God and love of neighbor. Love of God implies a personal relationship with the Cosmic Entity. Love of neighbor implies a personal relationship with a particular expression of the Cosmic Entity. We are all made in the image of God and God exists in every image. From the perspective of spiritual realization, one is equal to the other. This has been the teaching of great spiritual masters throughout history. As P. R. Sarkar asks, "If all human beings are the offspring of the Supreme Entity, how is it possible that only Muslims are the favorite children of Allah, and only Hindus are the favorite children of Náráyańa?"[9] As far as religious leaders are concerned, they tend to oppose spirituality because it defies their political authority. It reduces the need for a priest class to tell people what to think and how to act.

Why do we say religions are political organizations? Politics is embedded in all religions because they are human institutions. The priests (or any religious leaders) define what is good and what is bad, what is right and what is wrong, and in so doing, the priests create rules and regulations in order to impose their will on others. In this way, the followers of the priests, spouting a particular dogma, are led to divide themselves from humanity as a whole. Enemies are identified and dogmas waved like swords. When religions rule civilizations, as we have discovered in

*The Untold Story of Western Civilization*, they are not averse to killing "non-believers" and using their own dogmas as a justification for doing so. During the days of the Roman Empire, we saw Roman priests kill Jews and Christians for their beliefs. During the Middle Ages, we saw the Catholic Church kill the people of European tribes for not becoming Christian. During the Reformation, we saw Catholics and Protestants kill each other over competing religious dogmas, all of which were supposedly based on the same scripture. In the modern age, we see the followers of all religions killing each other in the name of their narrow image of God. Religious fundamentalists tend to be the most divisive and destructive people regardless of which religion they represent. In the name of their god, they would send everyone else on earth to a living hell.

Like corporations and armies, religions also seek to expand their wealth and power and to accomplish this they must conquer other peoples, either by indoctrination, force of arms, or colonization. The best that can be said about religions is that they hold out spiritual hope for people within their organizations. This is not unimportant because without hope people lose their will to live. The worst that can be said about religions is that their morality extends only to those within their own group. For the most part, religious hierarchies are self-indulgent and exist only to generate wealth and power for themselves. Of course, religions, like anything else, are composed of good and bad elements and good and bad people. There is nothing inherently wrong with rituals and stories so long as they do not divide and exploit people by placing one gender, race, class, or nation above another. But, unfortunately, all religions do this.

**Capitalism**

Today, the world is not dominated by warrior kings or priest classes. It is dominated by capitalists who control the world by owning money. Capitalists have their own ideology. Their main tenets are: (1) the religious justification of their own superiority (Calvinism), (2) the racist justification for their right to colonize and exploit other peoples (Imperialism), (3) the evolutionary justification for their exploitation of their fellow men (Social Darwinism), (4) the righteousness of limitless profit-taking

(Classical liberalism), and (5) the righteousness of unlimited consumption of the earth's species and resources (Consumerism). Capitalism is a gravely destructive system motivated by our most base carnal desires and by "the bottom line," which justifies corporations grabbing everything they can put their hands on and to hell with everyone else. Capitalism, ideologically, assumes unlimited material resources and if any resources become limited in supply, the capitalists will employ armed force to take what remains of them. Capitalism evolved in relation to the nation-state and thus nationalism and militarism go hand in hand with capitalist imperialism.

While the capitalists have given humanity access to goods and services never imagined, and while they have demonstrated a genius for mass production, the capitalist system has also resulted in wage-slavery, warring nation-states, mass migrations of refugees, climate change, and the exploitation of resources beyond the capacity of nature to reproduce them. It has led to the rapid decline of the planetary life support systems—arable soil, potable water, breathable air, protective forests, and the diversity of wildlife.

As society comes under greater environmental and social stress due to the war and greed of the powerful capitalist nations, conflicts between people become more extreme and polarization occurs. Adherents of conflicting ideologies blame each other for the misery everyone is feeling. The capitalists are powerful. They control the world and they control our lives. Capitalism is a self-centered ideology.

**Marxism**

Karl Marx was born about one hundred years after the Industrial Revolution had begun in England. He observed the impact that capitalism was having on society and began to search for answers as to its success. He walked through the polluted air and bumped shoulders with the ragged army of workers trudging to their factories in the industrial cities and came to develop the first comprehensive analysis of the capitalist system of production. He developed an ideology called communism that was antithetical to capitalism. Marx identified a "two class system" at work within the capitalist system. There were those who owned the means of industrial production and those who had to work for them to earn a living. He called the two classes the bourgeois (capitalists) and the proletariat (workers). Marx saw that these two classes were in perpetual conflict due to the fact that the capitalists profited by taking advantage of the workers' labor. Thus, the capitalists have no incentive to pay the workers a fair wage and use every means and opportunity to extract increased labor from the workers for less pay. They are always disposed to using machines instead of human workers. This conflict between the capitalists and the workers continues today as can be seen in the battle of workers to increase the minimum wage, and in the movement of the capitalist corporations to replace human labor with machines, robots, and artificial intelligence.

Marx referred to the relationship between the capitalists and workers as "class conflict" and he projected that the conflict of interest would become more extreme over time and that the workers would eventually rise up against their oppressors, overthrow the capitalist class, and form an ideal society based upon cooperation. This new world he called "communism." It was a world where everyone would work together in peace. To hasten the day toward the realization of his ideology, Marx espoused a worker revolution. This shows that Marx was not a utopian reformer. He was a practical man and he knew that a better world would not come about without revolution and the creation of a new economic system.

Marx was a humanist who sought the greatest good for the majority of people, but he was also a materialist. This was his tragic flaw because he did not consider the human need for mental or spiritual expansion. He was primarily concerned with meeting our physical needs so that we could continue living day to day and generation to generation. But this has never been enough for human beings.

Marx failed to realize that life is a psycho-physical phenomenon and that human beings are fundamentally psychological beings. Human evolution, in contrast to the evolution of all the other species that preceded us, is not primarily determined by biological changes, but by psycho-social changes. Unfortunately, to Marx, "consciousness" was only a cursory phenomenon. He did not understand consciousness as an absolute entity, but saw it only as a shadow of material reality reflected in the individual mind. Marxist ideology failed because of this fundamental flaw. His vision was not sufficient to encompass the scope of human existence.

Hobbled by his fundamental materialist perspective, followers of Marx have been unable to offer realistic solutions to the problems that they witness within capitalism. In fact, capitalism has proven to be much more dynamic than Marxism. Despite its predatory behavior, the capitalist system has allowed intellectual freedom and spiritual opportunity to people. When the Soviet Union collapsed and China converted to state capitalism, Marxist ideology found itself sidelined as a workable solution to the current problems of capitalist society.

Even so, we must credit Marx and the Marxists for having created an antithesis to the rampant exploitation of the capitalist class. We are also indebted to the Marxists for their analysis of how profit is formed by exploiting human labor and how capitalism creates a class conflict because of this exploitation. This reality has not diminished in the least. We also owe respect to the Marxists for being willing to fight for the downtrodden and risk all to free the people from capitalist exploitation.

**Conservatives and Liberals**

In the US today, dominant ideologies reflect the contradiction between conservatives and liberals, or more specifically, between the Republican and Democratic parties. Today, politicians are engulfed in internecine feuds that impact every issue of our lives. As we watch our social cohesion slipping away each day, our best minds are unable to unlock horns long enough to see the futility of their efforts to resolve mutual problems. This conflict between left and right has become a game to many of them, a game with which the average American, watching his or her life-style deteriorate, has become increasingly frustrated.

The conservatives appeal to the masses of society because they tell them religious stories that give the people hope. So long as the masses of people have blind faith in what their preachers say and what their politicians parrot, they hunker down to fight any new ideas or any social programs that go against the will of their religious and political programmers. While most conservatives are poor and their lives are in shambles, they are taught that while life on earth may be miserable, they will live eternally in heaven. Even so, most conservatives are angry people. They have lost their jobs and their status in society as a result of capitalist exploitation, but they have been led to believe that their loss is due to uppity women, Islamic terrorists, Mexican immigrants, and black welfare cheats. In fact, all their neighbors.

Religious conservatives constitute the majority of the American people. They also are the largest contingent within the Republican Party. As fundamentalists and evangelicals, they believe in a myth-ological personification of Christ that they call "the fundamentals." Not understanding that the divinity of Christ is available to all human beings by virtue of learning how to love, they embrace a mythological story of a Jesus who was born of a virgin mother, died for the sins of humanity, came back from the dead, and ascended bodily into heaven. In this way, the Christian religions, beginning with the early Catholic Church, have reduced Christ from a spiritual master to a mythical Roman god named Mithra with whom his myth shares so much in common. Like the priests of old, modern day preachers tell the people what to think and promise them life after death as a means of coping with their present miseries. There is nothing inherently wrong with believing in a mythical picture of god if it makes one feel closer to God. The problem comes when people feel they must impose their religion on others in a hurtful manner and persecute others who, according to their dogma, are supposed to remain sub-servient to the true believers.

Because of Calvinism, which influenced most protestant sects as they emerged, conservatives defend capitalism as a phenomenon sanctioned by God. Calvin said that the capitalists were the elect of God, and the working poor were only undisciplined minions responsible for their own miserable plight in life. Workers are here only to serve their capitalist masters and most will live eternally in hell as punishment for their human depravity. It does not take much of a stretch to realize that conservative ideology lacks the scope to serve as a universal ideology to benefit all.

Liberal Protestants, on the other hand, promote Jesus Christ as a wellspring of spiritual inspiration. They reject the conservatives' myth of Christ as "supernaturalism" and thus they are not as contemptuous or closed-minded when it comes to people of other faiths. They also support social service programs for the general population and the poor. In this respect, the liberal Christians tend to have a larger social consciousness than do conservative Christians. They reject the myth that the capitalists are an elite class sanctioned by God. Rather, like secular liberals, they condemn the capitalist exploitation of their fellow human beings. They have a deeper understanding of the political and economic mechanisms that cause human misery and are willing to fight for social programs to protect the people.

Liberal Christianity, unfortunately, also has its limits. For liberal Protestants, Christ remains largely an intellectual icon rather than a spiritual reality. They forget that Christ's ministry was not about defending religious orthodoxy, but was about showing people how they could merge with the Divine by nurturing love for God and for their neighbors. God is not realized by sitting in pews once a week, reading the Bible, believing in church dogma, or by asking for favors. God is realized by acts of love and the best way to show love is by serving one's neighbor.

The tragic flaw of the liberals is that in downplaying the spirituality of Christ, they have reduced him to a dry intellectual concept. They have taken the mystery and the mysticism out of Christ's spirituality and, in doing so, they have weakened people's sense of devotion and have failed to provide the people with eternal hope. Human beings need hope as much as they need bread.

The strength of the conservatives is the weakness of the liberals and vice versa. Having said this, both of these ideologies support the capitalist system. The only difference is that the conservatives want to return things to how they were in the good old days when white Christian men ruled every dimension of society. The liberals, on the other hand, want to improve the system for all people. While they may have a greater psycho-social perspective than the conservatives, they have less of a spiritual impact. The conservatives look backward while the liberals look to the future. Neither lives in the here and now.

Having said this, liberal Christians are more humane in their beliefs and in their relations with the poor, but liberal Christianity cannot serve as a universal ideology.

**Sustainable Development**

In the late 1980s, another ideology arose to confront the naked exploitation of the capitalists. It is called Sustainable Development. This theory evolved largely through the efforts of the United Nations. It linked the exploitation by the capitalists (national and international banks, multinational corporations) to dire environmental consequences. This ideology holds that capitalism is destroying natural resources at a rate faster than they can reproduce themselves, and as such, the planet is being destroyed. As proof, sustainable development scientists point to climate change, ozone depletion, soil and water depletion, and the destruction of forests and species. The ideology of sustainable development is the product of the world's secular intellectuals.

The benefit of the Sustainable Development movement is that it explains in quantifiable terms the negative impact of the capitalists' extraction of natural resources and exploitation of human labor. It bares the iron fist of capitalism that the main stream media keeps hidden in a velvet glove. It proves, in unequivocal terms, that to place corporate profits above human beings and the planet is a false ideology that only serves the wealthy few. While Sustainable Development has given the world a common vision and has broadened the scope of human responsibility to include the care of the nature world, it still does not rise above the material conditions. Its bottom line is based on the premise that if we do not stop the exploitation of the natural world, we will kill ourselves. Thus, like Marxism, it fails to address our psychological and spiritual needs. Because of its overtly intellectual and scientific veneer, it has also failed to capture the imagination of the masses and their need for eternal hope. It does not grasp that the poor have already been manipulated into believing that what happens to this world does not matter. In their religious programming, they have learned to believe that the only thing that matters is what happens in the next world. This is why the conservative mind does not care about climate change or the fate of natural world. Unfortunately, like capitalism and Marxism, sustainable development falls under the same category of matter-centered and self-centered worldviews.

## Progressive Development

During the 1990s, the United Nations and its affiliated non-governmental organizations (NGOs) were busy developing the vision of Sustainable Development. They were forming committees on social and environmental issues, writing reports, and holding world conferences. The "Earth Summit" was one such conference.[10] At the time, the authors were working with a now defunct nonprofit organization in New York City called the Progress Agency. Our purpose was to assist third world NGOs to strengthen the effectiveness of their organizations through management consultations. Our agency played an active role in the United Nations conferences to articulate the dimensions of Sustainable Development. Not being satisfied with its limited materialistic perspective, however, we proposed an expanded vision of sustainability that we called Progressive Development. Our worldview introduced a "human dimension" to the ideology of sustainable development. Instead of focusing exclusively on economic and environmental concerns, we added (1) personal, (2) interpersonal, (3) cultural, and (4) political dimensions to the discourse. If human beings are to succeed in improving social and environmental conditions, we felt that we must understand human behavior as well. Our personal dimension looked at how to take care of one's self through a nutritious diet, necessary rest, exercise, and some form of spiritual practice. The interpersonal dimension looked at behaviors that would improve our relationships with those around us, in our marriage, family, workplace, and community. The cultural dimension addressed our culture of sex and violence and the artificiality of a consumer culture. We advocated a culture based upon art, entertainment, communication, and leisure activities that sought to build community and spiritual unity. Finally, our political dimension looked at how we organized ourselves and offered an alternative to the two party political system. We advocated alternatives like democratically elected social boards at the local level.[11]

Although the impact of our ideas on the international proceedings was minimal, the exercise of developing a more comprehensive ideology led us more deeply into a historical analysis of human behavior, including the perspectives of third world intellectuals. We became particularly interested in the ideas of Prabhat Rainjan Sarkar, an Indian philosopher, social activist, and Tantric yoga master who, at the time, was having a noticeable impact on the intellectual and political life of India.

The starting point of Mr. Sarkar's philosophy is that the urge for wealth and power that drives the capitalist system is rooted in the human beings' relentless thirst for limitlessness. Our current problems stem from the fact that we seek to fulfill an infinite longing with resources that are finite, and thereby an impossible task. This contradiction has led us, as individuals and as a society, to the destruction of the environment and society that we are currently witnessing.

According to Mr. Sarkar, all of human history has been an attempt to satisfy the infinite longing for happiness within us. We want to be happy every second of our lives and when we die we want to be happy for eternity. Everything comes down to this. As a species, we are driven by this longing. It defines our nature. No other species reflects such a relentless urge. When animals are satiated, they lay down to rest. Not us, we always want more.

Mr. Sarkar sees our urge to accumulate wealth and power as a reflection of our attempt to fulfill this infinite longing. We think we can satisfy it by always achieving more. This behavior has become so ingrained in us that we do not even think about it. The longing never goes away. It is in our subconscious and hardwired into our DNA. We always want more. History teaches us, however, that the attempt to accumulate more physical wealth and power is only a blind alley, which never completely satisfies. No matter how we try to fill this aching hole within us by material possessions, we never succeed. In ancient times, warriors built large empires that existed for a century or more, but then sunk back into the sands of time even as they lay dead and buried beneath them. During the Middle Ages, priests created religion to captivate the minds of the people and therein gain their own wealth and power. The institutions of the priests lasted longer and their control over people was more complete, yet the priests also failed to secure enough wealth and power to salve the ache for the infinite that churned within their hearts. They too were laid to rest without accomplishing that for which they sought their entire lives. In modern times, the capitalists have gained control of the society. They achieve wealth and power by controlling the money upon which billions of people depend to secure their basic needs. But even by ruling over billions, and by having ten mansions in ten countries, they are not happy. Their children are not happy. In time, their wealth becomes meaningless even though they cannot stop their habit of accumulation. Mr. Sarkar defines this condition as a psychic disease. The incessant attempt to fill this infinite urge by possessing finite resources has been the driving force of human evolution, but it has not been recognized by existing ideologies. And yet, it remains the reason each of us gets out of bed each morning and the reason why human society continues to career blindly from one catastrophe to another.

Mr. Sarkar argues that our desire for unlimited happiness cannot be fulfilled by personal power or consumer goods because these are limited in their capacity to make us happy. Once the pleasure derived from them passes, we again seek new objects to satisfy us, but we never feel completely fulfilled. If such material acquisition had given us unlimited happiness, our thirst would have been slacked. We could have rested and been content, but this has never been the case. Only the mystics and spiritual masters have been able to solve this riddle and gain eternal peace.

Limitless happiness, according to Mr. Sarkar and other spiritual masters, is not derived from material wealth and power; it is derived from the personal experience of an Infinite Entity. In fact, the relentless urge inside us, that never goes away, demonstrates that it is our human nature, the very purpose of human existence, to seek the Infinite. Whether we want wealth and power or whether we want justice for all, we will never be able to achieve either of these goals by remaining confined within this psycho-physical reality. True, we must meet our basic needs, and this requires us to be practical in the objective world, but the fulfillment of our urge for limitlessness can only be achieved by a spiritual quest. By thinking along these lines, Mr. Sarkar's ideology of Universalism builds a bridge between religious and secular ideologies and between conservative and liberal ideologies. It provides a synthesis between idealism and materialism. And, as we shall see, it also provides a solution to the contradiction between capitalism and Marxism.

Presently, we face a civilizational crisis like nothing human beings have ever experienced. It is the carrier wave of all crises. It is more than a political-economic crisis; it is more than an economic-environmental crisis; it is more than a religious-interpersonal crisis; it is more than a personal crisis.

It is all of these and more. It is the rapid crumbling of Western Civilization. Current ideologies, because they do not provide a holistic solution to this crisis, will not be able to protect humanity or the natural world going forward. A revolution in gender, race, or class relations will not suffice, in and of themselves, to solve our overarching social and environmental problems. Wars between religions and wars between nation-states will not help us. For the first time in the history of the human race, we require something extraordinary. We require a holistic worldview, a Universal Ideology that has the capacity to mobilize the entire humanity for the benefit of all. Any ideology, short of this, will only continue to divide us and pit us against one another in a fight for quickly diminishing returns.

## Universal Ideology vs. the Limits of Factionalism

Because human beings are physical, mental, and spiritual beings, any ideology based exclusively on materialism or idealism is inadequate to serve our needs. Their interpretation of the dimensions of human beings and the relationship between the individual, society, and nature are not in balance. Only a universal ideology can help us know ourselves as individuals as well as understand our relationship to society and to the world in a balanced manner. A universal ideology points out the limits of our unworkable preconceptions. This is what we need if we are to address the destructive conditions that we have created due to our dependence upon old ways of thinking.

A universal ideology has the power to bring us together and give us hope for a better world. While it appeals to our reason, it is also able to create the waves of love required to soften the hardness of our hearts. A universal ideology recognizes that we are mind-preponderant beings and that our minds are capable of expanding into greater consciousness, the highest attainment of which is mergence with the Absolute Consciousness. This absolute consciousness is what people generally call God although their definitions remain too small.

A universal ideology is based upon the attainment of Oneness. Unlike current ideologies, which are either dogma-centered, self-centered, or matter-centered, only a God-centered ideology provides us with a unifying goal. Without such a unifying goal, factionalism dominates. This factionalism has become increasingly problematic as our world becomes smaller while problems become larger, affecting all of humanity. There is no use in chanting "Peace Now" if we cannot eliminate factionalism based upon competing ideologies. We can easily feel how unrest and conflict caused by factionalism exist just below the surface, and violently flair up in times of too much stress. Today, the world is barely holding it together. Wars and terrorism keep expanding, the climate is rapidly changing, and social instability is creating mass migrations that are spreading across the planet. Nations are closing their doors to other human beings and manning the walls. In the United States, conservatives and liberals can hardly look at each other because of their contrasting worldviews. As things continue to decline, pressures continue to build. The ideological factionalism that has produced our history, barring any changes, will destroy our future.

Neither dogmatic religions, capitalism, Marxism, conservatism, liberalism, nor sustainable development present a unified picture of reality. They are all examples of factionalism. Their perspectives of life are bound by "this versus that" and "us versus them." Certainly, we need to discriminate in order to act, but duality and factionalism cannot form the base of a universal ideology. Only spirituality can do that. Only a spiritual vision can overcome the primacy of dualistic thinking.

A universal ideology is based on the premise that our image of God, or who we call God, is actually the Cosmic Consciousness who permeates and enlightens all forms. Nothing exists outside of it. No person, place, or thing exists outside Cosmic Consciousness. Whether we call something good or evil, it all exists within it. Consciousness is the ground of being and the supreme unity from which all forms emerge and all forms return. Without a guiding belief in a supreme unity, we have no way to resolve contradictions; we have no way to relate to our neighbor other than by competition and dominance.

Up until this point in human evolution we have not yet created a true human society on this planet earth. But now is the time to do so. It has become a necessity to do so. Now is the time to adapt a belief system that is expansive enough to shelter each of us as well as the world we love.

Now is the time to adopt a universal ideology. But what would such a thing look like? What are its major aspects?

## Aspects of a Universal Ideology

First, a universal ideology, must address the nature of Absolute Consciousness and the nature of this universe in order to provide a context for our human existence. Secondly, it must account for the physical, mental, and spiritual dimensions of human nature. Thirdly, it must address the relationship between Absolute Consciousness and individual conscious-ness. Fourthly, it must address the relationship between the individual and society and between human beings and the natural world. Finally, it must provide a political and economic strategy to meet our needs in an environmentally and socially sustainable manner. A universal ideology must be mystical and scientific at the same time.

A belief system that can be supported by all must be able to identify our responsibilities to each other on the interpersonal, community, and planetary levels. From a political perspective, it must identify what we mean by a successful human society and offer common definitions of vice and virtue, sin and crime. Our ideology must identify a universal moral code that omits no one and upon which we can develop a new set of governmental institutions, a constitution, and laws. From an economic perspective, our ideology must include a practical theory that will allow us to meet everyone's basic necessities (food, shelter, clothing, health care, and education) as well as reward those who make outstanding contributions to realizing this goal. The gap in wealth between the poorest and the richest must exist within a socially acceptable range. A universal ideology must be built on cooperation and full employment. And it must also provide us with a strategy to bring this about. Without a concrete strategy to engineer this great transformation, we have only a utopian dream.

To adapt a universal ideology, we must reject narrow ideologies that are based on matter vs. spirit and faith vs. reason. We must also reject divisive sentiments such as racism, sexism, ageism, classism, nationalism, militarism, and imperialism. At the same time, our universal ideology must link the personal, interpersonal, cultural, economic, political, and environmental spokes of society to a spiritual hub. The question of the day is not whether we can develop such an ideology, but rather, given our current predicament, how do we, as human beings, make the next great leap as a human society. How can we continue our march to a loving Divinity and benefit the earth and society in the process? How do we satiate the infinite longing that relentlessly drives us onward while also creating a better world for everyone? These are the fundamental questions with which the spiritual masters of history have always wrestled, and in response have developed answers for their disciples which have lasted through time and space.

Given our look at human history in *The Untold Story of Western Civilization*, we cannot expect the owners of monopoly corporations or the leaders of central governments and central bankers to lead us through this great transformation. Rather, it is their desire to maintain the world as it is, even as they circle each other with weapons drawn in preparation for the end game. Domestically, neither Democrats nor Republicans have the solutions, nor do they even know how to think about a comprehensive solution to our problems.

Who, then, will lead us to our new world if we cannot depend upon our world leaders? The inevitable answer is that you and I must lead. Our friends and our neighbors must lead. We must join together, man and woman, one by one in the struggle for our very lives. Our revolution is a unique revolution. It is a nuclear revolution that begins in the heart and soul of each individual and spreads out from there into our families, communities, and eventually the world. It is a revolution that begins with a common belief system, a universal ideology.

Having a universal ideology will allow us to work for ourselves, our families, our neighbors, our countrymen and all of humanity as we strive to build a common human society. This book is an attempt to define the key features of such an ideology. It does not intend to be the last word in such an attempt, but hopefully it is a start. Each one of us possesses within ourselves the love and knowledge to build upon a universal vision and to manifest it in this troubled world. In this struggle, our leaders are ourselves. And it will be our love and moral courage that will draw the masses of humanity to our vision.

# The Main Components of Universal Ideology

In *The Untold Story of Western Civilization*, we attempted to discern patterns of human thought and behavior insofar as they related to God, Nature, Society, and the Individual, We also looked at the role that gender and race played in the evolution of Western Civilization. This comprehensive history allows us to understand the trajectory of Western Civilization and where we stand in the motion of history. It allows us to see the root causes of those forces that divide us as well as forces that bring us together as a human society.

In this book on Ideology, we will articulate the main components of a universal philosophy as propounded by the social activist and spiritual teacher, Prabhat Rainjan Sarkar. Mr. Sarkar's teachings to date are primarily disseminated by two organizations of which he was the founder. The first is Ananda Marga Yoga Society which develops social service projects and teaches meditation and other spiritual practices. The second is Proutist Universal which espouses a new socio-economic theory and creates local development models to manifest this theory.

When we began to analyze Mr. Sarkar's writings, we realized that he has created a synthesis of the best ideas derived from the most powerful social and religious ideologies in human history. Moreover, he had also created the connective tissue, if you will, that turned these philosophies from limited thought systems into a universal ideology. In doing so, Mr. Sarkar has provided humanity with a set of beliefs that comprise the most cogent ideas in our evolutionary trudge to perfection. As such, there is no need for us to reinvent the wheel, only to roll with it and improve its speed as we move along.

This book contains chapters on the following topics: (1) Social Psychology, (2) Human Nature, (3) Spirituality, (4) Politics, and (5) Economics.

Chapter One on social psychology argues that in order for an ideology to appeal to all people, it must be aligned with the driving force of human history, i.e., the dominant psychologies that groups of people use to survive and achieve wealth and power. The history of Western Civilization is divided into three great eras, each having its own ruling psychology. The ruling class always consists of that group that best adapts to the particular social environment of their era.

At the dawn of human society, the people were overwhelmed by the forces of nature. For hundreds of thousands of years, they had little ability to change their living conditions on their own. Things gradually began to change, however, when some began to develop a warrior mentality. They braved the impossible and, in doing so, became the heroines and heroes of the people. They built the rudiments of an early human society. The greatest warrior queens and later warrior kings and their courts constituted the ruling class in each society. As society changed from a matriarchal to a patriarchal system, the need for warrior skills took on greater prominence and the rule by men increasingly fostered the use of physical force to subdue one's enemies and the forces of nature. The period in which the women governed we call Prehistory or the era of the Matriarchy. The period in which patriarchy took hold, we call Ancient History.

After thousands of years, the warriors succumbed to the psychology of the intellectuals, who came to dominate the warriors and the masses by controlling access to the warriors' goddesses and gods. These priests not only controlled the labor of the people, they controlled their minds as well. In setting themselves up to interpret the wishes of the gods, they fostered the use of mental force in subduing the people to their wishes. The period in which the intellectual mentality ruled in western history, we call the Middle Ages.

With the onset of Modern History, the masses, warriors, and intellectuals succumbed to another psychology. It was the psychology of the merchant who came to control the coin of the realm. In time, everyone eventually came under the control of the money-lenders. The capitalists were born, and became the new ruling class of Modern History.

In order for a universal ideology to be credible, it must understand how these psychologies were used to both benefit and exploit people during the different ages of history and how they are being used today to dominate different aspects of social life. A complex human society requires the services of those who express each of these social psychologies. We need the common people, or the masses, who do not mind getting their hands dirty. We need warriors to defend what we build.

We need intellectuals to expand our minds and help us plan. And we need merchants to help us create wealth. We will need all of these psychologies and skills to build a new society. In chapter one, therefore, we analyze the dominant psychologies in society, describe their strengths and weaknesses, and demonstrate how people who are dominated by each psychology are able to achieve personal perfection while contributing to a world of benefit to all.

Chapter Two discusses what it means to be a human being living in society. It reveals how human beings think and how the myths, philosophies and dogmas of the past have programmed our thinking and keep us from moving forward as a human society. It looks at our mental capacities in the form of instincts, sentiments, rationality, and intuition and how these capacities influence our decisions and our judgments. The chapter looks at the differences between individualistic and collective tendencies and points out how the collective tendency dominates in our species. It looks at what happens when our collective tendency is governed by the sentiment of a group (groupism) and how, without the guiding force of reason, we are led astray by such sentiment and controlled by factionalism. The chapter distinguishes between *geo-sentiments* like nationalism and *socio-sentiments* like religion. It looks at the motivation of people who foster these narrow sentiments. Finally, the chapter looks at the principle of selfish pleasure and how it is used to create mental complexes and psychic exploitation in others, especially as it manifests in gender, race, and class relations.

Chapter Three addresses the meaning of "spirituality" and demonstrates why understanding our spiritual nature is now, more than ever, important in our individual lives and to our survival as a species. It explores in detail how our thirst for limitlessness is derived and demonstrates how it can only be fulfilled by merging with a limitless entity. It discusses the relationship between the soul, mind, and body and how our sense of identity arises. It looks at the difference between brain and mind, and between mind and soul. It looks at the relationship between unit consciousness (soul) and Absolute Consciousness (God). It defines absolute consciousness and discusses its existence in unmanifested and manifested states. It discusses the process by which the universe becomes manifest and of what it consists. It discusses the relationship of matter and form and the method by which unit consciousness gains liberation from form. It answers the questions: "Who am I and what am I?" and "What is my relationship to the universe?" It discusses the law of karma that governs our actions and its relation to the cycle of life and death. Finally, it discusses the need for spiritual practices and what constitutes beneficial practices and what does not. It looks at why we do not have to worry about the pain of giving up the vices we love. The purpose of this chapter is to integrate spirituality into our self-knowledge, regardless of our religious affiliation or lack of one.

Once the spiritual nature of the individual is defined, Chapter Four looks at the organization of human society. It examines the nature of politics and proposes six factors which can assure the success of any society. These factors are a universal ideology, a spiritual practice, an inclusive social outlook, a beneficial socio-economic theory, a body of practical knowledge by which to put a new system in place, and the availability of a teacher and leaders who embody the ideology. This chapter also looks at the requirements for creating a new form of government from the ground up. It looks at the role of government, political parties, the question of vice and virtue, sin and crime, and the tenets of a universal morality. It looks at the principles of a universal constitution and the laws required to support a true human society. Finally, it looks at the necessity of a new code of justice and the different motivations for criminal behavior.

Chapter Five looks at universal economic principles that are intended to create a balance between individual and collective needs as far as the accumulation of material wealth is concerned. These principles are intended to maximize the utilization and rational distribution of all resources whether spiritual, mental, or physical, or whether they are derived from human labor or the natural environment. These principles are based on the assumption that the universe is our common inheritance and that no one has the authority to abuse it or use it to take advantage of others. The chapter also looks at principles of economic justice and economic planning. Principles of economic justice hold that access to basic needs should be guaranteed to all and that the best way to do this is through a decentralized economy run by democratic participation. The chapter looks at the balance of agriculture, industry, and commerce in a successful local economy. Finally, the chapter defines a socio-economic planning unit and provides a strategy for organizing a local economy.

# Chapter One: Social Psychology

T HE UNIVERSAL IDEOLOGY OF Prabhat Rainjan Sarkar provides us with unifying principles, as well as a theory and practice by which to organize ourselves as a human society. More than this, it allows us as individuals, irrespective of religions, to experience a personal relationship with a loving Divinity.

As we traced the evolution of human society in *The Untold Story of Western Civilization*, we saw how the idea of God became an indicator of our mental evolution. "God" was, after all, the greatest idea that we could ever imagine at any point in time. Through the years, the idea of God evolved to become more encompassing. It was Shiva in the East who introduced the idea of God as a loving entity and attainable Perfection. In the West, Jesus Christ did the same. Historically, the God-centered ideology of these masters had only been practiced in Himalayan caves and monastic cells. According to common belief, it is only within such lonely places that men and women are able to realize Divinity and become enlightened. Our social conditioning by the priest class of our day teaches us that enlightenment cannot be achieved by the average person who lives in society and raises a family. As such, spiritual science has never been employed in the public interest. While some religions speak of the One God and are active in social service work, this is not the same as integrating spiritual science and social science as a means to achieve enlightenment. In this book on Universal Ideology, we will explore the thinking of the Indian mystic and social activist, Prabhat Rainjan Sarkar, who presents us with the vital link between social science and spiritual science and, in so doing, provides a common foundation for individual and social excellence. The marriage of these two sciences constitutes the base for a Universal Ideology.

The premise of Mr. Sarkar's social science is that human beings are mind-preponderant beings and, as such, human society is not driven primarily by material conditions, but by the strategies and methods that we use to master our social and environmental conditions. It is social psychology, therefore, that is the driving force of human history.

As we saw in *The Untold Story of Western Civilization*, those who possess different social psychologies have always developed ideologies to justify their dominance over society. Western history is divided into different ages and each age of history has been dominated by a different social psychology.

Mr. Sarkar explains the ages of history accordingly:

> The past may be divided into various yugas or ages: the shúdra yuga or worker age; the kśatriya yuga or warrior age; the vipra yuga or intellectual age; and the vaeshya yuga or capitalist age. In the future also these ages will come and go. People will reject the old social order and embrace a new one.[12]

In Ancient History, the warrior psychology dominated. In the Middle Ages, the intellectual psychology dominated. And in modern history, the capitalist psychology dominates. In each age, social and environmental conditions differed, and while people who reflect each psychology have existed in each age, those who excelled at mastering the existing conditions became the dominant or ruling class. This is true of the warriors, priests, and capitalists. Each rules under different conditions and by different means. The warrior controls by physical force, the intellectual by mental force, and the merchant/capitalist by dominating the medium of exchange. These three means of having social power cycle throughout history depending upon circumstances. As such, the current dominance of the capitalists will give way to the dominance of the warriors in the second cycle of the social system. In time, the warriors will again cede power to the intellectuals and the intellectuals once again to the capitalists. This rotation of the ages, Mr. Sarkar calls the Social Cycle.

There are also times when the masses (shúdra/workers) dominate in a society, but these are only in times of crisis and social upheaval. When the masses rise up, a revolution occurs. This might presage a simple change in administration or it could mean a change of such significance that a new era comes about and with it a new dominant psychology. The masses may help to create a revolution, but they do not have the means to administer or dominate a new social structure. They are content to get by. They only work to enjoy the simple pleasures of life: rest, sleep, sex, and oblivion. It is only when the masses are put under extreme stress that they arise to throw off their bondage.

People who express different psychologies form different societies and also different institutions within those societies. Social classes, therefore, are based on social psychology. In Mr. Sarkar's definition of social psychology, the term "class" does not mean a class or caste in the usual sense of the word. It does not mean a particular relationship to the means of production, nor does it mean a specific income status. Rather, by social class, he means the collective name of those people who are dominated by a specific psychology. In today's world, for example, the warrior class, i.e., those who predominately have a warrior psychology can be found in the military and police organizations. They are the members of the athletic clubs, the daredevils, the hunters, and the karate fighters. They dazzle us with their feats of physical bravery. They become our heroes and also our villains. The intellectuals, by comparison, serve in the churches, government bureaucracies, universities, the laboratories, and think tanks of big corporations. They are the ministers, social workers, scientists, artists, journalists, consultants, bureaucrats, and politicians. The merchants, on the other hand, are the small business owners, but they are also the great monopoly capitalists. As such, they are the hedge fund managers, bankers, investors, and corporate managers. They are the owners of capital. Their strongholds are the multinational banks and corporations. During the capitalist age, money becomes the main focus of everyone because without focusing on money a person puts his survival at risk and becomes subject to further exploitation.

A person is usually dominated by one particular psychology, but he or she can adopt more than one psychology if he or she is willing to expand his or her consciousness. For example, we can find intellectual warriors and warrior intellectuals. We can have warrior merchants and intellectual merchants. Because each of these psychologies represent a different way of having power in the world, the more social psychologies that an individual can master, the greater is his or her power in society. This is because such people have the skills to succeed, no matter the circumstances. If such people are not afraid to get their hands dirty, then they have added the power of the masses to their capacity.

As each age succeeds to the next, a new class is formed whose psychology comes to subjugate those who possess different psychologies. When the warrior age (the period of ancient history) evolved, the masses considered it to be a great blessing. They could not envisage that the warriors would become their exploiters. Similarly, when the warriors ceded power to the intellectuals during the Middle Ages, they did not realize that they had relinquished their wealth and power and would gradually be bound in chains like slaves. Still later, during the Renaissance/Reformation period, when the intellectuals began to sell themselves to the money of the capitalists, they at first did not realize that their value was going to be measured solely in financial terms.

It is typical for warriors and intellectuals to denigrate each other, or for intellectuals to think they are superior to money-grubbing capitalists, or for capitalists to hold the working class in disdain. This denigration of those having a different social psychology is a form of groupism. In actuality, it is self-destructive for a person to think less of another because of their social psychology. Rather, one should observe how other people think and act and, in so doing, incorporate their skills. In this way, people become more self-reliant and are able to help those whom they love. If physical force is required, they do not back down. If mental acumen is required, they do not feel inferior. If money is required, they know how to get it. If hard labor is required, they are not above the task.

Although *The Untold Story of Western Civilization* described how the ruling classes, imbued with the dominant psychology of an age, abused society by subjugating and exploiting the other classes, this abuse is not inherent in the Social Cycle itself. Despite the abuse and, at times, contemptible actions on the part of the different classes, each Age also brought us new ideas, new ways of organizing, and new technologies that have accelerated the evolution of humankind. Under the guidance of a Universal Ideology, the skills of each social psychology will become even more useful for advancing society instead of retarding it.

What is the value of analyzing society in terms of social psychology? In brief, having such a theory allows us to understand the different mind sets that contribute to a complex society. It gives us a clearer understanding of how people, possessed of such psychologies, think and act and by what means they gain wealth and power. It also allows us to interpret the intentions of the talking heads on TV, the politicians, economists, religious leaders, the newscasters, bankers, military leaders, and anyone who wants us to succumb to their point of view.

A study of social psychology also allows us to understand more clearly the basis of our own motivation and how we respond to challenges. It helps us to appraise our skill set and if we choose, it encourages us to gain mastery over more than one psychology. Is our propensity to be a warrior, intellectual, or business person? If we are intellectuals, for example, how do we develop warrior skills or business skills? If we are warriors, how do we develop our intellect or business acumen? How do we become more capable human beings, able to cope in any environment? Finally, a theory of social psychology allows us to better understand the flow of human society and to determine the conditions by which each social psychology succeeds or fails. Let us now look more deeply at the four psychologies.

## The Shúdra Age

**Psychic Characteristics**

At the dawn of human existence, when we first emerged out of the primal horde and came to identify ourselves as human beings, we all had the characteristics of the toiling masses. We were all shúdras. We were overwhelmed by the forces of nature and frightened by everything. Danger lurked everywhere and there was nothing on which to build a sense of trust. We cowered in fear and were thankful only to stay alive another day. Under such conditions, there was no potential to build a human society. The psychology of the masses has always been characterized by an inability to assimilate the waves of matter and gain control of them. In such a state, our minds did not develop any subtlety. We remained submersed in materialistic thought.

The material world overwhelms the shúdra mind and renders it unable to cope with reality. Such people cannot control anything, because the crudest waves, the waves of matter, control them.

Mr. Sarkar says:

> When the human race was in an embryonic stage and humans evolved from animal mentality to human mentality, human beings then, as today, found two paths open to them. The first was to become crude by ideating on matter—the path of shúdrahood; and the second was to overcome material and psychic obstacles by ideating on subtle things—the path of kśatriya-hood [warriors]. In those days people's minds were so full of material thoughts, due to living in a hostile natural environment, that at that early stage everyone necessarily possessed a shúdra mentality.[13]

## Shúdra Society

Those who have a shúdra mentality can collectively be called the shúdra society. After a long period in which mammals evolved into hominids and hominids evolved into humans, rudimentary social bonds were formed due to mutual self-interest, but the early humans were unable to build a social structure. Even kinship bonds remained weak. People had no sense of duty towards each other and therefore no social order could develop. Mr. Sarkar tells us:

> People generally felt uneasy if they came too close to each other. In fact, the shúdra society of that time could not claim to be much better than the present-day society of monkeys or dogs.[14]

The rudimentary idea of shúdra society, like that of merciless nature, is survival of the fittest. Where there is no love and compassion for the weak, there is no collective effort to preserve their lives. Parents take no responsibility for their children who, in turn, take no responsibility for their parents. So people are divided into innumerable groups and somehow pass their days. The joy of collective living for the shúdra, the expansiveness of many minds moving together, is nothing but an occasional "disquieting dream" for them.

The main sentiment in the shúdra social system is, "Let the living live better, and let the dying die quickly. Do not waste energy trying to save them." An attitude such as this produces a particular type of selfish social system, which, in reality, is neither a society nor a system. Because of their limited mental ability, this is as much as the shúdras have created and are able to create.

Human society in those days basically meant a particular individual's own body, his or her kin, and to some extent, children. As conjugal relations were based on sexual gratification, there was no sense of responsibility. Today there are still people with this propensity throughout the world in all societies.

Eventually, the people of shúdra society felt some parental affection for their children due to their physical contact with them, but once their children grew up and clashes of interest, typical of the shúdra mentality, would come about, they would not maintain their relationships. So, although mothers had a temporary affection for their children, the children had no sense of responsibility towards their mothers or close relatives.

Basically, shúdras live only for physical pleasures. They do not bother about ideas nor give any value to rationality. They have neither the time nor the inclination to think about the past or the future. Religion, spirituality, rationality, or a functioning social system have no significance for them. Whatever of these concerns we observe in shúdra society results from a mix of fearfulness and self-interest. They are not independent thinkers and are easily influenced by stronger minds. It was the women in their role as mothers who taught their children and their brothers and uncles how to advance beyond shúdra consciousness and create the conditions for a more stable environment. In other words, it was the mothers who brought humanity out of animality and provided the first examples of warrior consciousness.

In today's society, shúdras constitute the masses. Sarkar describes them as such:

> There are tens of millions of people in the world who live only for physical enjoyment. They are born; they eat; they preserve their lineage; they bring up their children to further their own interests; they look upon everything as objects of gratification; and they turn to others out of greed. Their past is dark and so is their future, and they block out the light of the present with the blackness of their petty selfishness. These are the shúdras. They live and die unnoticed, and unnoticed they carry about the burdens of their lives. Their birth, life and death mean nothing to the collective being of humanity. They cannot create any vibration in the human race through their actions, nor can they arouse sleeping humanity with a thunderous voice. No doubt they live in the world, but they are incapable of leaving any trace in its heart.[15]

## Shúdra Spirituality

In the earliest days of humanity, shúdra psychology elevated different natural phenomena to the status of spirits or gods. They worshiped the voices of their ancestors, trees, mountains, forests, seas, etc., out of fear and self-interest, but not out of the inspiration of the Supreme Being. As we saw in *The Untold Story of Western Civilization*, the first idea of a supreme being was the Moon Goddess, but this idea did not immediately exist in early human society. Furthermore, even at the time of the Moon Goddess, there was as yet no sense of subjective consciousness; and as such all experience was externalized.

## Shúdra Revolution

Shúdras, from the dawn of humanity to the present, have never constituted a ruling class in any age of the social cycle. They are not able to impose a structure on society because of their weak-mindedness. It is very difficult to create genuine awareness in shúdras. Generally, it is the warriors (kśatriyas) who make the masses (shúdras) do work and who temporarily inspire them to revolt. It is often observed that when shúdras are led by warriors, they readily support revolution or counter-revolution, like insects attracted to a fire and burnt by the flames. At work, shúdras act mechanically and do only what they are told and no more. Consequently, during the transition from one age to the next, as the masses rise up, chaos reigns as one ruling class overthrows another.

The shúdra revolution usually begins when the existing ruling class is at its most exploitive, and the other three classes become reduced to a disgruntled mass. For example, as the capitalist class becomes increasingly more exploitive, their behavior drives people out of the system. People lose their jobs, watch their lifestyle decline, and with each passing day have less to lose. The warriors and intellectuals, who once constituted the middle class, are now relegated to the position of the masses, struggling to survive. Every action they perform becomes dedicated to survival. As the capitalist age declines, all people, including the middle-class warriors and intellectuals and the lower class shúdras, all get reduced to the status of resentful and increasingly belligerent shúdras. It is then, under the weight of continued exploitation by the ruling class, that a shúdra revolution occurs. Shúdra revolutions occurred in Europe to bring the capitalist class to power. In the United States, the revolution did not change the social psychology of the ruling class, it just replaced the British capitalists with American capitalists. Yet no revolution can occur without the support of the masses.

Mr. Sarkar explains the reasons for Shúdra Revolution.

> Towards the end of an era, the collective psychology undergoes marked deterioration. Moral degeneration and social retardation cause psycho-social stagnation. Exploitation becomes rampant. This sort of unhealthy situation signals the end of an era. The different classes try to usurp social power and establish their hegemony by trampling on the rights of others. This conflict has been discernible from the dawn of human civilization. Through this clash and cohesion, human beings try to find the path of emancipation.[16]

In the modern world, capitalist exploitation is rampant almost everywhere. Capitalism is now rapidly moving into the final stages of degeneration. In the early part of the capitalist era, European society experienced certain advantages, but now society has become the victim of insatiable rapacity, unbearable hardship, and heartless deprivation. The shúdra class gains more members every day and those who suffer under the weight of capitalist exploitation move incrementally towards shúdra revolution.[17]

The proximity of shúdra revolution can be observed in the values that preoccupy the collective mind in this degenerative period of capitalism. Today the values of the shúdras are dominant again. Self-interest and survival of the fittest have become the ground for action. There is less compassion for the weak and less collective effort to preserve their lives. People are divided into innumerable groups. An attitude of "don't waste your energy trying to save others or to save the environment," leads to a selfish, cynical society that each day continues to disintegrate. During such days, demagogues rise to power to manipulate the fears of the masses. They become the bullies whom the shúdras take to be the strong leaders that will protect them from their fears. Everyone outside of their group becomes a threat.

## The Warrior Age

### Psychic Characteristics

The main objective of the warriors, like that of the shúdras, is to enjoy physical pleasure and thus the development of their finer sensibilities is limited. So also is any concern for those outside their group. While the warriors ideate on pleasure and comfort, unlike shúdras, they do not become subservient to matter, but instead control the waves of matter with their own waves. Their purpose in life is to overcome physical obstacles and conquer their enemies. In this struggle, the best of them value brotherhood, valor, honor, strength, and discipline. The worst succumb to cruelty, venality, drunkenness, sexual abuse, and racial hatred.

Nonetheless, the seed of physical greatness, that was dormant in the shúdras, germinated in the warriors. Shúdras are afraid of high mountains which they regard as a god and bow their heads before it. They try to dissuade the warriors from climbing the mountain, saying, "The gods will become angry if you climb the mountain." But the warriors go ahead and climb it anyway and after reaching the summit, they declare that they have conquered the mountain. Matter thus serves them and their acquired mental capacity to control matter through physical force is what creates the warrior psychology. Struggle is their nature. Since they spend all their energy controlling matter, they cannot think of or understand anything beyond matter. Their wont is to enslave nature. Today, human superiority over all living things exists because of the endeavors of warriors to conquer the animate and inanimate worlds, to dominate their environment by physical force.

In the embryonic stage of the human race, those who became the slaves of nature due to circumstantial pressure were the shúdras. But those among them, who came in contact with the harsh aspects of nature and made the effort to survive by fighting against them, were the first warriors. The physical clash of animal life resulted in the creation of shúdra life, and the physical and mental clash of the shúdras, created the minds of the warriors. Later on, those shúdras who made a habit of fighting against nature, due to the inspiration of the first warriors, were able to form the first warrior society. Therefore, the collective name of those who have warrior propensities is called warrior society. The strongest among the warriors who seek physical dominance over society are called the warrior class and as such, they develop a class-consciousness. The first warrior society were the clans, clan confederations, and tribes created by the women in their role as mothers in the period of Prehistory. In time, as the role of mother's-brother evolved and men gained more power in society; their rule was not as nurturing as that of the mothers, who originally set the conditions for social interactions.

The male warriors acquire fame, wealth, and influence by exploiting the shúdras' labor. Even so, the greatness of the warriors struck the shúdras with wonder. The cowardly and intellectually undeveloped shúdras accepted the superiority of the warriors and paid obeisance to their bravery and spiritedness. The shúdras also played a role in the warriors' conquest of the world, and their role was not unimportant.

But the credit went to the warriors, because whatever the shúdras did, they did under the leadership of the warriors.

To win the minds of the ignorant shúdras, the warriors praised them lavishly for their victories. This made the shúdras forget the fact that they had been exploited. During the post-revolutionary period, the shúdras, instead of thinking about their own interests, believed that the greatest achievement of their lives had been to be the standard-bearers of the deceitful warriors. Because of this mentality, the great warrior empires of ancient history were built.

During the Warrior Age, the different groups continually fought among themselves to establish their supremacy; hence, in the warrior society, love for one's group became more evident than in the Shúdra Age. The shúdras had fought solely to survive, whereas the warriors fought not only for their own survival, but also for the survival of others in their group and for their own prestige. The day that the warriors began to protect the shúdras constituted the beginning of the Warrior Age.[18]

The early warriors' main aim had been to secure food and protection by any means, whereas the later warriors' aim was to conquer with glory. This sentiment enabled the warriors to develop a subtler intellect and awakened their conscience and discriminative judgment. As their sense of valor increased, it went against the warriors' conscience to kill the unarmed, women, children, or old people, to kill those who had surrendered, or to kill a retreating enemy. In a word, the warriors' sense of valor transcended the animal level, and they began to appreciate the value of human beings.

While the warriors live mainly for physical enjoyment, a belief system and code of values is also important to them. Sometimes one may be a little more important, sometimes the other. Throughout all ages of history, we observe that people with a warrior nature go to their deaths gladly, or thrust their necks into a noose, or bare their chests to bullets, or, rather than face the humiliation of total defeat, kill themselves in an attempt to escape probable indignities. People with a shúdra mentality do not do this.

The heroic victories of the warriors were celebrated in the oldest civilizations and continue to be celebrated in societies today. The admirers of different warriors recount their tales of glory, while even those who opposed them on principle, nevertheless applaud their gallantry and heroism.

Time has three divisions: past, present, and future. Warriors only think about the past and the present. They do not worry about the future. Ignoring future consequences and inspired by their beliefs, they jump into the flames of a fire, leap out of airplanes, and take off in rockets to explore distant planets and moons. They want to conquer, to be conquerors, and not merely to survive.

Warriors also think about the past. They do not like to forget their traditions. The inspiration of the past guides their movements and they get inspired by the bravery of their group or their ancestors. They seek revenge against the enemies of their ancestors. It is not possible for them to decide on their course of action without first analyzing the significant events of the past.

## Beginning of the Warrior Age

The warrior age did not come about overnight. Numerous fragmented shúdra societies gradually accepted the authority of the warriors and began to unite under their hegemony. In other words, many shúdra-dominated clans began to unite into larger social systems. In the early days of matriarchy, and all through its existence, clans evolved into clan confederations, confederations grew into tribes, and ultimately tribes evolved into nations.

From the earliest stages of human evolution, brave and spirited women led the clans as group-mothers. These group mothers were the first warriors to unify the shúdras into clans and clan confederations. They defined our earliest social formations. Even as we transitioned out of the mammalian primal horde, they set the earliest laws (taboos) concerning who the clan members could eat and who they could not; with whom they could have sex and with whom they could not. The enforcement of these taboos was essential to stabilize a group and to define themselves as human. As humans evolved, the mothers chose a queen from among themselves who was the strongest woman and who could interpret the word of the Goddess for them. At this time, all the men and women in a group were named after the Queen, the matriarch. Once the social organization evolved into a tribe both the parents of a child kept the same identity. It was no longer necessary to keep separate identities, as had been the case during the period of clan confederations. When a matriarch died and a new matriarch was chosen, or when a group broke into sub-groups, it was only necessary to determine the identity of one's group-mother to determine one's heredity.

It was during the later days of tribes and before the onset of nations that the Warrior Age began. The acceptance of a warrior as the symbol of shúdra unity, which came about through a gradual process of transformation, represented the first step in the evolution of social psychology.

Warrior society emerged during the matriarchal period when men earned the distinction of being the "mothers' brothers." In this role, they protected the wealth and people of the tribe, took revenge on enemies, trained the older boys and young men, and went on raids to steal from their neighboring tribes.

In time, a male-dominated warrior society gained preeminence as the matriarchal societies began to decline and belligerent and war-like men proliferated. With the dawn of patriarchal society, a male warrior came to be the symbol of that new system. The nomadic Aryan tribes were the first people to renounce the matriarchal system and abandon the Great Goddess.

During the emergence of the warrior social system, it was, to a large extent, the sense of human value that elevated conjugal and domestic life to a higher level. Conjugal relations came not to be limited to the enjoyer-and-enjoyed but to include a sense of duty. As conjugal relations developed and a father's role in creating a child became known, a father's duty towards his children also awakened. This led to a reduction in the mothers' responsibilities to some extent and, as a consequence, women became partially dependent on men for their food and clothes, particularly during pregnancy and immediately after childbirth. As a result, although couples belonged to the same tribe, they began to form into families headed by men. Because families were headed by men, the tribes also in time became male-dominated and the matriarchs lost the power they had previously enjoyed.

Mr. Sarkar elaborates:

> In olden times, warrior societies began to recognize a
> man and a woman as husband and wife, although the

bonds of such relationships were not strong. As the society became patriarchal, even in the latter half of the
Warrior Age men kept many wives as they had in the
Shúdra Age. The only difference between the polyga-
mies of the two eras was that wives in the Shúdra Age
had no social ties to their husbands, whereas the ties
between the husbands and wives in the latter half of
the Warrior Age were socially recognized. Although
the social system which was formed in the first half of
the Warrior Age was to some extent strengthened in
the latter half, the stability of both conjugal and group
relations in the latter half depended more on the physical abilities and bravery of the group-father, or patriarch, and other males than on genuine humanism or a
sense of discipline. The maxim of the Warrior Age was
"Might makes right."[19]

Human beings are largely creatures of sentiment. In the earliest days,
the love of a mother and her brothers for her children developed. In
the latter half of the Warrior Age, a sense of responsibility also started
to awaken in children towards their fathers. Duty-conscious children
were careful to maintain the traditions and proclaim the heroism of their
fathers, and fathers also wanted their children to inherit their heroic
qualities, powerful personalities, and traditions. Thus, as the relationship between fathers and their children was strengthened, society was
also strengthened.

In order to maintain the traditions of the father-family, great importance was given to the selection of brides and grooms at the time of
marriage. As a result, in the Warrior Age, socially recognized conjugal relations gradually evolved, replacing the kinship system of the
matriarchy.

**Warrior Society**

Society means a group of people moving together. For the warriors, who
thrive on struggle, there was an undeniable need for unity within their
group and this was maintained by a high standard of discipline within

the group. As male-dominated city-states were formed, the warrior administration cared little for what the masses thought about their discipline or whether they were practically benefited by it. It was through the formation of groups and the maintenance of discipline within those groups that patriarchy society was established.

As Mr. Sarkar says:

> Under this system the chariot of exploitation may run over the weak without slowing down, the hunger of millions of people may provide opportunities for one person to live in great luxury, and a relationship of exploiter and exploited may be established among people instead of fraternal relationships, but it is still a system. Regardless of its merits and demerits, it is the nature of kśatriyas [warriors] to try to perpetuate the system they are living under.[20]

To maintain society, an administration is necessary and to maintain an administration a government is necessary. No one would submit to the administration of a shúdra. The warrior societies created administrative systems through brute force. The shúdras and the weak warriors submitted to the brute force of the stronger warriors and accepted the strongest patriarch as the king. Under the administration of this king, a social and governmental structure began to form.

The qualities of the warrior leaders were physical might, strength of arms, and mental cunning. After the death of a leader, one of his sons, or a man from one of the clans or tribes under his protection, who had the greatest number of similar qualities, was accepted as the next warrior leader.

In the course of time, the age of the warrior kings was replaced by the age of the monarchy. This transformation took place mainly for the sake of maintaining social order. After the death of a warrior king, there would often be a violent struggle for power among his sons and the men of the groups under his protection. Often, by the time this struggle was over and a new leader was selected, everything in the group was topsy-turvy, or the group had become fragmented into many smaller groups. A greater sense of discipline was obviously needed to save the group from such disorder and fragmentation. So, to avoid internal conflicts, the custom of appointing the son, particularly the eldest son, of the warrior leader as the leader's successor was introduced in most of the warrior nations. Once this became the system, monarchy was established in warrior society.

Warrior society also developed a finer human sentiment due to its tendency for hero worship. The weak submitted to the strong, and the strong protected the weak in exchange for their submission. That is why, in the warrior social system, it is considered a virtue to save those who are distressed and those who seek protection; and this type of dutifulness is an important mental outlook in the life of a society. For this reason alone, parents are looked after and protected when they become incapable of looking after themselves due to senility or physical infirmity.

In warrior society, people are divided as a matter of course into innumerable groups, which fight incessantly among themselves, but an unquenchable thirst for victory makes life somewhat like a game of chess, and the call to do battle and to display a powerful personality also gives meaning to life. Thus, it is not the tendency of warriors to carry the burden of all life's disappointments. Warriors enjoy the delights of collective living more than shúdras, because their collective sentiment inspires them to stick together in good and bad times and makes even the suffering of pain a sweet experience. The endurance of pain is a sign of physical strength and a mark of respect by one's peers.

**Religion and Spirituality**

The male warriors regarded the natural world as a collective embodiment of different forces. To their limited understanding, the idea of a synthesis of forces appeared possible, but to think more deeply than this was generally beyond their capacity. An outlook of enjoyment caused their minds, through physical clash, to move towards crudity, but sometimes it also moved towards subtlety in a process of synthesis.

The spiritual philosophies based on Abraham's God in the West and Brahma of the Upanishads in the East were the remarkable historical culmination of this process of mental synthesis. The idea that the polytheism of shúdra society might rest upon the motive of a single divinity (monotheism) first originated as a vague idea in the minds of the warriors, and that is why the concept of monotheism evolved within warrior societies. The first universal deity was the Great Goddess, who was worshipped during the matriarchal period and well into the patriarchal period of ancient history. Her functions of giving birth, nurturing, and then destroying all the forms of life were symbolized in her three aspects as Virgin, Mother, and Crone. Each annual cycle revealed these distinct aspects of the Goddess. In the spring, she was the virgin, in the summer, the mother and in the fall, the crone. In the winter, she descended into the underworld to emerge again as the virgin in the following spring.

Later, as patriarchy came to dominate human society, the Great Goddess was gradually replaced by male gods. The first identifiable male god was Indra, the god of the Aryans. Indra was a drunken, war-like god who carried a bolt of lightning and had long flowing white hair. He is referred to in the Rg Veda, the earliest Aryan texts, as the one who leads the men in cattle raids and steals the cows of the Great Goddess. In time, Indra lost prestige, when the invading Aryan culture began to synthesize many aspects of the more sophisticated, matriarchal culture of the Dravidians within the region of northern India. Once Lord Shiva came on the scene and introduced the idea of a Cosmic Divinity, both the Aryans and Dravidians worshipped Shiva as a divinity and Indra became ridiculed as a drunken sot. Slowly, but surely, the image of a single, loving "God the Father" emerged within the dominant societies of the Western world.

Warriors have a certain magnanimity of mind and a certain spiritual way of life based on that magnanimity. They pray to their gods for a son, a wife, riches, name, fame, and victory; they pray for fierceness and to be fearless. They want such things from their imaginary gods, not only for themselves, but also for those under their protection. However, they want to keep for themselves the right to distribute these things.

The spirituality of the warrior is not free from the influence of matter. Their spirituality is actually limited to the effort to acquire material things or the effort to conquer matter. It is not easy for their intellect to understand the meaning of spiritual progress. The high standard of personal discipline, which is necessary for the performance of spiritual practices, is absent to some extent in most warriors because their minds are extremely restless.

Basically, the warrior sense of spirituality stems from their desire to have more and to attain more and to freely express themselves to the utmost. Where altruistic values take second place, the factor of greed comes into play. The warriors' hope of wealth, born of their greed, later helped the intellectuals to achieve absolute power. The warriors ultimately came to sell their physical brawn to the absolute authority of the intellectuals, who in their role as priests, persuaded them that they embodied the will of the gods.

The age in which the warrior mentality was dominant corresponds to the period that Western historians call Ancient History.

Although we tend to view Ancient History as a time of barbaric tribes and brutal warfare, we must remember that warrior society had its beginning under the leadership of women in their role as mothers. It was the women who initially built complex social networks and the agricultural civilizations of Mesopotamia, the Indus Valley, and Egypt. They also were responsible for the great cultural achievements of ancient Greece and Minoa. These accomplishments accelerated the evolution of humankind and laid the base for the patriarchal empires that followed.

## The Intellectual Age

### Psychic Characteristics

Intellectuals have the need to understand how things work and to use this knowledge to control their environment. While the warriors control by physical force, the intellectuals control by mental force. Having said this, how does one achieve power over another by mental force? The main technique has always been to befuddle the mind of the less intellectually developed and make them feel inferior. The first intellectuals emerged as priest classes who created supernatural stories about their city-gods to fill the masses with wonder at the intellectuals' access to secret knowledge. Intellectuals use their pursuits of the supernatural, and administrative skills very effectively in this way.

The common people did not understand the culture of the intellectuals. Through their religion, arts, and myths, the intellectuals appealed to the common people's sentiments and induced them to pay homage to their superiority. The common people think, "Even though we can't understand it, it must be something great." With this mentality, they knelt obediently at the feet of the intellectuals. Whereas the shúdras and the warriors merely enjoyed material pleasures, the intellectuals' pursuits of enjoyment were more abstract and refined, resulting in significant advancements in the arts, science, and technology.

Another characteristic of intellectuals is that they enjoy the glory of victory while avoiding the ignominy of defeat, and, in their personal lives, they satisfy their desires for enjoyment without taking great risks. While the intellectuals are constantly engaged in struggle, their fight takes place only on the battleground of their intellects.

Speaking of the difference between the warrior psychology and the intellectual psychology, Mr. Sarkar says:

> The fundamental difference between kśatriya-hood [warrior-hood] and vipra-hood [intellectual-hood] is that the ego of the kśatriyas draws objects of enjoyment to itself through a physical struggle with all opposing forces, while the ego of the vipras or their desire for enjoyment draws matter to itself either by the physical force of others or directly through psychic clash....

> Any expression of genuine humanity in the intellectual age did not surpass the humanity of the warrior age. They merely covered the genuine humanity that was there with a veneer of religious fanaticism. [21]

However, in an intellectual society there is more scope for benevolence than in a warrior society. This is to say that intellectuals are somewhat more sensitive to the pleasure and pain of others.

The intellectuals in their role as priests would always support those who paid them respect. They would think up justifications as to why their supporters were the best available to hold government offices or to achieve a higher social status. For example, priests would often justify their assertions with quotations from the scriptures. Of course, these intellectuals would not jeopardize themselves for the sake of supporting others, no matter how great their spiritual obligation required it. They rarely supported anybody if their own benefit was at risk.

Another characteristic of intellectuals is their emphasis on the future. While common people are only interested in the present, and warriors are interested in the past and present, the intellectuals are interested in the past, present, and the future. This does not automatically mean that they maintain a balance among the three. Intellectuals may concentrate on the past and ignore the present and future, or concentrate on the future and ignore the past and present. By giving undue importance to the past they make dogmatic decisions concerning policy and religion. By concentrating on the past, at the expense of the present and future, many intellectuals, both liberals and conservatives, have harmed not only themselves but society as well, and continue to do so. By being blinded by their infatuation with the past, they oppose new ideas. Society may break down and the environment become uninhabitable, but such intellectuals never come to their senses. This is especially true for religious intellectuals who become incapable of reason because over generations they have staked their dignity to a blind faith in a mythological world that never existed.

Excessive concern about the future can also be destructive. We have seen how the religious leaders infuse imaginary ideas about heaven and hell into peoples' minds. They tell the people, not to worry about this life, but only concern yourself with the after-life to come. By doing this, these leaders also harm themselves. By ignoring the social and environmental crisis of the present day, they destroy any hope for a positive life for their children on earth.

As Mr. Sarkar says, "Disasters occur when there is a lack of balance between people's physical and intellectual efforts. If the reins of society are in the hands of people who suffer from such imbalances, society as a whole will suffer the consequences of those disasters."[22] A doctrine that emphasizes an imaginary heaven and hell and considers life on earth to be a false and illusory reality is extremely dangerous for society. It stands firmly in opposition to the teachings of the great spiritual masters, including Jesus Christ, who told his disciples to care for and love their neighbors.

Even if an administration run by intellectuals does not itself create disasters, it will not be able to prevent them from occurring. This happens because the intellectuals give their power of mind a higher valuation than the application of physical force. Thus, under a church or other intellectual administration with this type of prejudice, other people are forced to work to enhance the intellectuals' prestige and to maintain their standard of living, but they are not appreciated as equals. By losing contact with the people, they set the stage for destructive social divisions.

Typical of an intellectual administration was the Catholic Church in the Middle Ages. The Church hierarchy used myths and stories to appeal to the people's sentiments instead of their rationality as a means to control them. The church turned their myths and stories into religious dogmas to enforce their control. What exactly are dogmas? Dogmas are beliefs based on myths, stories, and twisted logic that become encoded in the sentiments of a people. Dogmas have no relation to rationality, logic, or reason and require only blind faith to ensure compliance. Dogma-centered ideologies are usually perpetrated by a priest class in order to control the minds of the people. They are intended to create either inferiority or superiority complexes among the masses. Through the repetition of dogmas, which are then reinforced by ecclesiastical and social laws, the people were forced to believe that whatever the Church said was true. Anyone who spoke against these dogmas faced the penalty of persecution, torture, or death. Church dogma went so far as to claim that the Church held control over a person's soul. One could not enter heaven without Church approval. To disobey the commandments of the church resulted in eternal damnation.

As mentioned earlier, typical dogmas perpetrated by the priests are the myths of heaven and hell, the Garden of Eden and the inferiority of women, the need to offer indulgences (i.e., pay money to get your sins forgiven), praying for favors, confessing your sins to the priests to receive forgiveness, holding mythical gods and saints up for worship, the myth that ours is the true religion chosen by God, and the myth that if you die in battle fighting for your religion or nation you will go to heaven.

But even as the Church's hierarchy was cementing its power by the creation of dogmas and laws based upon them, many priests employed their reason to justify belief in their doctrines and in the Divine. It is quite natural, actually, for intellectuals to follow religious rituals based on both sentimentality and intellectuality. But even when there is no intent to exploit others, religions are seldom based upon spirituality. By relying solely on sentiment and intellectuality, and not spirituality, religions become mechanical and ritualistic, regardless of whether they have any reverence for God or not. To follow rituals, like performing so many prayers per day, or going to church on Sunday in order to fulfill one's religious duty, is not the same as seeking union with the Divine. Rather than becoming an expression of their love of God and neighbor, such practice becomes nothing but routine habit. Fear of being inferior, fear of being alone, fear of failure, and fear of hell are what drive ritualistic religions.

In regard to social discipline, the intellectuals were more flexible than the warriors. In order to sustain their own prestige, they realized that it was occasionally necessary to change the social system in order to meet the needs of the times. In their social systems, the warriors demonstrated the obstinacy characteristic of dictators. There was never any exception to the rule of law. At least, the intellectuals do not make this mistake. The reason for this is understandable. The prestige of the warrior is derived from their dictatorship, and so by any means they want to maintain the system as is. But the prestige of the intellectuals is based purely on intellectual supremacy, and so, after ensuring that they are able to maintain the scope for intellectual exploitation, they are willing to grant certain considerations to the people.

The cornerstone of any political state is discipline and a sense of unity. The real purpose of discipline in a warrior society is to achieve success in battle. Although this type of discipline was established by the warrior kings, something was still lacking. A mentality based on brute physical force is not enough to construct a well-knit society. A modern society needs another factor in order to give it strength. This factor is a social consciousness based upon morality. This social consciousness was provided by the intellectuals during the Intellectual (Vipran) Age.

The purpose of intellectual discipline is to maintain and develop the social structure, thus it will never overtly go against the social consciousness. Rather, it adapts itself to the changes of time, place, and person, creating new myths and dogmas to justify its actions. This is the form of society as we have come to understand it today.

In summary, exploiting others through use of intellectual force, getting others to fight their battles, creating a future vision, instead of just focusing on the past and present, and incorporating a social consciousness and moral discipline within the social structure, are some of the main characteristics of the Intellectual Age.

## Beginning of the Intellectual Age

The Intellectual Age corresponds to the Middle Ages as defined by Western historians. It covers the period from the fall of Rome to the beginning of the Industrial Revolution. As described in Volume Three of *The Untold Story of Western Civilization*, it was a period of time in the West in which the Catholic Church came to power and established a political hegemony through the Papacy and the Holy See.

Because the history of the warrior empires was soaked in blood, it was seldom illumined by intelligence. Warriors displayed dynamic personalities and courage, but little wisdom or subtle intellect. Therefore, after the Warrior Age had lasted for some time, the intellectuals, in their role as priests and ministers, began to control the warriors with their keen intellect. Although the warriors remained vigilant and cunning, once they submitted to the intellectuals, the Warrior Age ended.

Those with intellectual power encouraged the warriors to look in directions that they had never looked before and repeatedly explained to them things they had never understood. They brought religion to the warriors and, in so doing, positioned themselves as the seers and sages who understood the will of the gods. After this state of affairs had continued for some time, the warriors began to submit to the intellectuals in their role as priests and ministers. Recognizing their intellectual superiority, they began to use their forceful personalities to carry out the intellectuals' instructions. The priests gradually wrested the leadership of society from the warriors and maintained their supremacy in society with the help of the warriors' power.[23] In Volume One of *The Untold Story of Western Civilization*, we saw the beginning of this intellectual evolution in the rise of the rsis' of the Aryan tribes. In Volume Two, we watched as different priest classes arose to serve in the city temples of the ancient Middle

Eastern civilizations. We saw the Jewish priests create the Torah and the Talmud during their Babylonian Captivity, and we watched the early Christian priests battle each other for control of the Catholic Church. We also must acknowledge the rise of secular intellectual society among the Greeks and Romans that gave us philosophy, polity, art, science, and great advances in engineering.

According to Mr. Sarkar, there are more dishonest intellectuals than dishonest warriors. Most of the capabilities of the intellectuals are employed in appropriating a share of the hard-earned wealth of others. Just as the warriors used the shúdras as tools, the intellectuals use the warriors and the shúdras in the same way. Hence, when the Intellectual Age emerged from the Warrior Age, and the warriors laid their weapons, with complete trust, at the feet of the priests, they did not realize that they had surrendered themselves to deception and manipulation. The illusion of escaping the misfortunes of this life and going to heaven or hell in the next clouded their simpler minds. All the special qualities, the strengths and weaknesses, and the incongruities of the warriors' mentality could be deciphered by the intellectuals. They used this knowledge to exploit the weaknesses of the warriors' minds, giving them condescending encouragement for their simplicity.[24] On the other hand, by praising their strength, the intellectuals destroyed what intellect the warriors did have and by doing so, gained control of the warrior's strength for their own purposes. Just as a small man can control an unruly elephant, the intellectuals controlled the warriors through an understanding of their inner weakness, which was the pride they had in their strength. The priests sent the warriors into countless savage battles to die willingly, proud they were fighting for the glory of Jesus Christ. In fact, they were only fighting for the glory of the Church hierarchy.

Intellectuals developed the alphabets and compiled the ancient documents. They wrote the glorious history of the warriors. But in that history, they made it clear that it was the purpose of the powerful warriors to worship the gods whom the intellectuals, in their role as the priests, represented and whose words they interpreted. The powerful warriors could not see through this ruse. In their simplistic faith, they submitted to the shrewd and deceitful intellectuals.

**Religious Exploitation**

In the ancient city-state empires, the priests polished the idols of the city gods and kept their temples clean. In time, they began to conduct rituals of worship in which they conveyed the god's intentions to the people. They introduced myths and stories of their gods in order to exploit the people and build their own wealth and power.

The priests announced that their words were not from their own mouths, but were the words of the God they worshipped. "God says that you must think this and not that. You must behave in this way and not that. The gifts to the temple are the same as offerings to God." The priests threatened the people to get them to obey. "If you obey our command-ments, God will bless you and you will go to heaven; otherwise God will punish you in unimaginable ways for all eternity." The intellectuals created the myths of heaven and hell and the fear of hell turned people into religious fanatics. In this way, the people were easily led astray and many remain fooled even to this day because people will always want to understand the cause of their fear and misery, as well as have a reason to hope for a better life.[25] It is the power of the intellectuals to understand and to fulfill this need.

On occasion, the priests developed their religions based on the teach-ings of true spiritual masters and used these teachings to establish hierarchical institutions by which the priests could control the masses by promoting the master's words. Such was the case with the Church of Rome, which became the Catholic Church. By such means, the priests set themselves up as the intercessors between men and God. As the definition of "God" expanded, so too did the power of the priest class. This occurred despite the message of the spiritual master, Jesus Christ, that spirituality is based upon a direct relationship between a person and God and while this relationship may require the assistance of a teacher, it requires no intercessor. But despite all the religious splinter groups and the wars between them, the situation always remained the same for the people who were exploited by them. The priests, rabbis, ministers, or imams would tell the people, "Your father deserves to go to heaven, so we need a proper funeral," or "The only way to get into heaven is to listen to my words and donate to your religion." In this way, the intellectual exploiters gradually turned the minds of the people from practical reality towards an imaginary void by preaching contrived philosophies. The essence of their message was that the world is an illusion; therefore, renounce this world and do not be concerned about the human misery that you experience. Become desireless, detached, and self-abnegating by offering all your wealth and service to the Church. Under this spell, the people never stopped to consider that if the world was so illusory why was the Church hierarchy so committed to increasing its own wealth and power.

Because the intellectuals wanted to exploit the people's sentiments, they never promoted the path of rationality and discrimination, because they knew these could not be used as a means of exploitation. The priests wanted to lead the ignorant masses down the dark alley of blind faith and make them totally dependent upon the intellectuals for the salvation of their souls. So, the priests wrote reams of social treatises and told countless stories of religious fantasies to sway the minds of the gullible masses. In the place of logic and reason to support their message, they offered pedantic religious injunctions in which they held up the specter of eternal hell and torture as punishment for those who did not bow to their majesty. Essentially, these injunctions were no more than a concoction of religious bigotry and dogmatism. Such dogmas still hold sway over members of religions today. Faith in God is not the same thing as faith in religious dogma. The priests of the various religions do everything in their power to confuse the two in the minds of the believers. Essentially, faith in God leads to mental expansion, while faith in religious dogma leads to mental stagnancy.

Once a priest class is able to seize control over a society, as we have seen with Jews, Hindus, Christians, Muslims, etc., these intellectuals would write new social codes to cement their power. These new codes justified the behavior of the ruling elite while oppressing the most vulnerable, including women, the poor, slaves, and religious or racial minorities, who were condemned as heretics and heathens. Their legal codes also specified the means in which wealth would be transferred to the Church. The history of the Crusades, the Inquisitions, and Witch Hunts testify to this reality. In order to maintain their control, the priests based their machinery of dominance and exploitation on their so-called spiritual scriptures, which they always declared to be superhuman revelations given by "God" and not slippery people like themselves. Thus, the intellectuals gained the subservience of the people through the institution of immutable laws. These social codes were above being challenged because they supposedly came from the mouth of God Himself.

Because exploitation was the fundamental imperative of the priest class, they always made sure that they had the mechanisms to do this. According to Mr. Sarkar:

> The intelligent vipras understood that the path of exploitation was not the path of rationality and therefore they never walked that path, leading the ignorant instead down the path of blind faith. So when they set themselves to formulate social scriptures, they did so with an eye to their own convenience. Instead of supporting their views with rational arguments, they propagated high-sounding religious injunctions.[26]

A typical technique used by the priest class to assert its superiority and create a sense of inferiority in the people, was to introduce the idea of supernatural phenomena in order to achieve their objectives. In the early days of human society, people attributed frightful or distressing events to the ghosts of dead ancestors or natural forces who wished them harm. The priests capitalized on this fear of ghosts by becoming exorcists and tricking the people out of their money.

While lacking genuineness, their religious practices are not totally devoid of a spiritual aspect. However, in most cases, their desire to establish their own personal prestige by dominating others overshadowed whatever spirituality they possessed. In their goal to bring the European tribes under control, for example, they reinforced the myths of the supernatural powers of tribal gods and goddesses by designating many of them as Catholic saints. By doing this, they fortified their emphasis on mythical stories about Jesus Christ, and injected the confusion of religion into spirituality. Mythical stories have no relationship with spirituality.

The Catholic Church, in its golden age also encouraged artists to build great cathedrals, paint murals, make sculptures, compose music, and produce paintings to awe the common people and embed Church mythology into their minds and sentiments. The art, while grand and inspiring, emphasized the sharpness of the intellectual's mind, which overwhelmed the common people and mocked the down-to-earth sentiments of the warrior culture. Consequently, the respect that the warrior tribes held for the sacredness of a women's homestead, her folk crafts, witchcraft (healing), and the care of animals and nature, which had been so vital to warrior culture, were gradually diminished and ultimately condemned as evil paganism.

The Church convinced the people that the dogmas created by a particular pope or council of bishops were the words of God, and thereby undermined the natural inquisitiveness and creativity of the human mind and made people intellectually bankrupt. They used their scriptures to convince the common people that no mere mortal could achieve the same proximity to God as had the Church authorities. This injection of an inferiority complex in the minds of the masses has remained until this day, and due to this inferiority complex, the masses will always follow religious teachings, not out of rationally, but out of sentimentality based upon nothing more than blind faith. Even warriors and other intellectuals have fallen into this trap and have been compelled to say, "The goal is achieved not by reason but by faith" or "There is no room for reason in religion." This way of thinking is the antithesis of spirituality and reflects only corrupt politics.

When religious intellectuals talk about the need for "religious education," or a "religious state," what they really want is to entangle the minds of children, which are naturally inclined towards reason, in a net of religious superstition, so that later they will become puppets in the exploitive hands of their religious leaders. While there are certainly well-intentioned priests and nuns, the history of religious institutions amply documents the exploitation of the common people through this approach.

### The Social Structure of the Intellectuals during the Middle Ages

A government is needed to maintain any society. The government established in the Warrior Age by brute force remained intact in the

Intellectual Age, except that now the warriors were subservient to the Catholic hierarchy. Even though the control of the government appeared to remain in the hands of the warriors, in reality, nearly all the kings were bound to the whispering of their ministers and were forced to live according to the beck and call of the Church of Rome. In almost every country, we observe that even the most powerful kings were only puppets in the hands of their intellectual ministers, who were usually bishops or cardinals of the Holy See. The history of the monarchy was to a large extent the history of ministers and priests. If a king disobeyed the pope, the Church would muster the Christian kings of other lands to attack him and seize the wealth of his land.

From the time of the Roman Emperor Constantine, to that of the great king Charlemagne, who conquered Western Europe on behalf of the Church, the warrior kings came to rule only at the behest of the Holy See of the Catholic Church. At its most powerful, the Catholic Church controlled all of Western Europe. While the warriors created city-states and nation-states, the intellectuals created a church-state that ruled over the city-states and nation-states of the monarchs. In addition to controlling the kings, the Church also controlled the people by declaring the Divine Right of Kings, a doctrine that kings derived their authority from God, not from their subjects. This of course gave the Church supreme authority insofar as they controlled the kings as the representatives of God on earth. The Divine Right of Kings dogma also protected the kings who served the Church by declaring any popular rebellion to be a mortal sin.

No matter how hard a warrior king tried to overthrow the Church's dominance during the Middle Ages, he could not because he lived during the Intellectual Age, when the intellectual psychology remained dominant and the intellectual/priests were the ruling class.

Though the Church recognized the warrior monarchs as the supreme head of their national government, the Church did not grant them the right to interfere in religious matters, because it was through the institution of religion that the Church found the opportunity to establish itself. So, the warrior kings eventually became the "defenders of the Faith" and the "servants" of His Eminence and the Holy Father in Rome.

Because the Catholic Church was unable to completely capture the allegiance of the people through manipulative means, it developed its membership through forced conversions. Charlemagne, as he swept through Western Europe, fighting in the name of the Pope, forced all conquered people to convert to Catholicism under penalty of death. This is how Western Europe became Christian. It had virtually nothing to do with the spiritual injunctions of Jesus Christ.

This is not to say that there were not some people who converted to Christianity through genuine spiritual pursuit. Such was the case, for example, of those who succumbed to the example of the mystic Irish monks who entered Europe to teach true spirituality.

## Religious Conflict

In any society where religious rule has lasted for a long time, different splinter groups, motivated by opposition to specific dogmas and doctrines come into being while under the aegis of the ruling religion. During the Intellectual Age, new philosophies emerged as a result of clash among the intellectuals who propagated different doctrines. The new philosophies always took on a spiritual appearance, by questioning the morality of the mother religion.

Because egotistical intellectuals believe that only they understand the truth about things, their religions and organizations always become divided into many groups and sub-groups, each with contradictory opinions. Once certain religious leaders broke with the Catholic Church, for example, they immediately began to fight among themselves. Each group was busy refuting the ideas of the others and fighting among themselves for superiority. Mr. Sarkar says that while these internal clashes have been responsible for a certain amount of intellectual progress in society, they actually contribute little to the development of the magnanimity of mind.[27]

Generally, the theologies and philosophies of the intellectuals encourage people to find fault with others. As a result, people become degraded. Even today the leaders of some religious organizations spend the majority of their time in meetings and conferences slandering and vilifying others by using religious or diplomatic language to conceal their exploitative intentions. As so-called spiritual leaders, they ignore spiritual philosophy and spiritual practices. Of course, they put the mask of spirituality on their high-sounding verbiage in order to further their own interests. In this way, the people lose the vital distinction between spirituality and religion.

When shúdras clash with each other, it is a clash of self-interest only. They live for physical enjoyment, and are concerned only about their personal and family interests. Because they are unable to generate a powerful vibration in society, they are considered by the warriors, intellectuals, and merchants to be of little value. When warriors clash, however, it is a clash of powerful personalities, fist against fist, sword against sword, cannon against cannon. And when intellectuals clash it is a clash of intellects, con against con, ruse against ruse, duplicity against duplicity.

Religious conflict has led to horrific acts of violence against men, women, and children. Fanatic Catholics, who regarded non-Catholics as unbelievers, burnt them alive; and many orthodox mullahs decreed that killing an infidel was not a sin. Within the Jewish theocracy, the Sadducees and the Pharisees demanded that the Romans kill Jesus Christ, who was an Essene. An attempt on the life of Lord Buddha was made by the priest Devadatta.[28] After the Renaissance in Europe, Catholics and Protestants died by the thousands as they fought and killed each other in religious wars that lasted for over a century. These are only a few examples of religious conflict in human history.

**Women: The Slaves of the Intellectuals**

Among the European tribes, prior to the coming of the Romans and then the Catholic Church, women were regarded as having equal status with men. They were co-helpers and co-workers each operating within their social roles. In the Intellectual Age, women became no more than maid-servants, reduced to servile, second-class citizens. Those that took the brunt of the Church's campaign against heretical beliefs were the women. In the Intellectual Age, the exploitation of women by men greatly increased. In the attempt to indoctrinate the tribes of Europe, the Church conspired in every way to destroy the power of women.

The priests fabricated "divine" commandments from their manipulative scriptural injunctions, dogmas, and imaginary yarns of sin and virtue. These commandments maintained that men alone, particularly the priests, were the chosen of God for whom women had taken birth only to provide enjoyment and service to men. As we saw in Volume Three of *The Untold Story of Western Civilization*, the priests burned women as witches throughout Europe as a means to control women healers and female spiritual teachers. In this way they "converted" the European matriarchal tribes to Christianity through torture and death.[29]

The suppression of women and the attempt to control every aspect of their bodies, minds, and souls still form a core dimension of contemporary religion. This is true of all patriarchal religions. It is undeniably the greatest impediment to social progress for humanity as a whole.

We have either forgotten, or more likely, never been taught that as far back as the dawn of human knowledge, it was the women who imparted knowledge to others. It was the women who taught us how to pray by composing the incantations and offering libations to the Great Goddess. Even after patriarchy evolved, the women still sat within the warrior tribes as equals to men. In the Intellectual Age, however, they lost all prestige as human beings and were, as a gender, forced to submit to slavery. They were stripped of their rights to live as equals to men, to study scriptures or gain knowledge, to heal, to speak in public, and were completely superseded by priests in the society. Women were to remain silent and lost all power to teach men about spirituality. Ultimately, there was no alternative left but to submit to the superiority of the priest class or be burned at the stake.

According to Mr. Sarkar:

> Their social respect and prestige lasted as long as they maintained their feminine charm and beauty. In countries where the women alone toil and the men spend their days sitting idle and eating, the feminine status is no better. Women are still kept under severe domination. Even in the advanced countries of the world, where the women are courteously respected as the "fair sex," the masculine society wears a long face when the question of equal rights occurs. So the masculine domina-

tion which characterized the Intellectual Age remained
unchanged in the subsequent Capitalist Age....[30]

In the Intellectual Age, due to loss of prestige, economic hardship, and
other environmental causes, prostitution as a profession came into being
for the first time. It did not develop in either the Shúdra or Warrior Age.
Mr. Sarkar points out that:

> Individual depravity may cause a certain amount of li-
> centiousness, but it is certainly not the reason for the
> emergence of a large number of prostitutes. The iniq-
> uity or sin of this lewd profession is the creation of the
> selfish vipras [intellectuals].[31]

By being economically crippled and with the pain of unrelenting social
penalty and threats of perdition in hell, the women became filled with
despair and developed a deep inferiority complex. Mr. Sarkar notes
that, "Few keep count of the millions of women who wept and sobbed
themselves to death in the darkness of many a sleepless night. They were
leveled flat like the soft earth under the administrative steamroller of
the vipras (intellectuals)."[32]

### End of the Intellectual Age

The dynamics of social psychology follow a long-established pattern. Where
there is more physical clash in life, physical force will increase faster than
the intellect or the expression of intellect. In like manner, where there is
more psychic clash, there will be an increase in intellectual expression.
This is usually coupled with a gradual but eventually severe case of physical
indolence. From a psychological point of view, people dominated by intellect in this way gradually become more and more atrophied. In time, they
lose their balance and the lives of the people whom they dominate become
inconsequential to them. In this way, whatever magnanimity existed at the
beginning of the Intellectual Age was lost by the end of that age.

The end result of the loss of magnanimity by the intellectuals/priests
is that the merchant/capitalist class began to challenge their rule and,
in so doing, became the dominant class in society. At the beginning of

the Intellectual Age, the priest sought means to protect society as well as exploit it. They took advice from others in their endeavors. By the end of their age, however, the priests only gave advice, but no longer accepted it from others. Within their own circles, the only advice they took was from each other on how to best exploit the people under their domination. The Crusades, Inquisitions, Witch Hunts, and the confiscations of land and wealth by those who challenged their authority had gradually sapped them of their humanity.[33]

## Secular Intellectuals

By the fifteenth century, religious intellectuals were so morally corrupt, they no longer were able to maintain their tight control over their critics. This gave rise to the Protestant Reformation and a hundred years of war between the Catholics and the Protestants. The conflict between religious dogmas eventually provided an opening for the emergence of secular thought during the period of the Enlightenment that followed the Protestant Reformation.

During this period, the legitimacy of governmental rule by the Church and aristocracy was challenged head on by the secular intellectuals. To free themselves from the rule of the Church and its puppet kings, these revolutionary intellectuals devised the idea of a state being governed according to a legal framework. Instead of operating according to the whims of the pope or the king, the secular intellectuals advocated that governmental procedures be based upon a written constitution. To enforce the constitution, they advocated a constitutional monarchy, and later a constitutional assembly, which then gave rise to democratic governments. The revolutionaries, who at the time were the progressives and the liberal thinkers, held that society should not give primary importance to administration, but rather to human welfare. This was also a contribution of the progressive intellectuals.

The great thinkers of the Reformation and Enlightenment periods developed ideas that still dominate society today. As a result, the prestige that these intellectuals have, due to their revolutionary ideas concerning religion, philosophy, science, political economy, etc., is much greater than the prestige experienced by the warrior kings in their day. But it must also be admitted that intellectuals do not always receive immediate recognition for their contributions to collective wisdom. Instead, they face many obstacles during their lives and often become objects of censure, humiliation, and slander.

Human beings have an innate attraction towards the past because they have learned to be comfortable with it. They do not fear the past as they do the future. This is why there are always more conservatives than progressives in society. When an intellectual reveals something new, the population does not easily accept it. People cannot easily assimilate the new information and prefer to stick to the "tried and true." Thus, progressive intellectuals, who develop something new, face conflicts, acrimonious attacks, and unwarranted criticism.

This is why people like Galileo or Copernicus were persecuted by the Church. Or why the Church fought the proponents of Humanism or Protestantism as they arose. When Rabindranath Tagore first started to write his poetry, the existing writers of Bengal suppressed and ridiculed him. Yet today he is universally loved and revered as the world's greatest poet. Karl Marx was also rejected in his time, but came to be revered by billions of people after his death. Many artists, writers, and musicians have faced the same situation, as have many scientists. But when new theories and discoveries have been around long enough, they become familiar to people and eventually become established.

The history books are filled with stories of great intellectuals just as there are stories of great warriors. During the Intellectual Age, warriors fought and died by the hundreds of thousands while the popes, cardinals, and ministers received the triumphant ovations. The names of the great intellectuals are blazoned across the pages of history, but such history did not record the suffering of the common people or the soldiers who fought and died on the battlefield. This is because history is only written by the intellectuals.

Although the Intellectual Age has passed, intellectuals still play a major role in the Age of Capitalists. Today, in the service of their capitalist masters, the "policy-oriented" intellectuals have led and are continuing to lead millions of people along the path of death and destruction. Self-serving intellectuals fan the flames of the capitalists' insatiable hunger for more wealth and power by coming up with strategies for confiscating the wealth of other nations and peoples. It is not the common masses or the warriors who are responsible for the millions of refugees now trying to escape the wars and man-made environmental catastrophes. The responsibility lies with that group of shrewd intellectuals who, out of petty self-interest, have instigated the warriors and the masses to commit their heinous wars and destruction of environmental systems for the benefit of the capitalist rulers.[34]

However, not all intellectuals today succumb to the power of the capitalists. Those people who, undaunted by either political pressure or threats of violence, have tried to save their religion or their ideology from extermination, should be regarded as intellectuals from a psychological standpoint, regardless of whether they are intellectually developed or not. Those people who have the desire to resist, protest, or retaliate against the forcible imposition of divisive doctrines and laws are also to be regarded as intellectuals.[35] Such intellectuals who are willing to fight for the general welfare are either warrior intellectuals or intellectual warriors. They possess a rare brilliance because they are willing to fight for their ideals.

## Positive Characteristics of the Intellectual Age

Not all priests and intellectuals have used their minds simply to exploit others in a quest to accumulate material wealth. Some also sought, and continue to seek, mental wealth for its own sake or to surpass the intelligence of others. For some others, the struggle to continually increase their knowledge eventually allowed them to reach the highest or "pinnacled" intellect. And this brought them near to the spiritual realm of intuition.

It is known to any true mystic, regardless of religion, that when someone does spiritual practices, it causes the crude mind to reach the realm of the subtle mind and the subtle mind to reach the realm of the intuition, which is the innate repository of infinite knowledge that enlightens the intellect. It is not by the worship of mythical characters and saints that one achieves divine knowledge. Faith in a god of religion may help start one on the spiritual path, but blind faith is hardly the path to enlightenment.

This heightened state of intuitional awareness is revealed in the words of the different mystics throughout history:

> The coming of the kingdom of God is not something that can be observed, nor will people say, "Here it is," or "There it is," because the kingdom of God is in your midst (Luke 17:22).

> Remember the clear light ... from which everything in the universe comes, to which everything in the universe returns ... the natural state of the universe unmanifested. Let go into the clear light, trust it, merge with it. It is your own true nature, it is home (*The Tibetan Book of the Dead*).

> Why run around sprinkling holy water? There's an ocean inside you, and when you're ready you'll drink (*Kabir*).

> The first peace comes within the souls of people when they realize at the center of the universe dwells the Great Spirit, and that its center is really everywhere, it is within each of us (*Black Elk*).

> Mystical experiences do not necessarily supply new ideas to the mind, rather, they transform what one believes into what one knows, converting abstract concepts, such as divine love, into vivid, personal realities (*Mother Jones*).

> The explicable requires the inexplicable. Experience requires the nonexperienceable. The obvious requires the mystical (Buckminster Fuller).

The awakening of the pinnacled intellect enables one to approach the highest stance of subtlety. It is what allowed Jesus Christ to say, "I and my Father are One."

Unfortunately, not enough intellectuals try to develop a pinnacled intellect or spiritual intuition? Most are busy accumulating objects of enjoyment with the help of others' labor and using every means at their disposal to exploit the members of society while at the same time putting on a show of honesty and moral rectitude. Although the intellectuals are proud of their learning and want to lead society, their aversion to manual labor turns them into a kind of social parasite. Therefore, to justify their existence to the people, some began to perform social service and share their knowledge. This redeeming quality attributable to a handful of sincere intellectuals, both men and women, awakened in the minds of the people a special type of love for these simple intellectuals. They thought, "What is the harm if the priests take a part of what I've earned through my bravery, strength, intellect, or physical labor; he is also sharing his precious gifts with us."

The belief that serving the priests was the stepping-stone to heaven became firmly rooted in the minds of the people. Regardless of whether this belief was good or not, it helped to build and maintain the solidarity of society. Although most common people did not understand it, their devotion to the priests or to their religion helped them to progress spiritually and to assimilate more subtle ideas. For this reason, it is inappropriate to condemn religious leaders in a wholesale manner and to refuse to recognize this important fact.

While some brave warriors fought to defend themselves, to protect others, and to create a social legacy, some priests, motivated by their love of God and altruism, used their intellectual power to protect the mentally-undeveloped warriors and common people and with the people's help, were able to survive and have their own needs met.

Some priests applied their intellect to develop the skills of debaters, logicians, and metaphysicians. While such mental expressions did not particularly address the spiritual world, and while these priests might have used their logic and verbosity to exploit society and present themselves as righteous, their ideology also could be used to refute superstitious dogmas and encouraged people to move towards the subtler psychic realm.

Inevitably, those treading the path towards the subtlest realm of intellect provided spiritual inspiration to the human race and helped to develop a spiritual perspective. Because of this, it was possible in the past; it is possible today; and it will be possible in the future for society to develop a class of people that Mr. Sarkar calls "Sadvipras." These are the spiritual warriors of whom we will speak in more detail in our next book on Revolution. These are the true spiritualists within human society.

They choose not to escape from society to perform their spiritual practices, but rather involve themselves in the problems of society, using all their skills and determination to serve humanity and motivate people to move toward Divinity for the benefit to all.

Despite our harsh criticism of the intellectual class during their age, we cannot overlook the fact that human fraternity, universalistic intellect, and the quest for the highest mental attainment were also contributions of the Intellectual Age.

# The Capitalist Age

## Psychic Characteristics

While there have always been merchants in society, the ascension of the merchant psychology to a position of dominance, at the dawn of the modern age, was something new in history and ultimately gave rise to a new ruling class. While those imbued with the warrior and the intellectual mentalities used different methods to accumulate the material objects they enjoyed, the emerging capitalist class was more interested in owning material objects than enjoying them. The ownership of wealth and just thinking about it gave them an immense sense of satisfaction. So, in the Capitalist Age, i.e., Modern History, the practical value of material goods gave way to the monetary value of goods. The ultimate goal of the merchant/capitalists is to profit from the sale of goods and services and then horde the accumulated profit for themselves. This is the greatest curse of the Capitalist Age, because social wealth is created by the movement of money in society, not by its hoarding. When money is hoarded, society stagnates and the common people suffer. In the Warrior and Intellectual Ages, it was rare for people to die of starvation while grain rotted in warehouses. As Mr. Sarkar says: "Warriors and intellectuals do not kick others into a pit of privation, poverty, and starvation while they themselves enjoy their wealth."[36]

The capitalists are risk takers. They remain ever attentive to their profit and loss statements and they astutely watch the ups and downs in society in order to determine profit-making opportunities. Thus, they develop the capacity to take advantage of a wide variety of situations. This is the key to their success. They are willing to take more risk than the warriors or intellectuals. And although they are just as cunning as the intellectuals, their cunning is focused almost entirely on the accumulation of wealth.

While capitalists may be fighters, they lack the powerful personalities of the warriors and possess weaker personalities than the intellectuals because morality or social consciousness has little credence in their view. They would not hesitate to sell out anything to make a profit whether it was their neighborhood, their nation, the prestige of women, or even themselves. If an intellectual and a capitalist ever engage in a purely intellectual fight, the intellectual will win. But if the fight involves financial gain, the capitalist will win. Mr. Sarkar says the capitalists will lock the intellectual's mind up in his iron safe.[37]

Capitalists view everything with a greedy eye. Therefore, they do not have the capacity to correctly or fully understand worldly issues. They remain unconcerned with social or environmental problems unless they can profit from them. If their corporations pollute the earth in order to create profit, they would rather hire intellectuals to deny or mislead the public, or, failing that, employ the warriors to ensure their business will not be interrupted. In a capitalist society, anyone can say anything they want about the capitalists and not be punished. But if those critics move beyond words and begin to take action, they will find themselves monitored, hassled, and their livelihood destroyed. They may even be killed by the capitalist's thugs, as so often happens to journalists and activists in third world countries.

Those with a capitalist mentality look at other people as the wellspring of their wealth. They are the sharks and humanity their victims. While the warrior controls by physical force and the intellectual by mental force, the merchant controls by dominating the money supply. The capitalists (vaeshyas) increase their share of the money by exploiting the physical and/or mental work of others, depending upon the situation. They know better than anyone that it is through the exploitation of labor and natural materials that wealth is produced and it is therefore their objective to squeeze as much vitality out of labor and natural materials as possible

to increase their wealth. In this respect, the capitalists are similar to
the intellectuals; however, while the intellectuals try to hide their greed
behind false logic, quotes from scripture, or fake indifference, the capitalists make no such pretense of their desire to become "filthy" rich.

As intellectuals are somewhat more inclined to develop a degree of
conscience, they do not always use their intellects strictly to accumulate objects of enjoyment. However, this is not true with the capitalists
who lack a social conscience. Occasionally, they may make a donation,
according to their inclination or business priorities, but only when it is
in their self-interest to do so. While engaged in business, however, they
will not tolerate even the loss of a single penny. As a consequence, the
mind of the capitalist becomes cruder over time as a result of his/her
desire to accumulate more material wealth.

**Beginning of the Capitalist Age**

During the Intellectual Age, those who lacked physical strength or
intellectual ability tried to discover an alternative way to live and gain
wealth and power. The particular type of psychic clash, which arose in
their minds due to their constant efforts to establish themselves, resulted
in their money-making intellect. This skill helped them to exploit the
strength and courage of the warriors and the mental power of the intellectuals. The more they succeeded in this exploitation, the more they
became recognized in the society as leading men.

The merchants' skill at trading, banking, and manipulating the
labor of others for profit, gradually gained them importance at the
time when the iron rule of the Catholic Church was drawing to an
end. Merchants proliferated in the cities where trade predominated.
The so-called Age of Discovery had increased their importance within
medieval society as they sailed their cargo ships around the world and
brought back goods, food, furs, gold, and other objects for sale in their
mother countries. The Church hierarchy and the aristocracy became
ever more enamored and desirous of the wealth that the merchants
brought back to the cities from their foreign exploits. To feed their
growing want of exotic goods and services, the rich gradually found
themselves more in debt to the merchant class. In time, the kings of

Europe became dependent upon them to increase their wealth and to help build their national armies. The wealthy merchants also began to make large donations to the Church to build its cathedrals and to furnish them with objects of art.

The merchants took charge of the financing, production, distribution, and sales of merchandise. They became the financial advisors and bankers to the king and the Church. In time, they were able to buy titles and land from the Church and nobility.

Some intellectuals became servant-priests to these merchants. They underwent austerities, performed worship services, and recited scripture on behalf of the merchants in return for money. Other intellectuals became clerks, accountants, managers, architects, artists, etc. The courageous warriors took upon themselves the responsibility of armed gatekeepers and began to salute the owners of the castle twice a day. They became the merchants' strong-armed men. The shúdras, who had served as serfs during the Middle Ages now became the servants and laborers of the merchants. As more people found themselves owing their livelihood to this new class, they had no choice but to gradually elevate the status of the merchants (the bourgeoisie) in society. In this way, the Capitalists Age developed in every European nation. With the manufacturing of steel and the use of fossil fuels, machines could be built to do work faster and increase production. The skills of artisans became antiquated and skilled workers found themselves working for the capitalists. This development led to the Industrial Revolution and the dawn of the Capitalist Age. This revolution occurred between 1750 and 1840 in most western nations and signaled the end of the Middle Ages. Modern history begins with the Capitalist Age and is distinguished by the establishment of the new capitalist ruling class.

### The Capitalist State

In *The Untold Story of Western Civilization*, Volumes 3, 4, and 5, we traced the evolution of the capitalist state through the periods of Mercantile, Laissez Faire, Monopoly, State Monopoly, and Global Monopoly Capitalism. When the merchant psychology first took hold in

Europe in the sixteenth century, society initially benefitted. The merchants provided a great service to the people by overthrowing the oppressive rule of the Catholic Church and the aristocratic leeches of the Middle Ages. They were able to do this because they had accumulated enough money to change the feudal economy to an entirely new economic system.

The opportunity to create capital in a massive and diversified way is a product of the Capitalist Age. For any business endeavor, capital, either in the form of money or material resources, is initially required. The European capitalists brought back this wealth to their societies by confiscating it from abroad and bringing it back in their ships during the Age of Discovery and subsequently through the creation of colonies around the world. With the help of this capital, production systems were created throughout Europe and increased wealth was generated to meet individual and collective needs. This is what happened in the early days of the merchant revolutions in England, the United States, France, etc. Initially, capital improved the general standard of living in European society in a way that could never have been done without the initial capitalization from foreign exploitation and slave labor. Some of this wealth was usurped by the king, who used it to create his armies and civil servants.

In time, the capitalists created a system of credit and debt to increase access to capital. For example, the Rothschild bankers made their fortune by inventing government bonds. When a king needed money for a project or a war, the Rothschilds would underwrite the king's debt and sell the debt to others.[38] The king would have to pay interest on his debt and also pay the fees to the bankers for underwriting and selling his bonds. This financial invention allowed kings or queens to do whatever they wanted whenever they wanted. In this way, capital became more fluid in society and greater amounts of money were generated. National bonds allowed for the creation of standing armies and continuous warfare. Ever since the Rothschilds' invention, governments have used bonds (IOUs) to fund their wars and domestic programs. It is precisely through this mechanism that capitalists came to control all nation states in the western world.

Prior to the evolution of the capitalists, those who possessed the merchant mentality were simply small business merchants. They made money from their own labor and built businesses for themselves. Once, however, the quantity of money that was amassed was significant enough to loan to others, economic relations changed dramatically and the simple merchant evolved into a capitalist, one who used his money to make money.

No matter how excess wealth is generated, it needs to be controlled by an individual and that individual controller is the capitalist.

In time, the capitalists were able to wrest control of wealth from the Church and monarchy and create their own political-economy. This created the base for a capitalist revolution and ultimately the capitalist nation-state. These revolutions occurred throughout Europe, beginning with England and then France. The American Revolution was also a capitalist revolution.

## Capitalist Exploitation

The capitalists, as a class, harnessed their materialistic intellects in order to increase their ownership of wealth. Because of their materialistic preoccupation, they were able to defeat the intellectuals and dominate society through financial machinations.

The capitalists clearly understand that their system of exploitation would fail without the support of the laborers, warriors, and intellectuals. To ensure that this support continues, they use their "policy-oriented intellectuals"[39] to develop positive public relation and advertising campaigns. The PR people, in their role as mainstream media executives and politicians, use their grandiloquence to convince the people that the capitalists are really working for their benefit. They tout the myth that democracy, liberty, and the pursuit of happiness drive capitalist societies, when actually it is the capitalists' wealth that determines every political decision. Thus, as a result of this psychological manipulation, the people continue to support those who, in actuality, are responsible for the financial misery in their lives. Through a process of indoctrination, the laborers, warriors, and intellectuals became enslaved to the capitalists and remain so today. Although some "value-oriented intellectuals" understand what is happening and offer resistance. However, after a short struggle, they also are compelled to surrender to the capitalists like flies caught in a spider's web. Without the help of the "policy-oriented intellectuals," it would be virtually impossible for the capitalists to force the laborers and the warriors to work for them.

The victory of money over intellect and physical force did not come about in a single day. Only after being entangled in the web of finance, and having their vitality exhausted in the struggle, did the intellectuals and warriors, having no other alternative, surrender to the capitalist system. They are now forced to sing the praises of the capitalist system while despairing of their own situation. Through the power of money, the capitalists gradually took over all the accomplishments achieved by the intellectuals, the sacrifice of countless warriors, and the physical work of millions of laborers. All have become slaves to the capitalist system.

## The Continued Exploitation of Women

As in the Intellectual Age, women tend to bear the brunt of capitalist exploitation. The exploitation of women that was institutionalized by the Catholic Church and other religions in Europe continued unabated under the capitalists. To this day, women struggle against impossible odds to achieve political, economic, and social rights equal to those of men. More pressing is the continual battle women face to control their own bodies. Men believe they have the right to deny a woman her reproductive rights regardless of the risk of mortality or her decision as to what is best for her. Even more destructive is the prevalent, harassment, rape, physical abuse, violence, and enslavement of women under capitalism. These violations of women are often committed by strangers, but more often they are committed right inside a women's home in the form of "domestic violence."

It was not until the late twentieth century when the "marital exemption" in rape laws was finally abandoned in capitalist countries. Even today, however, women are discouraged from reporting rape or violence by men because of the humiliation they face from the male authorities. If women obtain a court order to restrain a rapist, they still have no support because the police cannot protect them twenty-four hours a day and the men in the community will usually not lift a finger to help them. And even if they have the courage to take the kids, uproot their lives, and leave the abuser, where are they to go when there are no facilities to take them in?

Capitalist society fosters domestic violence. Rape and sexual abuse is epidemic in the military, universities, and within corporations. A recent study found that two-thirds of young women have been sexually harassed while at work.[40] When women speak up about being harassed and assaulted, they are called "hysterical" by the corporate media.[41] Capitalism does not defend women; rather it suppresses them, impoverishes them, and then humiliates them for their poverty and anxiety. We are living in a rape culture and very few men will organize to protect women from violence. Not white men, black men, brown men, yellow men, no men. In the meantime, the health care industry makes a fortune dispensing drugs to women for their depression while male counselors make millions "treating" their mental illness. It is estimated that each year in the United States $4.1 billion dollars is spent on direct medical and mental health care services for women of domestic abuse.[42] And these are only the reported cases.

Women receive hate mail if they want to run for public office or rise in the corporate world or in the military. They receive abuse if they want to earn fair wages or equal pay, to receive an education, or to have maternity leave.

It was as early as 1837, when a French Utopian Socialist, Charles Fourier, coined the term "feminism" to express support for women's rights within the capitalist system. Throughout the entire history of capitalism, women have had to battle against relentless institutionalized sexism. In some capitalist countries, women were not allowed to vote until late in the twentieth century. It was not until the 1960's, when the "women's movement" began to address the inequality and harassment that women face on a daily basis in the United States.

Without women being treated as equals, it will be impossible to progress as a human society. There can be no revolution. There can be no improvement in the human condition. There can be no dream of a better world. There can be no spiritual awakening.

For women, the struggle entails overcoming millennia of indoctrination that men have a right to exploit them. It means becoming again the warriors they once were and taking back what rightfully belongs to them.

For men, the struggle entails overcoming millennia of indoctrination that we are superior to women and that we are justified in sitting back while women are continually harassed, raped, and abused all around us. Is this what being a "real man" means?

## Manipulation through Fear and Desperation

Capitalists understand that, due to limited resources, only a few people can accumulate great material wealth. They know that their class will always remain small, while those who are the objects and tools of their exploitation will always be the great majority. Today, activists have acknowledged this division between the one percent who are the rich capitalists versus the ninety-nine percent of humanity.

The desperate feeling among people that we do not deserve to live a fulfilling life is the greatest accomplishment of the capitalists. To maintain their control over us, they nurture this feeling of desperation because it is the emotional base upon which they build their divide and conquer strategies to use against us. In our desperation, we lash out and blame each other for our miserable lives. We strike out at our neighbors if they are a different gender, race, age, religion, or nationality than us. The capitalists are ever engaged, through their mass media, in nurturing fear and desperation among us and turning us against each other. In the US, the capitalists create horrific wars in the Middle East and when people there try to escape the death and destruction to protect their children, the capitalists refuse them entry into the country, claiming they are terrorists who want to kill us. All the while, we remain servile to the capitalists, thankful to God that we have a job, even if it is a menial job that does not allow us to make ends meet. Still we humble ourselves because we believe it is better than to have no work at all.

Such a system of exploitation causes rampant sexism, racism, and xenophobia because the frightened workers think that women, racial minorities, and immigrants are going to take their jobs from them. In this system, those who are the most vulnerable to exploitation must be further suppressed if the white workers are to keep their jobs and their sense of dignity. While this is the situation today, the capitalists, in their greed, have not looked far enough ahead. They do not foresee the day when the masses, having nothing left to lose, will desperately leap into the fire of revolution. The Capitalist Age will then come to an end. Exactly when this will occur is difficult to predict because the downtrodden people must have no other options available to them. In the meantime, they lack the understanding that the capitalists are the parasites of society who are responsible for their misery. Their minds have been cleverly deluded by the mass media into thinking others are the threat. At the same time, their Christian religions are telling them not to think about their suffering in this life because they will be rewarded in heaven.

The capitalists increase their personal wealth by buying the back breaking work of the masses, the powerful personalities of the warriors, and the sharp intellect of the intellectuals, according to their need. The masses, reduced to chattel, provide their physical labor in exchange for mere subsistence. Because they sell their labor so cheaply, the capitalists become sinfully rich while society wobbles along, becoming weaker each succeeding month and year. The powerful personalities of the warriors build and maintain the social structure. They man the armies of the capitalists abroad, while domestically, they serve as the police and security guards who keep the people from acting out. While the motto of the police is "Serve and Protect" and while we must admit that there are some police officers who believe in these principles, the majority of the police have been indoctrinated to look upon the people as their enemies. Armed with military gear and more powerful weapons, they are willing to die to protect the capitalist system. At the same time, the policy-oriented intellectuals keep the people in a state of fear, accepting their oppression. The mainstream newspapers and TV news shows will say and do whatever the capitalists tell them to do.[43] Like the workers, the white male warriors and intellectuals also fear losing their jobs to the women, racial minorities and immigrants who have become the scapegoats of the media. On top of the social pyramid, miles above the human fray, the small class of monopoly capitalists sit on their celestial thrones eagerly watching for ways to manipulate the chaos below for profit. It is they who masterminded the governance structure of the modern state for the purpose of increasing their wealth and remain as indifferent as Greek gods to the continued suffering of the mere mortals below.

Society is only a money-making machine for the capitalists. And like a machine, the society works without protest. The capitalists are not punished for their crimes because they sit above the law. If a capitalist's crime becomes too obscene to be ignored, a scapegoat will be found to take the fall. Through their banks and corporations, the capitalists dominate national armies and national governments so no laws can be written to curtail their exploitation. The capitalists may be part of the social body, but they are not part of the money-making machine. They are separate. They supply the fuel for the machine, but they take far more from the machine than they spend on it. They think, "Because I provide the fuel for the machine the output is mine. My money built the machine, and when I no longer need it, I will destroy it." The capitalists are willing to plunder society and the planet to make a profit, and if they can no longer make a profit, they are willing to destroy both. This is their mental illness. They have become certifiable sociopaths.

When the capitalists encounter a setback or they see the people moving toward drastic reforms or rebellion, they adopt new forms of deception in order to protect their position. Until an actual *shūdra revolution* occurs, the capitalists will have their apologists working without rest to develop newer and more artful methods of deception. A "tried and true" device is to promote their magnanimous distribution of social welfare crumbs. Abroad, their foreign aid extended to poor nations during floods and famines will later be recovered with interest. The capitalists benefit from their apparent acts of altruism in various ways. First, they continue to make good money off of their businesses in those countries. Secondly, people who are disgruntled with the capitalists' exploitation are to some extent pacified and their wounded minds are temporarily soothed by the aid. Thirdly, it now becomes easier for the capitalists to exploit the people's vulnerability. They can now more easily sell loans to the government that will put the country into even greater debt and enslavement.[44] In time, they will privatize the infrastructure and the national resources of that country in payment for this debt. Because of capitalist "altruism," the entire third world has plunged into debt, while eighty percent of the human population has been impoverished.

In the meantime, the capitalists are benefitted by the "radical" intellectuals who maintain the welfare system and also by those who continually point out the capitalists' faults, but who will take no action to stop them. As such, their worthless words ring hollow and only serve to lead the capitalists to develop ever more subtle means of exploitation. This is essentially the role of the liberal Democrats.

## Ending Capitalism

Whatever human dignity people may have possessed, in either the Warrior Age or the Intellectual Age, is severely reduced in the Capitalist Age, where a person's worth is solely measured in terms of money. Money is superior to human beings. For example, the capitalist corporations weigh human deaths from known carcinogens in their products to the profits they can make from not eliminating the carcinogens that kill millions. To ensure profits they are willing to pay a fine for killing people.[45] The lies of the cigarette industry and the fossil fuel industry are good examples of this practice. The quality of a person's life is of no consequence in a capitalist society. The repercussions of this predicament have far-reaching consequences in all spheres of society.

Those intellectuals and warriors who once thought independently and who possessed a sense of dignity and self-reliance, cannot establish themselves in today's society unless they learn to flatter the capitalists in a psychological way. Those who hope for respect, or have gained it, depend, or have depended on, the financial manipulations of the capitalists.

The difficulties faced by those who try to destroy capitalism in order to rebuild society on a humanistic foundation are greater than those suffered by people who tried to reform the social structures of the previous ages. For example, those who wanted to destroy the Church had to fight only the intellectuals, warriors, and laborers in its service, but those who want to strike at the capitalist structure have to fight against the capitalists as well as the intellectuals, warriors, and laborers who are obedient to their masters.

The common people do not even understand what the "value-oriented intellectuals" are saying even though they may speak and act for the common good. And even if they understand them, they remain silent and withhold their support. This is because they owe their livelihoods to the capitalists' money and they will not risk losing their jobs no matter how low their pay.

The intellectuals exploited the masses during the Intellectual Age under the pretense of religion. The penalty for challenging the Christian religion was imprisonment, torture, death, and the threat of eternal damnation. The same dynamic occurs in the Capitalist Age, but capitalist exploitation is more devious. In the Capitalist Age, the intellectuals exploit others through religious and secular means in order to promote their own and the capitalists' interests. They tell the people that it is not the role of their religion to be concerned about their daily suffering, only with their "spiritual" needs. Or they tell the people it is useless to fight the system and sinful to break its laws because it is God's will that capitalism exists. Such doctrines help the capitalists to perpetuate their structure. Such priests and preachers destroy the personal integrity of people and make them the victims of the ruling elite. The common people, not knowing any better, willingly accept the falsehood that everything is preordained and that they must support the status quo.

Therefore, those who try to fight the capitalist structure and show the downtrodden people the path of liberation will have to first free the people from the pervasive lies of organized religion. It is interesting that Mr. Sarkar, like Marx, used the term "opium of the people" to describe religion. Concerning this matter, he said:

> A group of exploiters loudly object to a remark that was made by the great Karl Marx concerning religion. It should be remembered that Karl Marx never opposed spirituality, morality and proper conduct. What he said was directed against the religion of his time, because he perceived, understood and realized that religion had psychologically paralyzed the people and reduced them to impotence by persuading them to surrender to a group of sinners.[46]

Marxists are one hundred percent correct in saying that capitalism cannot be reformed from the inside, no matter how many liberals, progressives, and social democrats wish this were true. Unfortunately, it will take a revolution to dismantle capitalism, to curtail the ruling class, and to prevent the further rape of the earth and the continued terrible abuses to our fellow human beings. The political state that creates the rules and provides the muscle to ensure that capitalism succeeds will need to be demolished or abandoned, if we are to create a better world for our children.

The psychological manipulations by those who perpetrate the capitalist system will fail only when those laborers, warriors, and intellectuals, who understand capitalist exploitation, withdraw their support from the system. Unfortunately, most of these people, rather than choosing to become revolutionaries, become even more cynical and depressed by their own existence and the misery they see about them. Governed by such a destructive sentiment, they lose their rationality and discrimination. The day will come, however, when they will mercilessly smash the capitalist structure to pieces. How or why they do it, or how the new structure will be built, will never enter their minds. They will jump into the struggle because their desperation can no longer be contained. They will think, "Life is so miserable; I have nothing left to lose." In a state of anarchy, the condition of the laborers, warriors, and intellectuals will become almost the same. It will be useless to expect from most of them anything worthy of human beings. They will all submit to mob psychology. This is the lesson of history.

While we face a state of anarchy, perhaps in the near future, this is not to say that we will have a revolution. Without a plan prepared by a core group of strategic thinkers, and organized by people at the local level, a revolution will not happen on its own.

Since the dawn of capitalism, there have always been strong-armed dictators and intellectual bureaucrats who have tried to bring the capitalists under their control by putting the economy under the control of the state. But this has not proved successful because neither intellectual bureaucrats nor warrior dictators understand money as well as the capitalists. If a society's capital is entrusted to collective management without a clear business plan on how the capital should be used in a *sustainable manner*, poor utilization of the capital is inevitable in every circumstance. This was a major flaw of communism.

When large amounts of capital are placed under bureaucratic management, even a small miscalculation on the part of the managers will lead to gross misuse of funds. This is the main reason, for example, why the system of collective farming, or the commune system, failed in communist countries. They were so ineffective that farmers were willing to kill their own livestock rather than surrender their family's hard-earned wealth to distant party bureaucrats.

If a capitalist system is abolished by force, bureaucratic managers do not have the same control over that wealth as the individual owners did. This is one of the main reasons why capitalist countries developed faster than communist countries in the material sphere. In the revolution to end capitalist exploitation, we will need the help of people with capitalist skills, but their hearts must be in the right direction.

Having said this, if a state tries to increase its national wealth without stopping capitalist exploitation in society, it will only increase the individual wealth of the few people in power. Thus, although there may be an increase in the per capita income of society, the per capita income of the poor will not increase, while the per capita income of the Party functionaries or capitalists will increase.

While any state must be able to use capital to increase the wealth of the state, we can only approve the intervention of the state in the local economy if it actually increases the per capita income of every person that is governed by that state. Such a state, then, cannot be called capitalism. It would rather be an example of socialism. But even in this situation, a socialist state would have to depend upon people with a merchant psychology in order to be successful. The difference, however, is that the capitalists would work primarily for the benefit of society and not for their own self-aggrandizement.

There are some people who possess a merchant psychology who are willing to use their skills and knowledge for social service due to their humanitarian or spiritual inspiration. No doubt some honest capitalists are worthy of veneration by everyone. But like the king who lived for his people, or the humble monk who served the people out of love for them, such capitalists are rare in society. The majority are not interested in adopting the path of selfless service, nor are they eager to dedicate themselves to making their minds one-pointed to achieve God-realization. Mr. Sarkar, in discussing the average capitalist, tells us:

> They avoid or usually try to avoid the real purpose of
> dharma, for they do not have any sense of or feeling for

religion other than some degree of fear of God. If this fear decreases, they begin to behave like mean-minded demons. In such a state of mind they can commit any type of sin to satisfy their hunger for money.

A mind, which runs after money, moves in very crooked ways. Although this movement involves intense effort, due to the crudeness of its objective the movement cannot be straightforward: it is crooked, extremely crooked.[47]

## The Need for Revolution

It should be remembered that the capitalist system was not created in a day. The capitalists worked long and hard to create their political-economy and they will struggle to maintain it at all costs. To expect them to be won over by humanitarian requests, or to expect them to voluntarily renounce their profits and commit themselves to a life of service, is sheer lunacy. Even if the capitalists were to become inspired by a social consciousness, intelligent people should consider whether it is rational to allow the exploitation of the masses to go on until such an unlikely day arrives.

Until a revolution occurs against capitalism or until we meet that fateful day when they make society and the planet uninhabitable, the capitalists will go on making small concessions with their liberal face to keep the machine going. Through their corporate foundations they will support some charities and build some churches, etc. Thus complete social breakdown will come only when they completely lose their common sense due to excessive greed and try to suck society completely dry. Today, capitalism is at an advanced stage of a degenerative disease. Societies and environments are already breaking down. Millions of refugees from war and environmental catastrophes are already on the move. In the meantime, the capitalists hide their lack of conscience behind a wall of praise and support from their apologists in the mass media.

Mr. Sarkar warns us:

> Once the social body falls unconscious, the vaeshyas [capitalist] will die along with the rest of the body. Otherwise,

before allowing themselves to die, the exploited shúdras
[laborers], ksattriyas [warriors] and vipras [intellectuals]
can unite to destroy the vaeshyas. This is the rule.[48]

A dreadful calamity will befall society if those warriors and intellectuals,
who understand present conditions, squander their lives by running
after mundane pleasures instead of utilizing their energy to help human
society. There can be no social improvement until the exploitive capitalist
mentality is eradicated or rendered ineffective through circumstantial
pressure.[49] No political leader, no national congress, no non-profit
movement can create a better society if they neglect the fact that we are
being ruled by people who are ever vigilant for opportunities to enlarge
their wealth by continuing to exploit us. If the warriors and intellectuals
fail to take action, what can one expect but a badly deteriorating society
and our green earth turned to wasteland.

Society may degenerate into chaos and destruction, but we will not
create a revolution without moral leaders who are willing to take the
reins of society into their own hands. Who will these leaders be? Who
will be our heroes? Who will lead the revolution to create a sustainable
world on earth? This will be a subject of discussion in our next book on
Revolution. For the present, however, let us just say that the leadership
will depend upon you.

## Destructive Ideologies

When we look at the historical record, humankind has consistently
been under the sway of destructive ideologies. During the Intellectual
Age, a priest class promoted an ideology based on religious dogmas as
a means to control the people. This dogma is still in force in the West.
Most Protestant Christians still believe that the capitalist system is God's
design. In the Middle East, the Islamic fundamentalists employ their
own dogmas in order to destroy capitalism. They selectively use the
teachings of the Prophet Mohammed (upon him be peace) to justify
terrorism, torture, suicide bombing, the taking of other Muslims' lives,
etc., to force their dogma on others. They use snippets of the Quran

to brutally suppress woman. Islamic fundamentalists, using their own twisted interpretation of the Quran as a shield, are nonetheless resilient enemies against capitalism because they are inspired by more than material interests or love of country. It is not the winning of the battle that inspires them; it is the winning of heaven.

Narrow minded dogmas are severe liabilities that lead humanity astray from the spiritual path. They prevent the mind from expanding, from thinking creatively, and from reaching our full potential. They create a static society in which rationality or discrimination play no role. In effect, such ideologies are anti-human.

With the rise of capitalism in modern society, a new ideology developed to justify the merchant class's rise and dominance of modern society. At the time, they constituted the middle class, who were fighting to overcome the expensive taxes imposed upon them by the aristocracy and the Church in order to fund its fabulous lifestyle.[50] As such, the capitalists advocated personal liberties, limited government, private property rights, and belief in *laissez-faire economics*.[51] This ideology expanded its tenets and principles over time and eventually gave rise to the emergence of contemporary left wing and right wing ideologies. The right-wing conservatives continue to support "classical liberalism" and the privileges of the individual over the needs of society. They continue to hold onto the religious dogmas of the past. The left, composed of modern liberals and progressives, for the most part, broke with classical liberalism during the Age of Progressivism when they became aghast at the social abuses imposed by the capitalists on the average person. Since then, they have supported social welfare programs as a check and balance to the blind ambition and the continued exploitation by the ruling class. And yet they continue to whole-heartedly support the capitalist system.

Capitalism is a secular ideology. This means that it is not based on religious dogma even though it is supported by it. Rather, it is based on the *principle of selfish pleasure*. It is a self-centered ideology. The capitalists do not care about dogma, nor do they care about whether one is conservative or liberal. They will use all dogmas and all the postulates of the left and the right to serve their interests. They will tolerate any dogma and do not care if it is divisive or not, so long as it allows them to continually make money. It is only their selfish interest that matters. This is the fundamental intention behind the capitalists' relentless exploitation of people, places, and things for self-aggrandizement.[52]

Because the capitalists accomplish everything with money, their vital force comes from money. They take all sorts of risks in life to accumulate money. For money, they will sacrifice their conscience, their sense of good and bad, or right and wrong, at any moment. Therefore, in order to save humanity and the earth from the capitalists' money, it will have to be taken out of their hands. But even then, all social problems will not be solved because even if they lose their money, they will still possess their greedy, money-making mentality.

Thus, a new structure of society will have to be built in such a way that the greedy, money-making mentality of the capitalists is kept in check. A key component of a new society, therefore, must be the empowerment of local people to create their own local economies in which they will have direct control of the businesses required to meet their own basic needs. In this way, their livelihoods will not be dependent upon outside capitalists and they can keep a large portion of money rotating within their local economy. Under these tightly controlled conditions, those local people with a merchant-mentality will be led to serve society rather than themselves and they will be rewarded for their contributions to the people in their community. The tenets of economic decentralization and economic democracy are at the heart of sustainable development, Permaculture, the Green Party, Transition Initiatives, progressive socialism, and many other revolutionary organizations. People within these movements are not waiting until tomorrow. They have already started to create a new society. They make progress garden by garden, shelter by shelter, job by job, using local money and local resources. They firmly oppose all measures to oppress the people and the natural world.

A new society cannot be accomplished by trying to persuade the capitalists of its moral value or by engaging them in philosophical talks. The capitalists will have to undergo rehabilitation to save them from their own greed and make them productive citizens in society.

## Shúdra Revolution and Sadvipra Society

The inevitable consequence of capitalist exploitation is shúdra revolution. When the capitalist class, mad with excessive greed, completely loses its common sense and forsakes all sense of humanity, then a revolution by the masses will occur. Revolution will not occur, however, just because an opportune time has come. It requires proper planning, revolutionary organizations, and model projects for people to emulate.

Revolution will take place when only two classes remain in society: the exploiting capitalists and the exploited people. If no warriors and intellectuals get reduced to shúdrahood by the capitalists, shúdra revolution will not occur. The common people do not have the ability to bring about a revolution. They avoid struggle. And they do not have the personal and collective force to establish a new system. Therefore, shúdra revolution will ultimately depend on those shúdras who have sufficient spirit and are mentally warriors and intellectuals.

### Who Will Be the Leaders of the Revolution?

The Marxists, who want to bring about a proletariat revolution with only the help of manual laborers, will not succeed unless they take into consideration the mentality of the people. Shúdra-minded people do not understand their own problems; much less the ability to solve them. No matter how well labor leaders might explain their problems to them or how fiery their lectures on the need for struggle may be, it will not have any influence over their minds. They will spend their time eating, drinking beer, and watching TV. Shúdras do not even consider whether their families are eating properly or if their children are getting a proper education. If their bosses increase their wages, they will merely spend more on their old habits. Their standard of living will not be raised. This is why such people cannot bring about a revolution. It is foolish for those who want to bring about revolution to depend on them. Their static nature will thwart its movement and their cowardice will prematurely extinguish its fire.[53]

Neither can revolutionaries depend upon those warriors and intellectuals who are still wedded to national and religious traditions. It is extremely difficult for warriors and intellectuals to go against these traditions because they have been indoctrinated into them as children. Such people think, "What will happen is bound to happen, struggle will not accomplish anything." Or they think, "At least we are getting by, why should we get involved in other people's problems."

The Republicans have a point, although misguided, when they complain about the welfare state. As we have seen in Volume Four of *The Untold Story of Western Civilization*, the progressive era, which laid the ground for social welfare programs, only fortified capitalism and prevented revolution from occurring.

While we can respect most progressives and pacifists as honorable people, their philosophies are actually harmful to the people. Likewise, while we might respect the local priests and ministers for their empathy for the poor, their counsel to forget this life for a better life in heaven is completely inimical to any physical, mental, or spiritual progress of the people.

Therefore, the warriors and intellectuals who are true revolutionaries will have to be thoroughly prepared. They will need to suffer a lot and make great sacrifices for the people, most of whom may never appreciate what they have done for them. All the while they will have to fight against opposing groups and dogmas.

It is very easy to talk big about revolution. Audiences may be awestruck and applaud, but to actually bring about a revolution is not an easy thing. Mr. Sarkar says:

> Those kśatriya(warrior)- or vipra-(intellectual) minded shúdras who are the pioneers of revolution will have to learn to be disciplined, take proper revolutionary training, build their character, be moralists; in a word, they will have to become what I call sadvipras. A sadvipra will not launch a movement against honest people, even if he or she does not like them. But a sadvipra will definitely take action against dishonest people, even if he or she likes them. In such matters, it will not do to indulge any kind of mental weakness.[54]

The meaning of the word sadvipra is "a person who is a moralist and a spiritualist and who fights against immorality." Moralists and spiritualists can be found among all groups of people and in every locality, regardless of their income status. But in order to be Sadvipras, the rich will have to come down to the level of the middle class. They cannot live in indolent luxury on capital acquired by sinful means. They will have to fight against sin and injustice, and in order to conduct such a fight properly, they will not be able to keep their wealth; they will have to become middle-class. Thus, most spiritual warriors (Sadvipras) will come from the middle class, that is, the warrior and intellectual-minded shúdras. Certainly, Sadvipras can also come from the poor, but they must have the consciousness of a warrior or intellectual. They must have the capacity to think and fight. They must be disgruntled with their own impoverishment and the impoverishment of others. Such people will be the vanguards of the revolution. They will carry the message of universalism to every home in the world.

## Democracy and Capitalism

The capitalists support democracy as a system of government because in the democratic system, they can easily sway the vote of the masses of people who constitute the majority. It is easy for hired politicians to sail through the elections by delivering high-sounding speeches that are easily ignored after winning office. As we were told so explicitly in the Trilateral Commission's *The Crisis of Democracy*, it does not matter what a political candidate tells the electorate, once he is in office, he will have to accommodate the people who hold the real power.[55]

It can be unequivocally stated that if only educated people, instead of all adults, were given the right to vote in any country, the governmental structure of most democratic countries would change. And if sadvipras alone had the right to vote, there would be no difference between the real world and the heaven people imagine.

In the capitalist democracies, the situation of middle-class people has been in decline for decades.[56] An increase in the number of disgruntled warriors and intellectuals in a society is an early omen of the shúdra revolution. It is therefore the duty of those who want to create a world free of exploitation to help increase the number of such people. It will be harmful for the revolution if these people die or are transformed into shúdra-minded shúdras. All the sadvipras in the world should be vigilant to make sure that the number of such people does not decrease.

Revolution means a great change. In order to bring about such a change it is theoretically possible that there will be no killing or bloodshed. If the warrior-minded disgruntled shúdras are in the majority, or are most influential, the revolution will indeed come about through bloody clashes. But, if there are a large number of influential intellectual-minded shúdras, it is possible that there will not be bloodshed. But it is not wise to give much hope that this will be the case. In all the revolutions of history, the liberation of the people has generally involved bloodshed.

Some people claim that they will be able to bring about socialism or communism, or the liberation of the people, through democratic methods. However, history belies this belief. If the United States and the industrialized countries of Europe are progressing toward socialism, it is at a tortoise-like pace. Given the breakdown of societies and climate change today, this is not acceptable; speed is the most important factor.[57]

When the American forefathers were exploited by Great Britain, they did not waste their time hoping for more democracy, they revolted. They chose the path of shúdra revolution, and gained their freedom within a matter of a few years, not a few centuries. In a democratic structure, the people's progress is very slow. It cannot be called revolution; rather, at best, it is evolution; i.e., gradual change.

One of the most important features of progressive socialism (PROUT)[58] is the establishment of cooperative bodies in the administration. But these cooperative bodies will be meaningless unless they are run by honest citizens. If the public does not have a high moral and educational standard, we cannot expect to find many worthy people as representatives, ministers, or directors of cooperative bodies. Dishonest directors will exploit the people and dishonest representatives and ministers will indirectly support such corruption by deliberately refusing to investigate it out of fear of losing their administrative positions, or future votes. If such abuses continue, it will never be possible to build up cooperative institutions. Corruption will never be flushed out of the courts and secretariats, and progressive socialism will never be established.

Without a universal ideology and the leadership of spiritual warriors, it is impossible to attain the high moral standard necessary to establish progressive socialism within a democratic structure. This observation speaks to the limits of democratic socialism, which theoretically is not bad, but it is very unlikely that it will ever succeed in a capitalist-dominated world. The supporters of Bernie Sanders in the last US presidential election will come to understand the truth of this statement.

## Post-Revolution

Whether they are dominated by a warrior psychology or an intellectual psychology, the disgruntled shúdras who take over the leadership of the shúdra revolution are warriors in terms of their courage, personal force, and capacity to take risks. After the shúdra revolution, the leadership of society will pass to these people and the warrior psychology will remain dominant because the need to quell social unrest and establish order will continue. In the post-revolutionary period, such warriors can no longer be called disgruntled shúdras. By this time, they will have become the warriors of the second rotation of the social cycle. The capitalist age will have cycled into the second warrior age.

The Sadvipras among these warriors will then be tasked with keeping an eye on the new warrior class to make sure that they do not descend into an exploitative role. If the warriors descend into exploitation after a reign of power, the sadvipras will fight against them and establish the next Intellectual Age. If the intellectuals descend into exploitation, they will also fight against the intellectuals and initiate the Capitalist Age of the second rotation. And if the capitalists descend into an exploitative role, the sadvipras will once again inspire the disgruntled shúdras to bring about a second shúdra revolution.

According to Mr. Sarkar, the social cycle will rotate continuously.[59] Nobody can stop its natural rotation. If the post-revolutionary Warrior Age is called the thesis, the steps taken by the sadvipras against the warriors who descend into exploitation is called the antithesis. The second Intellectual Age, which evolves out of this conflict, is called the synthesis. If, in a later period, the intellectuals descend into exploitation after their reign of power, the steps that the sadvipras take against them is again called the antithesis. And the second Capitalist Age will be called the synthesis.

Nobody can stop the rotation of the social cycle, not even the sadvipras. Rather, they position themselves within the nucleus of the social cycle, vigilantly observing the process of rotation. One after another, one age follows the next: Intellectual after Warrior, Capitalist after Intellectual, Warrior after Capitalist. Sadvipras will never allow society to follow the process of natural evolution, which during the process of decline will cause great suffering to humanity. They will bring about social revolution whenever necessary in order to shorten the period of decline and create the next ascent. In order to protect humanity, the sadvipras will have no rest. A time will never come in the life of a sadvipra when he or she will be able to sit back in an armchair and say, "Ah, I have nothing to do today, I will have a nice rest." Their peace will come from God's reward for their selfless service.

**Sadvipra Society**

A Sadvipra society is one led by the pioneers of revolution who will be disciplined, have proper revolutionary training, who work to build their character, and who espouse a universal morality. Such a society has never existed within the first rotation of the social cycle in human history. In most countries, the last stage of the first rotation is in progress. In a few countries the post-shúdra-revolution Warrior Age has been established, and here and there the first indications of the Intellectual Age are beginning to emerge. As there is no sadvipra society, the social cycle is rotating in a natural way.

In every age, the dominant social class first governs, then starts to exploit. After a period of exploitation, revolution takes place. Due to the lack of sadvipras to lend their help, the foundation of human society fails to become strong.

In order for a Sadvipra Society to be established, the Sadvipras, who are now dispersed across the planet and are largely unknown to each other must develop a "class-consciousness." In other words, we must learn to identify each other, become aware of each other, begin to support each other, and together, in time, come to build a revolutionary organization together that reaches across the planet. They will be aided in their mission by possessing a shared Universal Ideology and a commitment to Divine Consciousness and the Creation.

May all rational, moral, and spiritual fighters immediately begin to build a sadvipra society without further delay. "Let the new human beings of a new day wake up to a new sunrise in a new world." With these good wishes Mr. Sarkar concludes his discourses on social psychology.[60]

In this chapter, we have gained a better understanding of the different social psychologies that have evolved in the human quest for greatness. We have seen how ruling classes, based upon these psychologies, have risen and fallen in history. In the next chapter, we will explore the attributes of our human nature that have made us susceptible to manipulation by these ruling classes. We will also discover how to free ourselves from being manipulated by others and how to stand among the greatest of spiritual warriors.

# Chapter Two: Human Nature

*We are all born in this universe. We are all grateful to the Almighty, because He has given us the chance to know Him, to realize our nature. That is the course of our journey. How can we forget the path? The path of knowing Him is so beautiful. P. R. Sarkar*

*Do not try to follow animal nature. But at the same time you have got to eat, you have got to sleep; that is your nature too. Having proper restraint over your animal nature, try to follow the true human nature; the true human nature is to know yourself. P. R. Sarkar*

UNLIKE OTHER SPECIES, WE humans are mind-preponderant beings. Throughout our entire existence, we have struggled to develop our minds and have welcomed whatever has been conducive to this development. We reject whatever stands in the way of our mental development. Even though circumstantial pressures may prevent us from doing so for a time, as soon as an opportunity presents itself for us to think freely again, we rise in revolt to destroy whatever holds us back. Human nature has always been like this. Throughout all the ages, we have fought to expand our consciousness. We have always wanted to be more. The well-wishers of humanity have always acted in accordance with this essential characteristic of our human nature.

In yoga philosophy, the term "dharma" means "nature." We have said before that the nature of human beings is to thirst for limitlessness, that is, to thirst for the Absolute Consciousness. Every created entity, whether cell, amoeba, fish, plant, animal, or human being is on the same evolutionary journey. This is because the Cosmic Nucleus is always attracting everything in the same way that a black hole in the center of a galaxy continually attracts all the stars in that galaxy. As unit consciousnesses evolve through different species over the course of lifetimes, the attraction between the unit consciousness and the Cosmic Consciousness increases. This continuous journey has been going on since the creation of the universe. Every single entity is moving inexorably toward the Cosmic Nucleus. This is the path of evolution. Human beings are the last species to evolve and we reflect the greatest consciousness. To continue our journey to Absolute Consciousness, we now require certain intuitional practices. In yoga philosophy these practices are known as "dharma sadhana."[61] For human beings, the purpose of dharma sadhana is to help us fulfill our nature and merge in the Absolute Consciousness. It is only through such practices that we are able to quench the inexorable thirst within us to always have more.

Each one of us is moving towards the Supreme according to our individual propensities. Our propensities are the "reactive potential" within us that are caused by our past actions. These propensities collectively are known as karma. Our individual karma is either propelling us towards or away from the Supreme Nucleus. If we forget our true nature as human beings, we are propelled away from the Supreme Nucleus, but if we act consciously to move forward, then we are propelled toward it. It is up to us to select which direction we want to take. Animals do not have this capacity to choose. They automatically evolve according to the laws of nature. As human beings, we are also moving toward the Supreme Entity, but we can choose not to. When we advance toward the Supreme, we act according to our human nature. When we distance ourselves from the Supreme, we forsake our human nature.

In order to make individual and collective progress, we must know our true nature. Once we know it, then we will be motivated to move along the path to the Supreme by doing intuitional practices. The horrendous problems that confront humanity today stem from the fact that we do not understand our human nature and we do not do intuitional practices. Throughout history, we have been programmed by religions to believe that simple faith in myths and stories was enough to merge with the Divine. But the reality is quite different. Spirituality is a personal relationship with the Divine. It is an internal experience independent of religion. Religions have spiritual value when they inspire us to act according to our human nature and move us toward the Absolute Consciousness. Anything else about religion is worthless and potentially dangerous. Many of us have been programmed by harmful religious dogmas that have led us to look down upon others, to exploit and hate others. Each of us must break free of such programming and begin to explore our true nature.[62]

Truth is achieved only by living according to one's nature. If we do not live by our nature, we will never understand the truth and where there is no truth, there is no victory.

By following our human nature, we will become true spiritual aspirants and by becoming true spiritual aspirants, we will come to know God within ourselves. This is the revelation of the great spiritual masters of history.

In order to perform spiritual practices, we must first observe moral precepts. Without a moral base, intuitional practice is impossible. We are talking here about a morality that is universal in scope, not a narrow morality that only extends to one's group and excludes other groups. By observing universal morality, we follow our true nature.

All men, women, children, every human being is inevitably moving towards the same Cosmic goal. Even if, by our actions, we temporarily move away from the Supreme, He will inevitably pull us back. There is no power on earth greater than this attraction for the Supreme. As Mr. Sarkar says, "No one has been deprived. Everyone has been given the chance equally. No one can say tomorrow, "Oh Lord, You gave a chance only to that person, not to me." No one is higher, no one is lower. All are equal in the eyes of God. No one is deprived; everyone has been given the opportunity to know Him. So, it is for us to grab the opportunity and try to become one in Him. That is why we are all here today."[63]

## Living Beings and Their Mentality

The reason that most human beings are easily programmed by negative ideologies and do not live according to their human nature is because we are governed by our animal nature that we inherited in the process of evolution.

Human beings are the result of an evolutionary process. In fact, we are a species in transition from animality to Divinity. We may say that God created the universe in an instant and this is a spiritual truth, but the nature of the created universe is that it exists within a time-space continuum and this means that all mental and physical forms are continually changing. Everything in the universe comes into being, is maintained, and then dies only to be reborn in another physical form to continue its evolutionary process. This is as true for a galaxy as it is for a tiny ant. Human beings are no exception to this rule.

Our brain and our mind are also a result of an evolutionary process. As our brain evolved so did our capacity to think more clearly. Today, human beings possess four distinct mindsets, of which the first two, we inherited from species that preceded us in the evolutionary process. The four human mindsets are instinct, sentiment, rationality, and intuition. Every human being in the world responds to internal and external stimuli based on these mindsets. Some of us are governed more by instincts, others by emotionality or sentiment, still others by rationality, and a few by their intuition. The higher mindsets, those of rationality and intuition, require a conscious effort to develop. These are the most subtle layers of mind that separate us from other animals. By developing these layers of mind, we come to know our human nature. Until one is able to develop rationality, for example, a person will continue to move through life unable to discriminate between what is truth and what is not. They will be guided only by their instincts and sentiments which are easily manipulated by others with ulterior motives.

## The Instinctive Mindset

The human brain evolved through multiple phases, the hindbrain, the midbrain, and the forebrain. As it evolved, human beings developed a greater understanding of themselves and their environment and this raised our level of consciousness. The evolution of the brain has been a process that did not just begin with humans. In fact, a rudimentary consciousness began with the most primitive life forms. As P. R. Sarkar says:

> Those creatures whose minds have just started functioning, whose ectoplasm has been activated—those unicellular entities instinctively feel: "This is my food,

that is not my food. Now is the time for sleep, now is the time for waking." These undeveloped creatures have only this narrow sense of the minimum essentialities of a living structure. This sense is as predominant in multi-cellular creatures as in unicellular ones, but the difference between the two is that, while the unicellular creatures are incapable of providing their own minimum essentialities, the multi-cellular organisms can do so quite efficiently. In the case of a multi-cellular organism, since many cells are functioning collectively, there is greater scope for clash and cohesion. As a result, the lower mind is powdered down and transformed into the subtle mind.[64]

In other words, the brain grew more complex as a result of the struggle to survive and evolve. The hindbrain, which is the most primitive part of the human brain, evolved in the process from unicellular creatures to fish, amphibians, and reptiles. The hindbrain or the "reptilian brain" is the oldest part of the human brain and it controls the body's vital functions such as heart rate, breathing, body temperature, and balance. These are functions that one does not need to think about. The hindbrain includes the main structures found in a reptile's brain: the brainstem, and the cerebellum.[65] As the reptilian brain evolved it got passed along to mammals and eventually humans who evolved later in time.[66] Automatic functions and thoughtless reactions like fight or flight have always been functions of the hindbrain.

### The Sentimental Mindset

As mammals evolved, the midbrain or Limbic system, which is considered the "emotional brain" developed. Our feelings originate in this part of the brain. As we learn:

> The limbic brain emerged in the first mammals. It can record memories of behaviours that produced agreeable and disagreeable experiences, so it is responsible for what are called emotions in human beings. The

main structures of the limbic brain are the hippocampus, the amygdala, and the hypothalamus. The limbic brain is the seat of the value judgments that we make, often unconsciously, that exert such a strong influence on our behaviour[67]

Marc Beckoff in his article, "Do Animals Have Emotions?" adds:

Limbic system structures are involved in many of our emotions and motivations, particularly those that are related to survival. Such emotions include fear, anger, and emotions related to sexual behavior. The limbic system is also involved in feelings of pleasure that are related to our survival, such as those experienced from eating, sex and child care.[68]

In short, the mammalian brain gives us the ability to feel, learn, and remember. It is worth emphasizing that the midbrain contains the amygdala. Scientists have discovered that neurons in the amygdala are responsible for fear conditioning. Fear conditioning is the learning process by which, through repeated experiences, we come to fear something.[69] This response is not rational. It is more primitive. It is what makes animals and humans wary of unfamiliar circumstances.

When one is ruled by emotions or sentiments, he or she is unable to distinguish between what is true or untrue; one merely is attracted or repelled by something and allows the mind to run after it or away from it. A sentimental person may run after something proper or improper. Being ruled by sentiment is a risky path because without the ability to make rational decisions, one can be easily manipulated by others or even destroy oneself. History has taught us that a person controlled by their "mammalian brain" may lead a family, a social group, a state, or an entire society towards utter destruction. Running blindly without the ability to discriminate between what is proper and improper is called "sentiment." Prejudice, bigotry, and other group sentiments are products of the mammalian or sentimental mindset.

In Chapter One, we have seen repeatedly how people who are dominated by their sentiments are easily controlled by others who possess a rational mind. The masses of people, throughout history have been controlled by ruling classes, be they warriors, intellectuals, or capitalists because these people knew how to manipulate peoples' emotions and thereby control them to do their bidding. Such methods of control include creating fear and feelings of inferiority or superiority in people, using divide and conquer strategies, conning, baiting, demagoguery, etc. These same methods are being employed today to promote sexism, racism, classism, nationalism, and religious dogma among the masses who are controlled by their sentiments.

**The Rational Mindset**

As human beings, we consider ourselves to be rational beings, yet much of what we do is driven by the hindbrain and midbrain. In other words, much of our reaction to stimuli is instinctual and/or sentimental. As vibrations from the external world strike our sense organs, our brain processes them and we instinctively or sentimentally react to them without even thinking. If, for example, we have been conditioned by racism, as soon as we see a person of another race, we may be filled with fear, anger, or hatred for that person. In order to overcome the power of our sentiments over our minds, we need to become conscious of our reactions and learn to control our emotions. We need to make an effort to reach a higher level of mentality.

Just as the mammalian brain evolved from the reptilian brain, so also did the human brain evolve from the mammalian brain. In doing so, our brain became more complex than that of mammals. While the forebrain (the neo-cortex) began to evolve in primates, it culminated in the human brain with its two large cerebral hemispheres that play such a dominant role in our ability to understand reality. These hemispheres are responsible for the development of human language, abstract thought, imagination, and self-consciousness. The neocortex appears to have infinite learning abilities.[70]

The forebrain is divided into the *diencephalon* and the *telencephalon*. The diencephalon is composed of the thalamus, hypothalamus, epithalamus, the pineal gland, and other parts. It is responsible for relaying sensory and motor signals to the cerebral cortex, regulating thirst, fatigue, sleep, and circadian rhythms. It links the nervous system to the glandular system and controls important aspects of parenting and attachment behaviors among its many functions. The hypothalamus is considered to be an updated part of the mammalian brain.

The other part of the forebrain is the telencephalon that contains the largest part of the brain, the cerebrum. The cerebrum occupies about two-thirds of the human brain space. It is here that language, abstract thought, imagination, and self-consciousness are grounded.

The cerebral cortex that forms the outer layer of the cerebrum consists of the gray matter of the brain. It is divided into two hemispheres. The right hemisphere controls the left side of the body and is involved in artistic, spatial, and musical thought processes. The left hemisphere controls the right side of the body and is involved in linear, rational, and verbal aspects. The cerebral cortex is also divided into four lobes, the frontal lobe, occipital lobe, parietal lobe, and the temporal lobe, each with their distinct functions.[71]

The forebrain is what has enabled human civilizations and cultures to develop.

As Robin Dunbar at the University of Oxford tells us, the ability to master the social interactions of group-living requires a lot of brain power. This is a skill that higher primates began to acquire by living in groups. Scientists, for example, note the enormous expansion of the frontal regions of the primate neocortex, particularly in the apes. Dunbar has demonstrated that a strong relationship exists between the size of the frontal neocortex in various species, the size of primate groups, and the frequency of their interactions with one another.[72] This tells us that the brain grows in response to more complex social environments. The more information the brain needs to process, the more it starts to identify and search for overarching patterns, a mental process that is a step removed from identifying the concrete, physical objects in front of us.

It appears that the ability to predict the behavior of other individuals within a group confers a larger evolutionary advantage. Language increased because it improved this ability.[73]

The rational mindset requires conscious reasoning. It employs logical, objective, and systematic methods in reaching a conclusion or solving a problem.

Rational thinking requires different skill sets in different situations. For example, the logic we use when interpreting a science experiment is not the same logic we need when comparing prices of buying a car or following a new recipe.[74]

Despite the remarkable development of the neo-cortex and our consequent ability to think rationally, when we look around us, if we are honest, we must conclude that most of our behavior continues to be governed by the instinctual and emotional parts of our brain.

The social consequences of having the majority of human beings governed by their instincts and sentiments is profound and requires greater elucidation.

## Types of Human Sentiments and Group Identification

Sentiment manifests in two ways, through individualism and groupism. There are animals that prefer to roam about the world individually. They do not have a group life. Such animals are tigers, bears, pandas, moose, rhinoceroses, aardvarks, etc. These animals are extremely sentimental, however, and their sentiment flows according to their individualistic mental tendency.

The majority of animals choose to live collectively. Among these are elephants, zebras, horses, buffaloes, lions, wolves, deer, beavers, penguins, flamingoes, and great apes. Generally, human beings also prefer to live in groups. As such, there is a strong inclination to be governed by group sentimentality wherein the sentiment of the group dominates the will of the individual. Any kind of rational thinking on the part of the individual gets overwhelmed by the group sentiment. In *The Untold Story of Western Civilization*, we have seen how kings, priests, and capitalists have manipulated this group sentiment to control people and bend them to their will. An example of group sentiment is male chauvinism or sexism, wherein the males in a group have been programmed to share a common sentiment that they are superior to women and will do everything in their power to keep women in an inferior position.

This may take the form of controlling their bodies, humiliation, harassment, violence, etc. Other examples of group sentiments include racism, classism, nationalism, political affiliation, religion, or consumerism. These group sentiments intermix on a daily basis in society to create a pseudo-culture that keeps humanity immersed in negativity and fear, unable to advance rationally or spiritually.

## Categories of Group Sentiment

According to P. R. Sarkar, there are three categories of "group" sentiment. Each of these enslaves human beings to irrationality and makes us susceptible to programming that restricts our minds and spiritual progress. These categories are *geo-sentiment*, *socio-sentiment*, and *humanism*.

The core of geo-sentiments is tied to a particular land base, for example, one's country, homeland, town, neighborhood, etc. As such, geo-sentiments can have multiple expressions based upon this land base, i.e., geo-economics, geo-politics, geo-culture, etc. One who is motivated by geo-sentiment will only identify and support those who live within his or her defined geographical area. As we have seen in *The Untold Story of Western Civilization*, this sentiment was prevalent in ancient history when people were tied to their territory as clans, tribes, and eventually nations. This sentiment gave rise to city-states. During the Middle Ages, this sentiment took the form of allegiance to nation-states. Today, we still see it manifested primarily as nationalism. "My country, right or wrong."

The second type of sentiment is the socio-sentiment. It also can have multiple expressions, but the core of this sentiment is tied to a particular social group. Religion is a typical socio-sentiment, as are sexism, racism, classism, etc. One who is motivated by a socio-sentiment only identifies with people within their social group. This sentiment began in ancient history with the birth of male chauvinism, race slavery, and the emergence of ruling priest classes and aristocratic elites. It spread in the West during the Middle Ages due to the expansion of the Christian and Muslim religions. People who are dominated by social sentiment based on religion do not act rationally. They are willing to torture and kill those of other religions because they are not members of their group and therefore are not seen as equal human beings. Jewish, Christian, and Muslim religions have all been based upon sexism, whereby women are oppressed by a male priest class. The myth of Adam and Eve in the Torah, which was repeated in the Bible and Quran, reinforced sexism or the male socio-sentiment against women. Racism also exists in religion, as we have seen in the history of Jews and Christians who consider non-whites as inferior beings.

The third type of sentiment is humanism. Humanists may seek the welfare of humanity, but they do not concern themselves with the welfare of other species or the planet. Geo-sentiments, socio-sentiments, and humanism keep humanity from reaching our highest potential.

## Geo-Sentiment

P. R. Sarkar tells us:

> The sentiment that grows out of love for the indigenous soil of a country is called "geo-sentiment." From this geo-sentiment, many other sentiments emerge, such as geo-patriotism, geo-economics, and many other geocentric sentiments, including geo-religion. This geo-sentiment attempts to keep humanity confined within a limited part of this world. But the innermost desire of people is to expand themselves maximally in all directions.[75]

Geo-sentiment is a materialistic sentiment that locks the mind into supporting only a particular group of people. Geo-sentiment manifests as provincialism, localism, nationalism, and any other sentiment that limits one's identity to a specific land base. The group's sense of morality only extends to those living in one's material environment. Other groups, who live outside one's environment or one's national boundaries, do not merit the same moral consideration. The so-called "patriots" living within industrialized countries today consider whatever their country does to be absolutely good no matter if it includes trampling on others' human rights. This is totally irrational behavior. It goes counter to human nature by preventing communication between the groups and thus the expansion of social consciousness. Human evolution has been greatly retarded by identifying with such sentiments. In this way, we allow our animal nature to dominate our human nature.

As we saw in *The Untold Story of Western Civilization*, a group's sense of superiority, when it is based upon geo-sentiment, is used to justify colonialism and imperialism. It allows war-like nations to exploit indigenous groups by identifying them as savages or as inferior races not worthy of human consideration.

People with a geo-sentiment based on economic exploitation, thrive on the lifeblood of others and justify their actions by saying that it is quite natural for human beings to do so. Their priests make up superstitions about the inferiority of conquered peoples even though these people might have a more evolved human consciousness. We have clearly seen this in the European's exploitation of indigenous African, South American, and Native American people who were often more advanced spiritually then were the whites.

Fascism is born from such a geo-mentality, as are imperialism, capitalism, plutocracy, oligarchy, bureaucracy, theocracy, and monarchy. Such group egotism prevents the progress of humanity. It curtails the expansion of consciousness and destroys spiritual potential.

Today, many members of the middle class in industrialized countries work for multinational corporations that ravage other peoples' lands in order to exploit their raw materials and cheap labor. When the people of exploited countries take a stand against these corporations, the capitalist countries employ their armies to subdue the weaker people. The local people are immediately labeled "terrorists" as soon as they offer resistance and, from then on, they lose their human status in the mind of the colonialists. As human beings, we must fight this exploitation based on geo-sentiment. Within capitalist countries today, we can see how the capitalist ruling class manipulates the nationalist geo-sentiment of people to get them to support the capitalists' rape of other peoples' land and labor. See Volume Five, Part One of *The Untold Story of Western Civilization* for an in-depth analysis of this phenomenon.

The capitalists, who do not govern directly, but who exploit indirectly, have mastered the art of exploiting people's geo-sentiment. Both at home and abroad, they purchase the politicians and the local ruling classes, who then do their utmost to please the capitalists rather then seek the welfare of their own people. Politicians win elections with the capitalists' money by outwardly speaking against social, economic, and political exploitation. But, in fact, they support these things. Sarkar calls such people "vocal revolutionaries." They deliver long lectures against exploitation, but in practice they covertly support the exploiters.

P. R. Sarkar warns us:

> In the past this geo-sentiment has caused enormous harm to many individuals and groups of people. Intelligent people must keep themselves aloof from this geo-sentiment and support nothing that is based on it, because it pollutes the devotional sentiment; it degrades human beings and undermines human excellence....[76]

Today the world is dominated by the geo-sentiment of US-based multinational capitalism that has stretched its tentacles across the entire globe. People, within the US, who work for such multinational corporations, will feel a conflict between their quest for God and their outer reality. As long as such people remain passive in the face of human exploitation, they may be able to secure their material needs, but they will never be able to make their human existence a thing of value. They can only achieve spiritual glory by rising above geo-sentiment and by helping others to also rise above it.

Under imperialism, geo-sentiment is substituted for rational thinking and superstition is substituted for logic. All the religious, economic, political, and social theories based on geo-sentiment are nothing more than superstition. The leaders of religious sects who mouth high-sounding ideals, but who are essentially motivated by geo-sentiment, believe that their religious group is superior to others. Their evangelism creates little more than reservoirs of blind faith. They submerge humanity in a quagmire of superstition, while accusing their victims of being less than human. In this way, people may struggle in this condition for ages; their evolutionary progress ground to a halt.

P.R. Sarkar tells us:

> Geo-sentiment is very cheap. The Supreme Consciousness is not attainable by superficial means. Something

very great is attainable only by greatness. One must pay a high price to buy a costly thing. The Supreme Consciousness is not so cheap; it is not attainable by geo-sentiment.[77]

## Socio-Sentiment

Socio-sentiment does not confine people to a particular territory, but instead it confines them to a particular social group. Instead of thinking about the welfare of a particular geographical area, people who are dominated by socio-sentiment, have been programmed to think only about the well-being of their identified group, to the exclusion of all other groups. They believe that their group is superior to all others and thus they deserve special privileges to which others are not entitled. Such groups may take the form of corporations, religions, or military units in which sexism, racism, and classism are given free reign. Men feel they must dominate women. Whites feel that they must dominate people of other races. The ruling class feels that everyone only exists to be exploited by them. When individuals confine their identity to a particular group, they do not hesitate to violate the interests and natural growth of other groups. As P. R. Sarkar says:

> This socio-sentiment has, in the past, caused much bloodshed and created enormous division and mutual distrust among human groups, separating one group from another and throwing them into the dark dungeons of petty dogmas. Humanity's movement is then no longer like a broad and flowing river, but like a stagnant pool.[78]

A group mentality based on sentimentality leads to religious superstition. This superstition expresses itself as a fear that certain things or events will bring bad fortune. For example, "God will punish us with environmental disasters because of the sinful behavior of gays."[79] Superstitions cloud one's human intellect. In the absence of a rational mentality, human beings are bound to harm other groups, and even subgroups of their own group.

Today both geo- and socio-sentiments are on the rise due to the manipulation of the people by the mass media and corrupt politicians. In the United States, for example, women, racial minorities ,and immigrants are increasingly being blamed by religious and political bigots for the disintegration of the economy. Rationality is not increasing at the same rate of speed. As a result, the number of killings, suicides, and mentally-disturbed people in American society is rapidly growing. Society is polarizing. We see this manifested in the West today in the increase of sexual violence, race hatred, teen suicides, poverty, etc. This is all due to being controlled by a group mentality based on sentimentality. The manipulation of a people's geo- and socio-sentiments by the ruling elite keeps us divided and antagonistic to each other even though we are all suffering under the same exploitation by the ruling elites.

## Mixing Geo- and Socio-Sentiment

As an example, of how geo- and socio-sentiments divide us, let us take a look at the sentiments that gave rise to Donald Trump. "Make America Great Again" is a vivid example of the blending of reactive geo- and socio-sentiments held by a group of people who are desperate to return to the past in the midst of social change and economic decline. Its main components are male superiority, white racism, American imperialism, and Christian fundamentalism. Let us look briefly at each of these in turn. The sentiment of male superiority is a socio-sentiment that has been around for a long time and it always becomes more virulent when men believe that women are threatening their authority. To Trump followers, women have commanded too much public attention recently and have become "uppity." This requires that women be put back in their inferior place. This is why Trump can insult and shame women without any negative reaction from his base. He can call for Hillary Clinton, a symbol of woman leadership, to be locked up. He can "grab women by the pussy" and degrade them in any way that he pleases. This is all acceptable behavior to Trump followers.

Many women followers of Trump, who are governed by racist, nationalist, and religious sentiment went along with Trump's sexism because they had long ago accepted their subordinated position in society.

The US has historically been predominately white and white people generally have thought of themselves as superior to people of other races. This sentiment of white racism has us believe that we can enslave or exploit non-whites at will because they are inferior to us. Anybody in the US who is not white is fair game for white abuse, including Blacks, Hispanics, Semitic, and Asian people. Trump went out of his way to nurture white racist sentiments among his base. His words and actions support "law and order" against blacks, building a wall to keep out Latinos, and refusing immigrants from Semitic countries. He also supports throwing minorities out of the country. Trump has even gone so far as to break up families and imprison children. Trump's lack of humanity was never questioned by his base who loved his outspoken honesty concerning their true sentiments.

The primary geo-sentiment that is a component of the Trump ideology is American imperialism. This sentiment of "My country right or wrong," is the base for Trump's slogan, "Make America Great Again." This is a code word that allows his followers to reinstate the conditions of the past wherein white supremacy, military dominance, rabid nationalism, and male chauvinism reigned. The optimum period for the expression of Trumpism was the 1950s. The sentiment of American imperialism gives US corporations its justification to expropriate another country's resources with impunity as well as to silence "insurgents" by the use of overwhelming military force. This sentiment justifies Trumps insults to the United Nation and to leaders of nations regardless of whether they have been foes or allies. "Make America Great Again" means America first and to hell with anyone else.

Finally, we have the socio-sentiment of Christian fundamentalism which essentially is blind faith in supernaturalism blended with a toxic mix of sexism and racism in which Jesus Christ is a supernatural white man who created Christianity to rule the world as the true religion. While Donald Trump is obviously not a fundamentalist, or even a Christian, he appealed to the racist and sexist sentiments inherent in this religion. The fundamentalist leadership would gladly support him, so long as he gave them freedom to legislate their religious dogma. This includes governing women's bodies and persecuting homosexuals.

When you put all these geo- and socio-sentiments together, you get the toxic ideology of "Make America Great Again." Each toxic strand reinforces the other to create a weave of hate and fear, coupled with a sense of liberation to express their pent up anger, among Trump's tribe. Those who believe in white, sexist, Christian fundamentalist nationalism are Trump's people. Trump is their thuggish, loutish golden boy. He knows his tribe and they know him. This is why he could say "I could stand in the middle of 5th Avenue and shoot somebody and I wouldn't lose voters."[80] To his supporters, Trump is incapable of error. They will follow him blindly because he spoke to their innermost sentiments like no one had ever done before and promised to make them great again. Trump does not need to be intelligent. He can be as small minded and vindictive as he wants. He can tell all the lies that please him. He can claim that any media outlet that challenges him on the truth is only spreading false news about him. His tribe will believe him and support him because he understands and speaks for them.

Trump supporters lack a class consciousness. They believe that a billionaire who has made his fortune screwing others can be their savior. This demonstrates that his followers have no sense of who their real enemies are. They falsely blame their problems on women and minorities who have supposedly gained power at their expense. They blame the government for empowering women and minorities through social service programs.

Because the Republicans in power have a strong class consciousness and seek to benefit the rich at the expense of the poor, they are able to use Trump's followers to push through their "reforms" of dismantling the government's social service programs. The poor whites go along with this because they think it will punish uppity women and blacks, not realizing until it is too late that they themselves have been screwed.

**The Sentiment of Humanism**

The third type of sentiment is human sentiment. Many well-intentioned people sincerely feel pain for the suffering of others and are moved to help alleviate their suffering. They possess an expanded consciousness, greater than those who are governed by geo- and socio-sentiments. Yet, strangely enough, such humanists may care nothing about the welfare of other creatures or for the life support systems of the planet itself. They do not care if an entire species is killed off or that human beings destroy the soil, water, air, and climate for profit. They do not respect or have any empathy for the suffering of anything that is not human and find nothing wrong with this. A humanist can easily hunt an animal for sport.

If we use our rationality, we will have to admit that we depend upon other species for our survival. We must eat certain plants and animals to stay alive. Other species serve many functions for humanity, but to disrespect them, abuse them, torture them, and kill them without regard for their sacrifice or for their God-given existential value, is a sin that leads us away from our spiritual goal.

Humanism fails because it is not motivated by any spiritual inspiration. Therefore, it is bound to become a mere formality, devoid of real sincerity. It may die out at any moment, like a river ending in desert sands.

Nonetheless, the consciousness of the humanist is larger than those controlled by geo- and socio-sentiments. But it must become more. As Mr. Sarkar says: "Now, if the same human sentiment is extended to include all creatures of this universe, then and only then can human existence be said to have attained its final consummation."[81] This expanded sentiment he calls *Neo-Humanism* or *Universalism*.

## Two Types of People Who Create Divisive Sentiments

P. R. Sarkar identifies two types of people who, by the manipulation of our sentiments, create divisions among humanity and prevent us from moving toward human unity. One type does so unconsciously. They do not realize the great harm they are doing to human society and to the plant and animal kingdoms. The second type knowingly and deliberately works to undermine humanity and the planet for their personal gain. Mr. Sarkar calls this second type "human chameleons"—those who change their colors frequently to avoid detection.

Often those who manipulate others by appeals to their geo- and socio-sentiments are conscious of the fact that they suffer from the same disease, but they still propagate these sorts of ideas because they are motivated by selfish interest. Many liberals fall into this camp.

There are others unwilling to change because they follow the ways of their ancestors, parents, or group leaders and are afraid of change. These are the reactionaries. They suffer from a fear complex. They may utter high-sounding phrases about the love of God and country, but their hearts are filled with fear. Even though they recognize the need for change, they want to slow it down as much as possible. They may recognize in their hearts that others deserve equal justice, but they are afraid to go against those in their group. They say we do not want to change things too quickly. Those who say, "Slow and steady wins the race" can never accomplish any glorious task. Conservatives generally fall into this camp.

If we were to go door-to-door to convey the message of human unity, we would run into two kinds of people—those who are eager to learn and grow and those will feel threatened by a greater idea. We can immediately work with those who realize their ignorance and want to correct their behavior in order to promote the general welfare. The others, however, stand in the way of human progress and must be exposed for who they are. They do not seek the welfare of humanity. Despite their pretense, they are controlled by the goal of selfish pleasure and they will do anything to fulfill this goal at the expense of others.

Those people who intentionally manipulate the sentiment of human beings for the purpose of ego-gratification and self-aggrandizement, even though they know that others will be harmed, are truly demons[82] in human form. These are the mighty capitalists and their intellectual and warrior elites. But they are also people who we will meet in our everyday lives.

We encounter them in every field of life. We find them working in businesses, teaching in schools, preaching in churches, sitting in squad cars, working on the docks, even sitting at our dining room table. We find such people everywhere secretly acting to demolish the welfare of others for self-gain. They state their support for the common good, but when their lies are discovered, they change their angle. These are the chameleons.

It is often difficult to identify human chameleons who change their appearance in order to continue to exploit others. Sometimes they shift their ground from one geo-sentiment to another geo-sentiment, sometimes from a geo-sentiment to a socio-sentiment, or from one socio-sentiment to another socio-sentiment. They are adept at manipulating every sentiment. To attain the support of the masses, one day a certain leader will say, "I will not allow my country to be destroyed by foreign immigrants." In this way, he exploits both the geo-sentiment and the socio-sentiment of the people simultaneously. All the people will clap their hands in joy and say, "He is the only hope of our country. We will follow his leadership." Then when the country is destroyed, not by immigrants, but by the ruling elite to whom he has given free rein to exploit the people, that leader will not open his mouth. He will prefer to observe a vow of silence. Later, he will merely say, "I am extremely sad, I remain with the people." This is nothing but a strategy to manipulate people's sentiments. We must clearly recognize the people who adopt such strategies and to do so, we must develop a greater degree of intellect.

Chameleons often present themselves as reformers. Such reformers are no better than outright liars and hypocrites. The reformer's stance is, "we can't have everything that we want so let us be content with the crumbs that the powerful throw at us." Actually, the reformers believe that the process of exploitation will continue without interruption. There are many so-called reformers in the world operating among the political parties, the universities, the human services, and non-profits. While they speak of the need for reform, in reality they do not want to improve the welfare of the society. They only want to guarantee that their job or status will remain safe. They do this by creating inconsequential patchwork improvements while also working to maintain the overall system of exploitation. It is sad to say that many middle-class intellectuals, on the left and the right, fall into this category.

Reformers lack courage and boldness. If they had the boldness to take a stand against exploitation, they would have become revolutionaries. But they lack such boldness and thereby do enormous harm to humanity by delaying revolution. P. R. Sarkar tells us:

> The reformists of any age are not the real well-wishers of society. Rather they seek to preserve the defects of

society by any means. They are motivated either by a
fear complex or by a despicable cunning. And when
awareness finally dawns on those who were so long exploited in the politico-economic field, the reformists
lose their prestige, and also their popular support.[83]

When the tactics of the exploiters are uncovered, they grow desperate. Through the mass media and social media, they utilize all their
verbiage, all their abilities, all the weapons they possess to survive
because there is no other way out. Perhaps, they may even express
a faint desire to rectify themselves—but if they do, they will realize
how despicable their entire past has been. According to the standards
of Universalism, they have betrayed humanity. And when conscious
people recognize the true nature of these chameleons, they will disown
them without remorse.

Those who control others by manipulating their sentiments may earn
temporary applause, but ultimately people will realize that they have been
used. The capitalists and the reformers have steered the society onto a
bad course and, as a result, society is being destroyed. Consequently,
those who once earned the highest positions of respect in different fields
of life will later find that their thrones of glory lie shattered in the dust.
This is the lesson that history teaches us.[84]

## Mental Complexes and Psychic Exploitation

Those who are able to manipulate peoples' geo- and socio-sentiments
usually perpetuate their exploitation by injecting an inferiority complex in the minds of those whom they want to exploit. People who are
dominated by their middle brain and thus their emotions are especially
vulnerable to such manipulators.

If you analyze the history of the world, you will find that whenever
one group exploited another in the economic sphere, they first created an
inferiority complex in the minds of the exploited masses. This complex
was usually based on language, gender, race, class, nation, and religion.

Psychic exploitation is a tool of the corporate mass media. The American people, for example, are kept in a constant state of fear. Fear of uppity women, fear of minorities, fear of Muslim terrorists, fear of losing one's job, fear of death, fear of going to hell. The fear complex is developed across many spheres of social life. In third world countries, you will see billboards written in a language not used by the local people. What is the purpose of putting up such a billboard? It is to generate an inferiority complex among the local people regarding their language and social position. The billboards show that the rulers' language must be respected. Subconsciously the people now think: "Ah! That is the language of the rulers!"[85] In this way the ruling exploiters create indirect pressure on the peoples' minds. Once this feeling of inferiority is generated, the people will continue to suffer from this mental disease.

The moment that the capitalist promoters are able to create an inferiority complex in the minds of the people, they can infuse the same inferiority complex in other spheres of their lives as well. Then psychic exploitation occurs as a matter of course.

In time, people forget their own rights, and even forget that they are human beings. They forget that they too have the right to live with dignity. Instead they worry, squirming in their daily misery, ever grateful for the few seconds of peace that their friends or family may afford them.

The manipulators also blame others for the evil that they themselves have created and, in doing so, the people become confused, powerless, and feel inferior. This is how the manipulators widen the social gap between the rich and the poor until the social framework is completely broken down. Eventually the ruling class's sociopathic behavior will backfire on them because each day their methods create greater discord and prevent a well-knit society from ever developing.

Knowing this, the reason why we cannot accept narrow sentiments based on culture, economics, politics, and religion is that they create a mental weakness in people which prohibits them from acting in a loving manner. It is not acceptable that people who belong to large groups feel that they can disparage and denounce smaller groups. It is not acceptable that so-called patriots demean those of foreign birth. It is not acceptable that male chauvinists disparage, harass, and abuse women, or that white supremacists harass minorities, or religious leaders denounce those who belong to other religions. It is not acceptable that capitalists continue to destroy our mother planet for the sake of personal profit.

# Types of Psychic Exploitation

In their attempt to exploit people, manipulators use different types of psychic exploitation. Following are some of the main weapons in their arsenal.

## Economic Exploitation

The most debilitating form of manipulation is economic exploitation. P. R. Sarkar tells us that economic exploitation is perpetrated in two ways: the first is *psycho-economic exploitation* (using an exploitive business strategy) and the other is *politico-economic exploitation* (using brute force). Where psycho-economic exploitation is combined with politico-economic exploitation, it becomes doubly dangerous. This is the path of US-based global capitalism.

Intelligent people should analyze this situation carefully. Whether by use of psycho-economic or politico-economic exploitation, the exploiters not only diminish the people directly or indirectly, but they gain control over local governments by buying off its leaders. This makes exploitation vastly easier for the capitalists.

In the past, most countries of the world were victims of politico-economic exploitation, and many remain so today. In order to save humanity from politico-economic or psycho-economic exploitation, P. R. Sarkar urges rational people to raise the people's consciousness, otherwise they will never be able to successfully resist this type of exploitation. Here Sarkar uses the example of India:

In India, the masses were inspired to fight for independence without arousing their consciousness. As a consequence, India ultimately attained political independence, no doubt, but the people have not attained politico-economic independence as yet. Even today, they are victims of psycho-economic and politico-economic exploitation.[86]

## Religious Exploitation

Besides economic and political exploitation, religion has a major influence on the sentiments of people. Religions are based on dogmas. According to Mr. Sarkar:

> The propagators of religion never cared about the universally applicable human dharma free from all narrowness—rather they always feared and avoided it. What have they preached instead? They have always declared, "I am not speaking with my own voice, I am speaking with the voice of heaven. I am the messenger of God. Don't take these words to be mine—they are the message of God, and so you will have to accept them. You must not question whether they are right or wrong; to question is a sin. If you question, your tongue will fall off!" They have tightened the noose of dogma around the people, so that they fear to take a single step over the line, thinking, "How terrible! If I do so I will be burnt in hellfire for eternity!"[87]

Those who seek to confine groups within the bondage of dogma by such methods are the so-called religious leaders or false gurus. They have done enormous harm to the human society. Millions of innocent people have died in bloody religious wars initiated because of incompatible dogmas. Their leaders, meanwhile, fulfill their own petty self-interest, by claiming their lies and dogmas are God's commandments.

As in the political-economic field, so in the religious field, one group tries to bring another group into its arena of exploitation. For instance, under capitalism, a corporation attempts to exploit a less-developed people as its colony. They want to obtain these people's raw materials and cheap labor. Religions use the same tactic. The propagators of religious faiths take their message of "a superior god" to the "savages" in an attempt to build their membership and make the local people accept capitalism. As we have seen in Volume Four of *The Untold Story of Western Civilization*, those who forced colonialism on less developed cultures were consistently accompanied by missionaries.

Although some of these priests exploited the people consciously, many well-meaning propagators of religion were not even aware of the fact that they were helping the exploiters. During the Middle Ages, the Catholic Church spread its dogmas under penalty of death. You either became a Christian or you were put to death. This is how most of today's Christian families came to be Christians. Their ancestors were forced into Christianity and their children adopted their parent's religion down through each generation. This was true in Europe as it was in Africa and Latin America.

Even today, there are many well-intentioned religious adherents among the priesthood and the laity who, in thinking that they are doing good, are actually promoting the continued exploitation of the people by church leaders and the capitalist class. It is necessary to awaken such well-meaning people and make them aware of what they are doing. They need to be introduced to a philosophy of Universalism which seeks the welfare of all, not simply those of a particular gender, race, class, nationality, or religion.

Once such people's intellects are liberated, they will be able to throw off their illusions and begin to act for the welfare of all. As for those religious people, who already know what is right, they must be supported in their spiritual path and in their fight against injustices within their religions. For example, all people who fight against sexism in religion take a stand for spirituality. A rational person will only find the statements made by religious leaders against women to be vile and loathsome.[88] Another example, of church injustice was the destruction of the Liberation Theology movement in South America where local priests and laymen, who wanted to help the poor people develop their own economic enterprises, were shut down by the Church in Rome on the grounds that as representatives of the Catholic Church they could only be involved in "spiritual" matters.[89]

As we have learned, the agents of injustice who deliberately propagate harmful dogmas will become furious and violent when they hear the words of truth. However, their downfall is the inexorable decree of fate. Their karma dictates a future of pain and misery equal or greater than the misery they caused the people during their lifetime.

## Cultural Exploitation

The subtler and sweeter expressions of human life are generally termed "culture." There may be many nations but there are not multiple cultures. There is only one indivisible human culture even though there are local variations in its expression. Human culture is like a bouquet of beautiful flowers. Although the flowers differ, it is still only one bouquet. A particular group, which is motivated to exploit others, will try to destroy the local cultural expressions of other groups. These exploiters are like pernicious weeds trying to dominate the rest of the garden. Such exploiters forcibly impose their language, dress, and ideas on other groups and thus pave the way for exploitation by paralyzing those people psychologically. This is how people guided by geo- and socio-sentiments perpetuate exploitation in cultural life. This is occurring throughout the world and it is the central precept of colonialism. In the United States, such exploiters are still attempting to destroy the culture of Native Americans.[90] In speaking about cultural exploitation of indigenous people around the world, P. R. Sarkar asks:

> Is it not your noble duty to save these simple and perse-
> cuted people from exploitation? Certainly it is. Those of
> you who did not understand this before, now do under-
> stand it clearly; or you will come to understand it later
> from others. Human beings must be saved. Why should
> innocent people be forced to live like sacrificial lambs?
> This must not be tolerated.[91]

As we know, the human mind has a strong tendency to degrade itself. It flows more easily downward than upward. When exploiters, by virtue of their wealth, impose inferiority and fear complexes on people and reinforce these complexes by crude mass media entertainment, films, and dramas, it weakens their minds and they will become mentally paralyzed. Such paralyzed people will never be able to stand united against cultural or any other kind of exploitation. They will never be able to do so, because mentally they will be completely dead—their capacity to raise their heads in protest will have been crushed.

Exploitation in the cultural sphere is accomplished by the propagation of pseudo-culture, which promotes consumerism and desires for material objects, while, at the same time, filling our senses with images that demean our intrinsic humanity. Every honest rational person must fight against this pseudo-culture and inspire others to do the same. If this is not done, the future of humanity will be bleak. It is proper for human beings to struggle for political freedom, for social emancipation; but if their cultural backbone is broken, then all their struggles will end in nothing. It will be like offering water to a man who has already died of thirst.

> If one's spine is shattered, it is impossible to hold one's head erect. Can those whose necks and backs are crushed under the weight of pseudo-culture, be expected to hold their heads high in any sphere of life? Hence it is the bounden duty of every rational person to save innocent people from pseudo-culture.[92]

## Pseudo-Humanistic Exploitation

Socio-sentiment taken to its most expansive stage is called "humanism." It is larger than nationalism and internationalism, but it is not the answer to our problems for two reasons. First, in this world, humans are not the only living beings. There are many other creatures as well. It is easy for humanists to destroy the animal and plant kingdoms, but this destruction is upsetting the balance among the plant, animal, and human worlds and is resulting in the catastrophic ruin of human life as well.

Secondly, even within humanism there is a broad scope for the exploitation of people. A group that is acting in a "humanitarian manner" may do so only to obligate another group so that it can later exploit it. This is the tactic employed by industrialized nations with their so-called "foreign aid."

Another pseudo-humanist tactic is to teach literacy to "educationally backward" people, but in doing so inject ideas into their minds that mentally paralyze them and make them easier to colonize. The intention is to develop them socially in a way that is desired by the exploiters and thus destroy their originality. This is geo- and socio-sentiment posing as humanism.

The pseudo-humanistic strategy is to outwardly act like well-wishers of humanity ("We want to make the world a better place to live"). Yet, while preaching the gospel of humanistic idealism, they stab others in the back. This situation is prevalent all over the world today. Those of us who are employed in UN agencies, especially the World Bank and the IMF, US agencies like USAID, international NGOs, and human service agencies must be ever vigilant that our organizations are not guided by pseudo-humanism.

Such adulterated humanism is not genuine humanism, nor is it performed in a true humanistic spirit. It has some affinity with the pseudo-reformist strategy, which says, "Yes, what the revolutionaries say is correct; but if their objectives really materialize, it will threaten my livelihood and disturb my individual pleasure." The pseudo-reformists speak of reform, but in their heart of hearts, they have decided not to allow any change to take place. The sustainable development movement has been stymied for years because of the many pseudo-reformers who mouth concern for humanity and nature, but who will not fight to create the necessary changes. They too are the slaves of the capitalists.

Depending upon the degree of economic expansion, some countries are called "developed," some "developing," and some "undeveloped." Now the interesting thing is that none of the so-called "developed" countries, the industrialized capitalist countries, can stand on their own legs. They have simply forced the developing and undeveloped countries to serve them by creating circumstantial pressures on them. The capitalist countries did not become developed by developing their own resources. They developed only because they exploited others. Europe grew by exploiting the wealth and labor of colonized people. The United States grew by exploiting the slave labor of Africans.

Once one's culture is controlled, one becomes, unknowingly or knowingly, a slave. The rulers and exploiters are able to use the guise of humanism to exploit people in all spheres of life—social, economic, political, cultural, and religious. This is the case in the United States. Hence humanism cannot be considered the panacea; it is not the remedy.

Another flaw in humanism, as mentioned above, is its disregard for non-human creatures—animals and plants. All animals and plants have their own urge for self-preservation; no creature dies willingly. They share the same emotions and sentiments that we do. Furthermore, the torture and killing of animals and plants creates the very tendency to torture other humans as well. This cruelty is in the blood of the exploiters. While they mouth high ideals, they torture and kill other species for sport and to fulfill their egotistical greed for more power and wealth.

When people want more land to build their towns and industry, they bring about large-scale deforestation. But no one bothers to think about the creatures that live in those forests. We destroy their natural habitat, the forests, but we never consider any alternative arrangements for their shelter. As Mr. Sarkar says:

> We have recklessly destroyed large areas of forests without caring to think that thereby we are destroying the balance among the human, plant, and animal worlds. And we never realized—and still do not—that this wanton destruction of the animal and plant worlds will be of no benefit to human beings. Rather it will be a great loss for human society, because each and every living entity, whether plant or animal has two types of value: one, its utility value, and the other, its existential value.[93]

Human beings usually preserve those creatures which possess an immediate utility value for them; for example, cows, sheep, pigs, and chickens. Since most animals do not serve human needs, their utility value is nil, thus human beings are not eager to preserve them.

If milk could be created by a chemical process, we would stop breeding cattle. We would either eat them or kill them in another way. Mr. Sarkar vigorously condemns this behavior:

> Who says that those creatures who have lost their immediate utility value have no right to exist? No one has the moral right to say this. No one can dare to say that only human beings have the right to live— and not non-humans. All are the children of Mother Earth; all are the offspring of the Supreme Con-

sciousness. Most creatures have existential value, although they may not be valuable to human beings, or we may not be aware that their existence has some significance. This existential value is sometimes individual and sometimes collective, and sometimes both. Oftentimes, we cannot know the utility value, or the collective existential value, of a creature; we wrongly think that it has no existential value. This is the height of foolishness. As human beings have not advanced very far in the field of knowledge, they are prone to this sort of error.[94]

Even those animals that have a negative utility value deserve to live. Take the example of wolves who threaten the cattle on ranches. Rather than killing them, we should create a congenial environment for them in which they cannot kill the cattle and harm people. If, in the absence of proper safeguards, those undeveloped creatures do harm to humans or cattle, the fault does not lie with those creatures but rather with the human beings. Human beings are endowed with developed intellect. We can make adequate arrangements to protect ourselves and others.

Mr. Sarkar adds that:

> non-human creatures have the same existential value to themselves as human beings have to themselves. Perhaps human beings can understand the value of their existence, while other living beings cannot: this is the only difference. Even so, no one has conferred any authority on human beings to kill those unfortunate creatures.[95]

As long as we remain in bondage to pseudo-humanism and other geo- and socio-sentiments, we will continue to be exploited by others who have more wealth and power. We will continue to be dehumanized through their strategies to manipulate our sentiments. As such, only Universalism has the power to free us from our bondage.

## The Principle of Selfish Pleasure

The reason we are so susceptible to the exploitation of our sentiments is that appeals to our narrow sentiments trigger our desire for selfish pleasure. All the social, economic, and geographical dogmas that are used to motivate us are entirely based on this. Human beings yield to dogmas with the sole intention of attaining selfish pleasure. Even educated people knowingly submit to dogmas, thinking, "I don't care whether it does good or harm to others, because at least I have got some pleasure out of it!" Being motivated by this idea, they enslave themselves to dogmas. Mr. Sarkar explains:

> In the civilized world, even educated people knowingly follow dogmas because they have a desire in the back of their minds to attain some mundane pleasure in this physical world. Even in this civilized world where so much progress has been made in the field of knowledge, people are still following these dogmas, as if they are blind. The snares of dogma will have to be shattered to pieces; the iron prison gates of dogma will have to be crushed to dust.[96]

Dogmas are always motivated by the psychology of exploitation. They can never be accepted as a path to perfection. If we want to experience "a better world for ourselves and our children," we must move ever forward beyond the confines of divisive sentiments. We must move beyond the programming that has bound us throughout history and kept us prey to the manipulation of the elites in society who have always been bound by the principle of selfish pleasure.

## Overcoming Exploitation by Rational Thought

To get beyond our obsession with selfish pleasure and thereby become less susceptible to being programmed and exploited, we must think rationally. Because of our larger brains and expanded consciousness, we are capable of judging between right and wrong. We can discriminate. However, to develop our rationality, we must consciously work at it. To do so we must develop knowledge. Listening to learned discourses or studying and understanding the perennial wisdom of humanity are just some ways of developing our rational capability. So also, is association with learned and enlightened people.

Animals, being less evolved than humans, are incapable of rationality or discrimination. They cannot follow the path of conscience. Even the most developed animals merely follow the path of sentiment. When an animal likes something, it runs after it; when it does not like it, it does not run after it.

Mr. Sarkar uses the following example to amplify this point:

> [A] bird catches sight of rice grains and alights on the ground. It thinks: "Let me go down and eat them!" So it is caught in the net. But had it pursued the path of rationality, it would have thought: "Hmmm, rice is strewn in such a remote woodland! This is unnatural. There is neither a village nor rice fields nearby—so this is indeed strange. Let me think this over for a while... Aha! A net has been spread and ropes are laid on all sides. I must not alight there!" This is the way of logic. But if it follows the path of sentiment it will alight and be caught in the net.[97]

So, as human beings, we should follow the path of rationality. This is a unique treasure of humanity that no animal possesses. We have seen that those who possess love in their hearts and follow the path of rationality become our heroes and heroines. We cheer their victory and know that they alone can accomplish worthy deeds in this world. In these troubled times, each of us must become a beacon of hope for the world by acting in a rational manner for the good of all.

As we develop our intellect, our dependence on inborn instincts and sentimentality gradually wanes although they will always remain with us. No one teaches a child to drink its mother's milk or to laugh or cry. It acquires all these things as inborn instincts. Undeveloped creatures survive only because of these inborn instincts, but not developed creatures.

Likewise, no one teaches a child to feel fear or hope or attraction for something. These feelings are already developed within our mammalian brain. Just as dependence upon instincts is lessened by the development of sentiments, so also sentimentality is lessened by the development of rationality. Blind sentiment or blind faith declines as we gain the power to think clearly and move toward a universal goal.

In human beings, the hindbrain, midbrain, and forebrain are all connected. This is why our lives are so complex. Take the example of a young man standing on a front porch with flowers in his hand to give to a girl to whom he is attracted. His urge to jump out of his skin, his pounding heart, and desire to run away are a result of his hindbrain. His feelings of dread, excitement, and love that are driving him crazy result from his midbrain. All the while his forebrain is telling him to relax and everything will be okay. "Just ring the doorbell." In this way, his rationality allows him to meet the girl of his dreams.

Because our brains contain these different mindsets, we live in a world of steady conflict, often not knowing what to do. Sometimes our rational mentality is victorious, sometimes our sentimentality. Sometimes our instincts override everything else.

As our rational mind becomes stronger, however, we will be less controlled by our emotions. We can then begin to take charge of ourselves. Even so, wherever groupism exists, sentimentality exists. People are swayed by the sentiments of the groups with which they identify. In such a state, they follow group leaders blindly. When their logical mind starts to develop, however, people can begin to question the truthfulness of what their group holds dear. They can begin to break through their programmed way of thinking and may realize to their dismay that "we blindly listened to such-and-such religious leaders or politicians who didn't contribute to the welfare of the people in the least." Or they may think, "We wrongly thought that person to be great, but now we find that he did enormous harm to society by propagating National Socialism."[98]

The reality is that all living beings of this world have originated from and will merge into the same source; everyone has the equal right to survive and fulfill his or her destiny.

## The Limits of Rationality

We have said that human existence is more mental than physical. As an example, if someone wounds our feelings and then offers us delicious food and drink, we will not be inclined to accept it. If someone speaks ill of us or reproaches us, we will distance ourselves from them because they have wounded our sense of self-respect. Animals do not behave this way.

As human beings, we pride ourselves on our rationality, which implies our ability to discriminate. Using rationality, we ask ourselves, "Should I do this or should I do that?" When discriminating between what is proper and improper, if human beings select the proper path, this is called *conscience*. When one is moving forward, guided by conscience, one comes upon innumerable alternatives. We have to constantly ask, "What is good and what is bad? What should I do and what should I not do?" When one has to examine both sides before taking a step, it is difficult to move quickly. There is advancement, but the degree of speed is slower compared to acting on instinct or sentiment.

To study a situation requires intellectual analysis. It means to assimilate internally the external events of the objective world. It may require research. Study, however, does not require that one be literate. Anyone can listen to another and weigh the truth of their words, although literacy is desirable.

Study also has its defects. These defects may be due to ignorance or to changes in time. For example, a teacher or the author of the book may be ill-informed and this defect is then passed from person to person. This is a defect due to ignorance.

The second defect of rationality is due to change in time. A teacher or a book expresses a certain reality according to a temporal perspective; but the moment there is a change in time, then that reality begins to lose its validity. There is also the risk of believing the propaganda of governments and corporations.

If we cannot trust what we are being taught, how do we identify those leaders who espouse geo- and socio-sentiments or pseudo humanism? If we cannot trust the mainstream media, how can we identify the liars and deceivers of humanity who deprive the people of the minimum necessities of life? No matter how difficult the task, we must continue to study the situation. As P. R.Sarkar says:

> You will have to identify them. You will have to ana-
> lyze each and everything in the proper perspective.
> Until you come to a clear conclusion after proper anal-
> ysis, you cannot rescue the people from the tightening
> noose of exploitation. Here the importance of study is
> tremendous—you will have to do it. You cannot afford
> to shut the pages of your books and remain like frogs
> in the well. You must enlarge your mental horizons and
> move ahead by shattering all social bondages.[99]

Rationality requires us to analyze the positive and negative sides of what we read or hear. We must weigh the pros and cons. If the positive side is predominant after verification, we can accept what we read, unless another analysis leads us to a more comprehensive view. This process is more than just reaching a "decision." It is reaching a "logical decision." These two should not be confused.

But even if we reach a logical decision about the truth or falsehood of something, this is not enough. We must also see whether what is being proposed is conducive to human welfare. Is what we read or hear for the benefit and happiness of all beings? Is it for the spiritual well-being of all? If it is, only then should we support and propagate that idea and devote ourselves wholeheartedly to its implementation. If, on the other hand, we need to reject an idea or action because it does not lead to the benefit and happiness of all, then we must reject this bad idea perma-nently. "My 'no' is final."

On the other hand, if we see that by proper analysis, the proposed idea may be used for human welfare with some changes, or in the future, then we can say, "My 'no' is not final – this idea may be used in the future." We must act according to our conscience. This process of discrimination is the rational approach.

Mr. Sarkar says:

> Now, what will you do to counteract geo-sentiment, to
> safeguard yourself and also the collective body? (It is

more important to protect the collectivity than to save yourself.) First, you will study. And what will you do to remove the defects in study? You will have to come to a logical decision after examining the positive and negative sides. And then, after reaching a conclusion, you will decide whether that conclusion will be implemented or not; whether or not you will materialize that conclusion will be decided on the basis of whether or not it is conducive to human welfare. When you reach this final decision, this final desiderative point, that is your conscience. Finally, through your conscience, you can successfully combat geo-sentiment....Keep your conscience ever-vigilant. Develop a firm rationalistic mentality, and no one will be able to deceive you by false geo-sentiment. This rationalistic mentality will provide you with sufficient inspiration and strength to fight against socio-sentiment, ordinary humanistic sentiment, and pseudo-humanistic strategy. You will not only gain vocal strength, but become strong in all respects.[100]

This wise counsel becomes more critical with each passing day as society continues to polarize and the media creates an "us vs them" mentality. It is just as difficult for the left to weigh proposals from the right as it is for the right to weigh proposals from the left. This is what the ruling elite count on. It is part of their divide and conquer strategy. Yet, if we want to develop our rationality and move beyond partisan politics based on sentiment, this is what we must do. It was not so long ago when liberal and conservative politicians were able to compromise on important issues.

## Intuitional Mindset: Awakened Conscience and Social Equality

Now that we have discussed the mindsets of instinct, sentiment, and rationality, we can discuss the fourth mindset of human beings, that of intuition. Intuition derives from a more subtle understanding of reality than rationality. It develops as our individual consciousness begins to merge in Cosmic Consciousness. By adhering to the precepts of universalism, we begin to sense that everything is an expression of the Divine. By seeking the welfare of all, we move closer to the Divine and, in doing so, develop a clearer understanding of what is true and also a more subtle love of life. The development of our intuition is synonymous with merging with Divine Consciousness. In other words, intuition derives from using the heart as the basis for acting. One develops a "good heart" by devotion to the Supreme and the welfare of the whole.

Because our inner strength is nourished by devotion to the Supreme, it makes perfect sense that we direct our minds toward the Supreme. But even so, we cannot neglect our rationality. We must continue to exert our rationality in the external or objective world. In the absence of rationality, even our internal thoughts will become disturbed. Therefore, the use of our rationality in the objective world is also required to facilitate our inward movement towards the Supreme Consciousness. We must be able to continually adjust to objective events while at the same time pursuing a spiritual approach internally. P. R. Sarkar calls this action "subjective approach with objective adjustment,"[101] wherein the goal of the subjective approach is the Supreme Consciousness.

Supreme Consciousness is the ultimate goal of everyone. We are all moving towards the Divine, both individually and collectively; but we will not be able to move ahead if we ignore the disparities and inequalities of collective life. We should always be working to eradicate these inequalities, while at the same time be moving together towards our intuitional goal. The progress of all would be accelerated if the inequalities were uprooted. By taking such an intuitive path, we will gradually outgrow our need for selfish pleasures. It will be replaced by a more satisfying inner peace and a feeling of spiritual bliss that comes with the realization of the Supreme Consciousness. We will learn how to love and, in so doing, experience a happiness unparalleled.

It is our *conscience* that helps us determine how to promote the welfare of all living creatures. Our conscience is the pinnacle of rational thought as well as the base of our intuition. The first step towards establishing an awakened conscience is study; the second step is strengthening our rationality. The third step is to open our intuition.

Having a strong conscience will open our intuition. As such, we will easily be able to identify the perpetrators of narrow, self-serving sentiments and counteract them. We will move beyond the principle of selfish pleasure and become an embodiment of the *principle of social equality*. This principle implies that not only human beings but all life is due equal respect and deserves equal protection. Everything has equal status from the perspective of Divine Consciousness. This universal worldview will help us fight against all narrow sentiments.

Mr. Sarkar says:

> If one avoids this [principle of social equality] and thinks, "I will be a virtuous person, I will be a devotee of the Lord, I will do all sorts of good deeds—but I will not raise my voice against injustice," I must say that will be foolish. Trying to do good while avoiding this sama-samája tattva [principle of social equality] is just like placing the cart before the horse. The cart should be placed behind the horse; it is foolish to place it in front. Sama-samája tattva teaches that the basis of dharma (human nature) is the collective march of all in unison."[102]

The endeavor to advance towards the Supreme Consciousness by building a society that is free from all inequalities, with everyone moving in unison, is the effort Mr. Sarkar calls *spiritual mentality*. It means the same as intuitive mentality. To develop a spiritual/intuitive mentality we must live according to the principle of social equality and not the principle of selfish pleasure. In this process, we must totally reject all hypocritical ideas, all narrow isms that are contrary to our basic intuitional (spiritual) mentality, and we must welcome all those ideas which help to cultivate it.

An honest person should never resort to hypocrisy in any sphere of life. Under no circumstances, must he or she compromise with any unjust theory. This is the rule; this is what is correct and proper. As Mr. Sarkar warns us:

> So you, who want to be real human beings, must con-
> tinue your sádhaná (spiritual practice) in you inner
> life and strive ceaselessly for God-realization, and
> with equal effort you must see to it that no irratio-
> nal, undesirable or detrimental theory is propagated
> in the external world, which can harmfully influence
> the human mind. You must be ever-vigilant in this
> regard. That is why I told you to be vocal against
> all sorts of injustice. Otherwise your goal will not be
> achieved.[103]

If we want to progress in our humanity, we should not dwell upon the misdeeds of our past. We should rather concentrate on building a new social order based on Universalism. When we have embraced the ideal of spirituality, when we have attained the physical strength, intelligence, and intuitional wisdom to materialize it, we will find ourselves as beacons of hope for humanity. We will play a leading rule in implementing this noble and sublime ideal.

As Mr. Sarkar puts it:

> Our coming to this earth and our remaining here, our
> every breath, every vibration of our existence—should
> this not attain supreme fulfillment? Should we not, by
> utilizing all our physical, psychic and spiritual powers,
> attain the pinnacle of human glory?[104]

Conscience is the base of our intuitional mentality and it is strengthened by adhering to the principle of social equality. Once developed within us, the principle of social equality will make all of our deeds positive, effortless, and heartfelt. No one can stop its movement. It is the desire of the Supreme Consciousness that this movement continues endlessly until it finally merges in Him. As such, the principle of social equality is nourished by a constant and perennial source of inspiration from the Divine.

## Universalism and Intuition

Universalism is the application of intuitional (spiritual) science within the material world. It acts as a bridge between the spiritual and material. In its expression, we see how spiritual values can impact the narrow sentiments that currently enslave human beings.

Everywhere people spout their self-serving "isms," and betray their intolerance by trying to gag each other's voices. Politicians and intellectuals spend their time criticizing and slandering each other. They befool the people by painting rosy pictures of their groups' contribution to human welfare. On the other hand, they themselves are moving far away from the path of selfless service and welfare. To emancipate people from the unhealthy influence of narrow "isms," there is no other way than Universalism. Only Universalism is free from the defects of any narrow isms because everything of this entire universe comes within its periphery. The morality of Universalism extends to all, not just to one's group.

It is only through the use of rationality and intuition that we can emerge from the shortcomings of current religious, political, and economic ideologies and move towards universalism with firm steps. By virtue of our rationality and our intuitional mentality, we can realize the nature of pure Consciousness and merge with the Supreme Oneness.

As people become more generous and broad-minded through adopting Universalism, they will rise above the narrow geo- and socio-sentiments that evoke violence, hatred, and meanness in this world. As we try to see the Divine in everything, the question of "mine" and "yours" will eventually dissolve. A universal outlook, however, does not occur without effort. Rather, the struggle for greatness occurs in stages.

### Intuitional Practice

Mr. Sarkar describes intuitional practice as a physico-psycho-spiritual process that helps us remove the defects of the physical and psychic world and moves us towards the spiritual goal in the quickest way possible. This movement towards the spiritual goal goes hand in hand with our ability to provide greater service to the people. Our journey begins with the desire to elevate the mind and ends in the attainment of the Supreme Goal.

Intuitional practice in the physical realm entails meeting our individual and collective needs, particularly food, shelter, clothing, health care, and education. But it also entails building social institutions upon which we can collectively depend to meet these needs. In the mental realm, it entails developing our minds through rational thought, use of discrimination, adherence to a universal paradigm, and meditation. In the collective aspect, it entails instituting policies, rules, and regulations that benefit all. Finally, in the spiritual realm, intuitional practice creates an intimacy with Divine Consciousness and engenders love for this magnificent creation.

It is meaningless to concentrate on attaining Divinity while ignoring the welfare of this creation. As Jesus Christ said, "Thou shalt love the Lord thy God with all thy heart, and with all thy soul, and with all thy mind." This is the first and greatest commandment. And the second is like it. "Thou shalt love thy neighbor as thyself." On these two commandments hang all the laws and the prophets."[105] Divinity is revealed in the workings of this psycho-physical world. By analyzing the inconsistencies and contradictions of this physical world, we will be able to solve many problems that cause harm to others and keeps them from progressing to their ultimate goal. There are many people with tremendous mental potentiality, but they do not have a clear line of thought. They are mired in sentiments and narrow ideologies and the outcome of their defective thinking is defective action. Such people have not been properly guided as to how to move in this relative reality. They have not been properly guided unto the path of the Cosmic Entity.

When someone commits a wrong, we have a tendency to condemn him or her at every step. We should realize that such a person suffers from a sort of mental ailment and to cure such an ailment, we will have to introduce him or her to Universalism. We have not done so in the past, and that has been a crime of humanity.

Mr. Sarkar says:

> To build a healthy human race we should have given
> people proper guidance in philosophy, in science, in

all branches of human knowledge—which we did not do. We have utilized science more for destructive purposes than for benevolent aims; we have distorted the thought processes of human beings; we have deliberately misguided the people instead of leading them along the proper path. We have taught people to think about how such-and-such bomb can annihilate so many millions of people at a time—but we have never propagated a philosophy to teach them to think how millions of people could be benefited by psycho-spiritual practices. Thus human beings of today are following a defective path, and there is a desperate need for a change in direction. The only remedy is Neohumanism.[106]

The key to understanding Neo-Humanism (Universalism) is that it begins as an internal, subjective process. The more we are established in Neo-Humanism, the greater the speed of our rational and intuitive development. And as our minds strengthen, we will be able to provide greater service to all of life.

## Proto-Psycho-Spirituality

Mr. Sarkar calls the movement of our intuition toward spiritual realization *proto-psycho-spirituality*. What does he mean by this? He says:

> . . . since it is the mind which advances towards spirituality, this movement is called "psycho-spirituality." And it is called "proto" in the sense that it is a flickering entity—it is like a flickering flame, not like a steady flame. It is not something unruffled or fixed; it is expressive of movement. Hence it is not complete psycho-spirituality but proto-psycho-spirituality. And the mobility portion within the systaltic of proto-psycho-spirituality is purely psychic; and the blissful staticity within the systaltic is purely spiritual. So it is a happy blending of psychic and spiritual strata. Thus I call it "psycho-spirituality".[107]

Proto-psycho-spirituality is a dynamic force. Movement is the main factor. If we become lethargic and lose our mobility, we will not gain the benefits of this spiritual force. But, according to Mr. Sarkar:

> Those who move along this path make their lives glorious and effulgent, and their sweet radiance illumines and glorifies all other minds in this harmonious universe. In that state, whatever they come in contact with in the world, they will be able to distinguish the pure gold from the impure, the true from the false. On these people alone can all of humanity rely. Their victory is assured.[108]

But how and in which direction do we move? Mr. Sarkar reminds us that the universe rotates around its nucleus; that is, the Supreme Consciousness. Nothing is outside its circumference, so it is not necessary to search for its nucleus outside. Each and every grain of sand, each and every blade of grass, each and every entity exists within the periphery of the Supreme Nucleus. This universe is controlled by one Center both collectively and on an individual basis. Therefore, if an individual makes his or her psycho-spiritual nucleus coincide with that Supreme Nucleus, then that individual will feel oneness with every grain of sand, with every blade of grass. This will become his or her psychology. Mr. Sarkar tells us:

> This very realization will make one's life-force throb throughout the entire universe. By means of this proto-psycho-spirituality one can fight against all sorts of socio-sentiments. The human chameleons who use socio-sentiments or geo-sentiments can also be easily detected in the light of proto-psycho-spirituality.[109]

Mr. Sarkar encourages intelligent people to use the principle of social equality and proto-psycho-spirituality as weapons to fight against dogmas and free the people from their bondage of narrow sentiments. He reminds us that:

> This must be done, for although there may be some individuals who, knowingly or unknowingly, are fighting

against these socio-sentiments, the majority of people are in darkness. That is why you will have to carry the collectivity with you, because the collectivity is yours. The collectivity is not outside you—your future is inseparably connected with the collective fortune. You must take the entire collectivity with you and move towards the sweetest radiance of the new crimson dawn, beyond the veil of the darkest night.[110]

As people advance toward their spiritual goal, their intuitive mind eventually expands to become all-pervasive. Such people can never think of harming others; rather they think only of universal welfare. In this elevated state of mind, they can easily detect those who seek to exploit others. After recognizing such people, it becomes the duty of the spiritualist to expose them to the public, to make people understand that they are repeatedly harming human society. It is not enough for one to personally unmask them; one must open the eyes of others also. Only in this way can the well being of the world be promoted. Thus, it will not be sufficient to keep one's mouth shut like a goody-goody and not make waves. One will have to become a warrior and act with courage.

## Devotional Sentiment and Spiritual Mission

Mr. Sarkar defines "devotional sentiment" as the love and respect that we carry in our hearts for all of life. It is this sentiment that helps us make progress toward God-realization. Devotion is not a narrow sentiment; it is a universal sentiment.

Sarkar says that devotional sentiment is the most valuable treasure of humanity. Its power, he says:

> . . . is to transform the sense of worldly existence into the supreme spiritual stance. If a materialistic philosophy contains any narrowness, like the geo-sentiment we discussed, an imbalance is bound to occur between the inner and outer worlds, and psycho-phys-

ical imbalance will be inevitable. That is why, in spite of possessing everything, people will remain poor and deprived.[111]

With devotional sentiment, however, we come to experience that everything in this universe, all atoms, electrons, neutrons, molecules; i.e., every form of life is an expression of the Supreme Consciousness. Those who keep this realization alive in their hearts are called "spiritual warriors" (Sadvipras). When ritual devotion becomes a devotional sentiment, when the underlying spirit of humanism is extended to everything, animate and inanimate, in this universe, Mr. Sarkar calls this idea Universalism or Neohumanism and says that, in essence, it is "the cult of love for all created beings of this universe."[112]

Our devotional sentiment must be preserved so that humanity will not lose its most valuable possession. We must not permit the spiritual progress that people have made to be destroyed. Mr. Sarkar tells us that whenever we see that the pressure of external circumstances threatens this life essence, we should appeal to the Supreme: "O Lord, please be kind enough to protect our inner vitality from total destruction. Save us from the agony of total loss."[113]

It should be remembered that the effort to elevate the planet does not just fall to God's devotees. It is also the intention of the Supreme Consciousness to elevate the planet and He/She will come to the aid of every devotee as surely as a mother comes to the aid of her child.

Mr. Sarkar says, "When this Neo-Humanism operates in the external sphere, then internal devotion as a principle is transformed into devotion as a mission."[114]

What is the benefit of having devotion as a mission?

> [W]hen this surging Neo-Humanism overflows in all directions, making all things sweet and blissful, unifying individual life with collective life, and transforming this earth into a blissful heaven—that very state of supreme fulfillment is the state of spirituality as a mission. That is the highest state of attainment in human life, the source of all inspiration.[115]

Again:

> Devotion leads humanity towards the stage of subtlety,
> and finally ensconces a person in the state of supreme
> bliss. That is why in the scriptures devotion has also
> been called puśti márga, that is, a path by which all of
> human existence becomes spiritually strengthened: the
> mind becomes more stable, one realizes more and more
> spiritual bliss—in a word, the whole of human existence
> becomes blissful.[116]

By adopting the path of devotion, human beings become resplendent
in their own glory. As such, the multiplicities in reality get reduced to
only two entities—I and the Supreme Consciousness. On the path of
devotion, there is no one to create barriers, no one to exploit, no one
to impose geo-sentiment or socio-sentiment—internally humanity is
one and indivisible.

Mr. Sarkar says:

> In that supreme Neohumanistic status, the universal
> humanity will attain the consummation of its exis-
> tence. Then nothing will be impossible for human
> beings; they will be able to do anything and every-
> thing.[117]

## Spiritual Essence

What does spiritual essence mean? If we consider the entire human race,
we will see that there is a collective human mind. This mind is not the
Cosmic Mind because the collective human mind exists only within
the purview of humanity. In this collective mind, we will have to create
a new wave of thought. When the collective mind becomes imbued
with Universalism, we will collectively gain a sense of spiritual essence.
Because of the manner of human thinking thus far, the pace of human
progress has been painfully slow. If the collective mind is free to act out
of love instead of fear, the speed of progress will be greatly accelerated.

When this occurs, Mr. Sarkar tell us:

> Humanity as a whole will become converted into a
> powerful spiritual force, and in that stage, no pseu-
> do-humanistic strategy will work. All other weapons
> will become completely powerless before this mightiest
> spiritual weapon.[118]

How do we develop devotional sentiment; how do we bring about spiritual essence? To do so, we must understand the theory and practice of
intuitional science. In the next chapter, we will explore the meaning of
intuitional science. We will look more deeply into the nature of Cosmic
Mind and the process of creation. We will investigate the evolution of
human beings, the cycle of birth and death, and the attainment of spiritual
liberation. In essence, we will explore the relationship of the unit mind
to the Cosmic Mind and the intuitional practices that are necessary for
the unit mind to become one with the Cosmic Mind. These topics fall
within the scope of Intuitional Science.

# Chapter Three: Spirituality

*The meaning of spiritual practice is to look upon every human being, every object of this universe as one integral entity. To jeopardize the unity of the human race by creating factions is not the purpose of spirituality. Spirituality is not a utopian ideal but a practical philosophy which can be practiced and realized in everyday life.* P. R. Sarkar

**M**ANY PEOPLE, WHEN THEY think of the word "spirituality," respond negatively, because they do not consider themselves religious; i.e., belonging to a particular religion or believing in the conventional conception of God. However, it is important to understand the concept of "spirituality" not as a religious expression, but, as P. R. Sakar defines it above, as having a universalist perception of life where we are all a part of the same creation and connected to and responsible for each other. This is the definition of "spirituality" that is used throughout this book, especially throughout this chapter. Also, when we talk about "love," we are talking about that attractive force that binds us to each other and to Absolute Consciousness. In Chapter 3, we also make the distinction between the conventional concept of God and Absolute Consciousness. As we learned in Book I, the idea of God was an evolving construct that changed with humankind's ability to comprehend reality in its greater complexity. So, to begin this chapter, we will review the changing perception of God through history.

## The Idea of God

As extensively covered in Book One of this Trilogy, the idea of God significantly changed over the course of human history. In fact, the story of our evolution as a species can be observed in our understanding of who God was at any particular place and time. As we evolved, our definition of "God" represented the greatest idea that the human mind was capable of grasping. In our earliest days, God was represented as the voice of our ancestors. In time, this voice in our minds was attributed to nature spirits. These spirits could inhabit any rock or tree, plant or stream. Spirits were not bound by form. An evil spirit, that wanted to harm someone could be present in a tree one day, and then in a stone the next. At the time, people thought that their own thoughts came from outside of themselves. Thus, they equated the thoughts in their heads with the voices of their ancestors, nature spirits, and, in time, the voice of higher goddesses and gods.

A great leap in our understanding of God came when women, who governed the early clans and tribes, correlated their menstrual period to the cycle of the moon. God became the Moon Goddess, who was responsible for the birth of children. Each month a woman either bled or the Goddess would mix her spirit with a woman's blood and make a child.

In time, the clan mothers began to envision the male God as a snake. The snake became the eternal phallic principle. The snake was viewed as an immortal being because of its ability to shed its skin and be born anew. As the myth of its power grew, the serpent eventually turned into a dragon, a snake that could fly and it came to control all the waterways of the known world. With the advent of patriarchy, the snake, which was identified with the Goddess, had to be slain in order for patriarchal male gods to ascend to power. Thus, we find male heroes killing dragons in myths all over the world. The snake even made an appearance in the creation myth of the Old Testament (Torah), which was written by early patriarchal Jews. These men taught that the snake was an evil deity who spoke falsely and led men and women astray from their patriarchal god Yahweh. Women, according to the male priests, were guilty of listening to the snake and were therefore responsible for offending Yahweh and causing the fall of humanity from paradise.

Before the advent of patriarchy, however, women had also discovered the annual cycle. They first discovered the lunar cycle and then the solar cycle. With the discovery of the solar cycle, the Great Goddess came into being, expressed as a trinity in the forms of virgin, mother, and crone. Each spring the virgin arose from the underworld, was impregnated by her consort, the snake, or later the sacred king, and gave birth to all the new plants and animals of the land. In summer, she became the mother who cared for her children, and in the fall, she turned into the crone after the harvest and as winter approached. During the winter months, she returned to the underworld to be reborn again the following spring. As the definition of the Great Goddess grew in meaning, the queen of the tribe came to represent the Great Goddess on earth and each spring she chose a sacred king who, because of his virility, became her consort and lover. After a year or so of living in luxury, he was sacrificed in the following spring to thank the Goddess for her bounty and to encourage Her to produce a bountiful harvest in the new year. The blood of the sacred king was spread on the fields to fructify them. As the women bled each month, so a sacred king was chosen to bleed each spring. After his death, he was honored as a god and often became a star in the heavens.

As men wrested control of society from women, the Goddess was gradually replaced by male gods. At first these gods were powerful forces of nature—storms, roiling seas, thunder and lightning, earthquakes, and volcanoes. In time, they became anthropomorphic. The most ancient and powerful anthropomorphic god was Indra. He led the patriarchal Aryan tribes on cattle raids and in battles. He was a great warrior and a drunkard.

As the warrior kings began to build their city-states during the ascension of the patriarchy, gods and goddesses multiplied, each reflecting the power inherent in different facets of life. In time, each city came to have its own chief god who oversaw the general well-being of the citizens of the city. This god, in the form of an idol, was cared for by a priest class who lived in his temple and interpreted the god's needs to the people.

The Babylonians were one of many empires who fought for control of the Middle East from their city-state located in present day Iraq. At the height of its empire, in the first century BC, the Babylonians brought the captured idols of the tribes they conquered back to Babylon. In time, their own city-god Marduk took on the qualities of all these other gods and became the first god to be considered the God of gods. The spirit of Marduk lived in a great idol that was kept in the Babylonian temple called the ziggurat.

Around 1200 BC, a massive volcano exploded on the island of Thera in the eastern Mediterranean Sea. So great was its destruction that it devastated all surrounding civilizations. As social order broke down, the Minoan, ancient Greek, Hittite, and Egyptian civilizations were wasted. The event was so cataclysmic, it staggered the minds of the civilized world and, as a result, the gods throughout the Middle East stopped talking to men. In the absence of the voices of the gods, the bicameral mind of human beings broke down.[119] As a consequence, within centuries, human beings began to develop a sense of personal authority with the emergence of their own "I-feeling." They no longer attributed the voices in their heads to external gods but to themselves. Some great kings even began to claim themselves as gods. Beginning with Gilgamesh, the Sumerian king, later kings and emperors came to declare themselves as gods to their people. By this time the word "god" had come to mean absolute authority and the emperors seized on this term to define their own power.

This transfer of authority, from god to one's self, created a revolution in human thought and human understanding of reality. For the first time in history, we began to believe that we had control over our own lives. The "I-feeling" was now the "doer" and was responsible for its own actions.

In the Western world, this development led to the next evolution in our idea of God—Zoroastrianism. Zoroaster, who lived about three thousand years ago, had a vision of a good god and a bad god. Human beings no longer needed pantheons of gods and goddesses whom they had to please in order to be protected from harm and have their wants and desires fulfilled. Life was now greatly simplified to a dualist perspective. There was only one good god and one bad god and people had the free will to worship one or the other.

Zoroastrianism became the dominant religion among the Persians, who, in their conquest of the Middle East, freed the Jewish priests from their captivity in Babylon and, in so doing, introduced them to the ideas of Zoroaster. This profoundly affected the Jewish priests in their understanding of God. Yahweh, who was an angry, vindictive, and merciless volcano god, became a more caring god and changed into the good god of Zoroaster. The Jews added their own twist on the story of God. Yahweh had an adversary, but he did not represent the god of evil who was independent of Yahweh. Rather the god of evil, Satan, was actually a creation of Yahweh who had disobeyed him. Thus, dualism was changed to monotheism, the worship of one Supreme Being. Those who worshipped Yahweh would return to paradise after death, those who did not would live in the underworld of Hell with Satan.

Among the various Jewish groups, who quested after the knowledge of God, was a mystical sect called the Essenes. The ascetic Essenes submerged themselves in the examination of the Torah and the words of the prophets and, in so doing, came to believe that Yahweh would return to earth and once more turn the Middle East into the Garden of Eden. This sect, due to its daily focus on a Supreme Being and its ascetic lifestyle, gave rise to a mystical leader of great power, who was called the Teacher of Righteousness. He lived approximately one hundred years before Christ. The Teacher had a personal relationship with the Divine. He understood that God was neither an external authority, nor the voice of his own ego. God was an all-powerful subjective entity who resided in everything. This was a huge breakthrough in the Western under-standing of God. We now moved beyond an object-subject relationship in which God was either an external authority or the voice of our own ego. Rather, with the Teacher of Righteousness, we witness a human being who identified a subjective-subjective relationship in that both the individual and the Divine were understood to possess a subjective consciousness. This spiritual insight led to the possibility of the emer-gence of one's individual consciousness with the Divine consciousness. With this understanding of a subjective-subjective relationship, true mysticism or spirituality was born in the West. Now, we have a God who is a universal person, who transcends all religions and, at the same time, resides in the heart of all human beings.

It was from the Essenes, almost a hundred years after the death of the Teacher of Righteousness, that another great Jewish mystic arose. He was called Jesus the Christ. Jesus further expanded our definition of God by teaching that God not only lives within each of us, but that he can be known directly through acts of love. Jesus loved his Divine Father and served his fellow men and women. This was his life and this was his mission. Whether people were poor, sick, insane, whether they were rich or poor, men or women, of this race or that, Jesus served them all. His message was simple. Love God, love your neighbor, and one is equal to the other. By loving God, we come to love our neighbor and by loving our neighbor we come to love God.

The teachings of Jesus Christ were spread by the Essenes throughout Israel. When the Romans sent the Jews into exile, the Essenes took their message to other countries in the Middle East, to ancient Egypt, Greece, and Rome. Those who grasped the mystical teachings of Jesus became known as Gnostics and nurtured their personal relationship with the Divinity through meditation, service, and a simple life. On the other hand, those who were more concerned with the organization of a church and the ability to govern the flock of Christians became the bishops of the Catholic Church. The Church eventually killed off the Gnostics because it did not suit the Church's hierarchy to have people believe that they could know God from within. This is not how a priest class could gain power. Christ's teachings were carried to Rome by Paul and Peter, where Jesus Christ took on the mythic qualities of Mithra, a mystery god of the Roman army. Many of the myths of Jesus' birth, death and resurrection were first attributed to Mithra.[120] After about three hundred years, with the rule of Emperor Constantine, Jesus Christ came to be the lead god in Rome and the "Son of God" came to replace the gods and goddesses of the Roman pantheon altogether. In time, the hierarchy of the Catholic Church came to pervert Christ's teachings to justify its military and political dominance of Western Europe.

In the East, the quest to know God was given a great leap forward by the teachings and example of Lord Shiva, arguably the first God-realized person to walk the earth. Shiva lived about seven thousand years ago and introduced spiritual practices to his followers. He introduced the intuitional science of Tantric yoga and the practice of meditate. At the time Shiva was alive, the patriarchal Aryans were in the process of taking over India and suppressing the indigenous matriarchal Dravidians. In this pressure cooker, Hinduism was born out of a combination of the Vedas of the Aryans and the Tantric practices of Shiva. Because of its universal nature and the fact that it is based on science and not blind faith, Tantra yoga became accepted by both the Aryan and the Dravidian people. In time, it also came to provide the spiritual underpinnings for Buddhism, Jainism, Sikhism, Taoism, and other religions and yogic systems of the East.[121]

It is important to understand this distinction between religion, which draws its strength from our sentimental state of mind, versus intuitional science, which draws its strength from our intuitional state of mind. The former has the perspective of God as distinct from humans and tends to divide humans according to the tenets of the various religions; Christians, vs Muslims; Buddhists vs Hindus, etc. Whereas intuitional science sees God as indistinct from humans where all humans are seen as manifestations of the same Absolute Consciousness; we are all connected. If we are to extricate ourselves from this critical situation, we now find ourselves in, we have to move past the perspective that we are all separate and distinct entities and begin to see ourselves as interconnected and participating in a mutual striving for self-realization and ultimately mutual participation in Absolute Consciousness. Therefore, for the rest of this chapter, we will discuss what intuitional science is and how we all can begin to develop our intuitional nature.

## Intuitional Science

Although there are multiple paths to developing one's intuitional nature, in this chapter, we will explore the intuitional science of Tantra, a well-developed path to attaining self-realization. In doing so, we will witness the roots of spirituality for which the East has long been famous and which has created so many enlightened masters. Its teachings correspond perfectly with those of the spiritual master Jesus Christ. Both Shiva in the East and Jesus Christ in the West constructed their message on the love of God and neighbor and the realization of Divine Absolute Consciousness.

Nonetheless, as religions, both Hinduism and Christianity eventually became controlled by a priest class that filled the people's minds with myths, stories, dogmas, and rituals that allowed the priests to control the minds of the people. They never encouraged the people to perform intuitional practices, but only to obey the priests, and pay them, for being the embodiment of the "official word" of God.

The intuitional practice of tantric yoga has allowed the East to produce an incredible line of spiritual masters because it distinguishes religion from spirituality and speaks in a clear and rational language. The intuitional science exists independent of and transcendent to religious and non-religious styles of worship even though its truths are embedded within any sincere religious effort.

In this chapter, we will discover the underlying truths that lie within the mystical/intuitional traditions of all people. While religions are many, intuitional science is one. It stands in witness to human unity regardless of gender, race, nation, or religion. Intuitional science provides us with the most advanced idea of God that has ever existed or exists today. It teaches us what it means to be a human being and what is required to become a self-realized or God-realized human being. Intuitional science is the greatest accomplishment of human society throughout all of history. It is expressed by all masters for all times, while, at the same time, its secrets have often been hidden by those who seek to control our thought for their own benefit.

Throughout this chapter, in addition to both Eastern and Western authorities, we will also refer often to P. R. Sakar, one of the great teachers of Tantra because of his genius for presenting intuitional science in a language that all people can understand. While we may worship within different religions, spiritual science demonstrates that it is not a particular religion that is the truth. Rather, religions are styles of worship where their truthfulness is dependent upon their capacity to reflect spirituality. Mr. Sarkar provides us with a philosophy that synthesizes the mystical traditions of the world and has the capacity to provide each individual with a spiritual path that not only leads to one's own emancipation, but also delineates our duties within the cultural, economic, and political spheres of human society. Mr. Sarkar demonstrates that there is only one consciousness and that is the Absolute Consciousness of which we are all but forms.

It is only by understanding our intuitional/spiritual nature that we become capable of realizing our highest potential as human beings. As Alfred North Whitehead put it: "This primordial nature is eternal and unchanging, providing entities in the universe with possibilities for realization."[122]

We can understand our relationship with the Absolute Consciousness through a rational analysis of the workings of our mind and our individual consciousness. This is not an original idea. Many have believed this. For example, it was Origen, one of the early Christian theologians, who said, "The return to original being through divine reason is the object of the entire cosmic process."[123]

Absolute Consciousness, or the "Cosmic Entity," stands in Its own radiance for all time and space and within every entity of the cosmos. Many contemporary Western scientists are coming to the same conclusion. Max Planck, one of the founders of quantum theory, states:

> I regard consciousness as fundamental. I regard matter as derivative from consciousness. We cannot get behind consciousness. Everything that we talk about, everything that we regard as existing, postulates consciousness.[124]

Only by ideating on the Absolute Consciousness will we be able to overcome the duality of mind and abolish the narrow isms that divide us. Only by meditating on our Supreme Oneness will we be able to fulfill our eternal thirst for limitlessness. It is Absolute Consciousness that is the source of unity of all things. As the ancient Greek Philosopher Heraclitus said, ""For those who are awake, the cosmos is one."[125]

To better understand this concept of unity, let us explore the case for the existence of Supreme Consciousness and the need for intuitional practice. P. R. Sakar, in his book *Ananda Marga Elementary Philosophy* observes that human beings possess a thirst for limitlessness that we mistakenly attempt to quench by possessing finite objects. He tells us:

> Human beings are the highest-evolved beings. They possess clearly-reflected consciousness, and this makes them superior to animals. No other being has such a clear reflection of consciousness. Human beings can distinguish between good and bad with the help of their consciousness, and when in trouble they can find a way out with its help. No one likes to live in misery and suffering, far less human beings, whose consciousness can find means of relief. Life without sorrow and suffering is a life of happiness and bliss, and that is what people

desire. Everyone is in a quest of happiness; in fact it is people's nature (or dharma) to seek happiness.[126]

In our search for happiness, people are first attracted toward physical enjoyments. We strive for physical wealth and power to satisfy our desire for happiness. But these things do not help us achieve happiness because we are never satisfied with what we have. We always want more. Acquiring something *limited* only creates the desire for more because our hunger for possessing something is *limitless*. The rich will not be satisfied until they can attain unlimited wealth. The powerful will not be satisfied until they can achieve unlimited power. The desire for unlimited wealth and power can never be fulfilled by the things of this world because they are finite and cannot fulfill a limitless desire. Throughout Book One, we have witnessed empire after empire achieve a measure of wealth and power only to fall into oblivion. Warrior kings fought warrior kings, priests fought against priests, merchants fought merchants and warrior, priest, and merchant fought each other for control of limited wealth. Yet, in each case, the desired peace and happiness for which the victors sought was short lived, if it existed at all. The thirst for power and wealth that drives the warriors, priests, and capitalists of this world to dominate their spheres of influence is the same drive that leads them to destroy anyone or anything that stands in the way of their envisioned conquest.

As Swami Krishnanda says, "The senses cannot give you satisfaction. Anything that you possess in this world can be lost. The possibility of losing even the best of things gnaws into your vitals and poisons the joy that you are apparently having through sense contact."[127] What then is that infinite, eternal thing which will provide everlasting happiness?

Mr. Sarkar answers:

> The Cosmic Entity alone is infinite and eternal. It alone is limitless. And because we have a clearly reflected consciousness, the eternal longing of human beings for happiness can only be satiated by realization of the Infinite. The ephemeral nature of worldly possessions, power and position can only lead one to the conclu-

sion that none of the things of the finite and limited world can set at rest the everlasting urge for happiness. Their acquisition merely gives rise to further longing. Only realization of the Infinite can do it. The Infinite can be only one, and that is the Cosmic Entity. Hence it is only the Cosmic Entity that can provide everlasting happiness—the quest for which is the characteristic of every human being. In reality, behind this human urge is hidden the desire, the longing, for attainment of the Cosmic Entity. It is the very nature of every living being. This alone is the dharma of every person.[128]

Because human beings have evolved from animals, we possess two aspects—the animal aspect, and the rational aspect that distinguishes us from animals. But we must not forget that we also possess a soul, an intuitional entity. As Nobel Prize winner John Eccles writes in his *Evolution of the Brain, Creation of the Self,* "we have to recognize that we are spiritual beings with souls existing in a spiritual world as well as material beings with bodies and brains existing in a material world."[129]

As a species, human beings are evolving out of animality and moving toward Divinity, Absolute Consciousness. Our animality draws us towards gratification of material desires, but our spiritual or intuitional nature remains unsatisfied because material desires are transitory and short-lived. While animals are satisfied with the limited, human beings are not. There is, therefore, a constant struggle in humans between our animal nature and our spiritual nature. The animal aspect pulls us towards instant earthly pleasures, while our spiritual consciousness, not being satisfied with these, draws us towards the Absolute Consciousness. Mr. Sarkar notes that if the carnal pleasures derived from the possession of wealth and power had been infinite and endless, they would have set at rest the eternal quest of human consciousness for happiness. But they do not, "and that is why the fleeting glory of temporal joys can never secure a lasting peace in the human mind and lead people to ecstasy."[130] Human history has been a tale of death and destruction for this reason. We are a maddened species, destructive of our own kind and all of life, because we have not yet learned how to free ourselves from our slavery to unfulfilling desires and the fear of others who are bound by the same desires.

Consequently, we are denied further progress as a species, as our minds wander blind and weary through this temporal existence. As Plato observed thousands of years ago, "When the mind's eye rests on objects illuminated by truth and reality, it understands and comprehends them, and functions intelligently; but when it turns to the twilight world of change and decay, it can only form opinions, its vision is confused and its beliefs shifting, and it seems to lack intelligence." [131]

As author J. R. Seydel puts it, "A person who has no control of his own wandering mind, has no control in Life's destiny because of the lack of focus and direction in Life. It can be compared to a rudderless ship that is constantly tossed by the rise and fall of the waves from the powerful ocean." [132]

Mr. Sarkar defines *dharma* as "nature, characteristic, or property." The nature of fire is to burn or produce heat. Similarly, the nature of a human being is to seek unlimited happiness.

If we know that it is our human nature (dharma) to seek infinite happiness, and if we know that finite objects do not make us happy, why do we continue to seek happiness in such objects? It is because we have been programmed by our evolutionary process and by our history as a species to want such objects. This programming is extremely difficult to overcome and impossible to overcome if we do not realize that we are its prisoners.

If we do not follow our human nature, but continue to be captives of our programming and indulge our animal instincts, we will continue to behave as animals. It is rationality that distinguishes us from animals. If this is so, it makes sense to use our rationality to reverse our destructive programming, which is now leading us to the brink of societal and environmental collapse. As Buckminister Fuller suggests in his *No More Second Hand God*:

> We have plenty, we have
> the means, the ability, the knowledge.
> Let us start the mechanism
> to creative account;
> not to vast and vaster destruction. [133]

Those who make use of their clearly reflected consciousness, their rationality, have earned the right to be called human beings. As we have seen, throughout western history, as far back as matriarchal society, there have been a few among us who understood what consciousness is and sought to understand our world in terms of higher states of consciousness. These have been the mystics, the spiritual leaders, whose quest to experience self-realization have shown us how to make the leap from animality to humanity and from humanity to Absolute Consciousness.

However, in order to make such leaps, we need to understand how the mind works and how we can begin to focus on our rational and intuitional nature.

## The Senses and the Mind

Our focus on what we desire is determined by what we believe is *real*. In other words, what we focus on creates our reality and we tend to focus on what we perceive to have value. Warriors value weapons; intellectuals value understanding; merchants value money. Some people value none of these things, but are instead focused on serving others. Mothers, for example, value a warm shelter, enough food to get through the winter, and healthy children above all else. Regardless of what we value, if we spend our lives entirely focused on this psycho-physical reality, we become bound by it. In this case, our intuitional nature is not considered to be real. Alternately, if we focus on our intuitional nature in our daily lives, this aspect of reality gains credibility and we begin to gain the insights necessary to progress toward enlightenment. Therefore, in order to overcome the programming that binds us to psycho-physical (relative) reality, we need to understand how our minds really work.

As we learned in Book One of *The Untold Story of Western Civilization*, the era of modern history evolved after millennia of being dominated by emperors and religious leaders demanding blind acceptance to their rule under penalty of death. With the dawn of the modern age, we witnessed the beginnings of "free thought." Once free to think beyond the confines of brute force and religious dogmas, people began to reject the laws of authoritarian kings and priests and sought meaning for themselves. This led to a philosophical split between the free-thinking progressives and the religious traditionalists who remained committed to their dogmas. This, in turn, led to a further split among the progressives, some of whom believed that faith or rationality defined reality and others who believed only sensory data defined reality. The philosophies of Idealism and Materialism arose out of this split in worldviews. Those who believed that only sense data could describe reality became the materialists, the naturalists, and scientists who focused entirely on what our senses could identify. Only what we are able to hear, see, feel, taste, or smell determines what is real. Everything else is just abstract thought, a weak shadow of the real. There was a common belief that, if you could not measure it, it did not exist. Enlightenment scientists, beginning with Roger Bacon, rejected the idea that knowledge comes from God, intuition, revelation, or *a priori* reasoning (i.e., reasoning without sensory data). Only sensory experience could produce valid knowledge. The scientific method is based upon the principle that when one makes a statement (hypothesis) about the nature of reality, it can only be verified by being tested by observation and experiment.[134] The hypothesis gains credibility when others come to the same conclusion by their own observation and experiment.

During the fifteenth and sixteenth centuries, when reality was what the Church wanted people to believe, the scientific method played a major role in confronting the Church's religious centric view of reality and demanded that scientific truth be something provable by observation and experiment. Today, however, many contemporary scientists still honor the scientific method, but they reject the simple explanation that only by the analysis of sensory data can we come to understand what is real. Many scientists today, like the idealists of the past, hold that sensory knowledge is based on the act of interpretation, a quality of a reasoning mind.

From a materialistic perspective every action that we take appears to have been executed by our *sensory* and *motor* organs. Sensory organs are skin, ears, eyes, nose and tongue (to taste), Motor organs are the feet, anus, genitals, hands, and tongue (to speak). But, while it appears that our senses are performing our actions, it is actually the mind that is performing them. After all, if the mind does not work behind them, the organs by themselves cannot perform any action. It is the mind, which works and the motor and sensory organs are merely the instruments through which the work is executed. The action, which originates in mind, only finds its external manifestation with the help of the organs.

It is common knowledge that people with robotic arms can still feel a sense of touch. This is a simple illustration of how the mind can perceive sensory data despite a lack of sensory input.[135]

To illustrate how the mind works, let us take the example of a person looking at a book. It is the mind that visualizes the book with the help of the eyes. If the mind does not work, the eyes will not be able to see the book. For example, in an unconscious state, a person is unable to see the book even though the eyes are not damaged. They cannot perform their function because their contact with the mind has been suspended. Mr. Sarkar explains that when the mind sees a book, what actually happens is that the mind itself, with the help of the eyes, takes the shape of something we call a book. The shape, which the mind takes, is different from the image, which is formed on the retina, because the mind can see and become like a book even when the eyes are closed. But the eyes cannot see when the mind does not function. So, it is the mind which takes the form of a book during visual perception. The portion of the mind, which takes the form of the book, is termed the mental screen of the mind (or in Sanskrit, the citta).[136] But, as the image of the book is produced on the mental screen, there must be something other than the mental screen which does the actual work of seeing. Mr. Sarkar calls this the "Doer I" (Ahamtattva), literally, the sense of doing. So also, according to Mr. Sarkar, the "Doer I" alone will not be able to see or do anything unless there is a higher level of the mind which directs the "Doer I" to perform an action. So, there must be a third part of the mind which is different from the mental screen and the "Doer I." This third part gives us the feeling of "I am" or "I exist" and is called Mahatattva, literally, the highest sense. The mental screen, the sense of I-do and the sense of I-am constitute the three levels of mind that are required to perform the action of seeing a book. Sarkar refers to this process as psychic assimilation.[137]

Without the feeling of "I am," actions can still be performed, but the actions are not attributed to the self. This is how animals perform actions. They have a sense of doing but no sense of individual discretion.

It was Descartes, one of the early Enlightenment philosophers, who said "I think therefore I am." His rationale was such: Thoughts exist. Thoughts cannot be separated from me. Therefore, I exist. If I doubt this, there must be a doubter. Thus, I exist, whether I believe or doubt. According to Tantric logic, Descartes should have said, "I am therefore I think."

So how does the perception of an object actually occur? According to basic physics, every object radiates waves. These waves radiate from an object and strike the sense organs, which in turn carry vibrations to the mental screen. In the case of seeing a book, the vibrations of the book strike the retina, from which vibrations are transferred to the mental screen, which then takes the form of the object, which the "Doer I" then recognizes as a book.

Similarly, when the "Doer I" wants to hear something, it puts the mental screen in contact with the ears, which then receives sound waves. The mental screen, on the impact of these waves, becomes the sound waves themselves and the "Doer I" hears that sound. The mental screen takes the form of whatever the "Doer I" desires or does. To put it another way, the mental screen manifests the actions, which the "Doer I" performs.[138] Thus, instead of the senses dictating what we perceive, it is really the mind that is responsible for perception. The idea that it is the mind that determines the nature of reality and not sensory data is becoming more accepted to western science as well. In his article, "Can Our Brain Waves Affect Our Physical Reality," Peter Baska writes:

> The one difference between us and a photon is that we can think, we are conscious. As such, we can choose which of the possibilities before us to collapse our wave function into. But more than that, since we are entangled with our environment we can thus affect that as well and influence the randomness, just as it can influence us. Since we are conscious, we can choose what part of the randomness around us to be affected by, and how we in turn would like to affect it.[139]

Stephen Hawking also suggests that reality is created in the mind. He states:

> There is no picture – or theory-independent concept of reality. Instead we will adopt a view that we call model-dependent realism; the idea that a physical theory or world picture is a model (generally of a mathematical nature) and a set of rules that connect the elements of the model to observations. This provides a framework with which to interpret modern science.[140]

> We form mental concepts of our home, trees, other people, the electricity that flows from wall sockets, atoms, molecules and other universes. These mental concepts are the only reality we can know. There is no model-independent test of reality. It follows that a well-constructed model creates a reality of its own.[141]

According to Robert Lanza, author of *Biocentrism: How Life Creates the Universe*:

> Custom says that what we see is "out there," outside ourselves, and such a viewpoint is fine and necessary in terms of language and utility, as in "please pass the butter that's over there." But make no mistake: The butter itself exists only within the mind. It is the only place visual (and tactile and olfactory) images are perceived and hence located. Explained in the language of biology, the brain turns impulses from our senses into an order and a sequence. As photons of light bounce off the butter, various combinations of wavelengths enter our eye and deliver the force to trillions of atoms arranged into an exquisite design of cells that rapidly fire in permutations too vast for any computer to calculate. Then, in the brain, this information, which as we previously saw has no color by itself, appears as a yellow block of butter. Even its smell and texture are experienced in the mind alone. The "butter" is not "out there" except

by the convention of language. The same is true for all
perceived objects, including the brain, cells, and even
the electromagnetic events we detect with our instruments.[142]

University of Oregon physicist, Goswami also believes that "Consciousness,
not matter, is the ground of all existence . . . He holds that the universe is
self-aware, and that consciousness creates the physical world. Relating it
to modern physics, he says, "Consciousness is the agency that collapses
the wave of a quantum object, which exists in potentia, making it an
immanent particle in the world of manifestation."[143]

While we are seeing western material scientists and eastern intuitional
scientists coming together in their definition of the role of consciousness
in determining the nature of reality, eastern scientists still go further than
western science when they define the nature of consciousness itself. The
mind, in its three phases of "I am", "I do," and the mental screen is the
extent to which Western science can currently reach. Intuitional science,
however, puts the mind in the context of consciousness as a whole.

The three levels of consciousness in the mind are encompassed by
an even higher level of the "I" which is the "witnessing I." It is this
"witnessing I" which knows that there is a mind. The existence of "I"
in the mind only proves that there is another entity which is beyond
the mind and which is able to observe the existence of mind. This "I,"
which is the witnessing entity, is called "unit consciousness" or *átman*
in intuitional science. In the west, we call this unit consciousness the
soul. Thus, through introspection one can observe that átman (soul)
and mind are distinct forms of the same I.[144]

To summarize, unit consciousness, or the soul, is the witnessing "I"
beyond the three permutations of "I" within the mind. It is reflected in
the feeling of "I exist" and thereby establishes its identity in this psycho-physical reality. It goes through a further permutation to become
the feeling of "I do." Finally, the "I do" feeling gets objectified into the
mental screen, or what some refer to as the "Done-I."

In the evolution of species, the first level of mind to manifest is the
mental screen. This level of consciousness can be witnessed in plants,
wherein the plants have the capacity to duplicate their own image as well

as reflect environmental stimuli. In time, the feeling of doing evolves within species. Animals possess the sense of doing. They have feelings and sentiments, but they have no sense of I that integrates their impressions or allows them to differentiate themselves from their environment. This sense of doing existed in human beings up to the point when we developed a sense of "I." At this point, humans began to differentiate themselves from their environment and identify the locus of authority within ourselves. Only when this sense of subjective consciousness evolved, were we able to say "I am" and thus, "I do," instead of attributing authority to spirits, ancestors, goddesses, or gods, or other external projections of our consciousness. Once this happened, the external voices of authority began to submit to the internal force of one's own mind.

To better understand how these levels of the mind and the unit consciousness come into existence, we will next need to look at how creation itself comes into being. First let us look at what Tantric philosophy calls the Cosmic Entity.

## What is the Cosmic Entity?

Since there are many unit consciousnesses, there must be an entity that reflects the sum total of these unit consciousnesses. The collective name for all these unit consciousnesses (or átmans) is Paramátman, (literally, all the átmans). Just as twelve units make a dozen, and the collective name for a large number of soldiers is an army, the collective name for all the unit consciousnesses is Paramátman. Because we refer to átman or unit consciousness as the "soul," in English, Paramátman may also be called the Universal Soul or Over Soul. Ralph Waldo Emerson describes what he calls the Over Soul as follows:

> "We live in succession, in division, in parts, in parti-
> cles. Meantime within man is the soul of the whole;
> the wise silence; the universal beauty, to which every
> part and particle is equally related; the eternal ONE." [145]

Since we know that unit consciousness exists, we must also recognize that the collection of all of these unit consciousnesses exists. This demonstrates that the Cosmic Entity does exist and that It exists as Paramátman or Universal Soul. Paramátman is the term for the collection of all átmans In addition to the Paramátman, there is an Operative Principle that must exist to transmute the Paramátman into the multiple individual consciousnesses. and Prakriti is the name of the operative principle. The combination of the two is called the Cosmic Entity.

Because the Cosmic Entity is subtle, we cannot visualize It. It cannot be grasped by the senses and we can only get an idea of it with the help of our subjective mind. Prakrti, as the Operative Principle, also can never be grasped by our senses. It can neither be seen nor heard. Therefore, the Cosmic Entity, as a combination of Absolute Consciousness and the Operative Principle, cannot have any form or shape. It is not possible to describe It or say what It looks like. The Cosmic Entity can only be experienced as the mind, through intuitional practice, expands into It.

When we use the words He or She to describe the Cosmic Entity, it is only to help our minds form an idea of consciousness. In reality, it is not limited by gender nor any other quality or form. We only use the idea of gender to help us visualize a Supreme Being in a form that is attractive to us. So for convenience sake, when the personhood of consciousness is discussed we will refer to the Absolute Consciousness as Him and Prakriti the Operative Principle as Her, although the opposite is equally valid.

We have substantiated that the different forms of the mind, "I Exist," "I Do," and the mental screen are dependent on unit consciousness for their existence. But the existence of unit consciousness or Parámatman (collection of unit consciousnesses) is not dependent on any of these forms. In fact, we cannot find anything on which the existence of consciousness depends. Consciousness is therefore absolutely independent. As we quoted Planck saying earlier, "We cannot get behind consciousness."

This means that Cosmic Consciousness is non-causal. It has no origin outside itself. Likewise, unit consciousness, as a manifestation of Parámatman, under the force of Prakrti the Operative Principle, is also non-causal. This negates the commonly held view within science that consciousness somehow evolves out of the increased complexity of the brain. As Paul Davies says in his *God and the New Physics*, "Simple statistics soon reveal that the probability of the spontaneous assembly of DNA—the complex molecule that carries the genetic code—as a result of random concatenations of the soup molecules is ludicrously—almost unthinkably—small."[146] In other words, the brain does not create consciousness, rather consciousness creates the brain.

If the Cosmic Entity is non-causal and without form, how can we know such an entity exists?

Since the Cosmic Entity is subtle, we cannot use crude matter to define It. All matter in this world is crude and can be classified into five rudimental factors. Matter may exist in an ethereal, aerial, luminous, liquid, or solid form. Related to these five rudimental factors are five inferences that allow us to sense their existence. These inferences are sound, touch, form, taste and smell. The presence of sensory inferences distinguishes something crude from something subtle, something physical from something mental or spiritual. A crude thing will always have inferences, while a subtle thing will have none. The cruder the form of matter, the more inferences it will contain. The ethereal factor or space contains nothing which can be visualized. Yet space carries sound and therefore it is considered to be an aspect of material reality. Air has two inferences—sound and touch. That is, air carries sound and may also be felt. Air is thus cruder than ether (space). The luminous, liquid, and solid factors are even cruder because they can be seen and have form. Matter, in the solid state, also contains the inference of smell. All the five rudimental factors in which matter can exist are crude. Since the Cosmic Entity is subtle, we can never use these factors to measure It. Therefore, material science will never be able to measure the Cosmic Entity.

Applying the same test to mind, which is distinct from matter, we find that mind is subtle. It does not contain any inferences. However, even at its most subtle level, that of I exist, the mind cannot even measure its unit consciousness. Therefore, it can never measure the sum of all unit consciousnesses, which is the Cosmic Entity. Mind can never think, feel, or grasp the dimensions of the Cosmic Entity.

Even if we expand the mind to its limits, something always exists beyond it which is incomprehensible to it. And because the mind can only determine the boundaries of something within its scope, it cannot measure something which is beyond its reach as is the Cosmic Entity.

If we cannot measure the Cosmic Entity, how then do we know what it is? In Sanskrit, the language of Tantra, the Cosmic Entity is called "Bhagavan",,which is a name for God.

All religions have their own names for God, including Allah, the Holy Trinity, Yahweh, the Over Soul, G-D, Uhuru Mazda, the Great Spirit, the Great Goddess, the Void, the White Light, etc. No matter what name we choose to describe the Cosmic Entity, the naming of it gives it a form. The very act of defining or measuring requires a form. Even though it is formless, we cannot speak of it unless we are able to give it a form. We give God a form commensurate with our style of worship. Our ideas of God, therefore, are all qualifications of Consciousness. In Tantra, qualified Consciousness is called Saguna Brahma, (literally, Consciousness bound by form). Therefore, whatever our definition of God is, whether we perceive God as male or female, a unity or a trinity, the sound of Om, a spirit, etc., our idea of God can never equal the actuality of Absolute Consciousness. The distinctions that religions make in their concept of God are inconsequential to the actuality of God. To force one's idea of God on another, or to be prejudiced against others for their idea of God, only demonstrates that the members of religions have not been able to distinguish their mental concept from the true reality of the Cosmic Entity. As such, people who condemn others as heretics or infidels do not actually worship the Cosmic Entity, they worship only their own or their group's thought projection. This is the limitation of religions.

Moreover, we must also admit that our concept of God, no matter how all-encompassing in scope, is still not the Absolute Conscious state because it is still bound in form. To know the Absolute Consciousness is to know consciousness unbounded by form. To know this Unqualified Cosmic Consciousness, one has to step beyond all the forms of God and God in all the forms. This reasoning leads us to understand that the Cosmic Entity has a dual nature, Unqualified and Qualified Consciousness.

Although we cannot measure or comprehend the Cosmic Entity with our minds, we know that it exists as the collective of all unit consciousnesses and we understand by reasoning that it is manifested in relative reality. So how does the Cosmic Entity, which has no form and is non-causal, become manifest in the universe?

## Creation

Because Absolute Consciousness is only a collective name for an infinite number of unit consciousnesses, it must follow that it is subject to the same principle as unit consciousness. The only difference being that the scope of unit consciousness is finite, while that of Parámatman Absolute Consciousness is infinite. Just as the mind (sense of "I exist") comes into being when the Operative Principle binds unit consciousness, so also the creation comes into being when the Operative Principle binds Parámatman or the Absolute Consciousness. When this occurs, Absolute Consciousness takes the form of the universe.

The Universe is Qualified Absolute Consciousness (what most religions refer to as God). This creation comes about because Absolute Consciousness allows itself to become qualified or manifested as the universe. As Plato said more than two thousand years ago, "God is the energy of creation; the ideas, the pattern of creation; matter, the stuff of creation.[147]

Because the Operative Principle is a quality of Absolute Consciousness, it is by Its own principle that Consciousness is influenced and qualified. Because there is nothing outside of Absolute Consciousness, the operating principle must therefore exist within Absolute Consciousness. As such, as the Operating Principle, it can never be separated from Cosmic Absolute Consciousness. Unit consciousness and its Operative Principle also can never be separated from each other, just as the burning principle of fire cannot be separated from fire. They are inseparable as the two sides of a sheet of paper. The only function of the Operative Principle is to continually create different forms by Her influence over consciousness.[148]

Duane Elgin, an American philosopher, who speaks on the topics of conscious evolution and the living universe, states: "Our universe is infused with an immense amount of energy, and is being continuously regenerated in its entirety, while making use of a reflective capacity or consciousness throughout."[149]  Oxford Professor David Bohm refers to the "implicate order, which can be thought of as a vast ocean of energy on which the physical, or explicate, world is just a ripple."[150]

The Operative Principle has the ability to bind Absolute Consciousness and unit consciousness into three levels of expression. Figuratively, she has three ropes or principles which, as applied, confine consciousness into form. These are the sentient principle, the mutative principle, and the static principle. The sentient level creates the awareness of "I exist"; the mutative principle creates the "sense of doing"; and in the static level consciousness changes into matter, the stuff that gets reflected on the mental screen. The process by which Absolute Consciousness manifests itself in the world is the process of creation. Creation begins as a movement from subtle to crude. Just as unit consciousness becomes cruder by being transmuted, by the Operative Principle, into the three levels of the mind, so Qualified Absolute Consciousness also becomes cruder as it descends through levels of cosmic mind and ultimately into material reality.

We have to accept the existence of Qualified Absolute Consciousness because the creation can be experienced every moment of our existence. As Carl Jung states; "In the history of the collective as in the history of the individual, everything depends on the development of consciousness."[151]

Just as unit consciousness maintains its identity even when it becomes manifested into the three levels of the mind Absolute Consciousness maintains its identity even when manifested into the creation of the universe.  It also possesses a witnessing "I," a sense of "I-am," a sense of "I-do," and a sense of what is done (the mental screen).


## The Density of Absolute Consciousness


The density of the infinite Absolute Consciousness is not the same everywhere. The Operative Principle qualifies Absolute Consciousness where She finds Him weaker or less condensed. Wherever Cosmic Consciousness is less condensed, She is able to dominate Him and creation springs forth.

Even though a portion of Absolute Consciousness may become qualified, He does not lose His essential consciousness. For example, due to an imbalance in climatic conditions, a part of the ocean may freeze into an iceberg, but the rest of the water remains in its original state. In the same way, wherever Absolute Consciousness is less condensed, it gets qualified by the Operative Principle into form, but the rest remains as Unqualified Consciousness.

So, once a portion of Absolute Consciousness gets qualified, it becomes the manifest universe. The universe begins when the Operative Principle creates, within Absolute Consciousness, the Macrocosmic sense of I am, I do, the mental screen and then into the further crudifications of the ethereal, the aerial, luminous, liquid, and solid factors. As the Operative Principle continues to bind Qualified Consciousness, its manifestation becomes cruder. Thus, the movement in the flow of creation at this stage is from subtle to crude.

Ether is the first stage of material creation, from which all other factors are created. Air is compressed ether, light and heat is compressed air, the liquid factor is compressed luminous factor and the solid factor is compressed liquid factor. The solid factor is the final stage in the transformation from subtle to crude. We can see this progression occur in the creation and life of stars.

The solid factor is the only factor that can be divided into distinct units. The liquid or luminous factors will not remain distinct once they are brought within proximity of each other. Two drops of water will merge. Striking two matches separately will produce two flames, but if the two sticks are held close together, they will merge into one flame. Thus, it is not possible to divide or separate fire. But if two handfuls of dirt are mixed together, it is possible to divide them into two distinct parts again. Thus, unlike water, fire, air, or ether, only when Qualified Absolute Consciousness assumes the crude form of solid matter does it get divided into distinct units. As renowned behavioral neurologist Dr. Jay Lombard states in his *Mind of God*,

> Creation entails an array of circumstances in which what
> appears indivisible becomes divided and partitioned. So,
> too, our brains allow us to perceive and therefore believe

that our existence is also one of division – separate and
apart, autonomous, alone.[152]

With this distinction, unit consciousness comes into existence. In other
words, unit consciousness is a particular form of Cosmic Consciousness.

It is due to the crudification of consciousness that the Universe comes
into being. With the creation of solid matter, Consciousness takes the
form of an inanimate object. There is nothing cruder than this and it sig-
nifies consciousness under the most extreme influence of the Operative
Principle. Absolute Consciousness can be crudified no further.

During the creation process, however, the static principle of the
Operative Principle continues to exert pressure on the solid state until
there remains almost no inter-atomic space within the solid body. Now,
if the static force exerts more pressure beyond this, the equipoise of the
component elements gets destroyed and there is a tremendous reaction
within the physical body that results in the structural dissociation of the
five fundamental factors. This is called jadasphota in Tantra.[153] Western
scientists call this phenomenon the Big Bang. Because consciousness can
only be divided into units in the solid state, it is with the Big Bang that
unit consciousnesses have their origin. It is at this point that evolution,
the movement from crude to subtle, begins.

Although it was explained earlier that every person has a unit consciousness which is non-causal, the history of the earth, however, reveals
that human beings are not causeless. We are not even the first living
beings that came onto the earth, which was a raging ball of fire in the
beginning. Gradually as it cooked down, it became full of water due
to the production of hydrogen and oxygen and then land appeared.
The formation of plants, fish, amphibians, and animals followed, and
it was only after this that human beings evolved. Human beings are,
therefore, dependent on the earth for our origin and cannot be said to
be non-causal. However, since unit consciousness is causeless, it could
not have come into existence with human beings. It would have had to
exist before humans. As Peter Russell describes it:

> If all creatures are conscious in some way or other, then
> consciousness is not something that evolved with hu-

man beings, or with primates, mammals or any other particular degree of biological evolution. It has always existed. What emerged over the course of evolution were the various qualities and dimensions of conscious experience -- the contents of consciousness. The first simple organisms -- bacteria and algae -- having no senses, were aware in only the most rudimentary way: no form, no structure, just the vaguest glimmer of awareness. Their picture of the world is nothing but an extremely dim smudge of color -- virtually nothing, compared to the richness and detail of human experience.

When multicellular organisms evolved, so did this sensing capacity. Cells emerged that specialized in sensing light, vibration, pressure, or changes in chemistry. These cells formed sensory organs, and as they developed, the ability to take in information increased. Eyes are not only sensitive to light; they react differently to different frequencies, and can tell from which direction the light is coming. The faintest smudge of the bacterium's experience had begun to take on different hues and shapes. Forms had begun to emerge on the canvas of consciousness.[154]

Unit consciousness therefore existed even before the evolution of human beings; otherwise how could we get a unit consciousness? It was only with the creation of the solid state of matter that Consciousness was able to divide itself into separate units. Thus unit consciousness is reflected in each atom or in whatever smallest piece of matter we discover. However, it is only with the evolution of humans that unit consciousness actually becomes reflected in the mind. Hence human beings possess a clearly-reflected consciousness.

As to the question of the relationship between consciousness and human beings, Mr. Sarkar reasons:

> If human beings have originated from the earth they must have also obtained their unit consciousness from solid matter. They could not have got it from any other entity and so there must also be consciousness in the earth. For

instance, butter can be obtained from milk only because it exists in milk.... Butter, when it exists in milk, cannot be identified as butter till it is separated with the help of a churning machine. In the same way, unit consciousness is unidentifiable or dormant in the earth and can only be perceived when the human mind is created to reflect it. It has thus to be accepted that there is consciousness even in the earth. The earth was created from the sun and the sun is only a ball of fire, the existence of which is dependent on certain gases found primarily in the aerial factor. Similarly the aerial factor is dependent on the ethereal factor, because if there were no ether there would be no space for the air to exist. Thus we can see that the ethereal factor is the source of the air, sun, earth and then human beings.[155]

If a human being has unit consciousness, the ethereal factor must also possess consciousness. If it did not have consciousness, how could a human being who has been created from it have unit consciousness? Although ether is called crude because sound travels through it, it is not composed of a crude substance. It is nothingness, just void or space. As stated earlier, when Absolute Consciousness became qualified by the Operative Principle, He became manifest as the macrocosmic sense of "I exist," then "I do," then the mental screen and further into the ethereal, aerial, luminous, liquid, and solid factors. Hence, the only entity which can be in the ether is consciousness. Just as we find water in ice because it is made of water and contains nothing except water, similarly ether, which contains nothing except consciousness, has to be made of consciousness. When we consider that the rest of the universe, all forms of air, fire, water, earth and the entire plant and animal kingdom, have been shown to originate from the ethereal factor, and since ether can be tracked back to Qualified Consciousness, the entire creation is only made of Absolute Consciousness. The Cosmic Entity alone is the cause of the creation of the universe. As Buckminster states:

"God is a verb,
the most active,

connoting the vast harmonic
reordering of the universe
from unleashed chaos of energy.[156]

Animate forms are surely more subtle than the solid factor and this suggests that after creation reached its crudest form in solid matter, it then advanced towards more subtle forms.  In other words, Creation gradually evolves from crude to subtle, as demonstrated by the evolution of plant and animal life on earth. During evolution, Consciousness gets expressed in cells, cell colonies, microbes, plants, fish, amphibians, reptiles, birds, mammals, and finally manifests itself in the human mind, through the stages of the mental screen, the sense of doing and then, eventually, the I-feeling. Thereafter, through the process of self-introspection, a human being is able to develop a sense of self as a witnessing entity that allows one to say "I know that I exist." By the process of introspection, human beings discover that our minds were always dependent upon the unit consciousness, because our sense of "I" exists within the periphery of the unit consciousness or soul. Because mind is present in every individual, we know that unit consciousness must also be present in every individual. There are innumerable individuals in this universe and unit consciousness is reflected in each one.  Because of this creation process, Robert Lanza, founder of biocentrism suggests:

> Our souls are in fact constructed from the very fabric of
> the universe - and may have existed since the beginning
> of time. Our brains are just receivers and amplifiers, for
> the proto-consciousness that is intrinsic to the fabric of
> space-time.[157]

In summary, human beings possess a "clearly reflected consciousness" because our minds reflect every vibrational frequency expressed in the creation. We are composed of matter, liquid, luminous, aerial and etheric factors. We are also composed of a mental screen, a sense of doing and a sense of "I exist." With these capacities we are able to project the existence of our unit consciousness and Absolute Consciousness.

The Cycle of Creation chart below shows the movement of Consciousness from subtle to crude and then from crude to subtle.

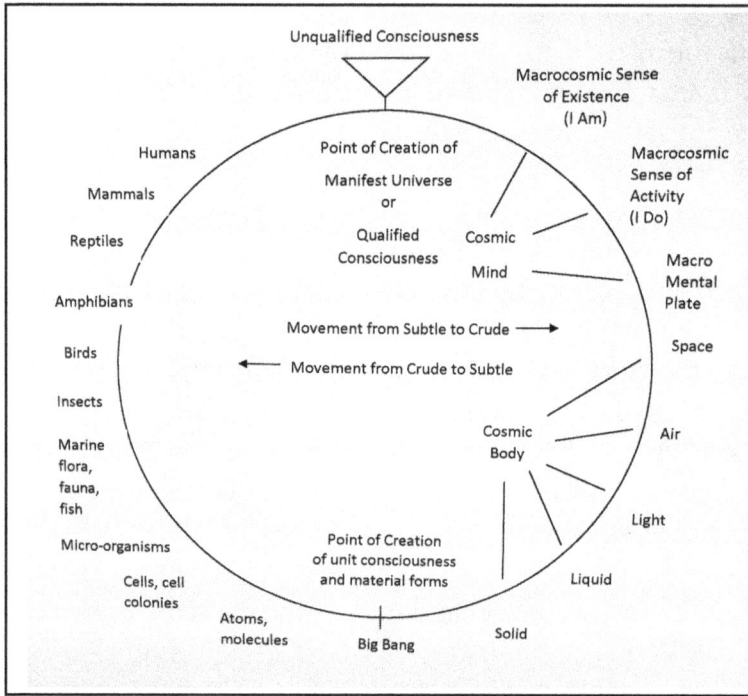

Unqualified Consciousness

Macrocosmic Sense of Existence (I Am)

Humans

Mammals

Reptiles

Amphibians

Birds

Insects

Marine flora, fauna, fish

Micro-organisms

Cells, cell colonies

Atoms, molecules

Point of Creation of Manifest Universe or Qualified Consciousness

Cosmic Mind

Macrocosmic Sense of Activity (I Do)

Macro Mental Plate

Space

Movement from Subtle to Crude ⟶

⟵ Movement from Crude to Subtle

Cosmic Body

Air

Light

Point of Creation of unit consciousness and material forms

Liquid

Big Bang

Solid

We explored in Book One, Volume Two of *The Untold Story of Western Civilization*, how the sense of "I exist" was formed in the breakdown of the bicameral mind around three thousand years ago. From that point on, humans developed an individual sense of self, having the authority to determine one's own actions. Once this occurred, it made possible the evolution of the mind beyond its instinctive and sentimental states, into the rational and intuitional states that allowed the mind to identify the soul and experience its connection to Absolute Consciousness. The mystical union between the Cosmic Self (Collective "I") and the individual self has been identified in both the East and the West. In the East, the Sanskrit word "yoga" means to yoke or join. It refers specifically to the process by which one links one's soul to the Collective Soul. As behavioral neurologist Jay Lombard states regarding the structure of the brain:

The drive to connect is deep within our biological makeup. The brain is an organ that is constantly striving for relationship for that which is beyond itself.[158]

And:

Each soul can be regarded as an integral fragment of divine light, the essential spark between a transcendent God and his immanent manifestation. The soul is what connects us to God, to each other and to ourselves.[159]

Yoga is much more profound that the Western interpretation of it as physical postures and mindfulness.

In the evolutionary process, human beings constitute the last physical form from whence Consciousness can again return to its pure Self. Humans are the highest-evolved beings on the planet and the ultimate stage in the evolution of relative reality. Before getting into how this evolution to pure consciousness occurs, we need to first understand the nature of this evolving universe.

## Of What is the Universe Made?

As stated earlier, the universe originated when Unqualified Cosmic Consciousness (God) became influenced by the Operative Principle. But if "God" created the universe, a very pertinent question arises about the availability of the material from which the universe was made. God material would be needed to create the universe just as the potter needs clay to make his pots. A potter obtains his clay from the earth. So, from where has Qualified Consciousness obtained His material? It has already been accepted that the Cosmic Entity is non-causal and all encompassing. Nothing existed before It or outside of It. If this is so, where is the material out of which Qualified Consciousness made this universe? The universe, which is so visibly existent, could not have been created out of nothing. The only material available to Qualified Consciousness for creation was Its own Self. Hence it has to be accepted that this creation is only Unqualified Consciousness metamorphosed into all that we find in the universe.

The entire universe is formed from Unqualified Consciousness, which becomes qualified and manifests as creation. Absolute Consciousness is infinite and eternal and nothing can exist beyond or before It. This means that every speck of dust in interstellar space and every grain of sand on earth is a manifestation of Cosmic Consciousness. It is everything that is.

There is nothing in this universe, no matter how crude and lifeless it appears, that is without consciousness. The solid brick, the dead wood, the asphalt highway, which are ordinarily regarded as crude and lifeless are not so. They are forms of the Cosmic Entity.

Yet, so much of the universe appears to be without any trace of consciousness. This is because Unqualified Consciousness is not able to expand His consciousness due to the influence of Prakrti, but the brick remains a form of consciousness nonetheless. Consciousness exists everywhere, even at the tiniest level of creation. As Duane Elgin states in his *We Are Living in a Living Universe*:

> Consciousness is present even at the primitive level of molecules consisting of no more than a few simple proteins. Researchers have found that such molecules have the capacity for complex interaction that is the signature of living systems. As one of the researchers who made this discovery stated, "We were surprised that such simple proteins can act as if they had a mind of their own.[160]

The greater the influence of the Operative Principle, the cruder Consciousness appears. As Her influence lessens, Consciousness appears in more subtle forms. Qualified Consciousness is a subtle entity, which can be appreciated only as an idea. Yet the moon, the sun, the stars, the planets, the atmosphere, and the earth, are made of this subtle Consciousness and are expressed in this creation. Logic leads us to believe that this creation has been formed of a subtle entity continually being crudified into forms.

Now we have a more difficult question to answer. How did a material universe get expressed? Although it sounds unreasonable, the only logical conclusion is that the material universe was never created! As Qualified Consciousness is subtle by nature, the crude universe could not have been created out of Him. Yet the existence of this visible universe cannot be ignored. Mr. Sarkar's conclusion is that this crude universe is actually only a thought-projection of Qualified Consciousness. He explains that when influenced by the Operative Principle, waves arise in the Qualified Consciousness that turn into infinite forms and that the entire creation is nothing but an imaginary entity filled with different thought forms. The first form created is the thought of "I am." In this way, the Unqualified Consciousness becomes Qualified Consciousness and the universe unfolds from this point as a projection of the I-feeling of Qualified Consciousness. Therefore, no crude stuff is required for its creation.

But if we accept that the universe is only a thought projection of the macrocosmic mind, why do we experience this world as a crude material construct? When a shape occurs on the mental screen of a person's mind, it is not always due to external vibrations. The mind also imagines forms. As long as a person is under the spell of imagination, every imagined object appears to be real. It is only after the spell is broken that he or she realizes the object to be his or her imagination only.

But how can an imagined object appear to be real? As explained earlier, the mind, which performs all actions, is the Doer-I and the part of the mind, which becomes the result of an action, is called the mental screen. When the Doer-I sees a book, the mental screen grasps the vibration of a book and takes the shape of the book itself. Similarly, when a person imagines a form, the mental screen has to take the shape of that form to enable the Doer-I to see it. For example, if Mr. Smith is sitting in Boston and thinking of Denver, he makes his Doer-I think of Denver and his mental screen then takes the form of Denver. At that very moment his Doer-I begins to see Denver in his imagination.

In order for the mental screen to take the form of Denver, it has to become like the state of matter of which Denver is made. If Denver is made up of buildings and streets, shops and people, the mental screen will have to become like these before it can take the form of Denver. Then alone will it be able to take a complete and proper shape. This is how an imaginary shape is formed in the mind and why it appears factual.

The mental screen takes different forms with the help of the physical organs. It is through the eyes that it grasps the shape-forming vibration of a book and takes its shape. But, in using the example of Mr. Smith imagining Denver, the help of the sense organs are not required because Denver is thousands of miles away from Boston and therefore beyond the reach of all the sense organs. Thus, when the mental screen takes the shape of Denver on its own, it loses its contact with the sense organs, which become non-functional and a person loses his sense of relationship and distinction of time, place, and person. Because his mental screen has lost contact with the sense organs and has instead taken the shape of Denver, it will not be able to receive vibrations from the immediate surroundings. This makes Mr. Smith see Denver in his imagination, although he may be in Boston at that moment. Since it is the Doer-I that is doing the imagining, as soon as the imagination of the Doer-I ceases, the mental screen also stops forming an image of Denver and the sense organs start functioning again. Then alone does Mr. Smith realize that the Denver that he had been seeing existed only in his imagination. Therefore, the imagined object appears factual as long as the spell of the imagination lasts. The moment that spell is broken, it appears to be imaginary and not real. While the imagination may not be "real," the mental screen did actually take a shape, and so, even if the shape is imaginary or unreal, the fact that the mental screen becomes like it makes it a reality.

In like manner, the universe has been created as a result of the imagination of Qualified Consciousness. Imagination requires a mind. The Cosmic Mind, like the unit mind is comprised of a sense of I exist, the Doer-I and the mental screen. The universe is thus created by the Doer-I of Qualified Consciousness making its Mental Screen take the form of the creation.

Because nothing existed outside of Qualified Consciousness, the Mental Screen could not take the shape of any external vibrations even if the Cosmic Doer-I wanted it to. The Cosmic Mental Screen therefore can only adopt the shapes and forms in the thought-waves or imagination of the Doer-I of Qualified Consciousness. The Cosmic Mental Screen forms the result of the actions (thoughts) performed by Qualified Consciousness and hence this universe is a result of these actions. This universe then is the imagination of Qualified Consciousness.

However, we are still faced with the question of how does the universe appear to be material, if it exists only in the imagination of Qualified Consciousness. We just explained that the imagination of Mr. Smith appeared to be factual as long as the spell of his imagination lasted. The imagination of Qualified Consciousness also appears to be real for the same reasons. Because the mind of the human being is only a unit of the Cosmic Mind, whatever appears true to the Cosmic Mind will also appear true to the individual mind. Although creation looks material to us, by using our rationality and intuition, we can see it for what it really is. Dr. Lombard states:

> Through God's metaphorical mind both our existence and our essence were created. It's through our evolution that we rediscover this essence through our own consciousness, and by doing so we discover the essence of God as well.[161]

In fact some leading cognitive scientists are now beginning to look at the universe, not as a physical entity but as a simulation. Bernard Haisch in referring to an article by Dr. Bostrom in "Philosophical Quarterly" concludes:

> . . . there is an even simpler view: that some transcendent consciousness has created not a physical reality, but a virtual reality based on its abilities to act like a vast mental computer. At first glance this might appear to be a trivialization of consciousness as a mere computer. But that is too literal. Think instead of an unbounded intelligence capable of unlimited concentration, able to dream up and keep in mind every detail of an entire universe governed by the laws and logic of that intelligence. The data storage and computation for such a Herculean simulation may be only a tiny part of the super abilities of such a consciousness if its potential is unbounded, or even infinite.[162]

Mr. Haisch, goes on to state that:

> It is almost a mathematical certainty that we are living in someone else's computer simulation. An alternate (and more optimistic) view is that there exists a great consciousness whose mind is the hardware, and whose thoughts are the software creating a virtual universe in which we as beings of consciousness live.[163]

R. C. Henry, Professor of Physics and Astronomy at Johns Hopkins University, in his article, "The Mental Universe," states:

> Physicists are being forced to admit that the universe is a "mental" construction. Pioneering physicist Sir James Jeans wrote: "The stream of knowledge is heading toward a non-mechanical reality; the universe begins to look more like a great thought than like a great machine. Mind no longer appears to be an accidental intruder into the realm of matter; we ought to rather hail it as the creator and governor of the realm of matter. Get over it, and accept the inarguable conclusion. The universe is immaterial-mental and spiritual.[164]

Jeans also commented in an interview in *The Observer*:

> I incline to the idealistic theory that consciousness is fundamental, and that the material universe is derivative from consciousness, not consciousness from the material universe... In general the universe seems to me to be nearer to a great thought than to a great machine. It may well be, it seems to me, that each individual consciousness ought to be compared to a brain-cell in a universal mind.[165]

Bernard Haisch in *Is the Universe a Vast, Consciousness Created Virtual Reality Simulation?* explains it this way:

This hypothesis could hardly be seriously imagined, say, even fifty years ago. But the amazing and rapidly expanding capabilities of today's computers clearly suggest where digital simulations can lead. It may be necessary to extrapolate computational capabilities by perhaps a hundred orders of magnitude or more, but the advantage of this view is that there is in the end only one thing constituting all of reality: consciousness, the very thing that we all are most familiar with. Nothing else would need to exist but that as the source of a realistic but simulated universe. All that remains is for the creative consciousness to enter into the apparently real life forms that evolution would provide. . . In this view we, as consciousness, are real; matter, as physical stuff, is a simulation.[166]

Today scientists are coming to believe that the phenomena of the world of physics would only appear to make sense if the universe was a virtual reality. Victoria Jaggard, writer for Smithsonian.com says "Today, modern mathematicians grapple with the reason math is universal—why is it that no matter when or where you look, 2 + 2 must always equal 4? Maybe because that is a fundamental part of the way the universe was coded."[167] V. S. Ramachandran, director of the Center for Brain and Cognition at the University of California, San Diego found using fMRI scans that the same cells in the brain light up whether we perform an action ourselves or watch someone else do it—which might explain why some of us find action movies so exciting. But these "mirror neurons" aren't activated just by the things we see. The effect also occurs when we simply imagine ourselves performing the action.[168]

The universe is a relative reality. Although the Creation appears to be material to us, with intuitional practice, we can see it for what it is, an ever changing thought form of Consciousness.

## Evolution and the Process of Liberation

As discussed earlier, in the phase of creation where Qualified Cosmic Consciousness moves from subtle to crude, the process results in Absolute Consciousness forming Itself into infinite unit consciousnesses. In the movement from crude to subtle, these unit consciousnesses evolve in their expression and scientists call this the evolution of species. The most evolved species on the planet is human beings because we have clearly reflected consciousness. As physicist Brian Swimme characterizes it:

> . . . the intimate sense of self-awareness we experience bubbling up at each moment is rooted in the originating activity of the universe. We are all of us arising together at the center of the cosmos. We thought that we were no bigger than our physical bodies, but we are discovering that we are beings of cosmic dimension, part of the flow of continuous re-creation of the cosmos. By becoming aware of that stream of life in our direct experience, we become conscious of our connection with the living universe. [169]

The thirst for limitlessness that goads us as a species is actually the desire of our Collective Consciousness wanting to free itself from the influence of Prakrti and return to the blissful state of Unqualified Consciousness. To accomplish this, He must liberate each of us from the dominance of the Operative Principle. It is the intent of Qualified Consciousness to liberate all of the unit consciousnesses from the bondage of the Operative Principle so we can eventually be reabsorbed into Unqualified Consciousness. To attain the state of Unqualified Cosmic Consciousness is the highest status of our humanity. This union constitutes the ultimate state of freedom and ecstasy and is the goal of the evolutionary process.

As such, our liberation is dependent, in part, upon our own effort to move beyond the confines of our ego identity and achieve unity with Absolute Consciousness. The effort of the unit consciousness to liberate itself from the influence of the Operative Principle is called intuitional practice.

This requires an earnest effort and an intense thirst for freedom from the bondages of the qualifying principles of the Operative Principle. To make progress in this effort we must first realize that we are in bondage. The question of emancipation does not arise for those who are unaware of their bondage. It is only after one realizes this that one feels it is necessary to search for a method for self liberation; this method is intuitional practices.

Inanimate units, under the extreme influence of the Operative Principle, are incapable of even realizing their existence much less the means of emancipation. All species, except humans, lack a clearly reflected consciousness and therefore are unable to progress on their own volition toward liberation. The evolution of the unit consciousness through inanimate forms and non-human species is therefore dependent solely upon Qualified Absolute Consciousness. The minds of lower species evolve in the course of their struggle to overcome obstacles. In this struggle, their minds are refined by the process of clash and cohesion. Their minds grow by virtue of overcoming obstacles. But as humans, we are able to realize our state of bondage as well as determine a way out. This gives us the capacity to emancipate ourselves from material reality.

As stated earlier, it is the nature of every human being to seek liberation/self-realization. Yet many of us do not work for our liberation, even though we have become human beings expressly for this purpose. This lack of effort on our part defeats the very purpose of our existence. But where do we begin? How do we begin to see ourselves as spiritual beings whose ultimate destiny is union with Absolute Consciousness? There are two conditions. The first is that we must have a desire to be reunited with Cosmic Consciousness and the second is that we must exert an effort to achieve this reunion.

## The Spiritual, Mental and Physical Connection

Every human being has a unit consciousness (soul), a mind, and a body. Thus human nature is spiritual, mental, and physical. If human beings were souls/unit consciousnesses only we could not say "I have a soul," since there would be nothing to identify with the soul, and alternatively were we only bodies, we could not say, "This is my body." This demonstrates that, as human beings, we identify ourselves as something different from the soul or the body. The entity that we identify with and which appears to be the owner of the soul and the body is the "I" feeling of the mind. It is this entity that thinks "I" have a body. "I" have a soul. We perceive ourselves as distinct from the soul and the body and also distinct from the Creation of Absolute Consciousness because of this "I feeling."

Since the "I" feeling pervades every bit of the body, one feels the presence of "I" in every part of the body and yet our mind knows that our "I feeling" is distinct from the body because the body continually changes but the I-feeling remains the same. The physical body merely forms a shelter for the feeling of "I." A human being's feeling of "I" is thus neither his or her unit consciousness nor his or her body; it is only a mental creation of Prakriti the Operative Principle acting upon unit consciousness.

## What is the "I-feeling"?

The "I-feeling" in the mind is only a reflection of the subjectivity of the unit consciousness, which, in turn is only a reflection of the subjectivity of the Absolute Consciousness. It is because of the "I feeling" in the mind that a human being distinguishes himself or herself as an individual within relative reality. Just as the existence of a plank of wood is dependent on a tree, but cannot be called a tree, the "I" in the mind cannot be called unit consciousness. We saw how the evolution of the individual "I-feeling" occurred in human history beginning with the tale of the Sumerian king Gilgamesh and how this feeling of "I" proliferated as a result of the catastrophe of Thera when the voices of the gods ceased to exist.[170]

The feelings of I-me-mine distinguish us from our environment, whether spiritual, mental, or physical. It is the intent of intuitional practices to understand this I-feeling and to expand its scope so that it will ultimately merge with the Self Collective "I" of Absolute Consciousness and then into the Selfless bliss state of Unqualified Absolute Consciousness.

The context for this merger has already been discussed. In summary, Unqualified Consciousness is the supreme rank of Absolute Consciousness, and this status exists when it is not under the qualifying influence of the Operative Principle. However, once qualified (i.e., given form), Consciousness becomes (Qualified Consciousness), which is also called God by most religions because they qualify God according to their definitions of God.

The soul (átman) or unit consciousness, being a multiple of the Qualified Consciousness, is a multiple of Absolute Consciousness. Hence unit consciousness is also Absolute Consciousness, and on being released from the bondage of the "I-feeling," it merges back into Unqualified Consciousness to attain the supreme rank, which is its final goal, the fulfillment of its dharma.

## The Law of Karma

In order to attain liberation from the Operative Principle and merge with Unqualified Consciousness, we must be able to break free from the programming, which defines our sense of reality. It is our programming which determines our present course of action and makes it difficult to change direction.

In the quest for liberation we can either blame the Operative Principle for our state of bondage or we can blame ourselves, that is, our "I-feeling" for our actions. Philosophically, it works to hold either responsible for our bondage, but for purposes of making progress, it is better to hold ourselves responsible for our own actions.

What we know is that any exertion on our part to change our behavior for the better is met with resistance. It is a natural law that for every action, there is an equal and opposite reaction. For every step that we take forward, an equal force will push us back.

This is why it is so difficult to change our circumstances and why after millennia of competitive materialism, we find ourselves standing on the brink of disaster. Our present condition is a result of our past actions which, in turn, are an expression of our evolutionary and historical process. In Book One, we learned that it is impossible to change the course of history without understanding the course of history. In this Book, we are learning that it is impossible to change our individual course without understanding our own past history and the programming that we bring to any new situation. To change our condition, we will have to change ourselves. Yet each attempt to make progress in our life is met with an equal and opposite reaction to our efforts. This is why progress is impossible without the willingness to struggle. The bottom line is that the spiritual intuitional path demands that we become warriors who will stop at nothing to achieve our goal.

According to the law of karma, when an "action" is executed, one has to bear its consequence in the form of a "reaction." When the "I" orders the Doer to perform an action, the action is first formed on the mental screen and then activated in the physical world through our sensory and motor organs. In this process, the mental screen must take the form of any action performed by the Doer-I. This means that the mental screen leaves its normal form and is changed into the form of the action required by the Doer. The mental screen, in other words, becomes distorted in order to complete the execution of an action. The Operative Principle, being the dominating factor, causes a reaction to every action in order to bring the mind back to its former unvibrated status.

Karma constitutes our past thoughts, words, and deeds whose reactions have not yet been expressed and thus the mental plate remains in a state of distortion. The unexpressed reactions are stored in the mind as "reactive potential." Every action has a cause and effect. Good thoughts, words, and deeds create good reactions (good karma) and bad thoughts, words, and deeds create bad karma. For example, if you steal some money but do not get caught, the effect of this bad deed remains unexpressed in the mind. Similarly, if you give some change to a beggar, but are not immediately rewarded, the good deed remains unexpressed in the mind. The combined total of unexpressed actions is generally called one's karma.

It is by virtue of our past actions that the mind reacts to current stimuli. Because the effect of our deed still needs to be expressed, it is our karma which must be played out before we can gain liberation. Karma keeps our mental plate in a continual state of distortion and, like ripples in a pond, prevents our mind from clearly reflecting the full moon of Absolute Consciousness.

Karma is a product of the "I feeling". It is this sense of "I", not the soul or God that is responsible for one's actions. Let's take the example of Sylvester Stallone playing the role of Rocky in a movie. Rocky is not the real personality of Stallone. It is only a changed or assumed personality. As long as Stallone continues to act that role, he will be called Rocky and not Stallone. Similarly, as long as the feeling of "I" is a person's assumed identity, that person will be different from his or her divine self. The person with this feeling of "I" will remain only a changed or assumed form of unit consciousness.  As Mr. Sarkar says:

> It would thus be seen that it is a person's feeling of "I" which keeps the person away from his or her unit con-sciousness. In fact, it is this feeling of "I" which makes a human being a different entity from Bhagaván (Qualified Consciousness).[171]

In the above example, when the film is completed, Stallone, who played the role of Rocky, reverts back to his original personality and is called Stallone. In the same way, on release from this feeling of "I," the changed or assumed form of unit consciousness ceases to exist and unit conscious-ness assumes its own identity; that is, it becomes the I feeling of Qualified Absolute Consciousness. It is only the unit consciousness' attachment to the "I" feeling in the mind which gives one a sense of individuality. When the I-feeling in the mind is withdrawn into the unit conscious-ness, there is nothing to separate the unit from the Absolute and the unit automatically merges into the Qualified Absolute Consciousness. All sense of limited identity is resolved. This is why self-realization and God-realization mean the same thing.

Because the "I" in the mind is different from unit consciousness/God, neither the unit consciousness nor God can be held responsible for its actions or experience the consequences of its actions. The consequences of the actions performed by Rocky do not affect Stallone. Only Rocky will be affected, because the doer of the act is the assumed personality and not Stallone in his original personality. Stallone in his original personality would only witness all that the assumed form experiences. Similarly, it is the projected or changed form of "I" that acts and also experiences the results of all actions. The unit consciousness neither performs any actions, nor experiences any results. It only witnesses the actions and also the results thereof.

A fan at a tennis match will never get credit for winning a game, nor will he experience the pain of exertion. Only a player can be called the winner and only he or she will feel fatigued as a result of playing. Similarly, unit consciousness or átman is a spectator witnessing all the actions performed by the "I feeling" and the results experienced by it. It does not perform any action and hence does not experience any result.

The human being's feeling of "I" gives the mind the feeling of individual existence. Technically, it does not perform any action.  It is the "Doer-I" which works, and it is only the Doer-I which experiences the results of its action. On serious reflection, however, no action appears possible without the "I feeling" or the knowledge of existence that underlies each action. Without the "I-feeling," we would have a sense of doing, but we could not say "I do." Who else would make the "Doer-I" work? It is the "I feeling" which inspires the Doer-I to work. Thus, it is seen that although the "I feeling" does not actually perform any action, yet it is because of the "I feeling," that a person is able to work. The "I feeling" is therefore related to the performance of actions and is in this way related to the results of actions also.

Every action that the Doer-I takes toward liberation will be met by a counter force which consists of the accumulative reactions to previous actions. For example, if I have made it a habit of drinking late on Saturday night but now decide I want to improve myself and go to a religious service on Sunday morning, the negative reaction will be enormous. It would have been much easier to stay in bed than it was to get out of bed and go to a service when I can hardly think straight. The memory of how difficult it was to do this, will certainly weigh on me the next time I try such a stunt.

On the other hand, if I normally go to a religious service on Sunday morning, it is not difficult to get out of bed. Getting drunk on Saturday night would be the more difficult action.

It is by the law of karma, that a person will experience a reaction to all of his or her actions, whether good or evil. If a person steals and causes suffering to another, that person's mind will become distorted insofar as it has inflicted pain on another by stealing. To remove the distortion, the person inflicting pain must experience an equal amount of pain (mentally) as a result of his action. Similarly, if people by their deeds give happiness to others, they will, as a result of karmic reaction, experience an equal amount of happiness. Thus, the Operating Principle makes a human being bear the consequences (karma) of all his or her actions.

Throughout Book One, *The Untold Story of Western Civilization*, we witnessed multiple instances in which warriors, priests, and merchants performed evil actions in their quest for wealth and power. In some cases, we were able to witness them experience the consequences of their evil deeds. In other cases, we did not. Nonetheless, each of their actions was destined to create a consequence of pain in equal measure. In fact, Mr. Sarkar says that they will suffer greater pain as a consequence. Plato made a similar observation more than two thousand years ago:

> Those who through history have made the choice to harm their fellow-man to gain wealth or the "other allurements of evil" . . . then suffer even more than those they harmed. Why do those who knowingly inflict harm on others suffer more? Because there are laws that are universal, or higher than man-made laws – the highest law.[172]

The law of karma places us in an extremely difficult situation. To achieve liberation, we must be able to extinguish all the reactions to our past actions. But how is this possible? Common sense tells us that no one can exist without performing actions. Even when sitting quietly, one is still performing an action. The physical body may not be exerting itself, yet the ever-active mind is not still. The mind even without physical action engages itself in actions by thinking or imagining. A person may be thinking evil of someone; may even be planning to kill him; or, conversely, may be thinking of ways and means of helping others in their distress. All these thoughts are actions and do not need any physical exertion or movement. Physical action is only a further projection of mental activity.

It was explained earlier that all actions are performed by the mind and the ten organs, which are only a crudification of the mental screen. Actions performed by the mind with the help of the organs are physical, while those performed without their help are mental actions. Both types of action will cause a distortion in the mind and require a reaction. The reaction may not occur immediately, but it will occur inevitably.

Because we keep on acting right up to the moment of our death, any reactions that have not been experienced in this lifetime will need to be experienced after death. And according to the law of karma, only the one who commits an action will experience its reactions (karma); no one else can be substituted to experience them. This being said, how will a person experience his or her karma after death? To answer this question, we need a little context. According to Mr. Sarkar:

> The presence of the Operative Principle casts Her influence on unit consciousness and provides it with mind. Mind, which is an outcome of unit consciousness and the Operative Principle will exist as long as these two, Absolute Consciousness and the Operative Principle exist. Unit consciousness and its principle are inseparable counterparts of each other. Hence mind will exist with unit consciousness only. It is in mind only that one gets the feeling of "I," and as long as mind exists, the feeling of "I" will also be there. Since unit consciousness is immortal, the mind which is linked to it will not die either, and with mind the feeling of "I" will also be there. It will thus be seen that the feeling of "I" also permeates the physical body when unit consciousness (átman) takes shelter in a human body. At the time of unit consciousness leaving the body, the Operative Principle which is an inseparable counterpart of unit consciousness, also leaves the body. Mind, which is a creation of the Operative Principle, will naturally leave the body with Her. This results in the death of the physical body. Thus, death does not mean the death of unit consciousness and mind. It only means the death of the physical body. Unit consciousness (átman) and mind merely leave the physical body, which they had earlier adopted as a shelter.[173]

Some religions believe that when one dies with bad karma, he or she will go to hell, but one who dies with good karma will go to heaven. But this is irrational. No one's actions are purely good or bad regardless of how we define good and bad. Heaven and hell are only mythological creations that do not exist independent of physical existence because our minds cannot experience anything without a brain. If this is the case, what actually happens after death?

## Life after Death

According to intuitional science, the mind always takes the form of the physical objects or psychic ideas it encounters and unless the mind is liberated from these forms, through the extinguishing the totality of one's reactive potential (karma), the mind cannot achieve permanent peace. Therefore, death does not mean liberation from karma.

When the mind detaches itself from its body in the state of death, the mind becomes suspended in the unmanifested Operative Principle.[174] Karma cannot be resolved in this bodiless state of death because in order for the mind to function, it requires a brain. Therefore, karma that does not get expressed in this life will carry over to another life. In short, karma continues to exist after death and must be experienced once the unit consciousness and mind have assumed another body. Death, therefore, is not a supreme attainment because as long as a person has unfulfilled karma, there remains the inevitability of future rebirth. What is rebirth? Mr. Sarkar gives us a technical definition, "Material bodies disintegrate due to the inadequacy of the energy already acquired, and due to vibrational conflict. When this occurs, the reactive potentials lose their physical base and drift in the Macrocosmic flow. Later they are reborn as separate psychic waves as a result of clash amongst the different waves within the Macrocosmic body. The reappearance of these psychic waves is called rebirth."[175]

## Why We Die

In the above definition, our bodies die due to inadequacy of energy as well as conflict, but why does it have to be this way? Why cannot the unit consciousness continue its march towards the subtle with the same physical body until it finally merges in the Absolute Consciousness? This is because the human physical body gradually gets created as an assemblage of many particles formed at different stages in the movement from subtle to crude and crude to subtle. There will be some particles representing the ethereal factor and some representing the other factors—aerial, luminous, liquid, and solid. These factors are always moving from one level of crudeness or subtlety to the next. As we have seen, the ethereal factor moves on to the aerial factor and so on, until they become the crudest, which is solid. Therefore, the factors composing the human body must also be changing and therefore the human body cannot remain the same. This is another law of the Operative Principle that has to be followed. Change in the human body is inevitable and to bring about this change, death is necessary. If we assume that unit consciousness could continue in one body as its shelter until it merges in Absolute Consciousness, we are faced with the possibility of one body continuing for millions of years because the chain of actions and reactions may not free the unit consciousness earlier than that. This would result in a total stoppage of the evolution of factors in a body for millions of years because the chain of actions and reactions (karma) may not follow a direct course toward liberation. Most of us, for example, have not adopted a spiritual path toward liberation. As a result, we keep creating more karma with each birth that we take.

The necessary deconstruction of the fundamental factors, in order to evolve as units, makes physical death of the body inevitable. Everyone will have to give up this physical body. However, death, as we have just explained, does not mean the end of consciousness or the end of one's reactive potential. It only means the disassociation of the unit consciousness and mind from the body. The mind will always remain with unit consciousness. The individuality of human beings or the idea of one's existence is in the "I feeling" of the mind and will always remain with it.

However, the moment that the Operative Principle ceases to have Her influence on unit consciousness and is unable to maintain the existence of mind, the "I" will cease to exist and that will be the liberation of the individual.

The mind, which performs all actions and bears their consequences, survives to experience the reactions of the actions performed up to the very moment of death. Thus, it is the mind which acts and it alone will have to experience the reactions (karma). In order to do this, it must take on another body. This is the process of reincarnation. Reincarnation is not a purely Eastern concept. In Book One, Volume Two, Chapter Three, we showed how the subject was discussed in the Bible and how Jesus confirmed to his followers that John the Baptist was the reincarnation of the Prophet Elijah (Matt. 11:7-15).[176]

## The Mind and the Brain

Because the mind is subtle, it requires a crude base to be able to perform physical actions. This crude base is the brain of the human body. Mind and brain are so closely connected that one cannot work without the other. The brain without the mind ceases to function and, similarly, if the brain is not in proper order, the mind will not be able to work. A dead person's body has a brain, but it does not function because it is no longer associated with the mind. Similarly, when a person becomes unconscious or is made so with the help of anesthesia, his or her brain becomes non-functional for a time. As a result, the mind does not work, because its physical base, the brain, is not functioning. The unconscious state is not the state of death and so neither unit consciousness nor the mind leaves the body. However, even though the mind remains within the body, it does not work due to the brain not being in proper order and one finds oneself unable to conceive or perceive anything. It is, therefore, necessary for mind to take shelter in the brain as its physical base to be able to function and to experience the reactions (karma) of its actions.

In the process of rebirth, the mind and unit consciousness take shelter in a new body. Both are reborn. They have to take another birth to complete the experience of reactions to the actions of a previous life. Birth and death will continue to alternate as long as the mind continues to create karma. Thus, the mind and Unit consciousness may have to continue this journey through thousands of life times. They will keep on taking shelter in new bodies after discarding the old ones so long as karma still needs to be expressed.

## Misconceptions of Life After Death

We have said that the concept of hell or heaven as places where human beings live eternally is incorrect. Pleasure and pain cannot be experienced by the mind without the brain. Therefore, in the state of death, the mind becomes non-functional until it acquires a new brain at the time of rebirth. Heaven and hell only exist on earth and are created by virtue of one's karma. It is in this mortal world only that one experiences the pleasures of heaven and the sufferings of hell. The myth of heaven and hell was created by Catholic priests beginning in the second century after Christ's death. It does not appear in the Old Testament, the New Testament, Jesus' teachings, the Acts of the Apostles, Paul's epistles, or the other epistles in the canon.[177] For centuries, this myth has allowed the priest class to define what is good and bad behavior and thereby come to dominate people's minds. They point to spiritual reward as something that exists in another realm and therefore prevent people from fighting against the corruption that is holding them in thralldom. The people are told that their reward for subservience will be experienced after they die. This is the reason that Karl Marx called religion the opiate of the masses.

## The Force behind Rebirth

If unit consciousness and the mind have to seek a suitable body for the "I" to experience the results of its actions, what is the agency that selects this suitable body? Unit consciousness cannot perform any action and mind is also non-functional without a brain. Because one has to experience reactions according to the law of the Operative Principle, it is therefore the responsibility of the Operative Principle to make us experience these reactions by being reborn. Therefore, it is Prakrti that has to find the required shelter for the mind and its potential reactions.

Such a shelter may be available in a day or it may take millions of years to become available because the mind cannot take a new body until it suits the requirements of its potential reactions. Hence it is never possible to say where and when one is to be reborn after death. There may be innumerable worlds where life exists. Unit consciousness and the mind consisting of potential reactions may get a suitable shelter in any of them. Thus, it is not even necessary that one be reborn on this earth. We can only say that those reborn on this earth have found a suitable shelter here and that they have adopted a body only for the purpose of experiencing the reactions of their previous actions.

Although we may have to experience the result of our actions in a subsequent life, we will not be able to remember those actions in the next life, because our memory is not large enough to remember the deeds of past lives.

## How Can Human Beings Break the Cycle of Karma?

Given that we are imprisoned by the consequences of our actions, and that we commit actions up to the very second of our death, how is it humanly possible to gain emancipation and God-realization? If we are in a prison cell and there are no physical or psychic means to escape, what is to be done? According to the spiritual masters, the only way to break the cycle of action and reaction, death and rebirth, is to perform intuitional practices. But what does this mean?

We have said that the purpose of Absolute Consciousness, in the creation process, is to liberate every unit being. It is only with this intention, that, in the last stage of the evolutionary movement from crude to subtle, human beings appear with a fully-reflected unit consciousness.

We also know that the influence of the Operative Principle on the unit consciousness decreases when the human mind advances toward the subtle, but still we remain in bondage because the Operative Principle is always acting to maintain the status quo, and stop our ability to accelerate the movement towards subtlety. She does this through the law of karma.

So how does the mind free itself from the bondage of the Operative Principle if, every time we strive for liberation, Prakrti throws up obstacles, in the form of karmic reactions that set us back? To achieve liberation, we must recognize that there are two types of actions. The first type continually strengthens the I-feeling, and thereby keeps us separated from Absolute Consciousness. The second type weakens the I-feeling and moves us closer to realizing Absolute Consciousness. One must understand that it is not so much the action that leads to liberation or bondage, but one's ego attachment to that action. Actions that tend to increase the ego's attachment to crude objects further bind us; actions that decrease the ego's attachment to crude objects tend to liberate us. Therefore, to reduce the power of the I-feeling and prevent the continual distortion of the mental plate, one will ultimately have to give up one's attachment to the results of one's actions and surrender each and every action to the Cosmic Entity. This means that we envision the Cosmic Entity as the one performing our actions and therefore the fruits or consequences of those actions belong to the Cosmic Entity and not to our limited sense of "I." As Vanamali explains, "Thus, it is not the action that causes bondage, as is commonly misunderstood, but the desire that prompts it. If the motive is pure . . . it will cause no bondage and will lead to evolution." [178] For example, giving alms to the poor so as to gain public recognition or feel good about ourselves (ego desire), while seemingly good on the surface, is a bad deed since it results in greater attachment to the ego.

To act according to one's conscience, after proper consideration, creates good deeds. Evil deeds are just the opposite. They result from the wrong use of things and acting without conscience. However, both good and bad actions create a distortion in the mind, which must bear reactions. Hence, the need to surrender our attachment to the Cosmic Entity as well as the fruits of one's actions. This enlarges the reflection of Consciousness and accelerates the speed toward subtlety. In this way, can one extinguish one's reactive potential as well as eliminate the creation of future karma. It is the practice of intuitional science that gives one the strength and determination to surrender one's actions.

Since this is a critical point, let us make sure this concept of good deeds is clear. It is logical to ask, if we are to do good deeds to gain liberation, will not we just be creating more good karma? If so, is liberation possible if we just create more good karma? Good deeds that reinforce the ego are not good deeds, they are bad deeds. For example, going to church so that everyone sees how spiritual we are may look like a good action, but it is a bad deed. Volunteering to sing in the choir because we want everyone to hear our beautiful voice is not a good action, it is a bad deed. When we speak of good deeds from the perspective of intuitional science, we are speaking about those deeds that curtail or eliminate our attachment to the ego, that is, our sense of "I-do." Good deeds in this case mean deeds that we perform that are in service to humanity, but that we attribute to the grace of God. God is doing the good deed through us. We are only a vehicle. Good deeds are only those that we surrender to God. In this way our minds are always focusing on becoming self-realized and not on crude objects.

According to intuitional science, the quality or nature of the human mind is such that it becomes like the idea or entity to which it is devoted. For instance, if one starts thinking oneself to be mad, one actually becomes mad, as one's mind is largely given over to that idea. Similarly, if one is given to believe that one is suffering from consumption, one becomes so concerned with the idea that one actually develops consumption. The human mind is so made that it has the capacity of becoming like the object to which it is attached. As Dr. Jay Lombard states, ... neuroscience, which is now able to demonstrate a direct effect of brain cellular activity on our cognitive and emotional states. The biology is fact: What a person thinks, he becomes.[179] The unit consciousness that wants to return to Absolute Consciousness quickly has to become devoted to Absolute Consciousness, and this is devotion. "I am That" is the idea to which the unit consciousness has to be completely devoted in order to become "That" one day.

Those who do intuitional practices without developing devotion to the path of self-realization will gain nothing. But if there is only the smallest iota of love or devotion, they will gain everything.

Until one achieves this final state of selfless love, the attainment of Absolute Consciousness resembles any other loving relationship. The individual self and the Cosmic Self are in a relationship. In only a short time of ideating on Absolute Consciousness we develop a feeling of love (attraction) for it. As Dr. Lombard suggests, "The soul reveals itself through its will and engagement, an engagement that recognizes that its vitality and expression are contingent upon relationship with that which is beyond itself."[180]

Devotion is the method by which one becomes completely united with the Cosmic Entity. Love brings unity and when the unit consciousness merges with the Unqualified Consciousness, love becomes Absolute. The Supreme Self is no longer divided. And it is the purpose of intuitional practices to create that devotion.

As Mr. Sarkar says, "Devotion must be accepted as the highest mission in life: it leads humanity towards the stage of subtlety, and finally ensconces a person in the state of supreme bliss."[181] Dr. Lombard also believes, "One might even say that evolution's highest goal is the belief in the soul, for that belief not only provides the foundation for our inquiry into the meaning and purpose of our existence, it informs our actions and provides our life with its highest moral dimensions."[182]

## What Is the Aim of Humanity?

The thought-wave of creation originates in Absolute Consciousness, only to resolve back into It. Humanity, as the apex of evolution, forms the final stage of this thought-wave. Human beings are therefore bound to merge sooner or later in the subtle Absolute Consciousness and become one with it. Just as a drop of water merges in the ocean and loses its individual identity, so a unit consciousness merges in the Absolute Consciousness and, in doing so, loses its individual identity. The "I" is nothing more than an assumed identity of the unit consciousness which must be shed in order for the unit consciousness to merge with Unqualified Consciousness.

Until a unit consciousness merges with Unqualified Absolute Consciousness, it will not be truly liberated and may re-enter the Cycle of Creation and return again to the path of emancipation. Complete freedom from the bondage of the Operative Principle can only be realized by merging into Unqualified Absolute Consciousness. When this occurs, the unit will cease its cycle of birth and death, having fulfilled its ultimate intention. As such, the aim of humanity is not only to merge with the Qualified Cosmic Entity. It is higher than that. The aim is to achieve the supreme rank. This is the state of limitless bliss unencumbered by any form or contradiction.

## Concentration of Mind

To achieve complete freedom, an all-round effort to overcome the bondage of the Operative Principle is required. According to all the great mystics of history, the practice of intuitional science is the way to achieve liberation because it allows us to get beyond our ingrained programming. As we learned in Book One, Volume One, Chapter Three on Patriarchy, people felt that a divinity existed, but they did not know how to attain this divinity. They did not realize that divinity dwelt within themselves. Thus, they worshipped an external projection of their mind. People heard the voice of their god in their mind and took it for an external entity. The form that they worshipped could have been an ancestor, another species, a force of nature, or a human being who represented the Goddess or the God on earth. They did not know how to develop God-consciousness, nor make themselves fit instruments for the attainment of Absolute Consciousness. In the East, it was Shiva who prepared the path of spiritual practice for people, teaching them medicine, dance, music, marriage, the concept of dharma, and how to meditate. The fundamental meaning of Shiva's mantra has always been, I am one with the One. It is this ideation, performed with love in the heart, that moves people toward Divinity. It is this ideation which calms the mind and helps relieve it of its attachments. It is the nature of human beings to seek Absolute Consciousness and it is through intuitional practices that our divine nature is realized.[183] For the first time on earth, Shiva introduced the idea of intuitional practices. His legacy remains alive until this very day and underlies the great religions of the East.

In the West, we saw that it was the Jewish mystics (Essenes) who introduced the idea that the Divine Consciousness dwelt within and that it was possible to have a personable relationship with Him/Her. It was Jesus Christ who taught people how to intimately know the Divine through the act of love. Jesus made it clear to people that everything was Divine, but that one knows God from within. "The Kingdom of God is within you." At the same time, Jesus told people to love their neighbor. When asked what his greatest commandment was, he told people to love God and to love their neighbors and that one was equal to the other. Jesus knew that the Divine permeated all forms (The Holy Ghost) and that the love of God could also be realized by loving His creation. Again as Dr. Lombard reminds us:

> Knowing the Mind of God requires a shift in our own way of thinking – from beng a "theory" or belief to becoming a primary and fundamental axiom of mind, where to acknowledge God means to acknowledge the other within our selves.[184]

We also learned from the scriptures of the Gnostic Christians that Jesus gave intuitional teachings to some of his apostles, particularly Mary, James, and John. These secret teachings were specific practices that helped them know God directly through intuitive understanding. It was this understanding that they called "gnosis." Like the Essenes before them, the Gnostics also believed that they were custodians of the secret intuitional knowledge inherited from Jesus the Christ. This knowledge was not rational knowledge but intuitional knowledge. It was not derived from sensory data or rationality, but from the intuition, which revealed one's self as a reflection of Absolute Consciousness.[185]

The Gnostic teacher Monoimus said:

> Abandon the search for God and the creation and other matters of a similar sort.

Look for him by taking yourself as the starting point. Learn who it is within you who makes everything his own and says, 'My God, my mind, my thought, my soul, my body.'"[186]

The act of reducing external stimuli through sense-withdrawal allows the I-feeling to go more deeply within. Previously held captive in the mind, it gains the ability to identify itself directly with the soul, the nucleus of unit consciousness. The identification of the I-feeling with the soul is experienced as stillness or peace. Just as the reflection of the full moon can be seen when a turbulent pond is quieted, so also the full reflection of the soul can be seen when the mind is quieted. The soul and Absolute Consciousness, in reality, are one and the same, having been separated only by the waves of the mind, which result from one's karma that stretches all the way back to when one first became human and exercised free will.

As we observe the life of the mystics in history, we see that their enlightenment results from a disciplined practice of meditation, and service to suffering humanity. The ego does not like to do either of these things because it is too restless to slow down and remains immersed in thoughts of its own pleasure. The restlessness of the mind needs no description as everyone understands it well. As Mr. Sarkar explains:

> The perpetual restlessness of the Operative Principle makes Her creation – the unit mind – also disturbed throughout its existence. At times or in some places it may be more agitated, while at others it may be less disturbed. Restlessness, being a quality imposed by Prakrti, will vary with the influence of Prakrti. The mind is less agitated or disturbed where the influence of Prakrti is less. Her influence is the least in mahattattva (the feeling of I exist) and the most in citta (the mental screen), and hence the former is less restless than the latter. Sádhaná or intuitional practice lessens the influence of Prakrti on unit consciousness, and with that the restlessness of mind also lessens. Prakrti alone is responsible for imparting

disturbance to the mind, and with the waning of Her influence the vacillation of mind also lessens. Hence the vacillation of mind cannot be steadied unless unit consciousness is emancipated from the influence of Prakrti.[187]

Calming the restless mind and developing concentration of one's mind is the same thing. The concentration of mind occurs through the process of sense withdrawal, the relinquishing of doership, and the attribution of every action to Absolute Consciousness instead of one's ego. The concentration of the mind leads to meditation, which is a state of merger with Absolute Consciousness. Concentration of mind does not mean emancipation from the bondage of the Operative Principle. It is only the surest path leading to emancipation.

Ordinarily, the mind is absorbed in the things of the world. We are caught up in all the problems of being individuals. We are also faced with the societal and environmental problems that confront us as social beings. Being absorbed in the external expression of crudeness puts the mind under the greatest influence of the Operative Principle. People who make use of their free will by performing good deeds soon get back to Absolute Consciousness, because they direct their minds to the subtlest goal. Conversely, those who are addicted to material and psychic problems keep on experiencing the reactions of their actions. They roam directionless in the thought-waves of Qualified Absolute Consciousness, never reaching ultimate satisfaction. To overcome this addiction to material and psychic phenomena one has to perform intuitional practices. For those who want to truly make a significant impact on this world in crisis, through their service and leadership, concentrating the mind on the path of self-realization is a must.

## What Exactly Are Intuitional Practices?

Intuitional practices consist of the following activities: (1) Devoting one's self to the attainment of Absolute Consciousness (bhakti yoga), (2) Meditating on the fact that one is Absolute Consciousness (raja yoga), (3)

Selflessly serving the Creation which includes all creatures, human and non human (karma yoga), (4) Increasing one's knowledge of the intuitional science (jinana yoga), and (5) Keeping one's body healthy (hatha yoga).

Acts of devotion consist of doing anything that makes one feel close to the Absolute or the attainment of self-realization. It may be singing, dancing, praying, worshipping, attending church services, or spending time alone in meditation. It may be consciously relinquishing the ownership of your thoughts and actions so you can move beyond ego attachments. By such acts one is saying, "Lord I am yours. Everything that I am is yours. Everything that I do is yours." By acts of devotion, a person develops their love for God and God expresses His love for his sons and daughters in return. Acts of devotion build a personal relationship with others as well as the Absolute Consciousness.

The purpose of meditation is to merge one's mental vibration with the vibration of the Absolute Consciousness. It is not to calm the mind or to increase one's ability to be mindful. Its intention is not to give us additional clarity before going into a business meeting. Rather the purpose of meditation is to merge with the One Collective Consciousness. This is achieved by repeating a sacred mantra in harmony with your breathing. It is not achieved by concentrating on a candle flame or any other material or psychic object. A sacred mantra always means "I am That" or something akin to this.

Serving others in a selfless manner is critical for spiritual progress. The object is not to get noticed or rewarded for your service, nor is it to feel better about yourself for acting in a magnanimous fashion. The purpose of serving others less fortunate than you is to see the Divine in them and to serve the Divine out of love. Selfless service breaks down the ego and with it the wall between you and external reality. Inside and outside begin to merge in the act of performing selfless service. You will begin to see how Absolute Consciousness flows within all things.

To increase your knowledge of the intuitional science you can read the books of those who have extensive experience in its practice. Some of these books are available on Amazon. You can also read about the lives of great mystics or the scriptures of different religions. You will find nuggets of truth all around you once you begin to understand what truth is. Of great importance is to find a spiritual teacher who understands the intuitional science and will teach you how to perform spiritual practices. It matters not whether the master is incarnate or not.

Because your mind is dependent upon a healthy body, you must take care of it and not ignore or abuse it. To care for your body means eating nutritious foods, getting adequate rest, exercising, performing breathing exercises, and doing yogic exercises (asanas).

Eating nutritious foods is a pre-requisite for a healthy body. Junk foods destroy the body. Adequate rest is also required to keep from burning out. Regarding breathing exercises, it is important to learn how to breathe with your diaphragm not with your chest. While deep breathing relaxes the body and reduces stress, these effects are not the main reason for learning how to breathe deeply. The primary reason is that it will improve your meditation. By being able to take deeper and longer breaths you will improve your concentration and slow the vibration of your mind.

Yogic asanas keep your spine flexible and tone your glandular system. They are unique postures designed by Lord Shiva and developed over millennia by yogic masters. Asanas should not be an end in themselves, but rather a means to improve your ability to meditate and serve others. Basic asanas are those that stretch your spine in all directions, for example, head to knee, the lion pose, and the spinal twist should be done daily. The shoulder stand should also be done everyday to tone your glands and bring blood to all your organs. You can add additional asanas as needed to address weaknesses in your body or give yourself more energy. Again, it is always preferable to have a teacher instruct you in the proper performance of asanas and to learn what individual asanas are most appropriate for you.

In the past, people withdrew from society to engage in these intuitional practices. Asceticism has been a legitimate path for centuries. We have seen this in the East and the West. The monks living in monasteries and desert huts and the yogis living in caves attest to this. Mr. Sarkar, however, calls on spiritual warriors today to give up asceticism and become engaged in the struggles of society. This is because the problems of humanity are so great today that the need for spiritualists is also great. Mr. Sarkar advises that:

One will meditate on the Supreme to become one with
the Supreme, and at the same time, to purify one's mind,
one is to render selfless service to human society. Without
rendering selfless service to society, one cannot come
close to attaining self-realization. And without practicing meditation, one cannot render selfless service to
the society.[188]

As we can now imagine, the intuitional path is not for the faint of heart.
Neither armchair philosophers, egotists, nor couch potatoes can follow
the intuitional path. Only those with the disciplined mind of a warrior
can free himself or herself and others from the bondage of Prakrti. Only
they can succeed in creating a new society based on love and cooperation.

When Abba John the Dwarf told his teacher, the ascetic Abba Poemen,
that he had found peace without any problems, the old man told him,
"Go, beseech God to stir up warfare so that you may regain the affliction
and humility that you used to have, for it is by warfare that the soul
makes progress." So, when warfare came, he no longer prayed that it
might be taken away, but said, "Lord, give me strength for the fight."[189]

Don Juan Matus, the spiritual master who guided Carlos Castaneda,
put it this way: "The basic difference between an ordinary man and a
warrior is that a warrior takes everything as a challenge, while an ordinary man takes everything as a blessing or a curse."[190]

Struggle, therefore, is not something to be avoided but something
to be embraced on the path to liberation. It is by wrestling with obstacles that we gain strength. Jesus told his disciples that the ones who
will inherit the kingdom of heaven are the ones willing to suffer in
the service of the Lord. Those who are the dedicated fighters for the
liberation of themselves and others, Mr. Sarkar calls sadvipras or
spiritual warriors.

## The Teacher of Intuitional Science

The purpose of performing intuitional practices is to achieve emancipation and not to fulfill one's ego desires or gain spiritual powers. In

order to fully understand the special techniques of intuitional practices, they need to be taught by one who knows these techniques. It is not possible for anyone to learn this science on their own. They must have someone who can teach them or whom they can imitate. Hence, the necessity of an intuitional master.

One who is in bondage cannot release others from bondage. One with shackled hands and feet cannot remove the shackles of others. Only the one who has become emancipated; i.e., obtained freedom from the qualifying influence of Prakrti, is capable of becoming a preceptor.

Mr. Sarkar says:

> Only that person can be a preceptor who by his or her sádhaná (intuitional practice) has attained the supreme rank but also has, at his or her own instance, taken human form again for a predetermined period for the welfare of living beings. Such a person will be under the influence of Prakrti as long as he or she maintains his or her physical body, and on relinquishing the body with death, he or she will return to the supreme rank – the Non-Qualified Supreme Entity.[191]

This means there is no difference between a true preceptor and God. The true preceptor perfectly reflects God-consciousness and, having taken human form, cannot be any other entity except the Qualified Supreme Entity (Saguńa Brahma). The wish of the Qualified Supreme Entity is to obtain emancipation for each of Its units and it is with this intention that He brought forth the creation. However, because Absolute Consciousness is formless, it cannot directly help humans to achieve emancipation. It has to assume a human form to help His units, and that is the form of an enlightened spiritual master. Unfortunately, such Sadgurus are not very common. Aside from a spiritual giant of this quality, we will find many yoga teachers and mindfulness teachers, we will find many monks and nuns and others who are looked upon as spiritual teachers. How do we know that they will not lead us astray if we put our faith in them?

A spiritual teacher in the Toltec tradition of mysticism had this to say about his own teacher, don Miguel. He realized that don Miguel possessed enormous spiritual powers but that he never used them. The student could not understand why this was so. He said:

> As I journeyed into this question about don Miguel, I saw the amount of refrain he had in the use of Power. What I then saw was behind this motivation of refrain. I saw that don Miguel had no desire to change anyone, or their life. He only loved and accepted people just the way that they are. His love was/is, so unconditional, that he loves people just the way they are. In that unconditional love, there is no desire or need to change anybody.
>
> This is when I saw the real nature of don Miguel. I understood what unconditional love was. It means not needing to change anyone, and that includes yourself. This realization became much more powerful to me than any act of power could have performed. His unconditional love and respect was more powerful than any Ceremony, or act of Power or change could ever be. He loved me just the way that I was. I didn't have to try to be anything any more. I was lovable. I was good enough just the way that I was. He loved me no matter what I was. And in his reflection, I began to love myself just the way that I was. No conditions.[192]

The Buddhists have a guide for spiritual initiates they call "the Four Reliances." These reliances help the students make spiritual progress regardless of the teacher: First rely on the principle, not on the person. Second, rely on the spirit, not the letter. Third, rely on wisdom, not conditioning. And fourth, rely on complete teaching, not incomplete teaching.[193]"

Mr. Sarkar has this to say:

> Although it is difficult to find a true preceptor in human form, it is not necessary to search for one in jungles, mountains, and caves in accordance with popular belief. Because the purpose of God in manifesting

the creation is to obtain emancipation for each of His units, God will have to appear before anyone who has a yearning for emancipation. This yearning or state of mental uneasiness caused by the intense desire for emancipation heralds the arrival of the opportune moment. The Qualified Supreme Entity, in the form of a great preceptor, will appear to those who have reached this opportune moment by virtue of their intense desire for liberation. If this were not so, the purpose of the creation would not be served; it would be merely a trap, and the Creator, the Qualified Supreme Entity, would become the cause of bondage. Hence to wander through jungles and over mountains in quest of a great preceptor is futile. What is most essential is to kindle in one's heart a yearning, an intense desire for emancipation.[194]

As Abba Arsenius, a Christian monk in ancient Greece, said, "'If we seek God, he will show himself to us, and if we keep him, he will remain close to us."[195]

## The Qualities of a Master of Intuitional Science

What are the qualities of a great preceptor? Mr. Sarkar says that a great preceptor is an emancipated person and is master of all the supernatural powers, but does not have to display them to be recognized as a preceptor.

It is vital to understand that nothing can be achieved by merely depending on the preceptor. Everyone must also do the work required by intuitional practices. Emancipation is not possible without taking action. Some people have the erroneous impression that they do not have to make an effort; that they will attain emancipation due to the grace of the preceptor alone. Although it is true that liberation is not possible without the great preceptor's kindness, to deserve the grace of the preceptor, one has to follow the science of institutional practice with devotion and discipline, and not assume that the great preceptor will freely give everything without any effort on the part of the disciple. Other people think that because they are the disciples of a great preceptor and because he or she has come to elevate the fallen, he or she will take them all along when leaving, in the same way as a cowherd gathers together all grazing cattle before leaving the pasture at dusk. This way of thinking is not correct. A great preceptor does not come into this world to herd his disciples like cattle. The great preceptor comes to liberate people, to elevate them to the realization of Absolute Consciousness.

It is as Swami Yogananda said:

> A guru's only interest is to help you progress spiritually. If the teacher wants something from the disciple, he is not a master. The master's only desire is to give, not to take. But if the disciple has the wish to help the work of the master, that is to his credit—he is helped by giving to God's cause.[196]

## Why Are People Afraid of Intuitional Practice?

If intuitional practice is the duty of everyone, why don't people do it? Certainly, there are risks and obstacles on the intuitional path, but these are not the reason that people are afraid of intuitional practices. Rather, it is because people believe that they would have to give up their worldly life in order to do spiritual practices. They think they would need to surrender their job, their house, or their marriage. What would happen to the children? People believe that emancipation is only for the privileged ascetics and that it is not attainable by normal people. This is a false and dangerous assumption.

Giving up one's life and retreating to a desert hut or mountain cave will not set one free. Our karma will go with us wherever we go. A rural person may find living in a city disturbing. So also, a person who is used to the city life may find the silence of the country disturbing. In the beginning, one will find it difficult to practice meditation no matter where they live. But a person will get used to it after a short time. Becoming an ascetic is not necessary.

Let's look at the question of forfeiting one's worldly life in order to avoid temptations. If a person is tempted by greed, it can only be overcome through spiritual practices. Merely forsaking the world and retiring to the wilderness will be of no avail. We may argue that staying away from temptation may help us lessen our attachment, but by forcing ourselves to renounce a temptation may also cause greater mental agitation and cause us to get sick. In truth, forcing ourselves to leave a worldly life, only to keep away from its attractions, will serve no purpose.

Rather than giving up our worldly life, it is better to develop strength of character and firmness of mind. The spiritual warrior lives among temptations in order to face and overcome them step by step rather than avoiding them due to fear. Spiritual practice means waging war on negative forces and to win this war one has to face the enemy instead of running away or appeasing it.

Looked at from another perspective, some people may want to run away to a Himalayan cave because their normal life requires them to meet their obligations to their dependents. We have to earn money to provide for them. We must suffer diseases and the other trials of life. We have to face interpersonal problems and societal problems. All this creates the desire to run away from worldly life and be free from all responsibilities except to oneself. But this only amounts to the evasion of one's duty. One who runs away from worldly life avoids obligations and only demonstrates extreme selfishness. Evasion of duty and selfishness are negative actions, which will have negative consequences, and until the reactions have been completely experienced, emancipation will remain impossible. Thus, it is false to believe that one is unable to perform intuitional practices unless one runs away to a cave, as it is false to believe that one is unable to perform intuitional practices if one stays in their home.

Only by diverting the mind towards subtlety can we become victorious. The influence of negative forces decreases only due to intuitional practices, not to the act of escape. Therefore, we do not need to become ascetics to fight against negative forces; we can do this in our normal worldly life. Certainly these negative forces will disturb us in the beginning, but as we gain strength to overcome them, they will become less of a hindrance to us.

There is yet another great advantage in living a worldly life. It provides us with the opportunity to serve humanity, an important aspect of intuitional practice. Selfless service is best practiced at home and in one's community.

Therefore, the fear that people have of giving up their normal life to achieve emancipation is irrational.

Another reason that people fear doing intuitional practices is that they think they may have to become celibate and give up sexual relations. Such people have been misled by centuries of religious indoctrination that unless one is celibate, he or she cannot get close to God. Certainly, one can become overly obsessed with sex and, in doing so, create an obstacle to one's spiritual progress, but if one attempts to see the Divine in one's partner, it is not necessary to give up one's conjugal life in order to begin intuitional practices. Sexual obsession will diminish naturally once one gains spiritual force. Lust will be replaced by more love. It is by intuitional practice, not taking a vow of celibacy, that one becomes a spiritual warrior.[197]

Other people do not do intuitional practices because they think that it is better to start them later in life, after they retire, because there are less distractions and their income is secure. People are afraid that they may face difficulties in their old age if they do not accumulate enough wealth before their bodies become weak with age. They regard the prime of life as the period intended for earning money, and old age, with its decreased capacity for hard work, as the time to remember God. Such people think that hard work and intuitional practice are incompatible. They ignore the fact that hard work is necessary to perform intuitional practices. Such people also fail to grasp that one is constantly approaching death, not knowing when it will come. It is never certain that one will live to grow old.

Anything important should be started early in life, and so should intuitional practice.

Finally, and perhaps the main reason that people avoid intuitional practice is their fear of giving up all the pleasures and enjoyments of the world. This fear is also unfounded. It was explained earlier that the objects of earthly enjoyment are created under the influence of the static principle of the Operative Principle, and that we regard them as real due to our attachment to them. By performing intuitional practice, the mind is diverted towards subtle things and, in this process, worldly pleasures and enjoyments lose their attraction. They do not need to be given up; they evaporate on their own as our mind gains spiritual strength. Initially people may feel tormented by their absence, but in short order they will actually feel relieved to be without them. They will experience a freedom from desire. If we do not desire an object, we will not miss it when it is not there. An alcohol addict will be tormented if he does not get alcohol, but a non-addict does not feel its absence. As the mind gets diverted towards subtlety through intuitional practice, it no longer enjoys crude pursuits. Not to pursue intuitional practice for fear of having to stay away from earthly pleasures and enjoyments is irrational.

Therefore, we have seen that the fears that hold us back from doing intuitional practices are without foundation. Today the world needs spiritual warriors more than ever. It is harmful to oneself and to the world to avoid intuitional practices out of unfounded fears. Rather, it is better to take up the fight for humanity and move ever closer to the bliss of Absolute Consciousness.

# Conclusion

So ends our summary of the description and practice of intuitional science.

In this short exposition, we have learned what constitutes human nature, what is the Cosmic Entity, what is this world, who I am, and what is my relation to Absolute Consciousness and to this world. We have also learned how to live in this world and why the performance of intuitional practices is required. We have uncovered the mystery of the thirst for limitlessness that goads our every action and causes us to seek wealth and power. We have learned how our karmic programming keeps us in chains and what we must do to emancipate ourselves from it. The implication of this knowledge is profound. It is the culmination of the long human quest to experience the Divine that has characterized the history of humanity.

We have also learned that while spiritual practices may be cursorily addressed by mainstream religions, there is a big difference between intuitional science and religions. Myths, stories, relics, rituals, dogmas, and blind faith are the attributes of organized religion. On the other hand, universalism, intuitional science, rationality, and service to all are the attributes of intuitional science. Having provided this caution, true spiritualists are able to use most religions as styles of worship. To determine the spiritual strength of a religion, however, one only needs to determine if it has produced God (self)-realized human beings.

The only way to create the world that we all want is to put spirituality in the hub of our daily activities. This is the meaning of nuclear revolution. Revolution is not just an alternate way to meet our ego needs, adjust our interpersonal relations, deal with politics, economics, culture, or environmental concerns. Spirituality (intuitional practice) is not just another spoke on the wheel, another thing to do. Spirituality is the nucleus. It is that which infuses every thought, word, and deed with love, understanding, and the will to fight. As we saw in Book One, the mystics, regardless of their religion, have always claimed that God teaches through love. It is love that determines the value of a human being. In talking about Muslim mystics, Dr. Alan Godlas, professor at the University of Georgia says:

> After nearly 30 years of the study of Sufism, I would say that in spite of its many variations and voluminous expressions, the essence of Sufi practice is quite simple. It is that the Sufi surrenders to God, in love, over and over; which involves embracing with love at each moment the content of one's consciousness (one's perceptions, thoughts, and feelings, as well as one's sense of self) as gifts of God or, more precisely, as manifestations of God.[198]

It was the Christian Paul who said, "Love worketh no ill to his neighbor; therefore, love is the fulfilling of the law" (Rom. 13:10). Saint Teresa of

Avila told us, "Accustom yourself continually to make many acts of love, for they enkindle and melt the soul."

And as the Jewish mystics remind us, "In order to love someone else, you must first love yourself!"[199]

Although the fact that we need a spiritual preceptor to learn how to practice intuitional science is absolutely true, we should not wait to begin our intuitional practices until we meet a perfect master in the flesh. There are teachers at every level of accomplishment who can move us along. If we outgrow them, we know it is time to move on and find someone who knows more and loves more. That being said, the intuitional science of Mr. Sarkar is being taught by thousands of monks and nuns around the world if this suits your desire.[200] If not, there are different spiritual paths that lead to the same goal. The important thing is to begin the work, or if you are on the path, work harder. But remember, intuitional practices are not for the lazy or faint of heart. It is not an easy task to become one with the Supreme Divinity—to seize Perfection from imperfection.

While intuitional science concerns itself with the subtlest dimensions of consciousness, it is not an abstract construct. Rather, it is an applied mental construct. Its ramifications have the power to transform the relative world. If we believe that reality is essentially a material condition, as materialist do, we remain locked in a world in which consciousness is atomized, and we find ourselves alone, vying for resources in a competitive "dog-eat-dog" world. This is the world we have created for ourselves. By making the assumption that we are exclusively physical beings, we crudify our consciousness and limit our capacity to grow. The logical flaw in materialism is that it limits the mind to duality—body and brain, inside me and outside me, me versus you, us versus them. It completely ignores the Absolute Consciousness in which we all participate. By not grasping what Shiva, Christ, and the other mystics have revealed to us, which is that Absolute Consciousness is the universe and can be known through intuitional practices, materialists categorically deny the fulfillment of our deepest longing—limitless love and happiness.

As long as we tend to see everything as different from ourselves and our group, we will never be able to achieve self-realization. The movement of society is based upon the collective karma of its citizens.

It is a result of our collective genius, industriousness, and creativity, but it is also a result of our greed, cruelty, cynicism, ignorance, and lethargy. The negative trend of our collective karma cannot be overcome by more ego-gratification, the condemnation of each other, the need to make more money, or the desire to escape our fears. As Martin Luther King reminded us, "It really boils down to this: that all life is interrelated. We are all caught in an inescapable network of mutuality, tied to a single garment of destiny. Whatever affects one directly, affects all indirectly."[201]

We cannot blame God for our condition, nor can we legitimately stigmatize or scapegoat others for our problems. Whether we are warriors, intellectuals, merchants, or manual laborers, whether we are men or women, in the majority or minority, we are each responsible for the part that we play in society. Now that we are awake to our spiritual/intuitional nature and our relationship with the Cosmic Entity and all creatures of this world; now that we realize our state of bondage; now that we can recognize racism, sexism, classism, nationalism, and religionism for what they are; now that we see our negative actions for what they are, we are able to understand why we must engage in the struggle to gain our freedom and to make the world a better place to live.

The current visions for social change, be they conservative, liberal, or progressive, are based on materialism and fear. These worldviews are too limited in scope to inspire a new world. By submitting to such visions, even if we are able to prevent or mitigate impending social and environmental disasters, we will still continue to see ourselves as material, competitive creatures with no more purpose as a species than to pursue sensory gratification. We will continue to live under the dictates of groupism as a protection against others.

In today's world, it is not enough to avoid a zombie apocalypse. We must change the course of history. We must change ourselves by helping the world around us. While we require a global revolution, the revolution must begin in the nucleus of our own being. It must begin in the spiritual/intuitional realm that lies within.

In his article, "Consciousness Creates Reality—Physicists Admit The Universe Is Immaterial, Mental & Spiritual," Arjun Walia expresses the following view:

In order to create and manifest a new reality for ourselves, our thought patterns and the way we perceive reality must change. What changes the way we perceive reality? Information does. When new information emerges, it changes the way we look at things and as a result, our reality changes, and we begin to manifest a new experience and open our minds to a broader view of reality.

We have been repeating and perceiving our reality this way for a very long time, with very little information about what is really happening on and to our planet. It's almost like we are robotic drones that are trained and brainwashed to accept things the way they are and to not question what is happening in our world and to continue on with the status quo, only caring for ourselves and our own lives. As Noam Chomsky would say, our consent has been manufactured. If we continue down this path and continue to perceive and view reality as "this is just the way it is," we will, in essence, prolong that type of existence and experience for the human race without ever changing it.[202]

Mr. Sarkar has also given us new information that has been acknowledge by a myriad of insightful people. This new information can help us emancipate ourselves and serve the world.[203] Each one of us, regardless of our politics, wants a world in which our basic needs are met in a safe neighborhood and in a safe world. And, regardless of the fact that war profiteers and the capitalist media continue to "manufacture our consent" to their atrocities, in our hearts we all know what we really want and we actually all know what Jesus would do. We are all children of the Divine. We are all brothers and sisters and like brothers and sisters we need to take care of each other.

In our service to suffering humanity, it is vital that we create an entirely new socio-economy to replace the existing models that are leading to our destruction. No capitalist, communist, socialist, or autocratic theocracy today has the required scope to bring us together as a human society. In the following chapters and in Book 3 we will look at a socio-economic theory that provides us with a strategy to generate our own economic and political power right where we live, at the local level. It identifies the kind of social institutions and economic strategies that we require to optimize our collective human potential. In addition to a number of practical applications to this theory, we will also look at P. R. Sakar's comprehensive Progressive Utilization Theory (PROUT) that allows for every person on the planet to meet their basic needs and live in harmony with their neighbor.

We now have a universal ideology, a human story that addresses our most fundamental questions. We know why we are here and what we must do. Our goal is to create the optimum conditions for ourselves and humanity to realize our true nature. In order to do this, we must also change the material conditions that presently keep humanity in poverty and fear of the future.

# Chapter Four: The Politics of Progressive Socialism (PROUT)

*PROUT is a socioeconomic philosophy to help take humanity from imperfection to perfection. To move towards the Supreme Entity is a continuous process for one and all. At the end of this process, you will become one with the Supreme Entity.* P. R. Sarkar

## Progressive Socialism (Balancing Personal, Social, and Environmental Needs)

M R. SARKAR OFTEN REFERRED to his Progressive Utilization Theory (PROUT) as progressive socialism or spiritual socialism. It is progressive because it places spirituality in the hub of all socio-economic activity. It is socialist because it places the needs of human beings above capital accumulation.

While capitalist democracy is a political-economic system where a person votes for a political representative that seldom represents one's interests, progressive socialism is a socio-economic system in which local people take it upon themselves to ensure that everyone in their jurisdiction has their basic needs met in a sustainable manner. These needs are food, shelter, clothing, health care, and education, as well as the necessary infrastructure to produce and deliver the goods and services required to meet these needs. Typically, when people think about democracy they think only about political democracy. Progressive socialism, on the other hand, includes both political and economic democracy.

Progressive socialism is the political and economic component of P. R. Sarkar's Universal Ideology. Along with an understanding of social dynamics, human nature and spiritual reality, PROUT provides a means to restructure political economies to free human beings to pursue their higher capacities and realize their full potential. The first priority of progressive socialism is that all local people should have their basic needs met in a sustainable manner. To create a political structure that will allow this to happen is the subject of PROUT politics.

Progressive socialism will not spread through the ballot box. Rather, it is spreading through local revolutionaries who support the principles of progressive socialism and who are willing to organize local efforts to meet the people's basic needs. It is also spread by those warriors, intellectuals, and merchants in every country who are the well-wishers of human society. Progressive socialism builds from the local level and spreads to nearby localities and to other progressive socialists working at higher levels of organization and economic integration. It has already taken root in the hearts of many people around the world who are determined to become a force for universal good.

## What is Politics?

Politics derives from the Greek word politicos which means "of, for, or relating to citizens." It is the process of making decisions that apply to all members of a group. Politics is exercised within different social formations, from clans and tribes of traditional societies, to the modern local, state, and federal governments within nation states, and even at the international level through organizations like the United Nations.

A political system is a framework that defines acceptable methods of governance and organization within a given society. For example, such frameworks include capitalism, communism, fascism, democratic socialism, and theocratic totalitarianism. The leadership of such systems control power and make decisions regarding domestic and foreign policy as well as control the means to enforce such policies, including the protection or suppression of citizens internally or through diplomacy or warfare abroad.[204]

The Code of Hammurabi is likely the oldest legal code known to man. It was authorized by the Babylonian king, Hammurabi, around

1754 BC and was written on a seven and a half foot stele and several clay tablets. The code consists of 282 laws, with scaled punishments depending on whether one was a slave or free man. Nearly one-half of the code deals with matters of contract; for example, the wages to be paid to an ox driver or a surgeon. Other provisions govern transactions, like establishing the liability of a builder for a house that collapses or property that is damaged while left in the care of another. A third of the code addresses issues concerning household and family relationships such as inheritance, divorce, paternity, and sexual behavior. A few provisions address issues related to military service. Only one provision appears to impose obligations on a government official; this provision establishes that a judge who reaches an incorrect decision is to be fined and removed from the bench permanently.[205] Ah, the good old days.

Normally, western institutions trace political theory back to Plato's *Republic*, Aristotle's *Politics*, and the *Analects* of Confucius.

Contemporary students of political science are generally concerned with formal political structures that operate according to a constitutional system of government with publicly defined institutions and legal procedures. Such systems of government depend upon political parties to make good decisions on behalf of the people, which we know is not always the case. In most cases, politicians decide issues of public policy, foreign affairs, and war according to the dictates of a wealthy oligarchy. Most people view formal politics as something outside of themselves, but which still affects their daily lives. The extent of most Americans' involvement in the political system, for example, is to cast a vote for a presidential candidate once every four years. They may also vote for a representative and senator to represent them in Congress. This is generally the extent of their participation in national politics.

On the other hand, all people are continually involved in informal politics, which includes the management of households, offices, or organizations. It may include forming alliances and exercising authority to advance some particular goal or idea. Informal politics are more often personal and face-to-face.[206] In this stage of their development, Proutists are, for the most part, engaged in informal politics.

## What is Progress?

The first thing to understand about progressive socialism is the meaning of "progress." Social change may or may not be progressive. We can only speak of progress in relation to a specific goal. If we move toward that goal, we make progress; if we move away from it, we do not.

Human existence has physical, mental, and spiritual dimensions. There is movement in all three spheres and therefore there can be progress in all three spheres. The main consideration is what is the goal or the aim of one's action? For progressive socialism, progress is defined exclusively as that which moves us toward the Supreme Entity. Only when movement is towards this supreme goal, can we call it progress. Where movement is not associated with the supreme goal, it only slows or delays progress.[207]

Let us explore this a little more deeply. The word "progress" in the physical sphere is generally associated with scientific inventions and a higher standard of living. For example, people think that the use of an automobile to replace a bicycle, or the use of an airplane to replace an automobile is a sign of progress. To take another example, people used to sleep on the ground, but now they sleep on spring mattresses. They used to light a candle or an oil lamp to see at night, but now they have indoor electricity. There are many examples of progress in the physical realm. Computers are considered progressive because they help us work faster and with greater detail. In other words, we define physical and mental advancements as progress when they make our lives easier or more enjoyable, or when they make business more profitable.

But, if we look more deeply into this situation, everything in this psycho-physical reality is based on vibrations and all vibrations contain a positive and a negative aspect. Every atom has a proton and an electron, every wave rises and falls. Every positive movement creates a negative reaction. This is the basis of dialectical thought. It is the basis of our concept of good and bad. With each invention that provides us enjoyment, there is also a negative consequence. For example, today people have more gadgets to amuse themselves, but at the same time are more anxious and depressed. We can feed the world, but the food we eat is also giving us heart disease, cancer,

obesity, and diabetes. We can heat our homes and travel around the
world, but the fuel that we use pollutes our soil, water, and air and
threatens climatic collapse. A deeper look at the definition of physical
and mental progress, therefore, leads us to believe that the pluses
and minuses in the material and psychic realms tend to cancel each
other out. Genuine progress only occurs when human inventions
allow us the opportunity to reach our spiritual goal.[208] Some physical
improvements may be progressive because they allow us more time
for spiritual practices. The invention of books, music, or theatre, for
example, may inspire us to be greater human beings. Most things,
however, that we consider to be progressive, only create change, but
no progress. Such change amounts to little more than bobbing up
and down on an ocean's surface, buffeted about by waves of pleasure
and pain.

Real progress has to do with decreasing the gap between one's
mind and the Divine Consciousness. This is spiritual progress and,
in fact, it is the only kind of progress. There is no negative backlash
to spiritual progress because the goal is not finite. It is immune from
the effect of reactive momenta because no new karma is created. In
the absence of negative reaction, every movement is progress. There
is no question of minuses; there are only pluses. Even so, spiritual
progress depends upon a firm physical and mental base and this
base has to continually adjust to the changing conditions of time,
place, and person.

If there is little in the physical and mental realms that can be
defined as true progress, it does not mean that we should stop our
efforts in these spheres. Rather, we should continue to create more
congenial environments for people so that spiritual practices might
become more accessible. This particularly includes all efforts to
ensure that people have their basic needs met. The only caution, in
this effort, is that scientists and inventors give more attention than
they presently do to the negative effects their inventions might have
on society, and make moral judgments accordingly. For example, the
creation of junk food that cause heart disease and diabetes cannot
be considered progress.

## The Main Purpose of Government

Any political entity must have a government and its viability depends on whether people support it or not. In other words, the value of a government should be determined by whether it helps or hinders social progress. If it is harmful to human and planetary well-being, then it is better for humanity to destroy it. If it is useful but requires changes, then people should work for its change. If it is very good or moving in the right direction, then people should defend it with their lives.

From the perspective of progressive socialism, the main purpose of government is to support human unity. Human unity will remove all the stress and conflict that currently occurs because of the divisiveness created by sexism, ageism, racism, classism, religious exclusivism, and national chauvinism. Admittedly, at this time in history, human unity does not exist on the material plane. It only exists in the ideological realm. Nonetheless, as far as there is a desire for human unity, it will also gain expression in the material world. As people accept and incorporate the idea of unity into their mode of behavior, the more it will materialize. If the government supports human unity, it is a positive sign that the government is operating according to its highest purpose. If, on the other hand, it encourages the exploitation of one group over another, or considers one gender, race, class, religion or national origin to be superior to others, the government is not functioning properly and it needs to be changed or destroyed depending upon circumstances.

## Current Political Values

Political values have traditionally been based on local customs, bigoted sentiments, or religious concepts of vice and virtue. Within capitalist societies, the left wing and the right wing espouse different values. The right tends to base its values on religious scripture and the rights of white people, while the left values science and humanitarian ideals. Both defend their values as being good for the people.

Despite the Founding Fathers' desire to separate church and state, traditional religious values still maintain a strong hold on contemporary political thought. Religious fundamentalists continue to impose their values on the American populace under the banner of "Religious Freedom." These values are based on religious scripture and absolutist dogmas, which are beyond reproach or change in time, place, and person. For others, however, particularly the Left, values are relative and subject to change. Let us look at the question of taking one's own life. Americans, on both the Left and the Right, customarily believe that suicide is one of the gravest sins. But this view is not universally accepted. According to the customary belief of Indians, suicide is considered to be a sin, but it is not a grave sin. The Japanese do not consider suicide to be a sin at all but rather a mark of honor. These beliefs affect the penal codes of these three countries. In Japan, neither suicide nor attempted suicide constitutes a crime, and thus neither is a punishable offence. In India today the attempt to commit suicide is a punishable crime, but suicide itself is not. In the United States, there are no laws against committing suicide, but there are laws against assisting suicide. This demonstrates that arguments about virtue and sin are not absolute; they depend upon the ideas of local people, or people within certain groups.[209]

Different concepts of virtue and sin also coexist in the same country. In the United States, for example, the Republican and Democratic parties each have their definitions of virtue and sin as can be seen in their views of women's rights. And while politicians may act as if their definitions are beyond reproach, a person in one place and time calls a behavior a sin that is considered a virtue by another person in another place and time. Under these relative circumstances, what should be the basis of a legal code? If legal codes are based on the different concepts of virtue and sin, professed by different groups of people, we will certainly run into the problem where two opposing sides become ever more ensconced in their opposing positions. And over time, particularly when times are hard, the polarization only increases. This is what happened in Europe prior to WWI and WWII and which is again occurring in the United States and western society today.

As a result of this observation, we cannot build a PROUTist legal code on traditional concepts of virtue and sin that are followed by different groups of people.

Within a progressive socialist society, those who think they can arbitrarily impose their judicial system or legal codes on people by using the power of the state are mistaken. The principles underlying the PROUT legal code are based on people's social needs and not on the whims of an individual or group or the biases inherent in their particular concept of virtue and sin.

Rather, in a progressive socialist society, we will have to define what does and what does not constitute a sin or crime in accordance with a universal moral standard. Generally speaking, we can say that an immoral act is one by which a particular group exploits another individual or group or the rest of society, or aims to deprive them of the right to self-reliance, in order to further their own personal interests. Behavior based on such immoral intentions will be a crime in a progressive socialist society.

## Sin and Crime

As we have been discussing, a government is built upon legal codes. When these codes are related to the ideals of a social system they are called a constitution. When they are related to governance or justice, then they are called regulations or laws. These regulations and laws, in general, are formulated so as to materialize the ideals of the people as indicated in their constitution.

Because human beings are social beings, we must follow legal codes; otherwise it would be impossible to organize a society. Aside from this, we must follow moral codes as well. When people form such codes, (the "dos" and "don'ts" of society), sometimes the "don'ts" are called "sins" and at other times "crimes." In general parlance, whatever violates the law of the land is called a crime and that which violates a moral principle is called a sin.

In a secular state, an act against the legal code is regarded as a crime. In a church, or in a government controlled by a priest class, it is called a sin. Depending upon the locality and the psychology of the people, there are different views regarding what is criminal and what is sinful. Under a secular government, different states and nations have different constitutions as well as different legislative, administrative, and judicial systems. If someone does not conform to the codes of these systems while in that state or nation, his or her acts are considered criminal (illegal) and he or she is liable to be punished.[210] In a religious state, like that of Iran, if someone does not conform to the religious laws, their actions are considered sinful and the priest class uses the power of the state to punish them.

Sometimes crime and sin coincide but sometimes they do not. It is often the case where a crime is also a sin. For example, in the case of murder, a crime is also a sin. But, in another example, let us say the charge of a high interest rate on credit card debt is not a crime within a secular state, but is considered a sin of usury in a church-state.

The law of the land is created by certain people who are elected, selected, or who have seized power by force. In today's complex nation-states, there are many people who create the "laws of the land." Their decisions may or may not be correct or moral. In fact, as laws are constructed to serve the interest of the oligarchs, they are generally immoral. The definition of crime varies from country to country and from locality to locality. In the US, the definition of crime varies from state to state, county to county, and town to town, although smaller jurisdictions are always subject to the laws of the governments above them.[211]

The concept of sin is based solely on religious dogmas and not on the basic human principles of spiritual science. Therefore, as a spiritual activist, it is always wise to use discrimination in judging the correctness of a legal or moral code. It is extremely harmful to submit to laws or dogmas in a thoughtless manner. In fact, we should keep away from such partisan legal codes and religious dogma and attach the highest importance only to cardinal human principles.

Cardinal human principles, as we shall see below, change little from age to age, but social values may change dramatically to keep pace with the dominant social psychology. Cardinal human principles are not based on legal codes or religious dogmas that prevent humanity from expanding its consciousness. Violations against cardinal human principles such as racism, sexism, classism, claims of religious or national superiority, etc., are all legitimized by dogma and legal codes. Such legal codes and dogmas are divisive forces that must be destroyed. In their place, we must enshrine cardinal human principles, which seek the welfare of humanity and nature and encourage expansion of the mind. To act according to the dictates of a universal moral code is to act according to cardinal human principles and to go against them is to act against cardinal human principles.[212] These principles are addressed in detail below.

From the perspective of cardinal human principles, any action, which checks the progress of human society, is a vice, and any action which accelerates social progress is a virtue. In a PROUT society, vice and virtue are viewed in this manner, whether one calls vice a sin or a crime.

In summary, according to progressive socialism, there should be no difference between sin and crime, and the legal code should be based upon cardinal human principles. In a Proutist society, to violate cardinal human principles is both a sin and a crime. Therefore, in framing the constitution and the laws of a progressive socialist society, revolutionaries should not base them on local faiths or customs, but should draft them in recognition of the welfare of humanity and the environment as a whole.[213]

## Causes of Sin and Crime

According to PROUT, both sin and crime are caused by the same three conditions. The first cause is a shortage of physical and mental resources (poverty). The second one is non-utilization of over-accumulated physical and mental resources (greed and hoarding). The third one is stagnancy in the physical and mental strata (refusing to keep up with the movement of life).

When human beings lack the basic necessities of life (food, shelter, clothing, health care, and education) it becomes very difficult to follow higher pursuits. Every waking hour must be dedicated to physical survival. When people live under such extreme pressure, their sense of discrimination is easily disturbed. Even with a little extra hardship, they become easily angered and depressed. If their deprivation lasts long, they will naturally tend towards lawlessness and brutality because they have nothing to lose. While stealing, burglary, and robbery are all considered sins and crimes, these are mainly carried out to meet basic needs.

When people are ignorant, they commit all kinds of mistakes. Prompted by greedy or power-hungry leaders, they do not think for themselves, but are easily manipulated to use violence. Among the poor and uneducated, where social consciousness is less, the people tend to be more immoral. Men abuse women and children and human suffering engenders less sympathy. In third world countries, warlords rule by force of arms or gain control of the people by "winning" fixed elections. Such beasts can become leaders when the intellectual standard of the common people is low.

Thus, when those physical and intellectual resources required to meet basic needs are lacking, people commit more sins and crimes. Among the three reasons for sin and crime, this is the first and primary one. It is prevalent everywhere in the world although it is less evident in a few affluent countries where the majority of people have their basic needs met.[214]

Non-utilization of over-accumulated physical and psychic resources is the second cause of sin and crime. To satisfy the greed of the rich, the poor become slaves, and to meet their own meager needs they become criminals and sinners. The rich steal the physical and intellectual wealth of the poor to satisfy their baser propensities. Then, as we saw in Volume Five of *The Untold Story of Western Civilization*, on Contemporary History, they create monopolies to drive up prices and hoard their profits in nameless bank accounts. In society today, the big capitalists sit in the background; but in the foreground we find the bloated bellies of malnourished children and the masses of people unable to meet their basic needs.

Human beings actually have few needs. Primarily we need food, clothing, shelter, health care, and education. Most people do not even want much more than this. In cases of over-accumulation of resources by the rich, the majority of the people's basic needs are not met and there is no proper utilization of resources. Moreover, where there is over-accumulation, the rich tend to misutilize wealth by indulging in their baser propensities. Therefore, you will see that most members of the ruling classes throughout history, the kings, the aristocrats, and the wealthy of today are generally sociopathic and mean-spirited. In addition, you will see that government officials and the military elite who do the bidding of the rich also lack moral and spiritual fortitude and become mean-spirited. It is natural for people to move towards sin if over-accumulated physical and psychic resources are not properly utilized. If people have developed intellects, which are not properly directed, and there is no moral leadership, they become highly polished sinners and criminals and inflict great sufferings on others.

The over-accumulation of wealth in the US negatively affects not only the middle and lower classes but also the rich and their children. Preoccupied with their material pursuits, the rich turn into sociopaths, unaffected by the suffering they cause to others, but ever wary of any signs of social unrest. In their preoccupation with accumulating more wealth, they neglect their own children. They find themselves unable to provide love for them or even understand what love is. Without love and guidance, many of the children become lost. Many turn into addicts and see themselves as social parasites. Others, by following in their parents' footsteps, also become burdens on society.

The third cause of sin and crime is stagnancy in the physical and psychic spheres. Stagnancy is due to society having to carry the monumental baggage of warn-out geo- and socio-sentiments that prevent us from moving forward. This stagnancy makes us psychologically sick because it perpetuates all the narrow vested interests that have divided us throughout history, but which no longer make sense. For example, we are still bound to the sexist ideology perpetrated by the Catholic Church in its witch hunts during the Middle Ages and also to the racist ideologies perpetrated by southern slavers in the nineteenth century even though these sentiments are crippling society and preventing human growth. Stagnancy is a slow death. If dynamism is the sign of life, where it is absent, there is only death. Without dynamism, people are harmed repeatedly by the same sins and crimes that plagued their ancestors irrespective of changing conditions.

Even though there is no lack of resources and no misutilization of resources, sin and crime can still occur due to stagnancy. Everything in existence has its purpose. All entities are moving according to their own speed whether there is progress or not. Yet, if there is a person or a group of people who are stagnant, it affects the speed and progress of society at large. When the human mind becomes inert and dormant, either due to being indoctrinated by regressive dogmas, or human frailty, or by the need to protect wealth and power, or by lack of proper education, we not only destroy ourselves, but we also affect the movements of others. We often see this stagnancy manifested in die-hard conservatives and indoctrinated religious fundamentalists. "My ancestors did this, and we must do the same." Racism, sexism, and many other narrow isms are based on this stagnant mind-set. The abuse and oppression of women is a product of such mental stagnancy. When things remain motionless, they decay and die. A society that is afraid to move forward and to expand is destined to die.

From a spiritual perspective, it is not acceptable to say, "The members of my family hold conservative views," or "That's just the way I am" as an excuse for inaction in the face of injustice. This should not be allowed. While there is a time and a place for conservative thinking, those who hold conservative views today are normally indoctrinated materialists or are mentally stagnant. They may be rich conservatives or poor conservatives. While there is no excuse for being a rich conservative, we must understand that poor people often become conservatives because they cannot afford to risk any change that might jeopardize their already precarious position. Even so, poor conservatives, if they have a good mind and a warrior spirit, are likely to become social revolutionaries because they are so sick of the lies and deceits of the ruling elites. They are put in a position where they have nothing left to lose. Such people can be persuaded to fight for a new society that draws attention to their suffering and abuse and champions their rights for social and economic justice. Motion and speed have to be infused in them before humanity and the planet suffer through more horrendous abuse.

## Solutions to Sin and Crime

To ensure that every human being has the physical and mental resources to survive, the minimum requirements will have to be guaranteed to everyone. If the capitalists and their governments do not allow people the opportunity to provide for their minimum requirements by their own labor, they are nothing but oppressors and their system needs to be destroyed. Because we have watched wave after wave of so-called political reforms wash back impotently into the ocean of capitalism, today, only revolution remains an option for those who seek the betterment of human society. Revolution means an end to the capitalist system. It requires speed of movement. The goal of revolution is to create an alternative as quickly as possible so as to prevent the continuous suffering of people as capitalism continues its inevitable decay. A strong moral government, led by those who possess the powers of the intellectual, warrior, and merchant will be required to create a political-economy that can supply the minimum requirements to everyone. Those capable of providing such moral leadership, P. R. Sarkar calls Sadvipras or spiritual warriors. He says:

> Social life cannot be elevated merely by speeches delivered from political platforms; political leaders cannot produce sadvipras by their rhetoric. Besides, who are those who deliver lectures from platforms? Are they not the people who sling the mud of political censure on others? Most of them are blind after power. What will they teach others? Mental and spiritual training alone can create sadvipras. Sadvipras are only those who are perfect in morality and aspirants of the Supreme Consciousness.[215]

We will discuss the topic of sadvipras more in our next book on Revolution. For the present, it is enough to say that in order to create a PROUTist society, we must be willing to take on the mantle of a spiritual warrior and encourage everyone to do the same. Our leaders must be women and men from every age, race, nation, and religion who are imbued with the skills and powers of every social psychology. In the absence of a moral leadership, society cannot make true progress; it will only continue to tumble downhill.

To stop the over-accumulation of wealth by the rich, which is responsible for the lack of basic needs for the people, both physical and mental force will be required. It is not permissible that, due to over-accumulation of wealth by the rich, people are forced to become sinners and criminals and wallow in misery or die due to shortages of basic provisions. This cannot continue. There should be a maximum utilization of physical and mental resources and a rational distribution that assures all human beings are provided the opportunity to receive their basic needs. Despite the myth that there is not enough to go around, it has been proven many times that the earth's resources are ample enough to provide all of humanity with their basic needs. The only obstacle is that the tiny oligarchy of the rich has created a system to siphon wealth from working people and now are hoarding it all.

Capitalists and dogmatic-minded people who support destructive geo- and socio-sentiments, do not meet the definition of human beings. They do not listen to reason nor do they use their rationality which defines us as a species. Many current leaders refuse to think or act rationally because by telling lies and by controlling others' emotions, they are able to exploit people for their own self-aggrandizement. Such people are the lowest among us and they do incalculable damage to humanity. According to Mr. Sarkar, "They are to be struck, and those who do the striking are Sadvipras. The striking is to be done with a hammer! They are to be hit not with a hammer, but with a sledge hammer."[216]

The horrendous economic conditions, the anxiety, the depression, and the suicidal tendencies suffered by the common people can no longer be tolerated. This is why it is the duty of spiritual revolutionaries to continually work for the appropriate moment to permanently remove such oppression from society. We must create a path for human progress and make it "straight, clear, and well-constructed."[217]

The elimination of the causes of sin and crime must be a goal of the revolutionary forces. Sin and crime can only be removed when spiritual revolutionaries are ready to fight against the oppressors with an iron will. Unless the capitalist oligarchy is confronted and their power removed by a strong moral leadership, sin and crime will continue to flourish even in a post-capitalist society.

## Party Politics

In a political democracy, party politics stands in the way of human unity. Political parties are formed by different groups, which are defined by different socio-sentiments. Because of party politics, all the refined attributes of the human mind, such as simplicity, humility, and the spirit of service, slowly get destroyed. The group sentiment of the party commands more respect than individual ability. Service to party and self-aggrandizement, rather than service to the people, becomes the primary motivation of politicians. Mass deception becomes the most common expression of party politics and the people are never told the truth.

Instead of rectifying themselves, most politicians justify their ambitions through grandiloquence. They harp on the weaknesses of others and resort to bombastic language that incites one group of people against another. They do this to usurp the seats of government power and remain in office. Under the hypnotic spell of power, politicians easily forget that true statesmanship cannot be acquired by merely mouthing high-sounding slogans from public platforms. They want to barge into every aspect of human existence seeking to control it. While not all politicians act in this way, many do and everyone will have to remain vigilant against this type of politician. So long as the current political ideologies control people's mentality, we will remain under the control of politicians who act in this manner.

Under such circumstances, it is better that honest and benevolent people, who want to promote human welfare, not waste their vital energy in the miasma of politics or in political conflicts. Rather, it is more productive to render social service directly to the people with a steadfast commitment and without any ulterior motive in mind. Progress is quicker at the local level where activists can form social boards to render service to local people and thereby begin to build a new system from the ground up. Regarding mainstream politics, revolutionaries should only focus on enlightening people as to the true intentions of the elites and on fighting for legislation that at the very least keeps the wolf at bay. Democracy cannot work without education. People should be educated to cast their votes for deserving human beings, not for those who simply represent divisive party interests.

In this effort, remember that both Democrats and Republicans are capitalist parties. They both protect the capitalists' right to exploit the people and they both hide the capitalists' role in creating human misery. While the Democrats may have a more progressive domestic platform than the Republicans, both parties are more than happy to create wars abroad to usurp other people's wealth and labor.

## The Limits of Political Democracy

After the rule of the Catholic Church and the monarchies of the Middle Ages were abolished, the government of nation-states gradually changed into republics. The function of the republic was to free people from the whims of the Church and the kings and to establish laws that were more just and egalitarian. It was an impressive leap forward in governance that can be attributed to the growing merchant class of the day, who sought a greater voice in politics. In the beginning, only landowners were allowed to vote but, over time, suffrage was extended to greater numbers of people. This march toward universal suffrage did not, however, curtail the power of the landowners or the merchant class. This is to say that the democratic form of government that was created by the merchant class still serves their class interests today. In modern democratic republics like the United States, people elect government representatives who are chosen by political parties to address their interests. Yet, in order to run their campaigns, these political parties depend on the money of corporations and wealthy sponsors and, as such, are beholding to them once they get their politicians elected. A republic is called a democracy when the people elect the head of government. This is why democracy is called government "of the people, for the people, and by the people." In actuality, however, it is government by representatives of the people who owe their allegiance to the funders of their campaigns rather than the people who voted for them. It is the funders who rule America. Therefore, in the United States we live under an oligarchy and not a democracy.

Under this system, politicians are never held accountable for the promises that they make to the people when they were running their campaigns. This situation will never change under capitalism because it is not in the interest of the oligarchs to change it.

Although we do not want to admit it, democracy in capitalist countries is a farce. The majority of politicians are bought and sold by corporate money and once in office are never held accountable for their campaign promises. Under such circumstances, what is the value of voting for those who do not look after the people's interests and who do not cherish democratic values.[218] In the US, the low percentage of voter turnout is indicative of this situation.

Another problem with US democracy is that the right to vote depends on age. In the United States, we are permitted to vote at the age of twenty-one. This assumes that all of us who are twenty-one or older understand the basic problems of the people and can vote intelligently for those who will best serve the people. In reality, however, many people above the age of twenty-one remain ignorant of the cause or solution to social problems because they lack political consciousness. They are easily manipulated by high-sounding speeches.

Logically, the right of suffrage should not be based on age; it should be vested in those who are educated and politically conscious. Education and proper knowledge is essential for a successful and smooth-running democracy. By political education we mean a fundamental self-knowledge of what we should do to make life better for everyone and for the well-being of the planet. If people were taught and followed a universal ideology, this would make democracy viable. Furthermore, if people controlled the means of production to meet their own basic necessities, no national or global capitalist or politician would ever have the means to exploit them.

Undoubtedly, the greatest flaw in Western democracy is that it only pertains to the political realm and not to the economic realm. Under capitalism there is no, nor will there ever be, economic democracy. Even so, the people genuinely require economic democracy in order to meet their basic needs in a sustainable manner without fear of being unemployed, being fired or finding themselves incapable of paying their bills. Generation after generation, we are led to believe that there is no better system in the world than political democracy. Political democracy only gives people the right to vote for people who do not serve their interests, and it denies us the right to economic independence and self-reliance. Consequently, the unconscionable disparity between the rich and the poor continues to grow, leading to large-scale unemployment, poverty, and wide scale insecurity in society.

During their campaigns, politicians give lip service to the people's dire circumstances, blaming the other party for their plight while genuflecting at the altar of the rich by deflecting the people's attention from the root cause of their constant exploitation. The two party system serves only to divide the people while the rich continue their conquest. As we have seen in Volume Five of *The Untold Story of Western Civilization*,[219] the rich do not identify with the left or the right. They only care who serves them and who does not. They will fund whichever party has the sentiment of the people at the time. When the people get tired of the Democrats for their inaction, the rich fund the Republicans. When the people tire of the inaction of the Republicans, the rich fund the Democrats. We have by now lived under this system of political democracy for generations.

In the US, and almost all countries of the world, the masses lack political consciousness. In such a state, the cunning, erudite politicians continually play on people's sentiments in order to confuse them, while they themselves attain personal power. Consequently, the standard of morality in society continues to decline while honest people are relegated to the background. Moral leaders have less chance to win elections because election results are rigged through corporate financing, intimidation of women and minorities, gerrymandering, voting machine manipulation, and even the use of brute force. In the present democratic system, all sorts of immoral and corrupt practices are unleashed on society. The present system favors the capitalists and relegates our government to the control of immoral and corrupt politicians.

## No Scope for Exploitation

There should be no scope for exploitation in society. If the government, or a political party, is complicit in exploitation, a new movement must be created to safeguard the interests of the exploited people. But as well-intentioned organizers know from experience, to seek social justice for exploited people in a capitalist society by attempting to reform the government, has, by and large, proven to be a waste of time because the governance structure of capitalism primarily exists to protect the legal right of the rich to exploit the poor. The right of the 1% of humanity to exploit the other 99% is the basic rationale for capitalist governments. Capitalist governments do not work for human progress or to seek human unity. As such, they do not deserve public support or the right to exist in the name of the people. Even if a well-meaning politician desires a more equitable distribution of wealth, he or she will try to use the government to support the poor. But even if successful, the fruits of such actions are not long lasting and the money is seldom enough to remove the people's underlying economic anxiety.

Therefore, we should look at creating a new governance system within capitalist countries. The same can be said for contemporary communist and theocratic governments. If the people allow such governments to continue in their destructive path, abuses will only continue. This will lead to greater misery for the people and greater destruction of the earth.

## Criminal Justice

In capitalist countries, the criminal codes are framed by politicians according to the desires of their capitalist masters. This is why most men and women in the United States are in prison for "street crimes." These are basically crimes committed in order to survive. The criminal justice system is set up to imprison the poor. By contrast, "white collar criminals" who through fraud and embezzlement steal millions and billions from society are normally acquitted with the payment of a small fine. Of greater significance however, is that most of the sins and crimes of the capitalists are never punishes because there were never any laws created to stop their behavior. Under capitalism, a capitalist can finan-cially destroy the life of a person or their family or the entire population of a country and its all just part of a good day's work. As for the poor, they are punished for stealing a loaf of bread. Punishment of the poor, rather than rehabilitation, is the general norm. Thus the present-day legal codes are not written in the interest of the people. They are not based upon humanitarian values. This is why rational people should never follow legal codes blindly, but only follow the cardinal human principles of Universalism.

Political democracy promises peace, prosperity and equality, but, in reality, creates a venal and morally bankrupt ruling class that is above the law. It encourages exploitation and throws common people into an abyss of depression and anxiety.

In order for "a government of, by, and for the people" to succeed, there must be economic democracy so that economic power is vested in the hands of the local people and the minimum requirements of life are guaranteed to all. This is the only way to ensure the well-being of the people.

Under PROUT, economic and political powers are intentionally divided. Just as the separation of church and state was key to the founding of the United States, so the separation of economic power and political power is key to the founding of a post-capitalist society. Progressive Socialism advocates political centralization and economic decentralization. While political power will be vested with moral leadership at every level of government, up to and including a global confederation, economic power, on the other hand, will always be vested in the local people. This is the only way to ensure that local people cannot be manipulated from afar and their labor and resources drained to serve a global ruling class. The principal goal of today's spiritual revolutionaries is to remove all the impediments and obstacles which prevent the economic needs of the people from being met.[220]

## The Question of Revolution

Even as well-intentioned liberals and progressives work domestically to keep the wolf at bay by contesting the continual attacks of the capitalist system against the welfare of people and the planet, PROUTists realize that progressive socialism can never be created by reform movements. Rather it can only be established by two methods: (1) intellectual revolution and (2) physical revolution.

Intellectual revolution involves the propagation of ideals, but to materialize these ideals will take years, decades, perhaps even centuries. Suffering humanity cannot wait for this. Therefore, intellectual revolution is only possible in theory. When the welfare of a majority of people can no longer be fulfilled within a capitalist democratic framework, a physical revolution is sure to take place. Such a revolution, although undesirable, is inevitable and irreversible. This is because the masses of people will have nothing left to lose, and will revolt with or without leadership.

For moral leaders and Proutists, physical revolution denotes a fight against any and all factors, which go against the principles of public welfare. As such, these progressive socialists will inaugurate a new era of revolution against all sorts of divisive tendencies, narrow isms, and social evils. If a country's laws are not strong enough to rectify the conduct of rich and powerful immoralists, the Proutists will help local people create the systems to meet their own basic needs, establish economic freedom, and eliminate capitalist exploitation.

Due to narrow groupisms that currently preoccupy the majority of people, we suffer numberless social injustices every day. A new governance structure is required to address these injustices. We cannot depend upon the existing government structures of capitalism, communism, fascism, or theocratic totalitarianism to solve our problems because these structures are based upon faulty premises and create more harm than good. In every case, power is taken from the hands of local people and placed in the hands of a ruling elite whose intention is to control the people for their own self-aggrandizement. While we must move as quickly as we can to create a new government system, Mr. Sarkar, repeatedly emphasizes that:

> Even if there is no acceleration in our speed, we will have to bring with us all those people who are moving slowly or who have lagged behind. If, while moving with all, my speed decreases somewhat, this will have to be

accepted. But we must move together; this is the Supreme Truth. Those who wish to move together with all require sufficient physical and psychic strength. In addition to that, if they really wish to move collectively, they must possess some additional strength as well. That is why I tell you that you must not be like average people: you will have to be above average. It is not enough to move alone, you will have to take others with you, and for that you will have to acquire additional strength. You must prepare yourself accordingly.[221]

# The Goal of Progressive Socialism

The politics of progressive socialism (PROUT) at this time is largely informal, but in time it will also include formal politics. Even so, its mission differs from all other political parties or political philosophies. Progressive socialism consists of the policies and actions required to create an ideal society for all. In this mission, it seeks to accomplish two primary goals: (1) to ensure that every human being on earth is able to secure their basic needs of food, shelter, clothing, health care, and education at the local level and (2) that this is achieved in an environmentally sustainable manner. To accomplish this, also implies that the needs of all species and all natural systems must also be met. The first goal cannot be met without caring for the natural world in which we live.

Let us now look at the factors that are required to assure the success of such a society.

## Common Ideals

Currently, human beings are governed by the administrations of nation-states. The legal standing of these existing nations is based upon such factors as: (1) common history; (2) common tradition; (3) common territory; (4) common race; (5) common faith; (6) common language; (7) common sentiments; or (8) common ideals. Although these are relative factors and may not all be present in every nation, they remain the considerations that currently justify a nation's standing within the world community. From a Proutist perspective, the eighth factor, common ideals, is the most essential factor in the formation of a Proutist socio-economy and government. These ideals include life, liberty, and the pursuit of happiness, but the highest ideal for progressive socialists is the ideal of Cosmic Inheritance. This ideal holds that the universe is the creation of the Supreme Entity and, therefore, the ownership of the universe lies with the Supreme Entity. Human beings and other species have the right to enjoy and utilize the Creation, but we cannot declare that anything is our own possession. Everything is our common inheritance. None of it can be "owned" by any group, corporation, government, or individual. This is to say that under progressive socialism, private property will not exist. Personal property will exist, but the rights of land use and decisions about the utility of resources will be determined by the people within the local community (Samaj) in accordance with the goal of optimizing the living conditions of the whole.

Capitalism is a total violation of this ideal. Capitalists seize, or steal everything they can, including land, water, air, minerals, forests, species, human labor, etc. and "privatize," these resources to increase their wealth by which they continue to exploit human beings and the environment even more. Communists and current socialists, for their part, want to control resources using the state as the apparatus of ownership. This is no better than capitalism because the communist party controls the state and, for all intents and purposes, "owns" its resources. Theocracies that are run by priest classes want to own resources in the name of their religion. It is the same situation. All these systems are tragically flawed because none seek the welfare of humanity as a whole. They seek only to enrich the capitalist class, the communist party, or the ruling priest class.

The acceptance of the ideal of Cosmic Inheritance will allow us to unify our economic intentions across different countries and utilize natural and human resources for the common good. Proutists will promote this ideal within every action performed for the general welfare. As human society becomes more unified, humanity will eventually come under the banner of this common spiritual ideal.

**Six Factors to Assure Social Progress**

In order to create a strong society that supports the well being of the people, numerous factors are needed. According to progressive socialism, the following six are the most important of them. As a society incorporates these factors, the more sustainable it becomes and the greater the well-being of humans and the planet. These six factors constitute the ideological infrastructure of a progressive socialist society.

Universal Ideology

As a human species and human society, we require a universal ideology to guide our individual and collective behavior. Much of our energy is currently misdirected due to ignorance about ourselves and the destination towards which we are moving. We are unable to move together given the divisive political ideologies based upon group sentiment. In each country, the ruling class uses these political ideologies and organizations to divide and keep the people oppressed. This causes our nations to move about like rudderless boats that are always crashing into each other. For the first time in history, we now have a clearly articulated universal ideology with which to build a cooperative human society.

Intuitional Science

The purpose of intuitional science is to transmute physical energy into mental energy and then into spiritual consciousness. The practice is a psycho-biological process by which we are able to develop a healthy body and a healthy mind and ultimately a loving consciousness. The manner in which we accomplish this process is the subject of intuitional science. It entails practices related to diet, breathing, rest, sense withdrawal, self-discipline, meditation on the Divine, selfless service, and devotion. Through intuitional practices, we reduce our attachment and dependence on material pleasures and engage in more subtle pursuits that bring us closer to the Cosmic Entity and to a state of bliss. Without intuitional practice, it is virtually impossible to develop a clear conscience or to maintain the inspiration required to struggle against the forces of negativity. Only by intuitional practice can we achieve human progress individually and collectively. Only by intuitional practice can we create Sadvipras.

## Social Outlook

The third factor that we need is a universal social outlook. All living creatures in this manifest universe are the children of the same Cosmic Entity. As such, we are bound in a matrix of symbiotic relationships with the earth, all species, and with all human beings. They are us; we are they. This is the central spirit of a universal social outlook. Without this feeling of love and respect for all beings, a socio-economic theory will only regress to the perpetration of self-interest. As all human beings have experienced, without a universal social outlook, the strong perpetrate atrocities and injustices on the weak while powerful groups exploit powerless ones. Under such circumstances, it becomes the duty of virtuous people to wage war on the oppressors but to do so we must be organized. It is of no spiritual value to sit quietly in church pews, waiting indefinitely for moral preaching to bring results. All virtuous people, regardless of their religions, will have to become united and fight without rest for the common good.[222]

## Socio-Economic Theory

The fourth factor required by our new society is a sound socio-economic theory. Before we begin the work of creating a new society, we should know what kind of socio-economic structures that we want to build and how resources and wealth will be distributed in such a society. If this knowledge is lacking, we won't be able to build a firm foundation on which to construct our new society. PROUT provides the necessary theory and practice for this work.

## Body of Knowledge

The fifth factor for the welfare of our society is to have a body of authoritative teachings. Our society should have a body of literature, film, drama, video, etc., that inspires us and elevates us within all areas of human pursuit, including, spiritual, psychological, physical, cultural, environmental, economic, political, historic, scientific, environmental, etc. There is also a need for the company of elevated persons, master teachers, in all spheres of life to educate us about the qualities of existence, progress, and bliss. This is a role to be assumed by the great minds of our society, including entrepreneurs, managers, teachers, scientists, writers, artists, military strategists and tacticians, etc.

## A Spiritual Teacher and Moral Leaders

The last factor is for society to have a leader who understands the needs of society, who serves as an example of its ideals, who embodies the principles of Universalism, who is God-realized and who provides a model of fearless action. The leader can be acknowledged, chosen, selected, or elected. In the absence of a leader of this caliber in the flesh, we will have to create boards of our most disciplined and knowledgeable spiritual warriors to function as our leadership.

The social structure of progressive socialism depends on these six factors for success. A society, which possesses these six factors, will last forever and will continually produce good leaders and an inspired people.

From ancient times, many societies and civilizations have come into existence. Their strength lasted only to the degree to which they included these six factors of success. For example, the Roman civilization was considerably developed. Yet it lacked a universal social outlook. There was no feeling of fraternity or equality. The slave system was rampant and human feelings were on the wane. Furthermore, the lack of a proper socio-economic theory generated a kind of fascist mentality in them. Those rolling in luxury and adverse to labor became indolent. They eventually were defeated by a stronger and more strenuous force.[223] The present American empire also suffers from a lack of a universal social outlook and a balanced socio-economic theory. It too will fall, not to foreign invasion, as did Rome, but to its own corruption and environmental destruction. This will eventually trigger a revolution by its own people and the people of the world who have become economically enslaved to the US banks and corporations.

In the future, for want of these six factors, the extinction of nation-states is sure to happen. But where these six factors are present, where the movement is towards universalism and the Cosmic Entity, the people will triumph and create a human society for the entire human race. [224]

## Government from the Ground Up (Samaj)

Because a political system based on competing nation-states has led to world wars and economic depressions and has proven catastrophic for humanity and the planet, we require a new political system if our intention is to meet the basic needs of all human beings in a sustainable manner. Such a system will never depend upon international bankers and national governments but must be developed and controlled by local people and operate from the ground up.

A local socio-economy in a progressive socialist system is called a samaj. Samaj means a group of people who are moving together toward a common goal and who are willing to stand up for each other.[225] A samaj is not an abstract entity. Rather, it defines a socio-economic unit and therefore constitutes the base for socio-economic planning. When local people want to stabilize their lives by working in harmony with nature and each other, they will need to organize themselves into a socio-economic unit. These units may coincide with existing political boundaries or they may not. It depends on what the local people want.

It is important to remember that the fundamental understanding of samaj participants is that everything comes from the Cosmic Entity and everyone is moving along the same path towards the supreme culminating point. Therefore, circumstances should be created to give everybody the feeling that they have a future and that their children have a future.

Regarding the psychology of samaj members, Mr. Sarkar says:

> Some may have moved far ahead; some may have
> lagged behind. Some may be unable to walk due to pain
> in their legs. Some may have fallen on their faces. Those
> who do not even care to look after their companions

trailing behind them are not worthy to be called members of society. The proper thing is for all members of
the society to move in unison; and while moving together, each member should feel a responsibility for every other member of society.[226]

A samaj will be built at the local level by local organizers and led by
those who are imbued with moral integrity and who have dedicated
their lives to the Supreme. In other words, the effort will be led by people
who are the most committed to the welfare of others. The purpose of a
samaj is to make local people self-reliant in the meeting of their basic
needs. As the samaj movement expands and the pool of moral leaders
expands, they will begin to select representatives from among themselves
to serve on local boards. These boards will be responsible for planning
and organizing the meeting of people's basic needs.

Some characteristics which typically influence people to identify
themselves as a samaj and work together are: the same economic
problems and potentialities, a common sentimental legacy, common
customs, common cultural expression, similar geographical features,
etc. This is to say that a samaj is not only a geographic area but is also
a socio-economic group. The fundamental scope of these groups is
social, cultural, and economic, but not religious, racial, or linguistic.
People within a samaj must work to overcome their narrow sentiments.
This will be easier to do when everyone is working for the same goal,
in cooperation with each other.

Samajs or socio-economic units are built on the principles of economic decentralization and economic democracy. These are the means
to allow the local people to obtain all the requirements necessary for
their physical, psychic, and spiritual progress. More will be said about
these local socio-economic units in the next chapter.

A samaj that is led by spiritual revolutionaries is called a sadvipra
samaj. It is a society created for the benefit of all through relentless
selfless service and spiritual practices on the part of its leaders. In a
sadvipra samaj, people voluntarily choose to work together to provide
the minimum necessities for all community members, as well as to share
common feelings of joys and sorrows, and to struggle collectively against
wrongs and injustices. The sentiment of a sadvipra samaj is, "These are

my people and I commit myself to their welfare and happiness." People who live in the geographic boundaries of a samaj but do not choose to participate in its welfare, will in time become outsiders and it may be necessary to protect the resources of the local community from being exploited by such people.

One may theoretically object to the policy of giving social boards the authority to select their own leadership on the grounds that all people should have voting rights in the election of such leaders. After all, this world is the common inheritance of all, and every human being has the right to enjoy and utilize all the physical, mental, and spiritual resources. The position of progressive socialism, however, is that just because everybody has the individual right to enjoy everything, it does not follow that everybody has the individual right to run the government of a country. For the good and the welfare of the people in general, it is not fitting to leave the onus of the administration in the hands of all. We have already discussed the drastic shortcomings of such an approach. It must be remembered that moral leaders are not a closed class. Anyone can become a leader if they are willing to steadfastly serve others. Obviously, the more moral leaders there are, the better for everyone. As such, sadvipras will want to create as many sadvipras as possible. They will want to see everyone become a sadvipra. Rule by those who act in the interest of the whole is the only solution to the problem that plagues the current system of democracy. [227]

Progressive socialists will accept only leaders who have been involved in the process to improve the welfare of the people in the samaj and who have earned the faith and trust of the local people. When progressive socialism becomes established within the framework of democracy, then and only then will democracy be successful because it will include both political and economic democracy.

It must be understood from the beginning that rule by moral leadership is not a power that can be seized by forces or idle political campaign promises. Rather, it will only come about through the systematic and rational application of progressive socialism by many highly intelligent people who include warriors, intellectuals, and business people in their ranks. Under progressive socialism, leaders are not appointed by political parties; rather they are approved by the local people because they do not seek personal profit but rather the people's welfare. It is, therefore, the duty of the first wave of leaders, those who serve in the vanguard of a post-capitalist society, to educate the local people as to why building a local economy is their only solution to a stable local economy and a just living wage.[228] This process can only happen face to face at the local level. As such, the leaders should make an all out effort to raise the consciousness of the people as soon as possible.

This can be accomplished by:

1. Starting study circles and popularizing the ideology of universalism. This is the first phase of ideological education and is directed at the moralists, the future leaders of a new society.

2. In phase two, a socio-economic platform is created by local people and the general population of the area is mobilized to support it.

3. Simultaneously, the progressive socialists will begin to form social boards that will develop land-based projects to meet the people's basic needs. These projects may be local farms or food buying clubs, building shelters for those in need, establishing local wellness clinics, setting up classes to learn basic skills and strategies, etc. Members of the social boards need not run for election but will educate the people as to the most respectable politicians running for office at the local level and will encourage the people to vote for them.

4. Once a local socio-economic unit is well established and local boards are in operation, a Prout party, with the support of the local people, can begin to run candidates for public office in local governments. It should be remembered, however, that progressive socialism cannot thrive in a capitalist democratic framework. It can only thrive when the progressive socialists have begun to put a local economy on the ground to meet the people's needs. This can only occur in an economic democracy, which is the subject of the final chapter of this book.[229]

# The Role of the Local Government in a Progressive Socialist Society

As the socio-economic unit becomes functional, its local government will provide executive, legislative, and judicial functions, primarily as they pertain to the production, use, and distribution of resources for the meeting of basic needs.

The samaj government is not the same as the local governments that exist under capitalism, which must abide by state and federal legislation, including the rules and regulations that prohibit the growth of local businesses. Rather the PROUT local government develops alongside the mainstream government and acts only for the benefit of those people who are consciously committed to creating a local self-reliant socio-economy. No one is to be excluded from a samaj who desires to work for the benefit of the local people. The PROUT government will follow the recommendations of the local people who have developed their own economic Master Plan and who have supported the planning boards in its development. The local PROUT government will then facilitate and oversee the process that has been created by the community to achieve its goals. The government is responsible for balancing all the economic interests of the local people so that all local people eventually have their basic needs met in a sustainable manner.

In time, as more local people join the PROUT socio-economy, the PROUT government will take on additional roles. It will assume the protection of the local natural environment—the minerals, materials, soil, water, air, plants, animals, etc., upon which the people depend for raw materials to meet their basic needs. Unless we act within the guidelines of nature laws and the ability of resources to be recycled or reproduced, we will not be able to create a sustainable society.

A third role of a samaj government will eventually be to manage key industries. Key industries are those industries upon which all other occupations depend. For example, energy, water, raw materials, and education may be considered key industries. The people can determine what the key industries are in their local economies. The control of these industries should never be in the hands of private capitalists. Nor should they be in the hands of government exclusively. Rather, initially, they should be in the hands of a local quasi-governmental body composed of sadvipras and PROUTists who are members of the local samaj. Some of these sadvipras should be active in local government and others in local organizations. Key industries will operate on a no-profit, no loss basis to allow all other sectors of the economy to increase the purchasing capacity of the local people. By helping to reduce production costs, goods will become cheaper and the purchasing capacity of the local people will increase.

In addition to the above roles, the governance structure can address any other issues that the people may desire.

## Guidelines for Governments in a Progressive Socialist Society

As we develop our post-capitalist society, our governance structure will grow from the local level and eventually expand to the global level. Our decentralized socio-economies which are geared to meeting local basic needs will in time mature and grow, but the economic decisions regarding the meeting of local basic needs will never migrate outside the locality. The local people will always be in control of meeting their own basic needs. This "basic needs" component of the larger economy we call the People's Economy. The People's Economy is always controlled by the local people. This is the only way to ensure that local people will always be in control of their lives and not fall prey to outside forces.

As the local socio-economies grow, they will naturally begin to link with bordering socio-economies in order to increase efficiencies, improve infrastructure, protect the environment, and trade certain goods and services. While control of the economy will always remain local, the political structure will expand beyond the local level. A decentralized economy, coupled with a centralized political system, constitutes the basic structure of a universal human society. Such a structure will move us beyond divisive isms, as well as ensure the best use of the earth's resources and the care of planetary life-support systems.

As the government structure of progressive socialism grows from the local level to the state level and ultimately to a global level, it will always follow certain guidelines. These are:

## Meet the Minimum Necessities of Life

The first and foremost factor, as discussed, is that the minimum necessities of human society will be guaranteed to all. It is the role of the local economy to meet the needs of the people living within that socio-economic unit. This is to say that the minimum wage must be equal to the purchasing capacity required to meet one's basic needs.[230]

## Promote a Common Philosophy of Life

The second factor for successful governance is a common philosophy of life. People require a common ideology to move in unison. Unless we take responsibility at the local level to promote a universal ideology there will be little chance of social synthesis as we proceed to link with others. In the absence of a universal worldview, in-fighting between human beings will continue without opposition. Hence a common philosophy is essential.

Among the different political perspectives, we find that the cruder the philosophy, the less social cohesion it is able to generate. This is the lesson we have learned from capitalism, communism, fascism, and religious totalitarianism. When people unite for a subtle motive (i.e. a universal ideology), their worldview becomes subtler and social ties become stronger. A universal philosophy must be centered on the Cosmic Entity because He/She is the nucleus of all. It connects all. Only by ideating on such an Entity can we materialize permanent peace and tranquility on this planet. Without it, we will not succeed.

## Encode Universalism in Constitutional Law

The third factor of good governance is that the ideology of Universalism be encoded in constitutional law. Historically, as we have seen, constitutions and legal structures were based upon local traditions and the local people's belief in virtue and vice. Under a constitution based on Universalism, our legal structure will engage in a never-ending process to minimize the differences between sin and crime and between different moral codes. If the goal is universal welfare for all, the law should be one for the entire world

## Develop a Common Code of Justice

The fourth factor in PROUT governance is a common code of justice. Our constitution will address the need for such a code.[231] Our laws and regulations will be based upon principles of rehabilitation rather than punishment. Even in committing a heinous crime, no one should be subject to a death sentence, because as human beings, we are incapable of understanding another's motivation. This is the role reserved for the Cosmic Entity.

# Morality and Cardinal Human Principles

Today morality is a product of groupism thought. Every group comes up with its own definition of what it means to act in a moral way. Morality is thus dynamic and not static. Even within the group, it can easily break down under circumstantial pressure and the morality of a person may disappear at any moment. It cannot be said with any certainty that the person who has resisted a bribe of twenty dollars would also be able to resist the temptation of two thousand dollars. This is why morality is not the goal. It cannot be said that the ultimate aim of human life is not to take a bribe or commit a theft. What is desirable is that the tendency to commit theft should be eliminated.

Universal morality, not groupism morality, is the foundation of progressive socialism. While moral conduct is not the culminating point of the spiritual march, it is the foundation and its ultimate purpose is to attain Oneness with the Cosmic Entity where no desire to take a bribe or steal exists and all tendencies toward ego gratification disappear. It should be clearly understood, however, that morality is only an effort to lead a well-knit life. It is not spiritual attainment.

Universal morality is an attribute of a good citizen and it is the starting point on the spiritual path. This is its value. A universal morality is benefitted by performing intuitional practices, which creates harmony between oneself and one's environment. Those who do not follow a universal morality should never be allowed to become revolutionary leaders because they will only bring harm to themselves and to others.

Insofar as the concept of virtue and vice is concerned, progressive socialism simply states that "Doing good to others is virtue and doing harm to others is vice." Or "That which leads us to the Cosmic Entity is virtue and that which leads us away is vice." The central characteristic of virtue is to serve the collective interest and to accelerate the progress of the collective body. The central characteristic of vice, whether it be called sin or crime, is to slow social progress by exploiting people in the name of personal profit or the collective interest.

Human existence is an interpenetration of three dimensions: physical, mental, and spiritual. In this interaction, we have to prioritize our actions at every step along the way. To guide us in this endeavor we have cardinal human principles which are of primary importance for human progress toward the Cosmic Entity. The moral code of progressive socialism is based on cardinal human principles. Cardinal means "of basic importance". The importance of cardinal human principles in forming a strong society can be understood if we look at the mentality of people.

As explained in Chapter One, the great majority of people cannot transcend the limits of their physical existence. Meeting their basic requirements is their daily obsession. Worldly pleasures such as food, sleep, warmth, sex, alcohol, and drugs are their only enjoyment. They embody all that is animalistic in nature and remain tormented by carnal desires. Usually, the subtle feelings of life, the subtle expressions and practices, are beyond their reach.

Other people are more concerned with the enjoyment of their minds. They are guided to act within the guidelines of reason. By virtue of their mental clarity, they create art and music, architecture, gardens, scientific experiments, etc. They express the finer human feelings of mercy, sympathy, compassion, friendship, concern for others, etc.

Still others are concerned with their spirit. They believe that the mind flows for the sole purpose of attaining the Infinite, and hence they focus their energies on the contemplation of the Cosmic Entity. These are the spiritual aspirants. Drawn by the magnetic attraction of the Cosmic

Consciousness they speed forward and reach the stage which marks the end of mental limitations and the beginning of spirituality. Everything that they think, do, or say for the benefit of the people is an act of service to the Divine Entity.

According to Mr. Sarkar:

> At that stage [the meeting point of the mental and spiritual strata] one is no longer a human being, one is a veritable god. It is the duty of every person to reach this confluence of the mental and spiritual strata. It is the pinnacle of human progress—the point where humanity ceases to exist as it merges in divine beatitude. The culminating point of animality is the commencement of humanity. The highest peak of human progress is the beginning of divine bliss. Where animality ends, humanity begins, where humanity ends, divinity begins. The meeting point of the highest attainment of humanity and the blossoming of divinity is the base on which the cardinal human principles are established.[232]

From this perspective, cardinal human principles are the most important of all human principles. As such, only a universal moral code based upon these principles is able to create balance and progress within society and between society and the individual. Cardinal principles, according to universal ideology, take the form of certain observances and abstinences.

These observances and abstinences, therefore, constitute the moral code of a Proutist society. They are the tools by which human beings achieve self-control and social cohesion. No individual can make progress without self-control. And collectively, no samaj can make progress without a ceaseless struggle for the welfare of every one of its members. The ceaseless struggle for all-around welfare is a collective responsibility. Those who provide leadership in the social struggle must be strongly established in the observances (yama) and abstinences (niyama) of this universal moral code. If our leaders are not established in these principles, they will weaken and abandon the struggle. They will lose their way in the heat of battle. Those who maintain the struggle until victory is achieved are the true spiritual revolutionaries, the true sadvipras of society. They are the champions of cardinal human principles.

Spiritual revolutionaries are created by a continuous endeavor to expand one's consciousness. The ceremonial recitation of holy scriptures, being of noble birth, or making mountains of money, are of no interest to Cosmic Consciousness. The important thing is to continue spiritual practice. While being a moral person is not the end of the spiritual path, nonetheless, human society as a whole cannot advance without a moral base.[233]

## Moral Observances

The moral observances (yama) consists of five principles: Seeing everything as God (Brahmacarya), Discriminating truthfulness (Satya), Non-harming (Ahimsá), Non-stealing (Asteya), and Living simply (Aparigraha).[234]

### Seeing Everything as Cosmic Consciousness (Brahmacarya)

The meaning of Brahmacarya is "to remain attached to the Cosmic Entity." Whenever people work or think of doing work, they look upon the object with which they come in contact as a crude finite entity. Because of their constant desire for control over matter, their consciousness becomes crude. To practice Brahmacarya is to treat the objects with which one comes in contact, as different expressions of Cosmic Consciousness and not as crude forms. By means of such an ideation, even though the mind wanders from one object to another, it stays attached to the Cosmic feeling. As a result of this, physical work is converted into spiritual work and spirituality replaces materialism.

### Discriminating Truthfulness (Satya)

Satya means the proper use of mind and words with the intention of welfare. It has no English synonym. The word "true" or "truth" in English means to "state the fact." The spiritual warrior is not asked to follow the path of stating the fact. He or she is asked to practice Satya.

In the process of living on earth we must deal with our surroundings. Humans are rational beings: we possess, in varying degrees, the capability to do what is necessary and good for humanity. In the realm of spirituality, such thoughts, words, or actions are called Satya.

Mr. Sarkar gives an example of using Satya instead of "stating the fact":

> For example, a person rushes to you for shelter. You do not know whether he is guilty or not, or perhaps you know for certain that he is not guilty. He is followed by a ruffian bent on torturing him. If this terrified man seeks refuge in your house, and then the ruffian comes and asks you regarding his whereabouts, what should you do? By adhering to rta or truth you would inform the ruffian of his whereabouts. Then if he is murdered, will you not be responsible for this murder? Your mistake may have resulted in the murder of an innocent person. By adhering to rta or truth you become indirectly guilty of this heinous crime. What would be your duty if you followed the correct interpretation of Satya? It would be not to reveal the whereabouts of the person and rather to misguide the aggressor so that the refugee may safely return home.[235]

## Non-Harming (Ahimsá)

Ahimsa means not inflicting pain or hurt on anybody by thought, word or action. Some people mistake this principle to mean that it is not permissible to defend oneself or one's loved ones. Some think it means not using a plow to farm because it kills insects; or that one is not allowed to swat a mosquito even as it sucks your blood. This irrational perspective is against human nature. Even the act of breathing involves the death of numberless microbes. Does this mean we should stop breathing to follow Ahimsa?

Today, the popular definition of ahimsa is non-violence or non-application of force. This too has not been thought out. In all actions of life, whether small or big, the mind progresses by surmounting opposing forces. Life evolves through the medium of force—thesis versus antithesis.

The champions of non-violence are often the self-interested exploiters themselves who use hypocrisy and lies to turn their victims into passive sheep. If the people of one country are conquered by another country using brute force, should they remain passive and non-violent? No, they must use force to regain their freedom. Such a use of force may be physical or intellectual and as a result, both the body and mind of the conquerors may be hurt. The best that can be said of using non-violence as a moral principle is that the leaders of the oppressed believe they must wait until they are stronger to be victorious against their enemy.

Does it make sense to demand that the police or the army be non-violent? These organizations are necessary for the governance of a country. If these organizations do not use force even in case of necessity, their existence would be meaningless.

Those who are not adequately equipped to oppose an evil-doer should make every effort to gain power and then make the proper use of their power. If an individual lacks the ability to resist evil, or does not even try to resist evil, but declares himself to be non-violent to hide his weakness, it may be politically expedient, but it will not protect the sanctity of righteousness.

Anyone who, by the use of brute force, tries to take possession of your property, harms your spouse or children, comes with a weapon to murder you, sets fire to your house, or wants to take your life by administering poison, is an evil force and must be fought against. If any nation wants to occupy all or part of another country, the use of physical force against such invading forces is not against the principle of ahimsá. It is right action.

Ahimsa depends upon one's intentions. If one desires to harm others with the thought of cruelty, revenge, or murder, it is against ahimsa. If it is to create justice or righteousness or protect the defenseless it is not against ahimsa. The use of force against an aggressor is valorous and desisting from the use of force is cowardice. Wise people will assess their strength before indulging in violent conflict with a powerful aggressor; otherwise, if a fight is started without acquiring proper strength, injustice may triumph. But, if you find that the aggressor is bent on destroying you, whether you use force or not, it would be proper to die at least giving a blow to the best of your might without waiting to assemble the adequate forces.

It is not right to pardon aggressors before correcting their nature because this will only encourage their continued injustice.

A parent correcting a child does not violate the principle of ahimsá because there is no intention of causing harm or pain to the child. The purpose of such punishment is not to make the child shed tears; the purpose of such action is only corrective. Whether it is a thief or an exploiter or a friend or anybody else, any action with a true spirit of rectification will not go against ahimsa, no matter how harsh it may seem.

**Non-Stealing (Asteya)**

Asteya means non-stealing. Stealing may be of four types:

> 1. Physical theft of any material object. Ordinarily, those persons who steal material objects are called thieves. But thieves are not the only people who steal your wealth or resources. Whatever is taken by brute force, strength of intellect, or financial cunning, whether it is money or goods, amounts to theft, because behind such actions there is the intention of taking others' property deceitfully.

> 2. Psychic theft is also planning to take material objects. Only the fear of law or of adverse criticism prevents one from doing the action physically. Even so, there are negative karmic consequences for committing psychic theft.

> 3. Depriving others of their due physically. Even if you do not take possession of what belongs to others, but you deprive others of what is their due, you become responsible for their loss. This is also stealing. For example, you may take a subway train ride without buying a token. You do not directly steal money from the department of transportation, but you deprive it of its due.

> 4. Depriving others of their due mentally. If you do not actually deprive anybody of what is justifiably their due, but you plan in your mind to do so, that too amounts

to theft. Even to do so mentally carries karmic repercussions.

All these tendencies to steal are contradictory to the code of asteya. In
many cases, even educated people act knowingly against the principle of
asteya or do not want to accept that petty stealing violates this principle.

There are people who believe they are moralists because they won't
cheat any individual but consider it okay to cheat organizations, businesses, or the government. In the course of revolution, one will by necessity need to redistribute the wealth of the rich that was taken from the
poor, but to think of cheating someone for one's personal gain beyond
meeting one's basic needs is against asteya.

## Living Simply (Aparigraha)

Aparigraha is non-indulgence in the enjoyment of such amenities and
comforts of life as are superfluous for the preservation of life. We all
have basic needs like food, clothing, etc. It is also necessary to provide
for old age and have some resources for one's dependents. Therefore, a
number of factors have to be taken into consideration to determine an
individual's basic necessity for the preservation of life. While different
individuals will have different needs, it is possible, nonetheless for society
to set a standard for minimum necessities.

For example, the laws of society can dictate that no one shall accumulate more than a certain amount of money or no one shall possess
more than a certain number of houses or no one shall be owner of more
than a certain amount of property. But it is not possible for the society
to fix the minimum limit in all spheres. Big eaters may eat too much.
Sick people may spend too much on health care. This is why it will be
better if the individual and the society can work together cooperatively
to establish aparigraha. Those items of personal requirement, which are
left to the discretion of the individual, generally depend on his or her
concept of happiness and comforts. These should always be considered
in relation to the ability of the samaj to meet the basic needs of all.

Aparigraha will also change according to time, person, and place.
For example, one person may easily bear certain physical hardships,

while another person, under the same circumstances, may possibly die. Under these circumstances the latter requires more comforts of life than the former to remove his or her difficulty and this will not go against aparigraha. The time and place must also be considered in order for society to maintain the principle of aparigraha.

We can say that aparigraha is an endless fight to reduce one's own objects of comforts out of sympathy for the common good, after ensuring that one is able to maintain a balance in the physical, mental, and spiritual lives of themselves and their dependents.

In practicing aparigraha, the objects of pleasure will increase or decrease with person, place, and time; but the definition of aparigraha will be applicable to all persons, in all countries, and at all times. For example, if people are to throw off the shackles of debt imposed upon them by those with a capitalist mentality, they must know how to use material objects wisely. If people violate the cardinal human principles and incur debt due to their extravagance and, as a result, must approach society for relief, this will not be beneficial. Therefore, if a society is duty-bound to give relief to individuals by collective efforts, then the collective must have some say over the conduct of individuals regarding their expenditures. Not to consult anybody at the time of spending money, but to ask for help from all when in debt cannot be encouraged.

To put the above cardinal observances into practice in society, we must give permission to each other to speak openly about our weaknesses and not take such feedback as disrespect or as a slight. Basically the moral observances of progressive socialism are simple tenets—see everything as God, be aware of what you say to people, don't harm people, do not steal from people, and live simply.

## Moral Abstinences

The moral abstinences (niyama) consist of five principles – Cleanliness (Shaoca), Penance (Tapah), Contentment of Mind (Santosa), Understanding Spiritual Topics (Svadhyaya), and Taking the Shelter of God (Iishwara Pranadana).

## Cleanliness (Shaoca)

Shaoca means purity or cleanliness. It means abstaining from that which causes filth or impurities from affecting oneself or one's household. It includes both internal and external cleanliness. External cleanliness includes keeping your body, your clothes, your house, your neighborhood etc., clean and ready to use. Internal cleanliness, or purity, means keeping the mind clean of negative emotions like jealousy, greed, or vanity.

If the impurity of selfishness is making the mind weak, it has to be removed by the force of intuitional practice. People who are tempted by material objects should practice an opposite indulgence. Those who are greedy for money should form the habit of charity. Those who are angry or egoistic should cultivate the habit of being polite. Only selfless service to humanity and the effort to view the world with a universal outlook can cleanse the mind.

## Peace of Mind (Santosa)

Santośa means to maintain a state of mental ease. It requires one to abstain from running after finite pleasures. The longer one lives, the objects of enjoyment keep increasing in number and abstraction and this is why one's mental flow never gets any rest. Achieving the desired objects may give one pleasure for a short time, but that will not last long. The mind will again run in pursuit of new objects, leaving behind the objects already tasted. This is how the mind works when goaded by finite objects.

To remain content requires a mental effort to keep aloof from external allurements. There are two effective methods to detach the mind from such tendencies; one is auto-suggestion and the other outer-suggestion. If anyone concentrates on the opposite of their desires for finite objects, their nature is bound to change. This is auto-suggestion. A change in one's nature is also brought about if some external agent repeatedly conveys such ideals to one's ears. This is called outer-suggestion. This is why good company is essential.

In our effort to simplify our desires, it is not acceptable for us to forgo our right to self-preservation or our legitimate duties in life. We have to go on fighting with concerted efforts for the establishment of our rights. But we must also try to avoid wasting our physical and mental energy under the lure of material objects.

## Self-Sacrifice (Tapah)

There is no word for tapah in English. A substitute word is penance, but this is not quite accurate. Penance is not the issue. There is only one purpose behind the practice of tapah and that is to shoulder the suffering of others to make them happy, to free them from grief, and to give them comfort. Tapah means to abstain from wanting a reward for helping others.

Tapah is more than selfless intention. It requires physical work. To serve the sick who are in great pain is tapah. But to serve them with the goal of getting something back is not tapah. The practice of tapah leads to mental expansion. Those who perform it are the servants of humanity and the service rendered by them is their spiritual practice.

The practice of tapah yields great spiritual progress, but we also have to be circumspect in our service. We cannot let our work be misused by exploiters who want to use it to serve their own selfish ends. By unconsciously serving the exploiters, we deny our service to the real sufferers who truly deserve our help. Therefore, while following the principle of tapah, we should first determine whether the person we are going to serve really needs our service. A general rule is that, in practicing tapah, we should always give consideration to those who are less fortunate than us and not to those who are wealthier. Our responsibility is greater for those who are weaker, poorer, less educated, more ignorant, and downtrodden in comparison to us. To banquet the rich is of no use when we should be giving food to the starving. There is no need to send presents to our superiors when we should be sending medicine and food to the sick. We should not waste our time in flattering the rich; it will yield no result. Rather, we should win the hearts of the underprivileged by our sympathetic behavior and accept them into our company.

**Understanding Spiritual Topics (Svádhyáya)**

Svádhyáya means the clear understanding of any spiritual topic. In days past, students learned their lessons in the hermitage of the rishis, gurus, or religious teachers. Monks and nuns studied in their monasteries and convents. But the circumstances have changed and the term Svádhyáya has lost its meaning with the passage of time.

Nowadays reading religious scriptures without even grasping the meaning is considered to be Svádhyáya. Religious professionals have misguided the public by saying, "It doesn't matter whether you understand the meaning of scriptures or not, you only have to believe what I say." Or they say, "If you cannot find time to read books, simply touch your head to them; or if you have no time to hear religious sermons, light a candle to your favorite saint, or make a monetary offering to the church." Some people are taught to memorize holy books without understanding a word of what they are memorizing.

Svádhyáya means to read or hear a subject, and also to understand its underlying idea otherwise the proper spirit will never be realized. The same words may carry different meanings in different contexts. We have to be vigilant of those with vested interests who want to keep the public away from the true spiritual meaning of the scriptures in order to exploit them. It is necessary to abstain from such misleading attempts by others to control us.

**Seeking the Shelter of Cosmic Consciousness (Iishvara Pranidhána)**

Iishvara means "the controller of this universe." He who controls the thought-waves of this universe is Iishvara. It is another name for the Cosmic Entity.

Pranidhána means to understand clearly or to adopt something as a shelter. Therefore Iishvara pranidhána means to establish oneself in the Cosmic ideal—to accept the Cosmic Entity as the only shelter in life. It means to abstain from placing your faith in anything but God as your ultimate shelter. As Mr. Sarkar says: "Only that entity which neither comes nor goes, which has an unbroken existence from beginningless to endless time, can be your permanent shelter."[236]

Iishvara praṅidhána is completely based on ideation—it is a mental effort in its entirety. God is the subtlest Entity; therefore He/She can be realized only through love and by no other means.

Iishvara praṅidhána can be practiced both individually as well as collectively. In collective Iishvara praṅidhána, the combined mental efforts work together, and so give rise to the expression of higher consciousness in less time. The indomitable mental force aroused as a result of collective Iishvara praṅidhána will help you solve any problem, great or small, on this earth. It is for this reason that we should always be zealous to attend spiritual gatherings regularly. Like all other aspects of spiritual practice, Iishvara praṅidhána should be practiced both alone and collectively.[237]

The five abstinences cited above cover the actions of maintaining cleanliness, serving others selflessly, maintaining peace of mind, understanding the meaning of spiritual topics, and placing oneself in the security of the Divine Consciousness. When combined with the five observances, they constitute the cardinal human principles and the moral code of progressive socialism. All government structures, their constitutions, laws, and codes will be based on these cardinal human principles in order to best serve people, contribute to their progress, and maintain their respect.

## The Government Structure of Progressive Socialism

For reasons discussed above, the government structure of progressive socialism will not be based on party politics. Moral leadership is built upon a sense of devotion, self-improvement, and the welfare for all, not on party interest.

Even so, it is difficult for people to imagine an alternative form of government. They doubt whether honest people can really succeed in forming a government. Today, in the US, people have become extremely polarized between Republican and Democrat, between fascist leaning and socialist leaning tendencies. And yet, there remain decent people on both sides of the political spectrum who sincerely want the best for their communities. If honest people really want to promote human welfare, they can no longer afford to see reality through the divisive lens of left or right politics. Rather, in the spirit of mutual cooperation, we will have to break down

our fences and begin to govern ourselves. In the spirit of mutual cooperation, we should begin immediately to form ourselves into local boards
for the purpose of creating self-reliant communities. The purpose of these
boards is not to contest mainstream elections. Rather, the purpose of our
local boards is to provide the basic needs to the local people. To begin the
process of local self-reliance, local board members will be composed of
those moralists who take it upon themselves to serve the people with their
skills and expertise. Such people should lead the people in developing a
local Master Plan to meet their basic needs. Under progressive socialism,
economic democracy takes precedence over political democracy. In other
words, politics will focus on meeting people's needs, not on left or right
issues that serve only to keep the capitalist structure in place.

An important question that needs to be addresses is how will a new,
local, self-reliant economy be capitalized. The economies of the capitalist
countries were all capitalized by using the exploited resources of colonies
and by slave labor. Insofar as samajs will not have access to such capital,
the only viable substitute is the local people's own resources and labor.
It is only by building mutual trust and cooperation that such capital will
become available for public use. This is why the selflessness of the samaj
leadership is essential and why ideation on the Supreme is essential.
Without the experience of Oneness with the Supreme, the ego will continue
full-strength and individual selfishness will continue to reign supreme.

Those who are most dedicated to the welfare of the people will automatically rise to positions of leadership. In the realm of informal politics, authority always goes hand in hand with responsibility. In other
words, those who do the work gain positions of authority. In time,
board members should chose the best leaders they can, based upon
their knowledge, moral integrity, and good works within the specific
fields required to meet people's basic needs. At the local level, it will be
easier to identify those people who act according to a universal moral
code and those who do not.[238]

## Social Boards

Once again, mainstream politics is not the main focus of progressive
socialism. Rather political power will be invested in local social boards

composed of moral leaders. The purpose of these boards will be to create the economic infrastructure to meet the local people's basic needs. A local, moral leadership, dedicated to the people and skilled in service to the people, will fight ceaselessly against all corruption and exploitation. The greatest chance of creating a sense of economic security among the people lies in the collective endeavor of a moral leadership because they alone understand and represent the genuine aspirations of the people.[239] In the event that the people or board members become dissatisfied with a particular leader because he or she has acted immorally or in a manner that does not benefit the community, they can be replaced.

According to progressive socialism, authority should not be invested in one person or one institution. Rather, the political system should be based upon the creation of social boards that consist of people who are conversant and experienced with various branches of management that are required for the development of a People's Economy. These boards will address areas such as food, health care, education, social welfare, finance, energy, transportation, water, etc. Once established, and with the people's consent, the leadership of these boards, thereafter, will be responsible for selecting its future members and for electing representatives to higher boards.

Local boards will eventually evolve an administrative structure that includes a Supreme Board, Executive Board, Legislative Board, and Judicial Board, as well as maintain their own issue-specific boards. All oversight boards should be populated by our most moral and intelligent leaders.

The local Supreme Board will be a body elected by the revolutionary leadership. It will have the last word in framing policy and in supervising the functions of the executive, legislative, and judicial boards in the local community. The Supreme Board shall have final approval over any controversies.

The Executive Board will be elected from members of the local social boards and will consist of those moralists who have an exceptional knowledge of the principles and strategy of universalism. The Executive Board will be responsible for enforcing the policies and laws framed by the Legislative Board. It shall also supervise the work of selecting and nominating the personnel who shall be employed in the local government. Finally, it will also supervise the work of the various sub-boards established for different branches of the local government. This will ensure maximum cooperation between the different sectors of the local economy.

The Legislative Board will be elected by members of the community social boards who have a talent for taking the principles and practice of universalism and putting them into rules, regulations and laws. It will frame the laws according to the cardinal human principles of progressive socialism and the policies approved by the Supreme Board.

The Judicial Board shall be elected by members of the community social boards who have a keen sense of human motivation and an under-standing of criminal intent. (See A Universal Code of Justice below). It will ensure that the laws created by the legislature are followed. It will also frame the rules and procedures for the appointment of judges and different personnel of the judiciary.

As sub-boards are created to carry out the functions of the Supreme, Executive, Legislative, and Judicial boards, their members will be chosen from a list of names prepared by the Executive Board and forwarded to the Legislative Board. The Legislative Board shall recommend the list, after amendments if necessary, to the Supreme Board. The Supreme Board shall have final approve of this list.[240]

## Federated States

In time, as progressive socialism expands and samajs begin to link, the local oversight boards will send representatives to sit on similar boards at the next highest level of government. For example, when a local socio-economic unit begins to engage with other units in nearby localities for the purpose of trade, building infrastructure, etc., and if there is a desire to work together, the boards from each locality will send members to form higher administrative, legislative, and judicial boards to coordinate activities between the local boards. These higher oversight boards will have the welfare of the whole in mind. In time, local units may decide to form a permanent relationship and create a federated state government. Local representatives will then be sent to participate on federated state boards. Representatives of these boards, in time, will be sent to the World Government. In this way, the World Government shall be built from the ground up.

A federated state (federation) will be a political entity that will be composed of local samajs who have joined together for political reasons. The relationship between the samajs and the federated state will be based upon a universal constitution that may not be altered by a unilateral decision of any government in the federation.

The federated state, insofar as it is composed of self-sufficient economic units or samajs, will be initially formed on socio-economic and geographical considerations. Because there is a tendency for economically developed areas to exploit economically undeveloped areas, the federated states will maintain a balance between the samajs within their jurisdiction. They will address any issues of conflict between the samajs, including boundary disputes, environmental protection, infrastructure maintenance, as well as issues related to internal trade between the samajs.

The federated states will have the political authority to redefine or rename samajs to ensure social justice, but in no way will the redefinition of a samaj limit the local people's ability to be economically self-reliant.

Only representatives of federated states will be able to hold positions on the social boards of the World Government.

## World Government

Today, nationalism is rapidly being replaced by internationalism and in the near future, internationalism will be replaced by universalism. The feeling of nationalism will lie dormant within the scope of internationalism and the feeling of internationalism will lie dormant within the scope of universalism. As humanity becomes more secure, we will give up the narrow isms that plague us today.[241]

To materialize the concept of universalism and build a human society, a World Government is required. This World Government will be a confederation of all the federated states of the world. The World Government will not be a federation. Rather it will be a confederation of all the federated states. A confederation is a union of sovereign states that are united for a common purpose. The World Government, as a confederation, will address global issues. For example, these may be defense, foreign relations, trade, environmental protection, support of the federated states, etc.

Many people say that divergent national interests are the only impediment to the formation of a world government, but this is only a minor impediment. The main obstacle is the fear among national leaders that they will lose their positions of wealth and power. With the establishment of a world government, the total domination, which they exercise today in their respective nations, will cease to exist.

Not only the national politician, but also the people of the world, are generally skeptical about international capitalists controlling the formation of a World Government. To allay the fears of the people, the task of building a World Government should be carried out step by step, from the ground up. It cannot be created from the top down. Obstacles between people in different locations will have to be negotiated and the World Government will have to be strengthened gradually, not suddenly. In actuality, a World Government will not even appear on the radar of local people until they have established their local samajs and are secure in their ability to meet their own basic needs; and until they have already begun to organize themselves into federated states.

In the initial stage, the World Government will only be a law-making body. Local representation in the Legislature of the World Government will occur as follows. There will be two houses: a lower house and an upper house. In the lower house, representatives will be sent according to the population of the federated state. In the upper house, representatives will be sent state-wise. Bills will be placed before the lower house, and before their final acceptance they will be duly discussed in the upper house. If there are small states, which cannot send a single representative to the lower house, they will have the opportunity to discuss the merits and demerits of proposed acts with other states in the upper house.

The Legislature of the World Government will draft the World Constitution. It will be based upon cardinal human principles and serve as the basis for all laws that will be created and enforced. The first beneficial effect of such a world body will be that no samaj or federated state will be allowed to frame laws detrimental to the interests of its minorities should such a situation arise. The execution of laws developed by the World Government will be vested with the local governments and not with the world government.[242]

The federated states and local samajs may or may not fully execute the laws of the World Government but they must not go against them. The World Government will, however, have some executive power for limited and defined purposes, namely, for maintaining peace and settling disputes between the federated states.

The World Government shall also maintain a world militia under its control. By the same token the federated states will also maintain a militia and the samajs will maintain a police force to ensure internal law and order.

To summarize, in the government structure of progressive socialism, economic units (samajs) will be governed by boards composed of local sadvipras, those spiritual warriors who have the best interests of the people in mind. These boards may form higher boards, and even a federated state which will have its own boards. These federated boards will govern the different federations. The collection of these federated boards is the World Government, which is a confederated board or body. It will look after the confederation as a whole, but will not ignore the interests of any federation.[243]

Neither the federated state governments, nor the World Government, after it is established, shall have any authority in the management of industrial, agricultural, trade, or commercial enterprises. As stated earlier, progressive socialism maintains a separation between political and economic entities. Management of their economy will remain in the hands of the local people. This is to ensure that capitalists, opportunists, or self-seeking politicians cannot take control of local economies and misappropriate public wealth.[244]

## Constitution and Laws

Human societies have historically developed social institutions to carry out their duties and responsibilities. The government is one such vital institution. It is intended to organize a group of people in a certain area of land, provide administration, legislation and justice, promote their welfare and oversee their well-being. This institution is powerful because it also enjoys sovereignty.

As we have learned, however, the accumulation of power is dangerous if it is not guided by a moral leadership, a vigilant populace, universal principles, and just rules. The guide book in which all rules, regulations, and principles for the proper conduct of a state are codified is called a constitution. Under progressive socialism, the constitution will provide samajs and states with principles and policies to render all-round services to the people for their rapid progress.

Constitutions today differ from state to state or country to country. For example, both France and the US have written constitution but they differ in substance. The French system is a presidential form of government where the president appoints the prime minister and all other ministers. In the US, the president, who is directly elected by the electorate, rules the country with self-appointed secretaries. There are no ministers, only secretaries in the US system. The British have no written constitution. They have only a collection of traditions and conventions and not a written document. The theoretical head is the crown queen or king. All power is vested with the crown, but in practicality, the rule of the country is exercised by the prime minister in a parliamentary form of government.

There is a major flaw in the US constitution which gives individuals and corporations unlimited power. This results in the detriment of the American people as a whole. The legal right of the individual and corporations to exploit the collective must be curtailed in an improved form of government. A constitution within a progressive socialist government would introduce social controls so that collective interests are balanced with individual interests. For example, in the US constitution, the purchasing power to meet one's basic necessities is not guaranteed to the people, but it will be guaranteed under a progressive socialist system.

Everyone has the right to physical, mental, and spiritual development, but national constitutions having been a product of the capitalist age, have been written to limit the all-round welfare of all citizens in favor of a ruling elite. A constitution should be fair and just. If it is biased against lower classes, women, or minorities, it will undermine the unity and solidarity of the country and thus disturb the peace and prosperity of the society as a whole.

The Universal Constitution under progressive socialism will include the following points:

1. It will provide a check and balance system between the Executive, Legislative, and Judicial branches and contain specific articles to ensure a well-functioning government.

2. It will require a high moral standard and integrity from leadership.

3. All living languages will have equal status before the state or the World Government.

4. All citizens will have equal rights before the law.

5. Basic physical requirements will be guaranteed to all citizens so that everyone will enjoy peace and equilibrium in collective life.

6. A high-level review board will be constituted by the Supreme Board of the World Government to continually review economic progress and development in the different parts of the world to ensure that some areas do not lag too far behind or expand to far ahead of the average level of samaj development.

7. A case can be filed with the Judicial Board against any person in the world, including the members of social boards, because every citizen in the country is equal before the Constitution.

8. Once samajs become a part of a federated state, if a group of people want the right of self-determination for a samaj or group of samajs within that federated state, their right may be recognized only on the basis of a plebiscite held in that area.

9. Public education will be guaranteed for all and education will be free from all political interference.

10. The law and the Constitution will be the same for the entire world and each and every individual will

be equal before the law and before the constitution. According to the Constitution, each and every federated state will enjoy the same powers.

In addition to such articles, the formation of a World Government will also require a charter of principles or Bill of Rights which will encompass at minimum the following four points:

1.  Complete security will be guaranteed to all the plants and animal species on the planet.

2.  Each state will guarantee purchasing capacity for all its citizens to meet their basic needs.

3.  The constitution will guarantee four fundamental rights. These rights are: (1) the freedom to perform spiritual practices, (2) the freedom to express one's cultural legacy, (3) the ability to have access to free education, and (4) the freedom to speak in one's indigenous language.

4.  If the practice of any of these rights conflicts with cardinal human principles then that practice should be immediately curtailed. Cardinal human principles must always take precedence over all other rights.[245]

In our analysis of the politics of progressive socialism, we see that decisions of governance are based upon: (1) cardinal human principles, (2) a universal moral code, (3) a constitution that is based upon these principles and code, and (4) laws and regulations that are in sync with the constitution and the bill of rights. Their viability will be based upon the moral fiber of the people and their leaders.

A World Government that is based upon these factors will pave the way for the greater unity of human society and the idea of Universalism will acquire greater speed. This reality should not remain a utopian dream. It should become a clear expression of our dedication to the well being of humanity.[246]

## A Universal Code of Justice

In the section above "Guidelines for Governments in a Progressive Socialist Society," we stated that one of these factors was the development of a Common Code of Justice.

As local people begin to create their local socio-economies, at some point, they will have to contend with people's actions that are contrary to the intention and to the rules and regulations of their samaj. In other words, they will have to contend with issues of social justice and the behavior of criminals. Thus a local police force is necessary.

From a spiritual perspective, we must remember that the significance of society lies in moving together. In the course of the journey, we should not go ahead leaving people in the lurch. If we do not stop and offer help, the spirit of society will be put in jeopardy. Thus, a person, whether he or she is considered a sinner or a criminal, is so only superficially. Inherently, everyone has the potential of being a great human being. The principle object of the local leadership, therefore, is to create the conditions to bring this potentiality to reality.

According to universalism, everybody has the right to point out or correct the behavior of everyone else. This is the birthright of every human being. No scholar can dispute the right of people to correct the shortcomings of those with whom they come in contact. The recognition of this right is indispensable for a healthy society.[247]

Corrective measures are a necessary part of social justice. Insofar as corrective measures are concerned, rehabilitation should always take precedence over punishment. Whenever some action is taken to punish someone, a sense of superiority and revenge arises in the mind of the dispenser of justice and stifles his or her human sentiment. So also, the one who is punished becomes resentful and makes plans for revenge. Hence, Mr. Sarkar suggests that the words "penal code" should be eliminated from the social life of humanity. If anybody, whether a judge or a common citizen, imposes justice on someone else, it should be corrective, not penal. Then the offender, no matter how great his or her guilt, will have no cause for accusing anyone or for building apathy or revenge against the local people. So also, regardless of any flaws in the accuser's judgment, it will not harm the accused in any way.[248]

Our code of justice therefore is a "rehabilitation code," which should be applied in the following manner. The first step in correcting another's behavior is to persuade the offender by compassionate words. Secondly, use harsh words in order to convince them. At the third stage, tell them that they are violating laws and will suffer consequences. The fourth stage warrants the adoption of legal measures against them. This is the humane way of dealing with offenders. If, however, a person's behavior is beyond the scope of corrective words, such as the act of murder or rape, it will be necessary to skip the initial steps and move immediately to stage four, incarceration.

Legal measures should not include letting a criminal waste his or her day in a prison cell. We must remember that they are suffering from physical or mental problems. Most can be cured through humane consultation, a congenial environment, and intuitional practices, Therefore, the environment of a prison should be as compassionate as possible. It should be a correctional center and not a prison.

Regarding capital punishment, sentencing people to death because society is unable to cure their ills is as much a crime as killing them oneself. We shall have to deal with criminals with a humane heart and guide them out of their ills. Some police or prison guards may scoff at such an approach, but they will also have to admit that physical violence and harsh punishments do not result in improved human beings. Our rehabilitation approach will prevent a government from imposing a violent, cruel penal system and an oppressive dictatorship on the people. Well-intentioned police officers and prison guards will learn to see the wisdom in this approach because it will make their lives less dangerous and more humane. In our approach, they will not be alone in their work. Judges, doctors, psychologists and sociologists will also be there to help them.

## Understanding the Mind of Criminals

In order to act in a compassionate manner toward criminals, it is necessary to understand criminal motivation. In our discussion of the three causes of crime and sin, we have seen that people commit negative acts because they are poor or because they exploit others or because they prevent social mobility. But to understand the individual motivation behind these acts takes a deeper analysis.

PROUT categorizes criminals according to their motivations and the nature of one's rehabilitation will be based upon their motivation. As such, PROUT recognizes five categories of criminals. These are: (1) born criminals, (2) habitual criminals, (3) criminals due to environment, (4) criminals due to poverty, and (5) criminals due to momentary weakness.[249]

## Born Criminals

Some men and women are born with a deranged mind. The cause of their mental derangement is due to defects within their brain and glands. Such people can be divided into two main groups. The first group is composed of people who are normally very quiet, but in whom truthfulness and performing service are against their nature. They derive malevolent pleasure from deception and harming others. They are generally poor at managing their daily affairs and incapable of comprehending the difference between good and bad. They act according to their limited mental capacity. They are mentally underdeveloped and are often deprived of the same kindness and compassion that others may receive. Such born criminals take a long time to learn how to walk and talk and to understand simple matters. Despite the sincere efforts of their parents and teachers, they fail to acquire any education. Even before they reach adulthood they manifest their base propensities. They generally become petty thieves as opposed to armed robbers. Although they have a bad character, they do not have the courage to perform antisocial activities openly. They commit offences on their own initiative and at the instigation of others.

The second group of born criminals is much more dangerous. These people revel in displays of cruelty whether provoked or unprovoked. They have a natural inclination to kill or maim others. They become members of criminal gangs and commit murder and other horrendous acts. Generally they do not become pickpockets, petty thieves or burglars. They consider such things beneath their dignity. In criminal circles, they are usually greatly feared. From their mode of thinking or lifestyle, it appears as though they were born only to commit crimes. They consider compassion and conscience to be mere frailties and the importance of such attributes is beyond their understanding. Although they may be slow when it comes to worldly affairs, they are not fools. At the time of committing their instinct-inspired crimes, they give ample proof of their intelligence. They demonstrate their intelligence through their knowledge of anatomy and psychology, and by their behavior when dealing with the police and the public. Even if they are born into a beneficial environment, this type of inborn criminal ultimately takes to a life of crime.

Born criminals are society's greatest burden and greatest responsibility. Although such criminals are born with human bodies, mentally they are sub-human.

Just as doctors quarantine those with an infectious disease to prevent the disease spreading to healthy people, similarly it is necessary to isolate born criminals from other people. The treatment of such criminals should be undertaken in a corrective center.

In the treatment of born criminals, psychologists will diagnose the mental disease and explain its origins, and they will also play a role in helping cure it as far as possible. Doctors will be responsible for curing the disease through medicine or surgery, insofar as it is caused by physiological abnormalities. Then sociologists will have to arrange for the social rehabilitation of the criminal after he or she has recovered. If psychologists only describe the nature of the disease, or if doctors only diagnose the physiological disorders and nothing more, it will not be possible to accomplish anything productive. Of course, the patient may not make a complete recovery despite the concerted efforts of psychologists and sociologists. This is because one's karma, which has developed over life times, may not be resolved in the criminal's present life time. So also, psychology is still in an underdeveloped state and surgeons may not as yet have acquired the skills needed to remove the physiological abnormalities responsible for mental disease. That being said, we must move in this direction to help cure born criminals. Born criminals should always be treated as patients with a stubborn disease.

Any disease can ultimately be cured through spiritual practices and yogic methods, but for this a congenial environment is essential. The environments of incarceration facilities should therefore be made more pure and more humane. Born criminals may not be put to death, but they may need to be sterilized to prevent another generation of born criminals.[250] Such a decision should only be made by a board of experts and moralists on a case by case basis.

**Criminals by Habit**

Where moral integrity is low, where no effort is made to develop mental force, or where social control is slack, people will be influenced by their lower propensities and will choose a path which enables them to express their propensities unchecked. Those who lack mental strength often knowingly commit crimes in an almost mechanical way, even though they possess a sense of morality. Such people who possess a sense of morality but lack mental strength normally keep their momentary mental weaknesses under control out of fear of what society might do, and as a result the health of society and the purity of individual life is upheld. But if a situation exists where there is low morality, weakness of mind, or lack of social consequences, people will tend to engage in antisocial activities. If there is nothing to confront them, they will gradually become increasingly addicted to such activities. In this way, people get accustomed to performing antisocial activities and finally turn into hardened criminals.

This type of criminal nature is often formed as an indirect result of people being forced to submit to strict control without being given any moral education or guidance as to how to develop strength of mind. For example, some parents do not impart moral education to their children, and do not help them to acquire strength of mind or teach them how to lead a virtuous life; instead, they beat their children with or without justification. It is the children of such parents who later take part in antisocial activities.

The diseases of habitual criminals are not congenital, so in treating these people there is little need for a physiologist or doctor. Habitual criminals can easily be treated if they are provided with a proper moral education, a method of acquiring moral strength, and a strictly regulated social environment. So during the trials of habitual criminals, the judge should focus more on strict rules and regulations rather than on compassion. This approach will better benefit society.

## Criminals Due to Environment

Many people in society do not become criminals because of hereditary factors or bad habits. Rather, there are many examples where honest people become dishonest due to environmental pressures. Such people could have been revered as ideal human beings with impeccable characters if they had been given a proper environment.

Parents are often to blame for their children's antisocial behavior. The honest son of a criminal father is compelled to participate in antisocial activities out of fear of paternal abuse. The daughter of a prostitute is forced to lead the life of a social outcast due to unbearable maternal abuse or circumstantial pressure. These are cases where people become criminals due to their environment.

Sometimes personal difficulties, such as financial hardship or poverty, compel people to commit crimes, even when they know they are doing wrong. Due to circumstantial pressure they also may encourage their children to do wrong and force them to commit crimes.

Those who are born with fairly healthy bodies and minds, who have not become dishonest as a result of circumstantial pressure, may still unwittingly take to the path of dishonesty because they keep bad company. They think, "I don't have to bother about the company I keep, as long as I am good myself. I am old enough to understand the difference between good and bad." At the same time, they become piqued if someone tries to dissuade them from keeping bad company.

A person of any age is invariably influenced by the company he or she keeps. Where goodness is predominant, bad people will slowly but surely become good, and where the opposite is the case, good people will become bad. This is the natural characteristic of the human mind regardless of what people may think.

The people involved in Alcoholics Anonymous certainly understand this truth. If someone wants to abstain from drinking, but continues to socialize regularly with a group of alcoholics, he or she will fail in their effort.

In the pseudo-culture that derives from a capitalist society, there are many films and other media which unduly excite the cruder tendencies of mind and have a degrading influence on children and young people. In this case, the pseudo-culture becomes the bad company which causes depravity. If their family ties are weak, or if they are their own guardians, or have no high ideals to inspire them, they will succumb to bad influences and it will be extremely difficult to save them from their mental degradation.

Nonetheless, if those who become criminals due to keeping bad company are not transformed into habitual criminals, they will return to their normal good behavior as soon as they give up the bad company.

During the trial of a criminal due to environment, who has not yet turned into a habitual criminal, the judge should not attach too much importance to the provisions of the penal code. If, after thorough investigation, it is discovered that particular people or circumstantial pressure have caused these criminals (whatever their age) to take part in antisocial activities, it will be the duty of the judge to remove them from that environment with the help of sociologists and psychologists. Such cases rarely require further corrective measures. But if those who are criminals due to circumstantial pressure become habitual criminals as a result of a long-standing habit, a change of environment alone will not suffice. Corrective measures will also be necessary. In correctional facilities, criminals due to environment who have already turned into habitual criminals, should be housed with great care, otherwise their disease will spread to others.

The only way to overcome bad influences on people is to popularize the ideals of universalism, spread moral education, and train an honest police force.

### Criminals Due to Poverty

Most crimes throughout the world are committed due to poverty. Of course, the tendency to engage in antisocial activities because of poverty does not manifest equally in all places or among all people. The degree of such crimes varies according to the moral strength of an individual. But no matter how strongly developed the moral consciousness of a person, if poverty threatens his or her very existence, usually the person will commit criminal acts to survive. This being the case, we must consider one's poverty as a legitimate excuse for one's crime. For example, during the Great Depression, mothers broke into supermarkets to steal food to feed their children. They were simply demanding their right to live, and, after all, it is upon this right that the justification for human society exists. Regarding people in poverty, Mr. Sarkar says:

> Throughout history, millions of people have died due to artificial famines created by other human beings. While walking along a road, weary, plodding legs have given way and a person has collapsed in a pitiful heap on the ground, yet he or she has refrained from stealing. Although a high standard of morality is one reason why the person did not make a last desperate bid for self-preservation, it is not the only reason. Starving people, particularly if they lose their vitality by slow degrees, do not have the moral courage to fight. Knowing the end is sure, they seek refuge in the arms of death. Basing their way of life on incorrect philosophical and religious teachings, they accept their miserable situation as destiny. Perhaps, at that time, if they were led by a spirited leader and inspired by his or her fiery lectures, or if they received guidance about the course of action to take, they would collectively attack the prevailing social structure. In such circumstances, their actions might perhaps be described as immoral, but they certainly would not contravene the dharma of human existence.[251]

Under such circumstances, if the judge looks only at the crime, or is indifferent to the questions of cause and effect related to the crime, such offenders, who may be more honest than most well-fed, well-dressed, or so-called honest people, will be thrown into jail and branded as criminals merely because of deficiencies in the capitalist system of production and distribution of basic needs. Due to the bad company they meet in prison and overcome with shame, hatred, and humiliation due to their punishment, they will gradually turn into habitual criminals after being released from jail.

Those who ignore their conscience and repeatedly commit crimes due to poverty, eventually turn into habitual criminals. If somebody steals or robs out of hunger, or is goaded by their propensities into some mean act, it will be the duty of society to find out what the person's needs are and then address them in some lawful way. But if society fails to do its duty and punishes such criminals instead, all feelings of remorse will vanish from their minds and in their place a sense of desperation will arise. They will think, "Since I am sinking, let me sink to the depths of hell." Those who have committed crimes due to poverty will blame society for their offences. They will claim that their poverty is the result of a defective social structure, and in most cases this allegation will be true.

Hence, the solution to many different antisocial activities lies in the creation of a sound socio-economic structure. The man who is despised as a thief or treated with contempt by society might have been a genius if he had been brought up in a healthy social environment. The woman who is shunned as a prostitute might have been respected as a leader in society or honored as an exemplary mother, had she received a little sympathy from others in the early part of her life. This is why we should understand that such unfortunate men and women carry a burden of sin that was created through the behavior of society as a whole and not simply by their own individual crime. They are not solely responsible for their sins, or if they are, their sins are considerably less, or at least no greater, than the sins of selfish, mean-minded people who call themselves honest. Mr. Sarkar admonishes the so-called honest citizens who forget the devastating impact that poverty has on people:

> It is doubtful whether the Supreme Creator, let alone humanity, has the right to punish those who commit crimes due to poverty. Still, from the moral standpoint, I cannot support criminal acts. I would suggest that before committing such crimes they should become revolutionaries. It is the duty of those with a good knowledge of morality to guide them in their revolutionary activities.

Let them separate the gold from the dross in the fire of revolution.[252]

Regarding those who become criminals due to poverty, honest people have no alternative but to exhort them to launch a revolution. In this situation, the position of a judge is only a figurehead. There are no corrective measures to be taken. He or she has nothing to say or do. Psychologists and sociologists also have very limited scope for action. The pathways that lie open to them are very circumscribed.

The solution to crime completely depends on a just economic foundation of the different countries as well as of the entire world. If anyone is at fault, it is the majority of the world's leaders. Their responsibilities do not end just because they gain political and economic power by creating false hopes and deceiving the common people with remote and unattainable dreams. As Mr. Sarkar says:

> Those whose stomachs are full can always forget about the hunger of others. The world has become accustomed to, but has experienced quite enough of, the procrastination and heartless histrionics of such blood-sucking brutes. By inventing crises, they force the needy to commit crimes; by hoarding grains, they cause artificial famines and indirectly incite starving people to steal; and by making people's circumstances difficult and subsequently enticing them with money, they encourage men to abandon their families and compel women to earn their living in an immoral way. Because they remain above suspicion and appear to be honest according to the laws of the land, which in many countries are enacted for the benefit of the upper stratum of society, ordinary people are unable to raise their voices in protest. It can be said that the only path open to them is the path of revolution.[253]

On the other hand, there are many instances of affluent people indulging in drink, drugs, gambling, licentiousness, luxurious living, gluttony, etc., in order to forget their psychic problems or to gratify their instincts.

Due to their addiction, they lose their wealth and fall into debt to finance their bad habits. Eventually, when it becomes impossible for them to pay off their debts, they get involved in a wide variety of criminal activities, which have a highly deleterious effect on society. Privation is clearly the cause of such crimes, but society is not responsible for this type of privation as it is entirely self-created. It is necessary to take corrective measures to reform such types of criminal. In order to be able to reform them; it is essential to cure them of their addiction.

**Criminals Due to Momentary Weakness**

Even if the economic structure is sound, other factors may cause crimes and jeopardize social peace and discipline. With the eradication of poverty, crimes caused by keeping bad company and by personal difficulties may be decreased, but the number of crimes committed by born criminals or habitual criminals may not decline.

Another type of crime occurs occasionally. This is a temporary criminal urge, a special type of mental disease which suddenly appears in a certain type of environment and again subsides after a short time. Kleptomania, for example is a mental disease of this kind. After committing a crime, kleptomaniacs may feel ashamed and are anxious to return the property that they have stolen. They may have sudden fantasies about abducting people, becoming drunk or indulging in decadent activities. But analysis shows that they do not, in fact, have the slightest personal interest in such things.

Crimes of momentary weakness are usually caused by weak-minded people who have witnessed theft, murder, or any other crime, and are deeply affected by their experience. Due to the ensuing extreme agitation that occurs in their minds, they deviate from the path of common sense. If the feeling of mental agitation reoccurs due to the influence of temporal, spatial, or personal factors, they will immediately commit a crime. Those who commit so-called crimes of passion may be included in this category of criminals.

Because of the difference in the motivation of criminals, a progressive socialist society will develop a universal code of justice that takes account of these motivations rather than simply creating a laundry list of crimes and punishments. While the role of the police to serve and protect will remain largely the same, the responsibility of judicial boards and legal personnel will now include an investigation into the cause behind the crime and make a determination as to the type of correction required based upon this analysis. Not only will the attorneys and judges have to take this approach but also psychologists, doctors and sociologists. The code of justice will be framed by a moral leadership based on the belief that it is better in all cases to seek rectification and not punishment. First and foremost, the needs of a criminal must be determined and efforts should be made to remove them.

Depending upon the maturity of the local samaj, the code of justice may initially be limited to upholding rules and regulations, but in a later stage, people will be trained in procedures of rehabilitation and the prison will gradually be converted into a correction facility. Also, in time, the world constitution and legal codes of the World Legislature will come increasingly into play.

In this overview of the politics of progressive socialism, we can envision how a universal ideology can impact the day-to-day rules and regulations of a functioning society. In the next chapter we will see how it impacts the meeting of people's basic material needs.

# Chapter Five: The Economics of Progressive Socialism

*PROUT is the socio-economic approach, Neohumanism is the psycho-intellectual approach and spiritual practice is the spirituo-intuitional approach. This three-fold approach will take human beings along the path of salvation.* P. R. Sarkar

I N ORDER TO BENEFIT humanity and the planet, a Universal Ideology must address our physical, mental, and spiritual nature, as well as our identity as individuals and social beings. It must address the optimum relationship between the human species and the natural world. As such, it must be able to present a clear socio-economic strategy by which to provide people with their basic necessities in an environmentally sustainable manner. Without having our basic material needs met, our mental and spiritual growth will be impaired. Without addressing the needs of the natural world, we will diminish our capacity to live in a secure environment. In this chapter, we will discuss the characteristics of a local socio-economy, based upon the principles of progressive socialism (PROUT).

A local socio-economy is: (1) decentralized, (2) locally planned, (3) regulated to prevent harm to individuals, community, and the natural environment, (4) managed to protect resources sustainably, (5) undertaken to meet basic needs, and (6) is based upon the principle of Cosmic Inheritance.

The ability of local people to provide for their own basic needs is dependent upon their access to land. Land is the source of food, water, medicine, clothing, building materials, energy, etc. Because of this, the goal of progressive socialism is to create an agrarian revolution whereby local people are able to meet their own basic needs in a sustainable manner. The basic needs are food, shelter, clothing, health care, and education. PROUT calls that part of the economy that addresses these basic needs, the "People's Economy." Only when local people have control over the People's Economy will they have permanent economic security.

There are many reasons why towns and cities that once lived through prosperous days now find themselves in a depression. For example, a raw material like trees, coal, or water, upon which the locality was dependent, may run out. Advances in technology may render established factories or businesses obsolete and eliminate the need for human labor. Another reason is that quite often human skills do not keep pace with advancements in technology. For example, when the German engineering company Siemens Energy recently opened a gas turbine production plant in Charlotte, N.C., ten thousand people showed up at a job fair for eight hundred positions. But fewer than fifteen percent of the applicants were able to pass a ninth-grade reading, writing, and math screening test. The chief executive of Siemens USA said, "In our factories, there's a computer about every twenty or thirty feet. People on the plant floor need to be much more skilled than they were in the past. There are no jobs for high school graduates at Siemens today."[254]

The same is true for other manufacturing companies. John Deere, for example, repairs million-dollar farming machinery with parts that contain dozens of computers. Fixing tractors and grain harvesters now requires advanced math and comprehension skills and the ability to solve problems as they arise.

President Trump made a campaign promise to bring back manufacturing jobs to working-class communities. He blamed bad trade deals for the loss of over five million US jobs, but according to a study by Ball State University, nearly nine out of ten manufacturing jobs that disappeared since 2000 were lost to automation, not to workers in other countries.[255] Even so, a strong case can be made that many corporations moved their jobs out of the country to take advantage of cheap labor. So the American workers are caught between a rock and a hard place. Automation replaced them and even if jobs return, a high school diploma is simply no longer good enough to get hired. This is never discussed by the Trump administration, but it is a fact.

In 2019, the employment level again approached full capacity, but jobs have moved out of manufacturing and into minimum wage jobs like personal care aides, cooks, waiters, and retail sales that pay only a third of the wages from lost manufacturing jobs. The loss of pay and living wage jobs, and the fact that many Americans in the middle and working classes now find themselves on the verge of poverty, has created the angry and resentment against the system that catapulted Trump into the Presidency.

The building of a great wall to prevent our southern neighbors from coming to the United States will never reverse the advancement of technology that is making human labor obsolete. President Trump's imposition of heavy import taxes on Chinese and Mexican goods actually slowed the American economy by making many food and many consumer items more expensive for working class Americans. At this writing, his actions may spark a global trade war.

The U.S. tried to impose heavy import taxes on foreign goods in the 1930s with a law known as the Smoot-Hawley Tariff Act. It backfired and plunged the American people further into the Great Depression.[256]

Whether or not American workers have lost their livelihoods to foreigners or to automation is of little consequence to a struggling family. The point is that people, who are dependent upon the global economy, are always dominated by forces from outside their communities. These forces are cold and calculating and do not have the interests of the local people at heart. As such, we can never be economically secure or self-reliant. This loss of local empowerment continues to worsen under advanced capitalism. We are now, more than ever, at the mercy of multinational corporations who, as has been proven many times over, care little for our suffering.[257]

The hard truth is that if we ever want to be economically secure again, we will have to take matters into our own hands. Few may want to consider this, but we have no choice if we want to better our lives and the lives of our children.

Let us look, for example, at the basic requirement of food. Of the minimum necessities required for survival, food production is especially vital because it provides the nutrients we need to give us energy, maintain our health, and keep us alive. We cannot be productive or healthy without good food and, under the present system, many people are not getting the good food that they need and deserve. Even in the United States, which is the richest country in the world, many Americans do not have the money to buy food that contains adequate nutrition. This situation has led to widespread malnutrition and diet-related diseases. Malnutrition, in the US, has caused 9% (27 million) of the population to have diabetes,[258] 11.5% (28.1 million) to have heart disease,[259] and 33% (78 million adults and 12 million children) to be overweight or obese.[260] These diseases are caused by eating junk foods and processed foods that contain large amounts of refined sugar, dangerous fats, and toxic chemicals while providing negligible nutrients. People are fed junk food because it is more profitable for the corporations to sell junk food than nutritious food. The quest for profit has led to a production process that strips whole foods of their nutrients in order to create standardized products, increase shelf life, and promote a better appearance. To meet these profit-oriented objectives, harmful chemicals are also added to the junk food. These chemicals are in addition to the toxic residuals from pesticides, herbicides, and other poisons added to the plants in the process of growing them. The US government then subsidizes this system by paying for its distribution to children in our public schools. The diets of the children are now dangerously short on fruits and vegetables that provide the vitamins and minerals required to produce the cells that keep their young bodies healthy.

The only way to solve the problem of malnutrition and the maladjustment and misallocation of natural resources is to develop and implement a local plan to feed people with good food that is produced locally.

If local people can meet their food needs, this will go a long way to creating healthy people as well as creating local jobs and a more self-reliant community. PROUT, as well as many other movements, have always focused on food production as a key ingredient in building local economies and rightly so. The only question is, how can local planners increase the scale of local food production to help more local people become healthier and have steady jobs? Unfortunately, this question has no answer within the capitalist system, which is controlled by multinational banks and corporations whose goal is to continually profit at the expense of local communities. An entirely new economic system is required to accomplish our task. And that economic system is progressive socialism (PROUT). Let us now look at the principles and planning strategies of this new system.

## Five Fundamental Principles of PROUT

PROUT theory is based upon five fundamental principles which govern all socio-economic activity at the local level. These principles are meant to create equilibrium between the needs of the individual and the community, and between humans and the natural environment. They serve as a guide to maximize the utilization of, and rationally distribute all resources, human and natural.[261] They are essential to the success of progressive socialism. The first principle is:

> No individual should be allowed to accumulate any physical wealth without the clear permission or approval of the collective body.

This principle states that as far as the accumulation of physical wealth is concerned, individual liberty is not permitted to violate the interests of the collective body. This will cause the capitalists to reduce their wealth, but it is the only way to ensure that the minimum requirements of life, as well as special amenities, are guaranteed to all.

This principle is based on the concept of Cosmic Inheritance, which asserts that human beings have the right to use and share resources, but not to own or hoard them. As such, local social boards and cooperatives will determine the economic requirements to meet everyone's basic needs. While certain amenities will also be provided for exceptional contribution to the welfare of the community, a cap will be put on individual wealth so that it does not prevent the meeting of basic needs and amenities of everyone. Ceilings will be put on salaries, inherited wealth, property, and land ownership.

This principle, obviously, applies only to physical resources and not intellectual or spiritual resources. The second principle is:

> There should be maximum utilization and rational dis-
> tribution of all mundane, supramundane, and spiritual
> potentialities of the universe.

Not just planet earth, but the entire universe is our common inheritance. Hence, all the mundane, supra-mundane, and spiritual potentialities should be utilized in the best possible way. Nothing should remain unutilized or underutilized, but the utilization of natural resources must be sustainable. We must also remember that all species have an existential value, beside their utility value that must be respected.

Mundane resources are those physical resources that we use in our day-to-day life. Supermundane resources are natural laws, eco-systems, the consciousness within each and every natural form and species, etc. Spiritual resources refer to the ability of nature to create a sense of wonder and awe within us, and inspire us to greatness.

Maximum utilization means to make the best use of resources while protecting the natural environment. It includes three considerations: (1) effectiveness—doing the right thing and choosing the right policy, (2) efficacy—getting things done in a timely manner, (3) efficiency—doing things in the most economical way possible, reducing waste, recycling, and doing more with less.

Rational distribution entails four factors. Resources are to be distributed in order to: (1) guarantee the basic needs to everyone, (2) meet the special needs of people due to disabilities or infirmities, (3) provide incentives for those who make greater contributions to the welfare of society, and (4) continually increase the purchasing capacity of the average person.

The third principle is:

> There should be maximum utilization of the physical,
> metaphysical, and spiritual potentialities of the individ-
> ual and collective bodies of the human society.

Whereas the second principle relates to the use of all natural resources, this principle relates to the use and distribution of human resources. Everyone is endowed with different physical, intellectual, and spiritual potentialities. Everyone should be encouraged to contribute to social and environmental welfare given their respective capacities. Likewise, organizations within a local socio-economic unit (samaj), as well as samajs themselves, should be encouraged to serve the larger human society.

According to PROUT, there is "no inevitable conflict between individual and collective interests. Rather, their true interests are shared." This principle does not support subordinating the individual to the collective, nor the collective to the individual. It seeks a balance between the two, so that everyone's interests are optimally met. Each person has an individual aspect and a social aspect to their existence. They simultaneously participate in society and also distinguish themselves from society. Neither aspect should be sacrificed to the other. In the event, however, when individual interest threatens the collective good, the collective good will prevail. Conversely, the institutions of society will be established with the purpose of protecting individual rights.

Metaphysical potentialities refer to our mental capacities. Such potentials are wasted when people lack education or are denied opportunities for mental expansion. We want a society that encourages each individual to realize his or her greatest potential and achieve their dreams. The perpetuation of narrow isms by a self-interested group wastes human potential. For example, the sins and crimes of racism and sexism are responsible for a staggering waste of human potential.

Spiritual potentialities refer to our deepest longing for Divine love, peace, liberty, harmony, wholeness, and happiness. Under the current conditions of capitalism, communism, fascism, and theocratic authoritarianism, such potential is suppressed and may even be punished. The samajs of progressive socialism will provide every encouragement for the fulfillment of spiritual potentialities. While everyone will be encouraged to worship in the style that they prefer, in any areas where a religious dogma or activity goes against cardinal human values, such dogmas and activities will be challenged, and if debilitating to people's well-being, prohibited. The goal of social institutions and enterprises under PROUT is to help people reach their fullest potential and therefore narrow isms will not be tolerated. Human potential will be optimized by providing learning and training opportunities, meaningful work, the opportunity for leisure, and a supportive social environment.

According to the principles of progressive socialism, people will be rewarded for their contribution to human society instead of being rewarded for exploiting it.

The fourth principle is:

> There should be a proper adjustment amongst these physical, metaphysical, mundane, supramundane, and spiritual utilizations.

This principle holds that the utilization and distribution of natural and human resources need to continually be adjusted so that a balance is always maintained. For example, the use of a natural resource like oil may reduce human labor, but if it is used unsustainably, or its supply is threatened, or it proves harmful to other species, then another resource that is more sustainable, including human labor, may be required to diminish the use of oil.

The prioritizing of resource distribution according to more rare and valuable qualities also pertains to natural resources. A wilderness area should be preserved instead of being drilled for oil. Substitutes for oil can be developed but the loss of species and eco-systems may be permanent.

Concerning the individual, if a person is endowed with physical, mental, and spiritual resources, but society is only using his or her physical resources, then this person will not be able to serve society in a maximum way. Individuals who possess intellectual resources are fewer than those who have physical abilities. In like manner, people who possess spiritual strengths are fewer in number than those who possess mental capabilities. So there should be proper adjustment in the process of encouraging service from individuals or groups.

The fifth principle is:

> The method of utilization should vary in accordance with the changes in time, place, and person and the utilization should be of a progressive nature.

This principle acknowledges that change is constant. Every change requires adaptation. This implies that we have to overcome our fear, resistance, traditions, dogmas, etc., to optimally take advantage of the changes to which we are subjected. Every obstacle is an opportunity. When a resource no longer represents the most efficient way to address a need, it will need to be replaced by a more efficient resource.

A sense of unity will be created in the local socio-economy by building consensus around the five fundamental principles of progressive social-ism.[262] While these principles indicate how resources should be used within the local socio-economy, the process of utilization and distribution will not be the same for all people. Better methods of utilization and distribution should be continually developed, but the five principles of PROUT will assure that the process of utilization will always be progressive in nature.

No rule, regulation, or institution, under progressive socialism is set in stone. Rather, a progressive socialist society will by guided by the five fundamental principles of PROUT and will employ them according to changes in time, place and person while attempting to remain consistent with cardinal human values.

## Socio-Economy vs Political-Economy

Progressive socialism uses the term socio-economy instead of political-econ-omy when discussing the activity of a community of people. This is because an economy that includes all the dimensions of a human community cannot and should not be controlled by a government structure. A socio-economy includes all the social aspects of human living. It is what people do to meet their basic needs as well as what they do for entertainment, culture, education, spiritual growth, etc. Under capitalism, the ruling class controls the economy and sets up the political structure to ensure public compliance with its requirements. Therefore, a political-economy normally only enriches the ruling class and their local representatives. A socio-economy, on the other hand, is created by a local people to define their needs and interests and is governed by them.

While the goal of a political economy is for the individual or corporation to exploit human labor and resources in order to enrich themselves, the goal of a socio-economy is to maximize the use of resources and rationally distribute them in order to meet the collective and individual needs of the community.

While a political-economy is profit based, a socio-economy is needs based. This is a distinguishing feature of progressive socialism that separates it from capitalism or communism. It represents a dramatic shift in worldview from that which we have been indoctrinated to believe for the last several centuries. We have been taught to believe that the exploitation of nature and another's labor was an acceptable means for a few to get rich at the expense of others. Today, more people are coming to the realization that cooperation and community self-reliance can never be based upon a principle of human exploitation. We have witnessed the destruction of species, of natural resources, and the climate under capitalism. We have lived through depressions and have witnessed the endless wars of exploitation. Today, the US is ravaging the Middle East for control of the oil supply. Such a system turns people of goodwill into hardened cynics and continuously sabotages any good intentions among people. Rather, a progressive socialist worldview is based upon helping each other meet our needs in a cooperative manner. By this switch in consciousness, we will achieve that for which we have always longed.

In a PROUTist local community, the economic domain is a part of the social domain in which local people interact and transact for the benefit of all. The economy does not stand apart from our lives, nor does it have dominion over us.

## What Does "Local" Mean?

P. R. Sarkar does not look to the corporations or the governments to solve human problems. Rather, he believes that local people should take matters into their own hands when it comes to their economic livelihood. He recommends that they form their own socio-economic unit (SEU), their own local socio-economy.

In this effort, it is necessary to define what we mean by local. When people shop at corporate chain stores instead of shopping at local stores, money leaves the area. Are chain stores a part of the local economy under PROUT? No.

Today, a "local" economy, under capitalism, especially in rural areas, is largely dependent upon national and international chain stores, the exploitation of raw materials for export, and government transfer payments, which include welfare checks, disability insurance, Medicare, veteran's benefits, food stamps, etc. Given this, can we truly speak of a local economy? No, we cannot. Rather, our economy is only an outpost or colony of the global economy, administered at the federal level and enforced at the state level. Local people are only wage-slaves in this system.

When enough local people support the idea of creating a "People's Economy," under their own control they will take the first steps to economic freedom. This idea is not far-fetched and will continue to grow as a result of the increased pressure on people due to economic decline and job insecurity. This being said, the impetus for creating a local socio-economy may be triggered by different local circumstances. In some communities, for example, local activists may create political pressure to support a shift in the economic paradigm. In other communities, there may be a system of strong, progressive political leadership that initiates the change. And in yet other communities, opportunities for change may arise in a context of profound economic crisis or disaster. In any case, the further we move along the trajectory of global capitalism, people's welfare will be increasingly put into jeopardy by resource depletion, climate change, environmental destruction, and economic collapse. Local reorganization will become imperative for survival. Therefore, the sooner local people begin to put a new local economy in place the better off we will be.

There are many groups and organizations involved in developing local self-reliance strategies, including the Institute for Local Self-Reliance, local Sustainable Development initiatives, Permaculture projects, Bioneers, Transition Town Initiatives, Local First, The Green Party, Communalism, etc. Each can provide local organizers with models and food for thought concerning principles and policies. For example, in our discussion below on "who will do the planning," we drew upon the planning process established by Transition Town Totnes,[263] which has been involved in creating a local socio-economy for the past nine years. This community has done impressive work in actually putting a local economy on the ground within a capitalist society.

Who are the local people? Local people, according to PROUT, are not everyone currently living within a given vicinity. Rather, they are those who have merged their individual socio-economic interests with that of the socio-economic unit in which they live. This concept of local people has nothing to do with physical complexion, race, gender, religion, political ideology, language, or birth place. The fundamental issue is whether or not each person or family has consciously identified their individual socio-economic interests with the collective interests of their neighbors and is willing to work for the common welfare. Those who will not make such a commitment should eventually be considered outsiders even if they currently live in the same locality or town.[264]

No outsider should be allowed to interfere in local economic affairs or in the system of production and distribution within the local socio-economy. This rule is necessary to prevent the outflow of wealth from the local socio-economic unit. If local wealth is exploited and sent out of the area, the local people will continue to be vulnerable to outside economic exploitation and the local economy will be undermined.

## Socio-Economic Units (SEUs)

A local socio-economy can also be called a socio-economic unit. It is a self-defined community of people living within specified geographic boundaries who have expressed their intention to work together to meet their common needs. In Sanskrit, samáj or "society" means a group of people who are moving together happily and peacefully.[265] Amitai Etzioni, one of the leaders of the current American communitarian movement, says that communities "can be defined as having two characteristics: first, a web of affect-laden relationships among a group of individuals, relationships that often crisscross and reinforce one another (as opposed to one-on-one or chain-like individual relationships); and second, a measure of commitment to a set of shared values, norms, and meanings, and a shared history and identity—in short, a particular culture."[266] PROUT theory adds another characteristic to the definition of a local community—the primary intention of the local people in working together in a cooperative manner is to meet each other's basic needs instead of working for personal or corporate profit.

## Economic Decentralization

Many people still believe they can depend on corporate and government planners to design and finance the profit-making enterprises required to meet their basic needs, but joblessness and underemployment always remain large problems under capitalism. Impoverishment is a natural by-product of capitalism. It is the result of the wealth being concentrated in a few hands. To keep impoverishment from undermining the status quo, corporations and the government have agreed to provide a minimum welfare system, enough to keep the poor from rioting. In the US, people point to food stamps, Medicaid, and other federal programs as a means to alleviate poverty, but these doles are always inadequate and can be snatched away at a moments notice as we have recently seen. People cannot depend upon the federal government to improve their lives. Neither can local people depend upon foundation grants or federal grants for their survival.

Under present conditions, PROUT rejects the premise that humanity's basic needs can be met through a global capitalist economy. Dependence upon multinational corporations has only served to increase the poverty of people. The capitalists move their money to those localities where labor is cheapest. In so doing, they expand that local economy with jobs, but as soon as they discover another locality where people will work for less or the natural resources are more abundant, they leave the first locality without jobs, resources, or any hope for a better life. This is what is happening in the US economy today. Through automation and the sending of millions of jobs to China and other countries, the capitalists have abandoned the American people. No government programs will ever be able to rebuild the American economy simply because the capitalists can make more money abroad.

As David McGraw, the author of The Economics of Revolution says:

> If you are struggling to get by and running up debt to make ends meet, it is not your fault. It is the intentional outcome of government policy and economic central planning. In the present economy, it is impossible for 70% of the working age population to earn enough income to afford basic necessities, without taking on ev-

er-increasing levels of debt, which they will never be able to pay back because there are not enough jobs that generate the necessary income to keep up with the cost of living. [267]

Such a pathetic condition can only be eliminated by local people taking matters into their own hands in a cooperative manner to meet their own basic needs. When we say that production under progressive socialism is to meet needs not profit, this is not to say that surplus value will not be generated, it is to say that surplus value will not accrue to corporate "owners," but to the community as a whole. Surplus value will be used to increase wages, improve production, reward individual initiative, and enhance the education, human services and culture of the local people or create conditions for more leisure for the people to pursue personal growth.

## Economic Democracy

In a PROUT samaj, economic planning and implementation is in the hands of local people. The capitalist system trumpets its political democracy as the best system the world has ever seen, yet without economic democracy, capitalism has proven unable to meet people's basic needs and protect the environment. It is estimated that currently only thirty percent of the population is benefitted from the capitalist system and this percentage continues to drop.[268] According to a recent study by Oxfam International, eight billionaires, including Bill Gates, Warren Buffett, Carlos Slim, Jeff Bezos, Mark Zuckerberg, Amancio Ortega, Larry Ellison, and Michael Bloomberg collectively hoard $426 billion dollars which is as much wealth as that possessed by half of humanity. Since 2015, the richest 1% has owned as much wealth as the entire humanity.[269] This horrific inequality has trapped billions of people in poverty and is destabilizing governments everywhere. As poverty increases more countries in the world assume a war footing. Global capitalism is a mortal sin against humanity and needs to be eliminated at the earliest moment.

There is only one way to stop such rabid economic exploitation and alleviate the plight of the people everywhere, and that is for people at the local level to begin to pool their resources and labor to implement their own economy. Of course, extremely poor communities will need help from outside the community and that is where selfless service comes in. As P. R. Sarkar tells us:

> When the members of a society come to a unanimous decision, "We'll move together, we'll live together in good times or bad," then their collective movement is known as Samaj or society. Some may have moved far ahead; some may have lagged behind. Some may be unable to walk due to pain in their legs. Some may have fallen on their faces. Those who do not even care to look after their companions trailing behind them are not worthy to be called members of society. The proper thing is for all members of the society to move in unison; and while moving together, each member should feel a responsibility for every other member of society. Those who are unable to move must be carried so that the rhythm of the collective movement remains unbroken.[270]

Economic decentralization means very little without economic democracy. Only by participating in the design and construction of one's own socio-economic life-support system will local people be able to guarantee the minimum requirements of life to its participants and protect their local environment. To put economic democracy into practice means that people will need to work together to assess their situation, make plans, and design the systems to serve themselves. Economic democracy also means that local people control their local businesses and that these businesses provide for the full employment of community members.

Economic democracy becomes manifest in a community when mutual decision-making enters the workplace. This is best realized by the creation of cooperatives in which all members have a vote in such key issues as wage scales, production targets, price of goods and services, work hours, etc. While there will always be a need for a division of labor, management will follow the decisions of all the workers regarding agreed upon issues.

## A Balanced Local Economy

A basic tenet of progressive socialism is that everything comes from the earth. Local resources consist of land that is composed of minerals, soil, water, forests, animals, farms, structures, small businesses, villages, towns, etc. To increase local employment and increase resiliency will require that we use local resources to create goods to meet the people's basic needs. Creating the goods and services necessary to meet the basic needs of the local people is the core activity of the people's economy. The people's economy will include not just farms, forests, mines, and gardens. It will also include pre-farm businesses like seed production, the manufacture of tool and technologies for growing, harvesting and processing, etc., and post-farm businesses like food processing, mills, all kinds of product development from local raw materials, distribution services, etc. In other words, we will need to create an agrarian revolution in order to transform the local economy.

Today, in the United States less than three percent of the population work on farms and this number keeps dropping. This is due to the continued use of fossil fuels, large scale farm equipment, genetically modified (GMO) corn and soybean crops, and the purchase of real food (especially vegetables and fruits) from outside the country. It stands to reason that in a PROUT socio-economy, the sustainable agricultural sector at the local level will be greatly expanded. This will also include urban agriculture. Permaculture activists, as well as many organizations involved in sustainable agriculture, have already made great progress in creating low-tech models for growing organic food under various conditions. This work will continue and expand under progressive socialism.

For a People's Economy, dominated by food and farm production, we will need to shift our idea of employment categories. Instead of having only three percent of the population employed in agriculture, as exists in the present US economy, this number may have to be thirty percent or forty percent within a local socio-economic unit. In addition, greater numbers of people will have to be employed in the pre- and post-agriculture industries. It is possible that as much as eighty percent of the people may be employed in agriculturally-related production. There will be a great need for a wide range of industries to support local farm

production. Currently, small-scale farm tools and machinery are difficult to come by and small-scale organic farmers must diligently search
for machinery, like small tractors, that often were produced only in the
1940s and 1950s. Organic seeds, fertilizers, and organic pesticides are
also difficult to procure at the local level and presently must be ordered
from across the country. These products will have to be produced locally
under a PROUT economy.

Pre-agriculture employment will produce all inputs for production including machinery, tools, heirloom and hybrid seeds, organic
fertilizers, etc. Post-agricultural industries will include value-added
operations such as flour mills, oil mills, cloth mills, paper mills, herbal
medicine factories, consumer goods, household supplies, food processing, distribution, storage, etc. In establishing such an economy,
many local jobs will be created. In fact, there will be jobs for every
available worker and in exchange for their labor, at minimum, they
will earn the provision of their basic needs. We will work together to
see that this happens.

In this effort, the urban areas within a developed socio-economic
unit, especially those containing colleges and universities with research
capacity, may be tasked with developing more jobs in pre- and post-agriculture, while the rural areas engage more in land-based production.

In time, the local economy will develop key industries to supply
energy, water, raw materials, and equipment on a no-profit, no loss
basis to local residents and industry. In our transition from a capitalist
local economy to a progressive socialist samaj, we must remember that
current government agencies will typically lack the vision and mission
required to facilitate such a broad ranging economic transformation.
Currently, government employees are acculturated into the status quo
and work according to regulations, guidelines, and practices set up to
facilitate the centralized economy. As such, they often over-regulate and
enforce laws that put local people at an economic disadvantage.

Having said this, efforts should be made to engage government
employees in the building of a local people's economy, but we should not
depend upon them for leadership or place the success of such planning
at their disposal. We must be able to move without them. Nonetheless,
it would be most beneficial if local administrations begin to explore

how to bring key industries, particularly energy, water, and local raw materials under local control.

While key industries are run on a no profit, no loss basis to minimize the cost of production for local enterprises, this does not mean that workers in those industries, will not be eligible to receive bonuses, if and when they contribute to the maximum utilization of a resource by saving time or materials. So also, a certain amount of income will be set aside by the key industry to improve its infrastructure.

## Dimensions of a Mature PROUT Economy

According to Progressive Utilization Theory, a developed economy will consist of four parts: (1) people's economy, (2) psycho-economy, (3) commercial economy, and (4) general economy.[271] This quadri-dimensional economic model greatly expands the contemporary capitalist and communist concepts of an economy. This is because PROUT's primary aim is to create the optimum conditions by which people can also manifest their mental and spiritual potentialities within the physical and social dimensions of society.

### People's Economy

The People's Economy deals with the essential needs of the people. It includes the financing, raw materials, tools and technology, labor, production, distribution, marketing, shipping, storage, recycling, and all related activities required to meet the basic needs of the socio-economic unit. The People's Economy is directly concerned with the provision of food, clothing, housing, medical treatment, and education to all local people. As such, it must also address the needs for transportation, energy, and water. Continuous improvement in and ready availability of the goods and services required to meet these needs is the main purpose of the people's economy.[272]

The basic needs will be guaranteed by ensuring that the minimum wage will provide the purchasing capacity required to meet these needs. This guarantee will be enshrined in the local charter and eventually in the world constitution as a cardinal human right. This will give the citizens of any socio-economic unit the legal power to rectify the situation if their minimum requirements are not met. As the people's economy will address the minimum requirements and people's subsistence problems, it must take precedence over other parts of the economy. As such, it is the first part of the local economy that is constructed.

The people's economy will be developed by local private businesses and cooperatives. Private businesses will be limited in size and scope to prevent monopoly production and exploitation. In time, private businesses engaged in the production of basic needs will merge with cooperatives. Private businesses, however, will continue to engage in the production of luxury items, the arts, special services, etc. If a private business becomes too large, it will be required to function as a cooperative. Cooperative industries are the best means of independently organizing people so that they may take collective responsibility for their own livelihood.

The People's Economy is based on the principle of employment for all. Its intention is to eradicate mass poverty. The people's economy will grow based upon a revolution in the agricultural sector. The goods and services required to provide food, shelter, clothing, health care, and education are all derived from raw materials extracted from the land. For this reason, a people's economy will depend heavily on rural areas.

**Psycho-Economy**

While the people's economy is concerned primarily with the provision of the minimum requirements of life, the psycho-economy is concerned with converting our desire for material objects into mental, and spiritual pursuits. Communism and capitalism are essentially materialist philosophies. Both encourage a psychology of material attachment, which, in turn, encourages the pursuit of money in order to purchase an endless stream of material objects of enjoyment whose production adversely affect the natural environment. Therefore, people living under these two systems develop the mental propensity to run after crude physical objects. This propensity is the inevitable outcome of the continuous externalization of our thirst for limitlessness, and as such continues to drive people from one object to another.[273] As we have seen, the unchecked psychic urge for material acquisition has resulted in merciless exploitation. Such inhuman exploitation has caused the deprivation of millions of people as capitalism has engulfed the whole world.

In a similar fashion, the psychic urges and desires in a communist society also tend towards material accumulation because the mind does not get any scope in an atheistic society to divert the flow of its propensities towards spirituality. At the same time, the totalitarian rule of the communist world also tries to suppress the tendency towards material enjoyment by brute force in the name of equal distribution. This proposition is basically wrong and illogical. Such urges and desires cannot be suppressed by brute force.

Both capitalism and communism are anti-human. Under both these systems, psychic urges and desires, instead of being properly channeled, continue to increase one's karma and create a negative movement within the mind.

What then is the answer to producing positive psychic urges and desires? First, psychic urges for material objects should never be suppressed; rather our psychic urges should be channeled towards more subtle pursuits through a proper psycho-spiritual approach. In this psycho-spiritual approach, the goal of psychic urges is always singular. With constant spiritual practice, the mind, with its thousand urges and desires, becomes one-pointed and inexorably moves towards the Supreme Divinity.

This inner channelization and one-pointed conversion into psycho-spiritual desire brings about radical changes in individual and collective life. It makes people strong and dynamic and inspires them to support the principle of social equality. This is the goal of the psycho-economy.

The psycho-economy has two branches. The first branch endeavors to eradicate exploitative and unjust economic practices, behaviors, and structures. It will counter all economic and psycho-economic exploitation and make people aware of how capitalists, individually and collectively, exploit society and create unhealthy urges and objects that crudify the mind and prevent its expansion. The first and foremost duty of psycho-economics, therefore, is to wage a tireless fight against all degenerating and dehumanizing economic trends in society. Many nonprofit groups today that are working against exploitation would be considered as being employed in the psycho-economy of PROUT.

The second branch of psycho-economy develops and enhances the positive psychic desires of the individual and collective minds. This branch is virtually unknown today, but it will become an extremely important branch of economics in the future. It will ensure equilibrium in all levels of the economy. It will find new and creative solutions to economic problems to nurture the maximum utilization of psychic and spiritual potentialities. Psycho-economics will add to the glamour of economics.

While the people's economy will initially be the main concern of local people, the psycho-economy will gain increasing importance in the future once the problems of subsistence are gradually solved. The psycho-economy will be of major importance in a highly developed and mechanized economy where people only have to work a few hours a week and have much spare time. Artists and writers, social event planners, recreation and leisure groups, organizers of spiritual gatherings, and producers of goods to promote positive psychic desires who are inspired by the vision of service and blessedness, will take the lead in this aspect of the economy.

## Commercial Economy

In common parlance, a commercial economy consists of the exchange of goods, services, and labor activities that have a well defined monetary value. Commercial economies are often contrasted with sharing or gift economies where exchanges may not have an assigned monetary value.[274] The commercial economy, for example, does not include activities such as childrearing, housework, family care giving, and other types of necessary domestic labor, which are typically performed on an unpaid basis. Progressive socialism, however, brings an entirely new meaning to the concept of commercial economy. In a local samaj, the commercial economy is concerned with the development of efficient scientific methods of production and distribution, which will not incur loss and where output will exceed input. The aim of the commercial economy is to ensure the maximum utilization and rational distribution of resources for the benefit of all.

The commercial economy will create efficiencies in the people's economy as well as set the stage for inter-samaj and inter-state trading. It will facilitate economic parity, communication, and administrative efficiency.

The commercial economy will facilitate the cooperation of two or more adjoining socio-economic units (samajs), who have attained a high degree of socio-economic development. In such cases, they will be able to merge and form a single larger unit known as a federated state. This will further the welfare of their respective citizens and enhance their socio-economic interests. Even though two or more samajs may merge into a federated state, they will have the option to maintain their own people's economies. Nonetheless political organization and the merger of other aspects of the economy will come under the guidance of a federated state. (See Chapter Four, section on The Government Structure of Progressive Socialism for a description of federated states.)

In this respect, PROUT does not favor the continued existence of many small samajs and states, each with its separate budget and administration. Once the people's economies are firmly established in the different samajs, those samajs should seek to merge with adjacent samajs to strengthen their economies and overcome problems due to unnecessary duplication. In other words, small samajs should be expanded into larger socio-economic units so long as local control of basic needs is not forfeited.

This process of unification, for example, may gradually result in the formation of one socio-economic unit for all of the Midwest, or even the United States or North America. Gradually, it may include all the Americas together. Eventually, the whole world may function as one integrated socio-economic unit. After reaching this stage of development, socio-economic groupifications will have attained a state of equipoise and equilibrium, and universal fraternity will become a reality. However, no matter the size of the SEU, the same principles hold true: the local SEU still maintains control over its local economy and economic issues will remain separate from political issues, which remain the jurisdiction of the federated and world boards. As SEU's merge with other SEU's they may or may not decided to form a federated state, but because of the complexity of the merger of multiple units, they most likely will create a federated state to handle common legislative and judicial issues.

If the universal sentiments of human beings are given prominence and human unity is made the base of collective development, diversity will enrich humanity rather than tear it apart. If each socio-economic unit is inspired by a comprehensive ideology and a universal outlook, human society will move ahead with accelerating speed towards a sublime ideal.

If a single person remains outside the influence of universalism or becomes a victim of exploitation, then the foundation of universal humanism will be undermined. Hence, PROUT has adopted a rational method to solve socio-economic problems, which may be characterized as "universal in spirit but local in approach." The Commercial Economy, based upon the principles of universalism, will be led by scientists, local and regional planners, environmentalists, trade experts, management experts etc., who will be charged with enhancing the productivity of the local economy and integrating it with its neighbors according to the guidelines of improving the maximum utilization and rational distribution of all human and natural resources in a sustainable manner.[275]

**General Economy**

In 1949, a French intellectual, Georges Bataille, wrote a book entitled, *The Accursed Share: An Essay on General Economy*. In this work, Bataille coined the term "general economy." His premise was that surplus wealth was destined for unproductive use. This unproductive part of the economy, Bataille called "the accursed share."

According to Bataille, the unproductive surplus would either be spent on luxuries such as sex, gambling, the arts, spectacles, or monuments or be destined for an "outrageous and catastrophic outpouring" in war or destructive or ruinous acts of sacrifice.

Bataille is worth mentioning as an economist because he employed the notion of "excess" energy that he found in the development of natural systems and applied it to a human economy. Unlike classical economists who saw only scarcity, Bataille sees an "excess" of energy. This extra energy can be used productively for a society's growth or it can be lavishly expended. Bataille insists that a society's growth, as with all living organisms, always runs up against limits of utility. The excess energy, or waste, created beyond utility he called "luxury." The form and role luxury assumes in a society are characteristic of that society.[276]

PROUT's theory of General Economy also recognizes the idea of excess energy in any productive process. PROUT's objective, however, is not to waste this excess or surplus energy on useless activities or on war, but to use it to improve the living standard of the people. For example, this excess can be used to create a wage scale that, at its base, allows a person to purchase his or her basic needs, but which permits additional benefits that are offered to people who make advanced contributions to the welfare of society. Under PROUT, for example there will be a minimum wage and a maximum wage, wherein, hypothetically, the maximum wage may be ten times the amount of the minimum wage. The greater the contribution one makes to society, the greater his or her monetary reward. There will, by necessity, be a cap on wages, however, to ensure that the base wage is sufficient to meet basic needs and also allow for an increase in the quality of life.

But we all know that money is not the only reward that humans value. We also value non-tangible things like social recognition, leisure time etc. These can be easily rewarded to those who merit the gratitude of the local people.

The general economy under PROUT will address more than individual rewards. It will include the organization of the industrial infrastructure at all levels to improve the collective welfare. For example, it will work to create efficiencies within PROUT's three-tiered industrial structure, which includes cooperatives, private ownership, and "key industries." The purpose of key industries is to increase the surplus wealth of all enterprises in the samaj.

In addition to increasing the production of surplus wealth in a sustainable manner, it will also explore the means by which to employ this surplus production for the good of all participants within the local socio-economic unit. This applies to the plant and animal species in the geographic region as well. This part of a PROUTist economy will require the expertise of a wide variety of experts, including those who are working in other parts of the economy. We might say that it will require the participation of every member of the local socio-economy by one degree or another.

The four dimensions of a PROUT economy should be integrated and adjusted according to the principles of universalism to ensure the maximum utilization and rational distribution of all resources, and to harmonize human progress with the needs of other life forms and the planetary systems.[277] According to current mainstream characterizations of economies, a PROUT economy, therefore, has elements of a market-based economy, a command-based economy, as well as a green economy. But its basic feature is that it is intended to meet the basic needs of the people as a means to increase their mental and spiritual potentialities. The opportunity to increase these potentialities is not a luxury to be wasted. Rather, it is to fulfill our human nature and our purpose for living.

## The Principles of a Local Socio-Economy

The most important economic issue today is how to increase the living standard of people throughout the world. This issue has never been resolved because of continued economic exploitation by the rich and powerful within the capitalist and communist nations.

Because the rich and powerful are not concerned about the welfare of the people, we the people will have to take matters into our own hands. We will have to create circumstantial pressure from all sides in order to limit the centralized economy's stranglehold over our basic necessities and establish decentralized economies to meet these basic needs. To assist us in this endeavor, the follow principles have been articulated:

### The Local People Decide

A socio-economy, based upon the principle of economic democracy in which local people make the decisions, is the only way to achieve our all-around welfare. Only by such an arrangement will we guarantee our economic prosperity and also pave the way for individual and collective psycho-spiritual progress.

Local socio-economies cannot be planned and controlled from afar. They are derived from the desire and hard work of the local people who choose to participate in them. A local planning board will help the people develop a master plan for their local socio-economy and, thereafter, social boards composed of moralists will help supervise the creation of the new economy. The people collectively will determine the quantum of products and services required to meet their minimum requirements and set a wage scale to ensure that these products and services can be purchased by the people to meet their basic needs. All agricultural, industrial, and trade policies will eventually be formulated by social boards in accordance with input from producer and consumer cooperatives. For example, the members of farmer cooperatives will have a voice in forming the policies regarding agricultural production, pricing, and the sale and distribution of agricultural commodities. The price of agricultural commodities will be fixed on a rational basis by taking into account the cost of labor, raw materials, transportation and storage, depreciation, taxes, the collective need, the purchasing capacity of the people, etc. In addition, the price may include a rational profit of not more than fifteen percent of the cost of production. This profit may be used to improve the production process, increase wages, or reward special effort depending upon the vote of the cooperative's members and the administrative social boards.

### "Women and Children First"

PROUT is adamant about the dignity and rightful status of women. A true human society can only be created when all its members, male and female, young and old, black and white, have equal opportunity to express all their potentialities in the mundane, psychic, and spiritual spheres. Under progressive socialism, all women, as well as men, will have access to advanced education and will have the opportunity to become economically self-reliant.[278]

Historically, women have always played the dominant role in keeping local communities healthy and vibrant. There is no doubt that many women will lead the movement for a local socio-economy. They will sit on planning boards and all social boards in equal, or in some cases, greater numbers than men because currently their sense of cooperation and intuition in often superior to that of men.

A woman's role in society, so long denigrated under church and state, will be honored within the local samaj. Sadvipras will fight for this development. The traditional role of women as mothers and homemakers will be honored and they will be compensated as any other worker. If they choose to home school their children, they will be paid as any other teacher. If they choose to form child care cooperatives with friends and neighbors that is their business. It is probable that child care cooperatives will be associated with farmers coops, producer coops, etc., so that husbands and wives can alternate in caring for the children. Men will also be encouraged to raise the children, if their wives are required by the samaj in other capacities. Men and women will be compensated equally for their work and no one will earn less than what is required to meet their basic needs.

Children will also become more integral to the local community because, in a samaj, all community members will realize that the children are their future. As such, children will find themselves with many more teachers and educational opportunities than they have now. The current education system was set up to train children to become compliant workers and specialists who are given piecemeal chores in factories and prevented from ever putting the whole picture together.[279] Children under progressive socialism will be provided with meaningful mental and physical "hands on" experiences according to the needs of the community. They will be allowed to think comprehensively and creatively. They will be trained in the principles of universalism and taught moral, caring behavior. They will be taught to be sadvipras and to serve their communities. Our children will soar under such conditions.

### All Natural and Human Resources in a Local Socio-Economy Will Be Controlled by the Local People

The third principle of a local economy is that all the resources in a local socio-economic unit will be controlled by the local people.[280] Capitalists typically gain control over the raw materials in a region in the pursuit of profit. This should not be allowed to continue. Rather, available resources must be utilized for the socio-economic development of local people.[281] In particular, the resources, which are required to produce the minimum requirements, must be in local hands, and all the industries based on these resources will have to be controlled entirely by the local people. Local raw materials will be fully utilized locally to produce all kinds of commodities necessary for the economic development of a socio-economic unit. This is completely different from the global economy in which local resources and local labor are controlled by distant multi-national corporations and federal governments.[282]

After meeting the minimum requirements of the people in the local area, surplus wealth can be distributed among meritorious people according to the degree of their contribution to society. For example, while a common person may require a bicycle, a doctor may require a car. But there will also be provisions in the economy to balance the gap between the minimum requirements of all and the amenities of meritorious people. For example, to increase the standard of living of common people, they may be provided with scooters instead of bicycles. Although there is some difference between a scooter and a car, the gap that existed between a car and a bicycle has been partially reduced. There should be a continuous effort to raise the standard of living of the common people to that of the most meritorious. This gap, however, will never vanish completely, but the gap should never be allowed to endanger the welfare of the common people. If this is allowed to occur, the common people will then be deprived. Exploitation will re-emerge in society in the guise of amenities. A decentralized economy leaves no such loophole because, on the one hand, the standard of the minimum requirements will continue to increase, and on the other, the provision of amenities will be assessed from the viewpoint of the collective welfare.[283]

## Local People Fully Employed in the Local Economy

All the local people who are ready, willing, and able should be employed in the local socio-economic unit. The process of building the local socio-economic unit should begin with the creation of agricultural, producer, and consumer cooperatives. In other words, a decentralized economy will be based upon an agricultural revolution.

Unemployment is a critical economic problem today and setting the goal of one hundred percent employment of the local people is the only way to solve this problem. Immediately, labor-intensive industries, based on food and/or farm production, should be started or made more productive where they already exist. Admittedly, food production is hard work, but the collective samaj movement and the realization that the surplus wealth will go to the local people will inspire their effort.

Nutritious food that is locally produced for local consumption will increase people's health and the growing of this food will meet their need for physical exercise.

Aside from farm production of food and fiber, cooperatives will also be created locally to provide farm inputs (tools, equipment, seeds, organic fertilizers, etc) as well as process raw farm products into value-added foods or other products. All these jobs will help to alleviate the unemployment problem in the local economy. The production of farm inputs and the processing of farm outputs may be handled in the urban areas of a socio-economy.

Cooperatives will provide employment for local people, and also ensure that the skills and expertise of the local people are fully utilized. Because the basic necessities will be provided to all, it behooves the local cooperatives to employ every able-bodied human being to contribute to the local welfare of the people. Educated people, whether of the merchant, intellectual, or warrior mentality, should also be employed in cooperatives so that they are not required to leave the local area in search of employment or move from the countryside to the cities.

For the development of agriculture there will be a great need for specialists and technicians, so educated people will have to train unskilled rural people in the skills to develop the agricultural sector. In addition, all types of pre-production and post-production industries will have to be developed according to the needs and resources of the local area, and these industries should be managed as cooperatives.

Local people must always be given preference in employment. If this policy is followed, there will be no surplus or deficit labor among the local people, and if too many people do come from outside areas, they may not be able to be accommodated in the local economy. Wherever a floating population exists in a particular region, the outflow of capital remains unchecked and the economic development of the area is undermined. This is why all people who live in a local samaj arena will be encouraged to join the local socio-economic unit or be considered outsiders who maintain their allegiance to the central capitalist economy.

As the People's Economy becomes sustainable and the psycho-economy has educated the people concerning their rights as human beings and has encouraged their participation in the local economy, people can begin to build the psycho-economy, commercial economy, and the general economy as indicated above.

## Production to Meet Needs Not Profit

The fifth principle of a decentralized economy is that production will be based on consumption, not profit. This means that producers will give first preference to those items which increase the standard of living of the local people.

This principle will be realized as the commodities produced by an SEU are sold in the local market itself. No commodity that is locally produced will be traded or sold outside the SEU until all local people have access to that commodity on a sustainable basis. This rule will guarantee the real social security of the people. Because money will circulate within the local market, there will be no outflow of local capital. As such, local capital will continue to increase and this will ensure that people's income will have an upward trend and their purchasing capacity will continuously increase. In time, as more people join the samaj movement, all the money currently being drained from the local economy by the multinational capitalists will eventually be retained in the local economy.

The possibility of economic catastrophes in the local economy will thereby be eliminated. In such a system, wealth will continually increase at the local level and people's purchasing capacity will also increase. No economic system in the world has so far been able to continuously increase the purchasing capacity of the people.

## Basic Needs Met for All

The primary purpose of creating a local socio-economy is to meet the basic needs (food, shelter, clothing, health care, and education) of every participant in the local samaj. The ability to meet one's basic needs will be facilitated by the setting of a minimum wage by the local social boards and cooperatives that will guarantee the adequate purchasing capacity to meet those needs. In the transition period between the capitalist local economy and the local economy under progressive socialism, paychecks can be supplemented by a local currency that can be used to purchase locally produced goods and services. The goal of the local planners is to remove all the obstacles that interfere with the people having their basic needs met.

## Organize through Cooperatives

The seventh principle of a decentralized economy is that production and distribution will be organized through cooperatives. This is the practical means by which economic democracy gets expressed at the local level.

"Operation" means "to get something done. When an operation is done by collective effort it is called "cooperation." Under progressive socialism, this implies that something is done with equal rights, equal human prestige, and equal social standing. Where cooperation is between free human beings, each having equal rights and mutual respect for each other, and each working for the welfare of the other, it is called "coordinated cooperation." Where people do something under another's control, then it is called "subordinated cooperation." Within a local socio-economy the goal should be to do everything with coordinated cooperation and always avoid subordinated cooperation.[284]

No economic system today is based on coordinated cooperation. Rather, they are based on subordinated cooperation, resulting in the degeneration of society's moral fabric. For example, in the United States there is a glaring lack of racial and gender equality and no coordinated cooperation whatsoever. This lack of proper equilibrium in social life is causing the whole structure of society to become unglued.

The creation of cooperatives in a progressive socialist economy is completely different than the commune system under communism. In the commune system, society is reduced to merely a production-distribution mechanism under a regimented system of control. Rather than increasing production, the commune system has led to a decrease in production. In the commune system there are no individual rights to decision-making or to the use of resources. Without a sense of personal "ownership," people do not work hard or care for any property. If farmers feel they have permanent usufructuary rights to the land, they will always produce a better product. Such a sentiment is suppressed in the commune system, resulting in sluggish production and psychic oppression. So also, in the commune system, intelligent people are forced to work in jobs unsuitable for them and are paid wages that have nothing to do with their abilities or contributions to society. Because there is no incentive system and because individual initiative by meritorious people is not encouraged, people do not work hard. Such a system can never solve society's economic problems, either in agriculture or in industry.[285]

Some critics also point to the lackluster performance of cooperatives within the capitalist system but P. R. Sarkar challenges such critics:

> One of the principal reasons for the past failure of the cooperative movement is economic centralization. It is extremely difficult for cooperatives to succeed in an economic environment of exploitation, corruption, and materialism, so people cannot accept the cooperative system wholeheartedly. Cooperatives are forced to compete with the monopoly capitalists for local markets, and the rights of the local people over their raw materials are not recognized. Such circumstances have undermined the success of the cooperative movement in many countries of the world.[286]

Another reason that cooperatives find it hard to function in a capitalist economy is that the "profit motive" psychology of capitalism stands completely opposite the principle of cooperation.

Cooperatives will succeed in a decentralized economy, however, because all the local people will be involved in decisions to increase the utility and rational distribution of their own products. Trade boards composed of representatives of each industry will act to create an equilibrium between the production of the different industries and the needs of the people. The availability of local raw materials will guarantee a constant supply of resources to cooperative enterprises, and their goods will be easily sold in the local market. This economic certainty will create greater interest and involvement among the cooperative members and the local people will become more confident of their economic security and the cooperative system.

As far as possible, agriculture, industry, and trade should be managed through cooperatives. The employment of local people in outside corporations should be gradually switched over to employment in local cooperatives. Only where production cannot be undertaken by cooperatives, either because of the complex nature or the small scale of operations, should it be undertaken by local governments or private enterprises.

While mainstream production will be handled through producer cooperatives, the distribution of commodities should be done through consumer cooperatives. This will facilitate the balance between production and consumption and increase the security of the people. Therefore, adequate safeguards for cooperatives will have to be arranged. According to progressive socialism, the cooperative system, decentralized economy, and economic democracy are inseparable.

### Always Meet Local Demands First

To facilitate the meeting of basic needs, the particular demands of the local area should be addressed first. Local conditions should be carefully studied and programs adopted as per the requirements of the particular locality. In many areas today, for example, local people are living through a healthcare nightmare due to public ignorance of nutrition and lack of access to fresh fruits and vegetables. Diet-related diseases like heart disease, diabetes, obesity, and certain cancers have reached epidemic proportions. As such, local planners will need to focus attention on the relationship between fresh, unprocessed, whole foods and the health of people. In the rural areas, they will need to build the infrastructure to train farmers and get their foods to local markets. Urban areas can develop industries that either provide inputs to agriculture or add value to agricultural products. Urban agriculture is also a viable pursuit. In any case, production should be planned to meet local demands first. A decentralized, needs-based economy never puts production for export first.

### Organize the Economy as a Three-Tiered Structure.

In over-industrialized countries like the United States, which are based on a centralized economic model, large corporations maintain their existence by exploiting the raw materials and labor of undeveloped countries as well as the rural areas within their own borders. This makes local economic self-reliance very difficult.

In a decentralized economy, the economic model will be different. Both labor-intensive and capital-intensive industries will be developed to increase the productive capacity of the local socio-economic unit. To accomplish this, PROUT divides the economy into three parts: (1) key industries managed by the local government, (2) medium scale cooperatives and (3) small-scale private enterprises. This system will eliminate confusion regarding whether or not a particular industry should be managed privately or by the government, and will avoid duplication between the government and private enterprise.[287]

Such an economic structure should be based on the principles of self-reliance, maximum utilization, rational distribution, decentralization, and progressive increases in the standard of living of all people. Through the never ending creation of new industries, new products and new production techniques incorporating the latest scientific discoveries, the vitality of the economy can be increased.[288]

## Key Industries

Under PROUT, a key industry is one on which many other industries depend. These may include electricity, raw materials, water, waste management, highways, education, etc.

To reduce the opportunity for key industries to become exploitive, they will be managed by the local government on a "no profit, no loss" basis.

Another reason to have key industries managed by the immediate government is that they are often too large and too complex to be efficiently run on a cooperative basis.

Every socio-economic unit, and every region within a socio-economic unit must strive to be self-sufficient in power generation. In the transition period, a local administration composed of government and non-government members will have to arrange for the supply of sufficient power to facilitate agriculture and industrial production through the creation of a key industry. The local administration will supply locally-generated power such as solar energy, thermal energy, bio-gas, hydroelectricity, or any other power which is easily available locally.

We may argue, in principle, that governments should not run commercial concerns, nonetheless, in those cases where it is not possible to run a concern on a cooperative basis, the government should take the lead. Aside from key industries like power, water, and waste management, Mr. Sarkar also speaks of governments running operations to produce goods if industrial cooperatives are unable to manufacture them. Under such conditions, however, he says, such concerns should be mostly assembly plants. The manufacture of component parts for these assembly plants, however, should only be done through industrial cooperatives.

To guard against exploitation by the government, Mr. Sarkar says that such plants should be run on a "no profit, no loss" basis as any other key industry. This status will reduce the possibility of labor problems that can result over the question of profits. It is, however, necessary to keep both financial and commercial accounts to ensure that the concern does not run at a loss. If any loss occurs in such a plant it should be converted into an industrial cooperative.[289]

Because key industries are run on a no profit, no loss basis, this will lower the cost of production for the cooperatives and small businesses and increase the purchasing capacity of the local people. Energy for transportation, communications, schools, colleges, and hospitals should also be supplied on a no profit, no loss basis to maintain social dynamism.

## Cooperatives

We have spoken about cooperatives above, so we do not need to repeat our discussion of the role of cooperatives in a local socio-economy. We will only say that the cooperative sector will be the main sector of the economy because they are the best means for local people to organize themselves to guarantee their livelihood, and enable themselves to control their economic well-being. As such, most medium-scale industries will be managed as cooperatives. These cooperatives will be guided by the needs of the local people for specific goods and services and not by monopoly production and personal profit.

Producer coops, service coops, consumer coops, child care coops, banking coops, housing coops, farmers coops, doctor and dentist coops, artist coops etc., may all exist and thrive within a local socio-economy.

Trade and distribution of goods and services in a decentralized economy will be organized through consumer cooperatives. Commodities can be exported from one socio-economic unit to another through cooperatives, but only when such commodities are surplus to the needs of the local people.

## Small-scale, Privately-owned Businesses

Most small-scale and cottage industries will be in the hands of individual owners. Small-scale industries will be confined mainly to the production of non-essential commodities or to the service sector. Though privately owned, they must maintain adjustment with the cooperative sector, in terms of wages, etc., to ensure a balanced economy.[290]

A rural economy should not depend solely on cottage industries in which there are many producers working from their homes, typically part time. Such a situation will never be able to address the economic welfare of the local people. However, cottage industries can be helpful in initially providing rural women with an opportunity to earn a decent livelihood. As such, cottage industries will be made a part of the socio-economic planning. Cooperatives and the local administration will be responsible for supplying cottage industries with raw materials so that they do not suffer from scarcity.

According to the wages policy of PROUT, wages need not be accepted only in the form of money. They may be accepted in the form of essential goods or even services. It is advisable to gradually increase this component of wages in adjustment with the monetary component of wages.[291]

## Maximize Agricultural and Industrial Production

In a PROUT economy, people will strive to maximally utilize and rationally distribute all goods and services. Priority will be given to the use of local, renewable resources in the production of goods and services. Planners will strive for zero waste while developing as many local industries as possible according to the availability of raw materials and local consumption. These industries will be environmentally sustainable.

Initially, local industries can be financed through a model like the Self-Help Association for a Regional Economy (SHARE) that provides loans to small businesses at manageable rates of interest. This mechanism allows local people to pool their own capital for the purpose of building their own economy.[292]

Another model is provided by Seed Commons, a national network of locally rooted, non-extractive loan funds. They provide loans to jumpstart cooperatives by factoring in social capital (e.g. what their contributions are to the community) into their loan decisions. Borrowers are not required to make interest or principle repayments until they are able to cover operating costs.

Another mechanism that can be used to finance a local economy is the creation of a local currency. By creating a local currency, people can ensure a sufficient supply of money to facilitate the exchange of goods and services and also ensure a determined rate of economic expansion. Ideally, the amount of money in the local economy will be directly linked to the costs of production and the needs of local people for goods and services.

While having a trustworthy medium of exchange and access to finance capital for expansion is critical, local farms and industries will also feel secure when they know that sufficient raw materials are available to supply their needs, and they will be able to plan their future production efficiently. By encouraging the growth of local farms and industries based on local raw materials, local activists will strengthen local markets and mitigate the drainage of capital that is vital for the local area's economic growth.

### Don't Import or Export Raw Materials

Agricultural and manufacturing industries will try to use locally available raw materials first and, if possible, will not import raw materials from outside the socio-economic unit. Raw materials are the basic ingredients necessary to make finished products. The design of local agricultural and manufacturing industries that are based upon the use of local materials will keep money in the local economy and contribute to local self-reliance.

If there are not enough raw materials in any socio-economic unit to meet the minimum requirements of the local people, and if no substitute material can be developed locally, then the necessary raw materials can be imported from outside the socio-economic unit. By the same token, local raw materials should not be exported. Their value is much greater if kept in the local economy rather than sold or traded externally.

### Don't Import or Export Finished Goods

By manufacturing finished products locally, a socio-economic unit will conserve its money and improve the purchasing capacity of the local people. Finished goods, therefore, should not be exported until all the requirements of the local people in a socio-economic unit have been met. If finished goods are exported they should only be exported to another socio-economic unit, which has no immediate opportunity or potential to produce them, in order to meet the requirements of the people in that unit. And even then, the transaction of importation and exportation must not be motivated by profit but by need.

Importing finished products that can be locally produced should also be discouraged. It is essential that the local population utilize the commodities produced in their own area to ensure the prosperity of the local unit.

According to P. R. Sarkar,

> [W]hile initially, local commodities may be inferior, more costly or less readily available than outside commodities, yet in spite of this, locally produced commodities should still be used by the local people. If local commodities do not meet the needs and aspirations of the people, immediate steps must be taken to increase the quality, reduce the price and increase the supply of local goods, otherwise illegal imports will be encouraged."[293]

With continued local support, the local industries will develop to a stage when they will be able to produce goods of better quality at a better price.

This is an important principle that needs to be diligently applied. If it is neglected, the local industries will gradually close down, local markets will go out of the hands of the local people, and unemployment will increase. Once locally produced goods are accepted in principle, not only will local industries survive, but with their further development, the local economy will thrive. This will check the outflow of capital from the local area and because it will remain in the local area, it will be utilized to increase production and enhance the prosperity of the local people. With the increasing demand for local commodities, large-scale, medium-scale and small-scale industries will all flourish.

## Remove Goods Not Locally Produced from the Local Market

In time, those commodities, which are not produced within the local socio-economic unit, but which are in competition with locally produced goods, should be gradually removed from the local market. In a decentralized economy, the application of this goal is very important. If it is neglected, the local industries will not be able to gain a foothold, local markets will remain out of the hands of the local people, and unemployment will again increase. Once locally produced goods are accepted in principle, not only will local industries survive, but with their further development the local economy will thrive.

## Keep Money Circulating in the Local Economy

Another important principle of progressive socialism is to always keep money in circulation and not hoarded. This will allow the economy to move with accelerating speed. The value of money depends on the extent of its circulation. The more frequently money changes hands, the greater its economic value and the greater the prosperity in individual and collective life.

As stated above, it is recommended that local planners create a local currency to augment the existing national currency. This is legal and there has been historical precedent as far back as the original colonies. Examples from across the country demonstrate that millions of dollars can be added to the local economy in this manner. A local currency will help buffer the new socio-economic unit from the negative influences of the larger economy while also developing value within the locality.[294] The local currency will gain its footing by being exchanged for goods and services by those people who participate in the formation of the local socio-economic unit.

## Taxes

In the local socio-economy, there will be no income tax, but there will be a tax levied on the production of each commodity in order to pay for general services that do not directly generate income. This may include aspects of education, health care, infrastructure and the investment in more advanced aspects of the local economy.

## Local Language

The people's local language is to be used in all local dealings and transactions. It should be used in the administration, the education system, the economy, and in cultural activities. All official and non-official bodies and offices of a particular socio-economic unit should use the local language as the medium of communication. This is an important point that should not be overlooked. The reason is that there is a close relationship between the economic prosperity of people and their psychic and cultural development. As P. R. Sarkar points out:

> If local people do not develop a sense of self-confidence in their economic activities, then they become mentally weak, and this inherent weakness becomes an impediment to their economic well-being. Such a community will become an easy victim of economic, political and psycho-economic exploitation by vested interests. This unhealthy situation must be firmly resisted.[295]

## Support Cultural and Spiritual Development

A local socio-economy will not be able to generate Sadvipras without cultural events and intuitional practices. It is therefore, necessary that regular social and spiritual gatherings be held and honored by the community leadership.

A local socio-economy does not exist independent of social interactions and the need for human companionship. This is why it is called a "socio-economy." There is a close relationship between the economic status of people and their mental, cultural, and spiritual well-being. Economic improvements in individual and collective life will lead to the all-round welfare of people. As people gain confidence in their ability to meet their own basic needs and as they gain security in knowing that the community is set up for their welfare, they will begin to develop a better self-image. They will also become more engaged in cultural and spiritual pursuits, especially as other dimensions of the economy come into existence. This is one of the great benefits of a local socio-economy. It supports our human nature and provides the opportunity to partake in recreation and higher pursuits.

After some time, advances in local productivity will allow labor hours to be reduced. A forty-hour work week, for example, may be reduced to thirty or even twenty hours. This time can be used by individuals and families to pursue opportunities for recreation or culture and perform their spiritual practices.

The overall well being of society is the ultimate goal of a decentralized economy. This is a universal ideal and should be established in each and every socio-economic unit. It will bring economic prosperity as well as ensure greater opportunities for the psycho-spiritual elevation of all members of society.

## Planning a PROUT Socio-Economy

Now that we have discussed the principles of a local socio-economy, let us look at the planning process. The first phase of instituting a local samaj, as has been stated above, is for local people, living in rural areas, to create an agrarian revolution whereby they gain control over that part of the economy that addresses their basic needs. This part of the economy is called the "People's Economy."

The agrarian revolution begins when local people begin to organize themselves into a "socio-economic unit" to produce their basic needs within a given area of land. The local people determine the area and boundaries of a local socio-economic unit based upon their assessment of common geography, the carrying capacity of the land, weather patterns, water, soil type, eco-systems, the availability of raw materials, as well as social factors such as common economic problems and potentialities, common socio-cultural ties, the people's sentimental legacy, etc. Once determined, the boundaries then constitute the planning site of the local socio-economic unit.

## Benefits of Local Planning

Successful planning for rural revitalization can never be done by men in suits sitting in an air conditioned office thousands of miles away from the place where the people live and work. A centralized economy can never solve the economic problems of the rural areas, small towns, and villages. Therefore, economic planning must start at the local level, where the experience, expertise, and knowledge of the local people and locally available resources can be harnessed for the benefit of all the members of a socio-economic unit.[296]

There are many benefits to local economic planning: (1) the area of planning is small enough for the planners to understand all the problems of the area; (2) local people know each other and can make real input into the planning process; (3) local leadership can address issues according to local priorities; (4) local planning is more practical and effective and will yield quicker, positive results; (5) through local planning, natural resources upon which the people depend for life and livelihoods are better stewarded; and (6) capital and credit can be generated from within.

Totnes, England, the first Permaculture Transition Town initiative, [297] is a good example of how local people can come together to develop a local economic plan for themselves. In this rural town, local nonprofit organizations, local businesses, and community groups all played an active role in mobilizing human and material resources to address local needs and local employment.

It is inevitable that there will be different plans for different socio-economic units. Weather, rainfall, availability of water, soil quality, land contour, economic issues, local culture, etc., all affect planning. A PROUTist approach to planning will take into account all these relevant factors before any new enterprises are implemented.

## Guidelines for Local Planning

Initially, local planners will have to consider the following four factors: (1) the Five Fundamental Principles of PROUT,[298] (2) the physical demand at present and the physical demand in the foreseeable future, (3) the physical supply at present and the physical supply in the foreseeable future, and (4) the maximum utilization of land.

To address these factors, the local people will need to develop a Master Plan for their area. A Master Plan may include the following information:

A study of the local demographics, including migration patterns.

A study of the carrying capacity of the land.

A detailed study of the surplus and deficit of labor trends within the SEU. If there is a surplus of manual labor, jobs should be created that make use of manual labor. The goal of an SEU is one hundred percent full employment. Labor can be paid for in local currency that can be exchanged for goods and services produced within the SEU.

A study of local natural resources including rocks, clay, sand, minerals, fuels, forests, plants, animals, etc., and a determination of how to optimize their use in a sustainable manner to meet the basic needs. The study should include a plan to expand local utility over these resources.

A definition of the specific goods and services required to meet the basic needs of the local population, as well as the processes and components required to produce them that can be organized locally. Seeds, fertilizers, hand tools, mills, etc., can be set up as local businesses and supported by SEU participants.

A study of the current land used by farms, industry, and trade, as well as the variety, size, and distribution of the available goods and services required to meet basic needs within the SEU.

A specific plan for food production. A food plan, for example, might define the calories required in the local diet and the composition of those calories in terms of proteins, carbohydrates, fats, vitamins, and minerals. Then define the foods required that can be grown locally to meet those needs. Depending upon the number of participants in the SEU, planners can then calculate the quantity of foods required, who among the participants will grow the food and handle their processing, storage, and distribution. In this manner, it will also be able to define the unit cost per food item.

A study of the housing stock and the materials and costs associated with retrofitting them to provide for the local population.

A study of the health services within the locality and a plan to shift some services to local businesses. The study should focus on prevention, nutrition, and plant-based medicines.

A study of how to improve the capacity of the education system to address local needs.

A determination of a minimum and maximum wage that meets basic needs and rewards exceptional contributions.

A model calculation of factors required to set up an agriculture or pre- and post-agriculture production unit. Factors to consider are: the labor requirements, the cost of production, availability of local raw materials, the productive capacity, the purchasing capacity of the local people, the collective necessity, and the environmental sustainability of the endeavor.

The creation of training materials to teach people how to set up and manage cooperatives.

A survey to identify the current local market for locally produced goods. All goods and services produced to meet basic needs should be sold only in local markets. If the local goods do not meet the needs or aspirations of the people, immediate steps should be taken to increase quality, reduce prices, and increase the supply of local goods to discourage imports.

A plan to meet the emergency food, clothing, and shelter needs of local people.

A marketing strategy to educate the local people about the benefits of buying local products (psycho-economy).

A plan to create a local currency to facilitate the exchange of goods and services. This may include a LETS system,[299] ROCS,[300] barter,[301] a local currency,[302] or combination of these methods. Each exchange that does not require dollars will add that amount to the local money supply and allow dollars to be used for exchange within the larger existing economy. Local money should be kept in constant circulation and not hoarded.

An exploratory strategy to involve local government in the development of the SEU.

A strategy to conserve SEU resources through non-use, reuse, repurposing, recycling, and retrofitting.

A strategy for creating events which allow people to partake in recreation and higher pursuits and to build trust in community. Holding public award events for those who have made extraordinary contributions to the welfare of the people in the SEU may be one kind of event. Events to share ideology, to educate the community, to increase culture, to have fun, to worship together are all positive events to bring people together.

A plan to ensure the security of the local people if a local police force is unable to do so. Local people have the God-given right to meet their own basic needs and any forces that intend to deny people this right threaten their survival and are to be considered enemies of the people and the people will have to defend against such enemies.

A short-term (six months) and long-term (three years) plan of action.

An initial financial plan and budget based upon the use of local labor and resources. A system such as SHARE,[303] a revolving loan fund,[304] or a credit union[305] will eventually have to be established in order to allow local people to invest in the local unit.

Local activists will initiate a planning process that is open and inviting. It will include farmers, land owners, local business owners, regional planners, local colleges and universities, business associations, non-profits, students, the unemployed, etc. It will include men, women, and the young. It will include those with warrior, intellectual, and merchant mentalities. It will include sadvipras and all those who are willing to fight for their families and for their local community.

It will not include employees or representatives of national or multinational corporations or representatives of state or federal governments.

Once a plan is approved by the people of the samaj, social boards, and trade boards will be established to develop the infrastructure required to meet basic needs as well as the administrative policies concerning development, investment, regulation, energy, and transportation.[306] Trade boards or trade associations are specific to an industry and work with the oversight social boards to ensure that their industry is in sync with the overall demands of the socio-economy. Trade boards will be composed of representatives of the cooperatives and small businesses involved in that industry.

## Attributes of Local Planning

In our planning process, service to local people is always the first concern. We will have to help people in our local area in good times and bad. From a moral point of view and from a humane point of view, the responsibility for helping our neighbors falls on us. Food pantries and cheap kitchens should be addressed in all local plans. We want to make sure that everyone, no matter how dire his or her straits, has food to eat and knows that their neighbors are there to support them. This is what builds community. This is the example that we want to set.

By adopting such an expanded approach to economic planning, people will be able to alleviate the suffering of others and learn to trust each other.

In all cases, local people will determine the quantum of minimum requirements and the basic policies related to their own economic well being. If this principle is followed, the problem of outside interference in the local economy will continually diminish.

In time, federated state social boards can be developed to synthesize and help to coordinate planning for larger areas of production. It must be remembered, however, that planning should be of an ascending order, starting at the local level. It is often too easy for people's plans and programs to be co-opted at higher levels by powerful people who have other interests to serve. There is no economic resilience or security for the local people if the production of basic needs occurs outside their locality.

Currently, localities are demarcated on the basis of political boundaries. Yet, the well being of the local people may not be maximally improved by using such boundaries. Local planning should take account of such factors as the physical features of the area, including river valleys, varying climatic conditions, topography, the nature of the soil, the type of flora and fauna, etc., as well as the socio-economic and cultural requirements of the people. The existence of local markets and resources also need to be considered. Thus, the boundaries of an SEU may cross county or state boundaries. Over time, "localities" should be scientifically and systematically defined on the basis of maximum utilization and rational distribution of resources.

When planning is prepared for the all-round growth of a local socio-economy, we may call it "intra-locality planning." Each locality develops its own plan. However, there will always be problems which traverse local boundaries and cannot be tackled or solved by one locality alone, such as flood control, river valley projects, communication systems, higher educational institutions, forestation projects, the environmental impact of development, the establishment of key industries, soil erosion, water supply, power generation, the establishment of an organized market system, etc.

Therefore, cooperation between localities is necessary. Planning between localities is called "inter-local planning." Inter-local planning is performed to organize and harmonize socio-economic development in adjoining localities through mutual coordination and cooperation.

At each and every level of planning, there should be short-term and long-term plans. It makes sense that the maximum time limit for short-term planning would be six months, and the maximum time limit for long-term planning would be three years. Short-term and long-term plans should be drafted in such a way that they compliment each other. The comprehensive goals of planning at each level are to guarantee the minimum requirements of the local people, eliminate unemployment, increase purchasing capacity, and make socio-economic units self-reliant.

The overall well being of society is the ultimate purpose of a progressive socialist economy. Because we are presently operating under the tenets and structures of economic globalization, many of the PROUT principles and guidelines cannot be presently implemented. Nonetheless, they should be used by local planners to help transition the economy from a global economy to a local economy.

## Factors of Local Planning

One of the main problems with local development, especially as it applies to food production, is that small farmers and growers do not take account of the true costs of production. They do not count their time accurately, or that of family and volunteers. There are other costs that they also ignore and records that they do not keep. If we are going to build a viable, sustainable food system we must account for the true costs and capabilities of operations. In this endeavor, we should be able to understand and keep account of the following factors: (1) the cost of production, (2) productivity, (3) purchasing capacity, (4) collective necessity, and (5) sustainability.

### Cost of production

If we are to build a sustainable food economy, farmers must account for all the expenses incurred in producing their crops and farm products. This is the only way to get an accurate calculation of a unit cost of production. Through farmer cooperatives, farmers' networks, trade boards, and community-based organizations involved in food issues, this information can be mutually developed. Once this occurs, if farmers share best practices with each other, they can help reduce unit costs and the prices for locally produced food can be lowered thereby creating greater demand. As the cost of food drops, more local people will buy it and begin to join the local economy.

The cost of production should be systematically determined and all effort should be made to continually reduce the cost of production through greater efficiencies, improvements in technology, etc. All industries, including agrico-industries (inputs) and agro-industries (value-added), must see that the cost of producing a particular commodity does not exceed its local market value. All production must be economically viable. The more we share information, tools, equipment, and resources, the more we will be able to keep production costs down. Reducing the cost of production will free up capital to be used for other means, including more leisure, or increases in pay. Cooperatives can facilitate this sharing. And the spiritual intent behind this economic work will help to ensure fairness in the development of pricing.

**Productivity**

This factor addresses the need for maximum production in order to meet collective needs. Any under-utilized productive capacity should be identified and plans made to bring these resources into production.

For example, we want to develop a food economy that has the capacity to produce more and more. This will require that money should be continually reinvested—that is, kept in circulation rather than hoarded —so that the collective wealth of the locality is continually increased.

If local people are guided by the needs and potentialities of each other, productivity will continually increase. Maximum production in the economy will provide a congenial environment for more investment, more industrialization, more employment, increasing purchasing capacity, and increasing collective wealth. Once basic needs are met and amenities are also produced to create a certain level of comfort for everyone, surplus wealth can be used to improve infrastructure or provide more leisure for people to pursue personal goals.

In developing its business plans, a farmers' cooperative will set its productivity goals in relation to the collective need of the local population for its line of products.

## Purchasing capacity

The goal of local planning should be to increase the purchasing capacity of every local person. The existing practice of considering per capita income as the indicator of people's economic well-being is a false standard that masks the concentration of wealth and the impoverishment of the majority of people. It results from a model of centralized planning. The genuine measure of people's economic advancement is increased purchasing capacity. To increase people's purchasing capacity will require stable prices, periodic increases in wages, and the increase of collective wealth.

There will be no limit to purchasing capacity other than those dictated by resource limits and a fair balance between the lowest and highest paid workers. The minimum requirements will be guaranteed to everyone, including the lowest paid worker, and will be increased occasionally as circumstances permit. The setting of a minimum and maximum wage will make this possible. A maximum wage, for example, may be ten times the minimum wage, to encourage individual initiative, reward excellence, and acknowledge extraordinary contributions to the public good. The maximum wage should not be so large, however, that it threatens the basic needs of those who are earning the minimum wage.

Farmer and producer cooperatives should coordinate their business plans with those of local planners to ensure that their prices, wages and expansion plans are consistent with projections of an increase in samaj members (the growth of the collective need,) the purchasing capacity of the people and the requirements of environmental sustainability.

## Collective Necessity

Cooperatives will produce their goods and services based upon collective necessity. Under the capitalist system, farmers are uncertain about the market and unsure of the price they will receive for their goods. Often, farmers produce at a loss or are forced to go into debt in order to expand their acreage or buy larger pieces of equipment to barely make ends meet. Under progressive socialism, the farmers will know what to grow and in what quantities. Their market will be guaranteed as well as their income.

## Sustainability

Sustainability implies the proper use of resources. It means using non-toxic materials when possible. It means using materials that are not derived from fossil fuels when possible. It means using renewable resources and renewable energy when possible. It means developing the soil so that it yields nutrients in a sustainable way, rather than depending upon chemical additives produced outside the local area. It means protecting our water and raw material base. It means caring for our natural resources, including all animal species. Sustainability implies leaving our children with the same resource base, or even an improved resource base. In this endeavor, planners will remember that all species, aside from their utility value have an existential value. Their creation is no less important to the Divine than is ours. We abuse them at our own detriment.

# Who Will Do the Planning?

We have stated that local people will create a Master Plan for their local unit but who exactly will do this work? In the first phase of development, a small group of people, perhaps seven to twelve in number, can begin to promote the idea of a local socio-economy to people in the community. They can do this by sponsoring public events like showing films about local development or by throwing parties, holding town hall meetings, or by whatever means the group decides. The original group, along with other key planners, will constitute a planning board responsible for creating the community master plan. They will begin by gathering ideas and visions from the community. With these ideas, they will begin to design a new economic system. The planning board will serve a role similar to a board of directors of an umbrella organization. Once the board has the attention and interest of the people in the community and volunteers begin to emerge, the board will facilitate the creation of teams to address the major aspects of the Master Plan. Each team will develop its section of the Master Plan. When a Master Plan is assembled, it will be presented for review by the larger community. Formal objections and responses will be considered. A revision or revisions will probably be in order. Eventually, the Master Plan will be approved by a general consensus of participants.

Once a Master Plan has gained consensus from the people in the SEU, additional social boards can be created to plan and implement projects in their areas of concern. For example, the social board whose issue is food may explore the links between local producers (within a thirty mile radius of the town), and retailers and restaurants within the town, or they may create a farmers market, community gardens, or food pantry. The intent of their projects, aside from creating income is to build confidence and trust between people at the local level.[307] In another example, the communications team may begin to visit people door to door to inform them of the local movement and enroll their participation. Within this initial stage, it will be beneficial for a representative from each social board to meet monthly with the planning board to coordinate and prioritize projects that are dedicated to meeting basic needs.

In the second phase, local planners will need to become more strategic about the construction of their socio-economy. As the social boards gain experience and visibility in the community, their research will need to become more sophisticated and it may become necessary to employ a more professional model and gain the assistance of local experts. For example, social boards may be established to guide development in various social and cultural arenas of life (education, health care, the arts, social welfare, etc.), while trade associations, each comprised of representatives of cooperatives and local enterprises within their respective economic spheres (agriculture, manufacturing, and trade), begin to create the cooperative framework for meeting the community's basic needs. As the planning process becomes more sophisticated, it will attract more funding and support from local businesses and institutions.

A good planning strategy for trade associations to follow is the "Local Economic Blueprint" that was developed by the Reconomy Centre for the town of Totnes and its environs.[308] Based on public data, this group of local professionals estimated the potential value of four key sectors of their local economy. These sectors were food, retrofitting of housing and structures, renewable energy, and health care. Through their analysis of each sector, they were able to determine how much money could be retained in the local economy if people supported local business and added local businesses in their sector. The planners were also able to determine how many new jobs could be created in each sector. For example, in their analysis of the food sector, they determined that if local people only spent ten percent more on local food rather than depending upon chain supermarkets, they would add almost two and a half million dollars annually to the local economy. This is a sizeable amount for a town with a population of only eight thousand people.[309] Once the planners had developed their Local Economic Blueprint, they built a coalition of partners to turn the economic potential they had discovered into opportunities for new businesses and more jobs.

In the PROUT model, the "coalition of partners" would form themselves into farmer cooperatives and/or producer cooperatives. Let us take the example of farmers' cooperatives. In the initial stage, agricultural cooperatives would be formed by the mutual cooperation of groups of farmers. Suppose A, B, C, and D are four farmers who have consolidated their land into a cooperative in the following proportions: A has two acres, B five acres, C ten acres, and D fifteen acres. The profits from the sale of their crops would be shared in proportion to the amount of land each gave to the cooperative, and the labor each rendered for the production of these crops. Farmers would receive dividends according to the number of their shares in the cooperative. As the productivity of the land increases due to the continuous development of improved scientific techniques, farmers can expect greater prosperity.

A record will be kept of the productive capacity of all the land included in the cooperative. Dividends would be allocated on the basis of this productivity. For example, if a farmer has thirty acres of land of which fifteen acres are highly productive and fifteen acres are of low productivity, then his or her dividend would take into account the differences in productivity.

During the transition period, while the cooperatives are still working within a capitalist system, the farmers need not sell their produce immediately after harvesting due to pressure of circumstances. In the individualistic or private enterprise system, most farmers have to sell their produce immediately in order to get sufficient money to survive. But in the cooperative system, farmers will enjoy greater financial security because the cooperative can advance money to individual farmers and sell the crops at the most favorable time for the best price. This is because farmer cooperatives will be able to pool money to build facilities to aggregate, clean, sort, package and store their products, as well as develop a distribution network. In the transition period between capitalism and progressive socialism, the cooperatives can determine how much to sell and when to sell in order to get the best profit. Cooperatives will also be able to fix the price of their own produce within certain price limits. Thus, cooperatives will get the profit which is taken by middlemen and profiteers in the capitalist system.

Once progressive socialism is established and the social boards are strongly in place, the farmers' cooperatives, through their boards of directors, trade associations, and social boards will continually refine their approach to the planning factors discussed above, that is: (1) the cost of production, (2) productivity, (3) purchasing capacity, (4) collective necessity, and (5) sustainability.

A cooperative board will also determine its profit margin (surplus value) and how it should be distributed. It may be distributed in the form of dividends, kept for reinvestment in a reserve fund, or used to purchase items such as tractors, manure, etc. The money in the reserve fund may also be used to increase the value of the dividend in the years when production is low. If this system is followed the authorized share capital will not be affected.[310]

The board of directors will be elected from among the cooperative's members, their positions should be paid and not be honorary. Care should be taken to ensure that not a single immoral person is elected to the board. All directors must be moralists.

By the third phase, more cooperatives should be developed and trade associations, which will be comprised of cooperatives within a particular sector of the economy, will be more efficient at planning and organizing economic sectors to meet basic needs. This will include the food sector, housing sector, health care sector, education sector, etc. All boards and planning bodies will be strengthened and regular meetings will be held with representation from all social boards and trade associations. This process will result in an experienced local development process that will strengthen the capacity of the local socio-economy to meet the people's basic physical, mental, and spiritual needs.

In the fourth phase, when the people's participation has been widely established, the civic, business, and governmental sectors of the local community will be brought more into sync, each having increased responsibility for advancing the integrated plan for the local economy.

The people will always have the opportunity to review any plan, which will always be made public, as well as have the opportunity to make their voices heard in regular political assemblies or forums. If the people do not approve of a plan or aspect of a plan, it should not be put into effect. If the majority of people do not approve of specific board members, they will be replaced by members proposed by the social boards and cooperatives.

## Economic Development Models

While there are many alternative economic development models from which lessons can be learned, we will now take a brief look at two economic development models pioneered by PROUTists around the world.

### Multi-Purpose Development Projects

P. R. Sarkar's approach to Samaj building was to identify the greatest poverty belts of the world. He spoke specifically about India, China, Viet Nam, Indonesia, Mexico, Honduras, Brazil, and Peru. In the Middle East, he spoke of the socio-cultural maladjustment in the oil producing countries, even though there is enough natural wealth. In Africa, he spoke of the poverty and suffering among large sections of the population because they could not even afford to buy rice and had to live on rats and mice.[311]

There are billions of hunger-stricken people throughout the world. They not only suffer from hunger and malnutrition, but also diseases, lack of shelter, lack of education, exposure to environmental disasters, and merciless war lords who make their lives a living hell. Mr. Sarkar's strategy was to send his monks and nuns to the poorest countries and to the poorest locations in the developed world, to serve the people who were suffering the most. In these countries and cities, his workers set up projects to serve the needs of the poor. Sometimes the projects were based on emergency relief, other times on welfare, infrastructure building, or other projects to meet basic needs. These included schools to teach and feed the children.

The most critical problem that the poor face is malnutrition. Mr. Sarkar told his workers "immediate food shortages must be solved as an urgent necessity. What are you doing about this? You cannot shirk your responsibility. The entire globe is waiting for you."[312]

Once emergency food shortages were addressed by his workers, Mr. Sarkar encouraged them to work with local people to implement what he called multi-purpose development schemes.[313] These "schemes" link local projects together. Their aim is to elevate the standard of living of the people by meeting their basic needs and by bringing about integrated local economic development. These multi-purpose development schemes help to form the material base of a local socio-economic unit.

To Mr. Sarkar, oppressed people exist in all countries, even the so-called developed countries. He said:

> We must not neglect the developed countries because they also suffer from shortages. By adopting such an extended and expanded approach to service, good people can do something for the suffering and downtrodden humanity. You will have to elevate the standard of both the downtrodden mass and the down-moving mass. You should chalk out a plan and materialize it as soon as possible.[314]

All people in local areas can benefit from help in times of calamity. Cheap kitchens and community gardens are appropriate everywhere. Depending on the situation, the distribution of clothes, medicines and school supplies, special housing arrangements for the poor, and education programs for the children are also of service. All localities can certainly benefit from the help of others who are willing to serve people selflessly.

Of equal importance to helping the poor, is to build a self-reliant community where you live. Samajs need to be created everywhere if we are to permanently help the "downtrodden mass and the down-moving mass." Today, in the United States, under capitalism, we risk leaving behind the majority of an entire generation, the Millennials,[315] who are faced with unemployment and an insecure future, while suffering under a debilitating education debt load and fewer job prospects. These are our children who are suffering as politicians continue to pretend that capitalism is a legitimate system that only requires a little tweaking around the edges.

In the rural areas of undeveloped regions, where a Master Plan cannot easily be put together, those local people who are dedicated to the welfare of their people can develop simple projects and begin to link them together in multi-purpose development schemes in order to form the building blocks of an alternative local economy. Such multi-purpose development projects may be benefitted by setting up a hub of operations called a "master unit."

## Master Units

Many Proutists around the world have learned from the examples set by activists in the Sustainable Development, Permaculture, ecovillage, and Transition Initiatives movements and have incorporated these strategies and models into their work.

Mr. Sarkar, however, made a unique contribution to local economic development that has not been implemented by any of the local sustainability movements, but which might serve as a development model for them. Mr. Sarkar called this contribution the Master Unit.[316]

Master Units are land-based centers, located on a minimum of five acres of land, that provide a nucleus for multi-purpose development schemes. The purpose of a Master Unit is to provide a hub of operations for a local socio-economic unit that will help local people meet their basic needs. The Master Unit also provides a laboratory for the development of products from indigenous raw materials. Key staff members include a nurse, a farmer, and a teacher.

There are five primary requisites of an ideal Master Unit which correspond to the five minimum requirements in PROUT—food, clothing, shelter, health care, and education.

Meeting Minimum Requirements

The first requirement of a Master Unit is to provide food throughout the year. The second is to develop sufficient local raw materials through agriculture and scientific farming. Raw materials will be derived from aquaculture, forestry, dairy farms, horticulture, sericulture, etc. They will be used to provide local cottage industries or cooperatives with materials that can be processed into finished goods. For local businesses, the raw materials must be developed from within the local economy. Local resilience will be impossible if these materials have to be bought from outside sources.

Secondly, there should be production of sufficient fibers and fabrics for clothing and textiles. For example, hemp, cotton, and other plants can be used for making clothing.

Thirdly, prekindergarten programs, primary, and secondary schools should be started on all Master Units . Higher education institutions should not be established in the first phase, but training programs to develop essential skills should be ongoing.

Fourthly, general and special medical units should also be established. Special medical units would also accommodate people who are invalids for a certain period of time because Master Units may or may not run big hospitals. Medical units should emphasize alternative medical treatments such as diet, exercise, rest, herbs, homeopathy, and first aid services.

Fifthly, Master Units should construct houses for extremely poor people. This special housing project will be of vital importance in the days ahead.

Mr. Sarkar wanted to see Master Units created in every locality of the world. He created his first model project in the Purulia District of West

Bengal India and called it Ananda Nagar ("City of Bliss").[317] Since then there have been many Master Units created within India and in other countries of the world. They exist at different levels of development.

Just as the monasteries, after the fall of Rome, provided the monks with their basic needs, Mr. Sarkar wanted all Master Units to be economically self-sufficient in all respects because local activists should not be dependent upon the capitalists for money.

Common Structures and Programs

There are certain required structures that need to be built on Master Units:

- Schools
- Hostels, (for the young, the old, and those that can afford them)
- Children's homes, (including student homes)
- Medical units
- Cottage industries
- Farm buildings

Special Features

Besides the common programs and structures, there are some special features of Master Units that Shrii Sarkar also recommended:

- A wheat grinding machine or flour mill to produce flour.
- A bakery to produce bread.
- A seed bank. Workers on a Master Unit should continually experiment with and save heirloom seeds that perform best in their area.
- A Cheap Seed Distribution Center. The center will collect good quality heirloom seeds and sell the surplus to local farmers at cheap rates. Seed may be purchased from local farmers in the market or cultivated at the Master Unit but the center should provide good quality seeds at cheap rates to the people.

- A Free Plant Distribution Center. This center will grow plants from seeds and seedlings. The process for doing so is provided in the endnotes.[318]
- Sericulture and silk weaving center.
- Bio-gas plant. This means that there must be dairy animals. Water hyacinths are also good for producing bio-gas.
- Butter production.
- Beekeeping.
- An Ideal Farm Training Center.
- A Wild Life Sanctuary

A Master Unit can be established as part of a local socio-economic unit's Master Plan. By the third phase of operation, it can be used as a hub of operations to begin the research and production of food and basic materials from which to build local cooperatives in meeting basic needs.

## Getting from Here to There

Now that we have a sense of the principles and planning strategy for creating an agrarian revolution, let us look at the phases required to transition from global capitalism to local progressive socialism.

According to Shrii Sarkar:

> Self-reliance is the main objective of our farming projects; hence they should be oriented towards production. They should not be dependent on outside resources. An integrated approach to farming should include such areas as agriculture, horticulture, floriculture, sericulture, lac culture, apiculture, dairy farming, animal husbandry, irrigation, pisciculture, pest control, the proper use of fertilizers, cottage industries, energy production, research centers and water conservation. This approach will help make farming projects self-reliant, and should be adopted.[319]

Currently, there are four distinct systems of agricultural production. These are private enterprise, the sharecropping system, the cooperative system, and the commune system. In regard to agricultural production to meet local needs, the cooperative system is the best; private enterprise is second, followed by sharecropping, and finally the commune system.

The commune system is the worst. In the commune system, individual rights are overlooked. In some countries, the right of individual ownership may be accepted in principle but not in practice. Under the commune system, there is no scope for workers to be inspired or incentivized to fully utilize their skills. There is no opportunity for them to enhance their working capacity. They have no opportunity to develop their minds, so their lives can never be elevated to a higher standard of living. People living in the commune system have no psychological or human relation with their work. Those countries, that have adopted the commune system directly or indirectly, have utterly failed in agricultural production. This can be seen in the fact that capitalist countries, where agricultural production is based on individual ownership, supply food grains to communist countries. Though the capitalist system is bad, the commune system is even worse. The whole system runs counter to human psychology, and consequently production never increases.

The sharecropping system is better than the commune system because people get more incentive and freedom. In this system the psychology of "If I can produce more I can earn more" dominates. But this system also suffers from some major defects. Suppose a sharecropper manages to get two hundred acres of land from five different landowners, he may not cultivate the total acreage due to idleness, lack of laborers, or financial constraints. Or, he may think that limited cultivation will provide enough food to meet the demands of his family for the year, so he does not bother cultivating the remainder of the land, nor does he give the land the proper attention it deserves. As a result, the owner of the land will be deprived of income or have his land abused.

The sharecropping system also suffers from another major problem that also affects land owners. If farmers in these two systems do not have enough capital, even if they have a large area of land, they cannot adopt modern agricultural methods for production. Tractors and power tillers remain beyond their means. By using outdated plowing techniques, these farmers can only cultivate the surface of the land, and are not able to increase its productivity. They cannot improve the soil, utilize better quality fertilizers, high yielding seeds, or proper irrigation systems. If they are small fruit and vegetable farmers, the government provides no incentives or insurance for them.

While there are more incentives for farmers in individual agricultural production than in sharecropping, there are still drawbacks to private enterprise. Under private ownership, it is generally impossible for farmers to increase agricultural production of infertile land, which then lies unutilized. If their farms are too small or, if they lack the proper equipment, they cannot pay their expenses. In the United States, most farmers have had to sell their land because they could not afford to farm it. Although private enterprise is better than the sharecropping and commune systems, ultimately farm families cannot compete and must give up their dream and even their land. Society is not benefited by such an approach. If an individual farmer has a large amount of land in his possession and access to finance, he may be able to keep his farm, but this situation leads to over accumulation of land and the impoverishment of other farmers.

In the modern world, the cooperative system is the best system for agricultural and industrial production. In the cooperative system, members have collective strength and can gain financial help and access to various resources to increase their production. They can pressure the government to provide better irrigation facilities and high yielding seeds and even make infertile land productive. Land with little fertility can be transformed into fertile farmland with proper care. This will increase total agricultural production and also help a community become self-sufficient in food production and free it from food shortages.

Among all the attachments human beings suffer from, attachment to land is one of the strongest. Farmers can donate large amounts of produce without hesitation, but they will feel tremendous pain if they are asked to donate a few square feet of land. Those who donate land do so for only three reasons: (1) to save the major part of their land, (2) for a meaningful humanitarian cause, or (3) out of spiritual inspiration.[320]

To begin the process of agrarian revolution and increase local food production, local planners will have to divide the land into economic holdings and uneconomic holdings, according to productivity. Economic holdings are those where the market price of the produce will exceed the cost of production including capital, labor, and machinery.

Uneconomic holdings are those where the market price of the produce is less than the cost of production after including all costs. Because uneconomic holdings are not profitable, the landowners usually refrain from producing any crops.

To increase production, all economic and uneconomic holdings must be reorganized and management of the land should be done through cooperatives. However, Mr. Sarkar cautions local organizers:

> It is not wise to suddenly hand over all land to cooperative management because cooperatives evolve out of the collective labor and wisdom of a community. The community must develop an integrated economic environment, common economic needs, and a ready market for its cooperatively produced goods. Unless these three factors work together, an enterprise cannot be called a cooperative.[321]

Therefore, PROUT proposes a four-phase plan to introduce cooperative land management. In the first phase, all owners of uneconomic holdings should be encouraged to join the cooperative system so that their land can become economic holdings. In this phase, cooperatives will only consist of those people who merged their land together to make uneconomic holdings economical. Private ownership will be recognized. For example, one person may own one acre, another two acres, and a third person three acres within the cooperative. Each cooperative member will be entitled to a dividend based on the total production in proportion to the land they donated to the cooperative. Each individual will retain the deed of ownership of their land, but agricultural activities will be managed cooperatively.

It is vitally important that members who purchase shares in the cooperative should have no power or right to transfer their shares without the permission of the cooperative. Their shares, however, may be inherited. If some cooperative members have no descendants, then their shares should pass on to their legally authorized successors, who will become members of the cooperative if they are not already members. The reason for this policy is that it prevents capitalists from purchasing large numbers of shares in a cooperative and speculating in the market place. So also, in the cooperative system there should not be any scope for interest earning shares. Rather, shares should be based on the production of the land. If there are interest earning shares in farmers or agricultural cooperatives, then these shares will be sold in the share market, capitalists will buy the shares, the rate of share prices will fluctuate according to share market prices, and cooperatives will again become commercial enterprises.[322] Rather the value of shares should be based upon the dividends received as a result of the productivity of a farmer's land.

Disadvantaged or minor landowners will also benefit by this type of cooperative system. A widow, a disabled farmer, or a minor boy or girl, who owns some land, will derive an income from the land based on the number of shares in the cooperative. In the system of private ownership their land would have remained unutilized, and they would have remained poor. Therefore, even if cooperative members are unable to do any work, they will still be entitled to an income from the total profit of the cooperative.

In the first phase of this plan, those owning land, which is productive as an economic holding need not be persuaded to join a cooperative. But if an economic holding comprises land which is dispersed in small plots, as is the case in many third world countries, the scattered plots should be consolidated into one holding under cooperative management. In the United States, this principle can also relate to urban plots.

Cooperatives have the right, and, in fact, are encouraged to employ labor for farming. In this case, fifty percent of the total produce should be distributed as wages to the agricultural laborers who work in the cooperative. The owners of the land will get fifty percent of the total produce and those who create the produce through their labor will get the other fifty percent. This ratio must never decrease—rather it should increase in favor of the agricultural laborers who work in the cooperative. In this way, local unemployment will be lessened and workers will be able to earn a wage that meets their needs. It must be remembered that PROUT advocates production to meet needs, not profit.

The cooperative should be managed by those who have shares in the cooperative. The managers will be elected by cooperative members. Managers will also be paid salaries according to the extent of their expertise. Their position should not be honorary. In addition, the members of the cooperative may also work the land themselves and for this they should be paid separate wages. Thus, cooperative members can earn income in two ways—as a dividend based on the production of the land given to the cooperative and on the basis of their own productive labor.

In this first phase of the socialization of land, PROUTists will not raise the demand for land ceilings, but the sale of uneconomic agricultural land should be prohibited and landholdings brought under cooperative management. The responsibility for cultivating this land will not lie with the landowners but with the cooperatives, ideally with the expertise and assistance of the immediate government.

In this phase, planners should determine how the rivers and streams in a village can be harnessed for the collective welfare. For example, by constructing embankments and small dams on the rivers, large-scale irrigation, electricity generation, and industries based on local needs can be established.

Also, in this phase, steps should be taken to alleviate population pressure on land. People living in towns should be encouraged to find employment in new industries that either produce inputs for agriculture (seeds, fertilizer, hand tools, etc) or process agricultural products (mills, canning, bottling, cottage industries, etc.)

Provisions should also be made for the preservation of crops by building stores and cold-storage units under the control of cooperatives or trade associations. The cooperatives should be supplied with tractors, manure, seeds, water pumps, and other farming equipment through producer cooperatives that will either produce these goods or, initially buy them in bulk from outside manufacturers. Consumer cooperatives will supply the commodities necessary for daily consumption to the rural population.

In this first phase, agricultural laborers and day laborers will come within the scope of cooperatives. In other words, the workforce in the cooperative system will be composed of the shareholding farmers and non-shareholding laborers. Both groups will benefit: the shareholding farmers will get regular salaries for their work plus a return on their shares, while the laborers will enjoy stable employment and favorable wages.

There are two types of non-shareholding workers in agricultural cooperatives—those who are permanent workers and those who are casual or contract workers. The permanent workers will get bonuses as incentives besides their wages, while casual workers will only get wages for their labor. Those workers who give the greatest service to the cooperative should get the greatest bonuses. Skilled workers should get paid more than unskilled workers. This will be an incentive for all to become skilled workers and to work harder. Bonuses should be paid according to the amount of wages, which should reflect both the skill and productivity of the worker.[323] Bonuses should never be issued until the socio-economic unit is able to first provide for the basic needs of all.

During this phase, the education system in rural areas should be thoroughly reformed. To arouse the cooperative spirit among the people, there should be extensive training and education, but moral education must take precedence over everything else so that trust and the willingness to serve others is continually being strengthened between local people. In order for a samaj to succeed it is important that each person feels that their individual desires should not be met at the expense of the collective interest.[324]

Beside farmers' cooperatives, PROUT advocates the formation of other types of cooperatives, including producer and consumer cooperatives. Producer cooperatives include industries based upon pre- and post-agricultural production as well as non-agricultural industries. As in farmer cooperatives, there should be dividend earning shares, but no profit earning shares as in bank interest, otherwise these cooperatives will also become commercial enterprises. If there are profit earning shares, the spirit of the cooperative system will be destroyed and cooperatives will go back into the hands of the capitalists.[325]

So, it is vitally important that there must not be any preferential shares in any PROUT cooperatives, only dividend shares. Dividend shares earn a dividend which is defined as a return on the basis of the net profit earned by the organization.

Shareholders must be people of high morality. In cooperatives, voting rights should be on an individual basis and not on the basis of the number of shares a person holds. In capitalist countries, shares in cooperatives can be purchased and thus economic democracy becomes a farce because poor people cannot fight this system.

## Workers Incentives

The permanent solution to people's economic fear and uncertainty lies in the implementation of the cooperative system and the socialization of land, industries, trade and commerce. In order to keep labor relations congenial, a bonus system of work and piecework payments should be adopted. The harder and better the people work, the more income they will receive.

The bonus system of work and piece work payments are two different things. A particular amount earned by workers from the profit of the cooperative on the basis of their labor is called a bonus. Normally, the time involved in the production of goods can be viewed from three angles—the time allotted to complete some work; the actual time taken to complete some work; and the time saved to complete some work. In the PROUT bonus system, the calculation of the bonus is based upon the time saved to complete the work. The money value of this calculation is given to the workers. This is the incentive in the bonus system.[326]

Piecework payments are something else. If a piece of work is completed before the fixed time, and in the remaining portion of time extra work is done, then workers will get extra payment for that extra work. This system is called piecework payment. To take a concrete example, if the time allowed for manufacturing a scissors blade is two hours and the work is actually performed in one and a half hours, the payment for saving half an hour's time is called the piecework payment.

As workers receive greater incentives, they will try to manufacture more machines to reduce their labor time and gain more income accordingly. This is not the case in state capitalism because workers get fixed incentives which become part of their wages. In all cases, incentives should encourage workers to work harder and improve the quality of their work. Therefore all incentives should be directly linked to production. If this approach is followed, the per capita income and the standard of living of the workers will automatically increase as they work harder. And those who develop improved ways to increase production using the same amount of inputs will receive additional rewards. When work is done according to the bonus system and piece work payments, there are few, if any labor disputes.[327]

In this manner, people will increase their standard of living, even though production is for consumption, not profit. Farmer coops and industrial coops are all based on consumption. As such, profits will be minimized, so capitalists will not get the scope to exploit the workers. Wealth will be rationally distributed taking into consideration the collective need and the rewards for outstanding performance.

## Consumer Cooperatives

Consumer cooperatives should also be formed by like-minded persons who will share the income of the cooperative according to their individual labor and capital investment. Those who are engaged in the management of such cooperatives will also be entitled to draw salaries on the basis of the services they render to the cooperative. Consumer cooperatives will distribute consumer goods to members of society at reasonable rates that are set using the research of the social boards and trade industry boards. Consumer cooperative salaries will be commensurate with salaries of farmer and producer cooperatives.

Commodities can be divided into three categories—essential commodities such as vegetables, grains, salt, clothing; demi-essential commodities such as coconut oil and antiseptic soap; and non-essential commodities which include luxury goods such as jewelry, art, one-of-a-kind items etc. If hoarders create artificial shortages of non-essential commodities, the common people will not be affected, but if they hoard essential commodities, then the common people will suffer tremendously. This situation can be avoided if consumer cooperatives purchase essential commodities directly from producer cooperatives or agricultural cooperatives. This will eliminate the middle man and keep prices down on consumer goods.

In a local economy, people will have to watch for those who want to hoard essential commodities and create artificial scarcity in order to extract the maximum profit. Under capitalism, it is common for middle-men and profiteers to create artificial shortages or set monopoly pricing of essential commodities, knowing that people will certainly purchase them, even by taking on more debt, but few people will take loans to purchase luxury goods. If the distribution of essential commodities is done through consumer cooperatives that are controlled by local people, middlemen and profiteers will be eliminated.

Consumer cooperatives should be supplied with commodities from both agricultural and producers cooperatives. Commodities which do not go directly from agricultural cooperatives to consumer cooperatives should be refined by producer cooperatives. In addition, non-farming commodities should be compulsorily produced by producer cooperatives. For example, agricultural or producers cooperatives that produce cotton or silk thread, should sell the thread to weaver cooperatives, which can produce cloth on their power looms. Hand looms can also be used where intricate design work is required, but generally weaver cooperatives should install the latest power looms. The weaver cooperatives will, in turn, supply consumer cooperatives to sell their products.

The number of items considered essential commodities should be continually and progressively revised and expanded with the changes in time, space, and person. Such revisions should be made by the governing social boards and trade boards and not by the board of directors of a particular cooperative. What is considered a demi-essential commod-ity today may be treated as an essential commodity tomorrow. Demi-essential commodities, which may be affected by artificial shortages that cause suffering to the local people, should be produced by producer cooperatives.

Essential commodities or services of a non-farming nature that come within the scope of producer cooperatives, but which require huge capital investments, should be considered key industries and managed by the local government. The railway system is an example.[328]

So, for the establishment of a healthy society, agricultural cooperatives, essential commodity producer cooperatives and essential commodity consumer cooperatives are a must.

## Service Cooperatives

Aside from farmer cooperatives, producer cooperatives and consumer cooperatives there will also be service cooperatives in the local socio-economy. This type of cooprative will not be in the arena of producers or consumers cooperatives. Rather, they are a more subtle type of cooperative coming within the arena of cultural cooperatives.[329]

Let us take the example of doctors and dentists. Doctors and dentists should start service cooperatives. Suppose a doctor or dentist is not able to open his or her own practice, he or she may form a cooperative with five or ten other doctors. Such a cooperative is a service cooperative. Such cooperatives will cut expenses, allow for the purchase of more sophisticated technology and allow for research into natural medicines.

Besides service cooperatives, there are several other types of cooperatives which include banking cooperatives, housing cooperatives, and even educational cooperatives.

The cooperative is vital to secure the needs of the local people and allow for our intellectual and spiritual development. In order to redirect our thirst for limitlessness, there must be the following: (1) psycho-spiritual education, without which, society will remain balkanized, (2) rule by moralists, (3) ever increasing purchasing capacity, and (4) a balanced socio-economic structure.

## The Issue of Monetary Inflation

In capitalist economies, production is for the profit of the capitalist and the profit goes to individuals and corporations. In communist economies, the profit goes to the state exchequer and a microscopic fraction of the profit goes to the actual producers. In both cases, capitalism exists, and whenever fresh financial investment is required, money is printed and inflation takes place.

Under progressive socialism, the printing and issuing of monetary notes that are not backed by labor, raw materials, or gold and silver bullion will be stopped immediately. Any notes backed by bullion will be reissued with new shapes and colors. No monetary notes should be issued by the government from then on without a clear assurance that it is prepared to pay the requisite amount of money in bullion. This can only be implemented by a PROUT government. All trade between samajs will depend upon an exchange of goods of equal value, preferably by barter arrangements. In the event that this is not possible, gold and silver can be used. A limit to the discrepancy in the value of the goods exchanged should be set. If this percentage is violated, the creditor will have the right to demand payment in gold or silver.

Under capitalism, inflation is often caused by capitalists buying and selling currencies, bonds, and stocks. Under PROUT, the stock market will be eliminated. No local currency can then be manipulative by currency traders. Stocks will not be bought and sold on the market. Rather they will pay a dividend only to those who are working in cooperatives at the local level.

In a Proutist economy, where production is solely based upon consumption, there cannot be any fresh inflation because the money supply cannot be manipulated. Rather, money will be created locally according to the need of the local citizens for income and to create liquidity in their exchange of goods and services. In time, the existing inflation will gradually die out and the purchasing capacity and the minimum requirements of life will be guaranteed to the people.

## The Issue of Production Inflation

While monetary inflation can be cured in this manner, socio-economic units will also have to curtail production inflation. Production inflation may occur, owing to the application of scientific methods, or due to other reasons, and certain commodities may increase in excess of the demand or need in a particular socio-economic unit or region. Then it becomes a problem to market or consume this excess. This becomes particularly troublesome when the products are perishable or have a limited "shelf life."

Given excess production, the question will arise, "Will this excess production increase purchasing power and elevate the standard of the people or not." In general circumstances, such production may not be a big problem, not a chronic problem, but if no measure is taken to find a market for such overproduction, then it may become an acute problem. Such a problem can be addressed by taking three measures.

First, there should be a free trade system so that overproduction can be consumed by other economic units. This trade will occur under the same guideline of meeting needs not profit. Free trade will allow different SEUs having overproduction or underproduction problems to make respective adjustments among themselves so that the overproduction of commodities may be consumed by under-producing samajs or states. In that case, the concerned SEUs will be benefited. Here free trade means that there would not be any imposition of export or import duties, and thus the prices of these commodities will benefit the consumers when they reach the market for actual consumption.

Secondly, there should be proper arrangements made everywhere for the preservation of food products that can not be immediately consumed. Processing factories should develop the capacity to freeze, can, or dry food products to extend their shelf life.

Thirdly, new means of consumption can be invented. That is, consumption should be of a progressive nature and the means of consumption should be diversified. For example, there may be only a limited utilization of peanuts at the moment in a given samaj, but if the peanut oil can be extracted it can be used as an edible oil. Hemp is a good example of a raw commodity that can be used in diversified ways.

In the existing world structure, geo-sentiment is an obstacle to the implementation of free trade. Neither the capitalist countries nor the communist countries like the free trade system because it is detrimental to their respective self-interests. While capitalist countries may espouse "free trade" in actuality they place high tariffs on many produces especially from third world countries. There are some free trade zones in the world which are bright examples of the success of this sort of system. Singapore is one such example.[330]

In a PROUT economy there must not be any import or export duties on consumable commodities. If this is done, then this earth will greatly benefit. Having said this, we should remember, that in the initial stages of creating samajs, no raw materials or finished goods should be traded to other areas, unless the people within that samaj have their basic needs met in full.

## The Question of Unemployment

The question of unemployment arises only within the capitalist system where agricultural and industrial production is for the profit of those who own the means of production. Under these circumstances, it behooves the capitalists to reduce human labor as much as possible in order to increase their profits. Under progressive socialism, where agricultural and industrial production is for consumption and not for profit, the question of unemployment does not arise. Here the goal is one hundred percent employment of local people and the number of workers will never be lessened. Rather the working hours will be reduced for the same pay and the remaining hours will be used in mental and spiritual pursuits. The reduction in the working hours depends not only on the amount of production, but also on the demand for commodities and the availability of labor.[331]

To solve the unemployment problem, in both the short and long term, there must be an accurate understanding of the surplus and deficit manual and intellectual labor trends within the samaj area. Under capitalism, if there is surplus manual labor or intellectual labor, unemployment will be high. In most countries of the world, there is a surplus of manual labor. So, initially, most samajs will concentrate on creating industries that are labor intensive. In some instances, where there is a deficit of labor, due to an expanding industry, retraining programs may equip workers with the necessary skills for employment.

The more that local people support the local economy, the less unemployment there will be. But, if due to economic, political, or psycho-economic exploitation, people purchase finished goods made outside their socio-economic unit, rather than those made locally, then local developing industries may be forced to close down creating unemployment and other social and economic problems.

Another way to help solve unemployment, especially in rural communities, is to utilize plants and trees for economic self-reliance. All socio-economic units have the potential to increase their plant and crop varieties by properly matching them with the soil, topography, and climatic conditions etc. in their units. Reforestation can reclaim arid and semi-arid regions, and some unique plants like the fern, which has the capacity to attract clouds, can help radically transform the rainfall and weather patterns of a region. Agro- and agrico-industries based upon the productive potential of different plants can also help solve rural unemployment by creating a range of new goods and services. There are many dimensions to this revolutionary program to increase the utilization of plants at the local level that are consistent with the ideals of Universalism.[332]

The development of local industries, under progressive socialism, will provide immediate economic benefits. The unemployment problem will be rapidly solved, and, in a short time, it will be possible to create permanent full employment. In truth, the only way to solve the unemployment problem and bring about full employment throughout the world is by developing samaj level agriculturally-based industries. The growth of such local industries will provide real social security to the local people, not in the form of a dole, but in the form of secure employment within a strong, self-reliant community. This situation will create greater opportunities for people's all-round advancement, because all their basic needs will be met.

## The Question of Timing

The world is witnessing the end of the Capitalist Age. It is occurring because the capitalists, in their preoccupation for profit, have hoarded the wealth of the world and, in so doing, have set the stage for global depression. There are two main causes for economic depressions. The first is the concentration of wealth and the second is blockages in the turnover of money. When capital is concentrated in the hands of a few individuals, most people become the victims of a handful of exploiters. As a result of this process of severe exploitation, a depression in the economic world occurs. The concentration of wealth is the fundamental cause of this economic depression.

The second cause of the growing depression is that the corporations are sitting on great piles of cash, unwilling to invest in the economy because as the depression expands, they see less opportunity to profit. This stagnancy in the money supply causes the depression to deepen.

The capitalist do not even think about the impact that this will have on the common people. As such, the situation becomes so dangerous that there are fewer buyers to purchase commodities with each passing day. This results in surplus labor and deficit production leading to more businesses closing and more layoffs.

The global depression will not spare any country because in today's economy all countries depend upon each other for exports and imports. As such, the only way to stabilize society is to increase the production of basic necessities within localities and set up barter arrangements with other localities instead of using dollars.

Economic depression is not a natural phenomenon. Pause is a natural phenomenon, but not depression. Under progressive socialism pause may occur but depression will not occur. To save society from depression, the approach of PROUT is to increase purchasing power by reducing disparities in wealth, by increasing production, and by keeping money in circulation. Empty slogans, demagoguery, and mass rallies will not solve the problem. The people will have to organize themselves at the local level in order to meet their needs to get through the next financial crisis that has already begun. Attention must be paid specifically to increasing the production of those goods and services that meet basic needs.

In capitalist and communist countries, the mode of production is defective. In capitalist countries, management does not work in the interest of labor. Furthermore, the capitalists do not allow the circulation of money due to their hoarding and concentration of wealth. In communist countries, labor does not feel one with the job and that is why there is sluggish production.

The cooperative model of progressive socialism is free from these defects. It is well-adjusted with human ideals and human potential. Without PROUT, socio-economic emancipation will remain a utopian dream.

As we near the last stage of the Capitalist Era, now is the opportune moment for creating an all-around revolution. We should make an endeavor, beginning now, to shorten the time span of the growing global depression, to stop wars based on securing fossil fuels, and to stop the rapid degradation of the material world due to climate change. If we do this, before the decline steepens, we can avert the ultimate disaster, and accelerate the speed of social movement towards a positive goal. As the world passes through this most critical phase, we should be more active and create an impact. It is time to meet the neighbors next door, both to the left and the right of us.

Under progressive socialism (PROUT), a local socio-economy is built from the ground up by local people through the creation of an agricultural revolution. To summarize how to creates this revolution, a four-phase approach is required. During the first phase of agrarian revolution, management of all uneconomic landholdings should be taken over by cooperative management for the benefit of both those who own the land as well as the agricultural laborers who work in the cooperative. In the second phase, all landowners should be requested to join the cooperative system. In the third phase there should be rational distribution of land and redetermination of ownership. Finally, in the fourth phase there will be no conflict over the ownership of land. People will learn to think for the collective welfare rather than for petty self-interest. This psychic expansion will create a more congenial social environment. Such a change in the collective psychology will not come overnight, but will occur gradually according to the rational and intuitive development of the local people.

A system based on agrarian revolution and spiritual values will, in time, eliminate the present conflict between the capitalists and the people that presently destabilizes human society. The capitalists will lose control over the people, and with this development, social conflicts and environmental crises will be lessened and eventually eliminated.

# Appendix A: Eleven Principles of Progressive Development

In 1990, the Progress Agency developed the Eleven Principles of Progressive Development as an attempt to articulate the dimensions of a Universal Ideology as purported by Prabhat Rainjan Sarkar. The eleven points are:

1. Spiritual Unity (Love)

The entire creation, whether animate or inanimate, is an expression of one universal spiritual consciousness, which when realized reveals the unity of all things. The desire for spiritual unity (love) begins in the human mind as a thirst for limitlessness. Yet, human beings, not recognizing this thirst as a spiritual longing, try to fulfill it by pursuing finite objects—material accumulation, sense gratification and mental pleasure, which never completely satisfy. The realization of spiritual unity (love) is the supreme happiness of life, its ultimate fulfillment.

2. Transformation of Consciousness

The process of realizing spiritual unity occurs in the individual as a transformation from ignorance to enlightenment. This process is the evolution of individual consciousness and occurs in the collective as well. Regardless of different expressions, languages, and cultures, human beings are, in reality, a single species. This understanding poises humanity for an evolutionary leap that will allow us to realize, as a collective, that we are all members of one human family in relation with all of life.

## 3. Birthrights and Basic Necessities

In order to realize the greatest human potential, we must first meet certain basic necessities. It is the birthright of every human being to be guaranteed the opportunity to work for food, clothing, shelter, education, and health care. No one should suffer from lack of, or be denied, these basic necessities due to illness, calamity, fate or greed. It is also the birthright of every human being to receive love and care, and to live in a clean environment which promotes growth and well-being without fear.

## 4. Personal and Social Responsibility

It is our personal and collective responsibility to fight for improved living conditions worldwide. Moral life requires each individual to act in the best interest of the collective and, in turn, for the collective to act in the best interest of each individual. Each person must realize that, in fact, every thought, word, and action carries consequences. It is not necessary to "know all of the answers" to accept one's personal and social responsibility.

## 5. Utilization of Resources

To improve living conditions worldwide requires restructuring the utilization and distribution of individual, collective and planetary resources. These resources are physical, mental, and spiritual and include soil, water, air, ozone, minerals, plants, animals as well as all human potentialities. There is an abundance of resources to meet world needs including the power and information to realize world progress. Yet, we are handicapped by dogmatic thinking that keeps us in conflict with each other and the environment. It must be recognized that all resources have intrinsic existential value over and above their utility.

## 6. The Environment

For all practical purposes our environment is the planet Earth, a unique and complex eco-system in which all life forms exist within a critical balance. Our environment is more than a store of resources for human consumption; it has an inherent value as an expression of spiritual consciousness. Our progress and future survival is dependent upon its care and protection. The meeting of human needs and desires must be balanced with the rights of the Earth and all species for all to survive and prosper. It is our personal and collective responsibility to utilize appropriate technology, renewable resources, and methods of conservation and recycling for sustainability to ensure the protection of our environment for future generations.

## 7. Economics

The quality of life on Earth is being destroyed by conspicuous consumption, waste, and toxification due to human greed, cynicism, war, and ignorance. In reality, we work within a world economy in which goods and services are exchanged between people worldwide. There is a direct link between our economic behavior and the destruction of our planet. An economy which is based solely on the profit motive, without respect for human and natural resources, exploits and endangers life. A sustainable economy would allow for the ability of all to work for the provisions of basic necessities and amenities as well as promote individual incentive and expression without jeopardizing the collective and planetary well being. Moving society to an improved standard of living while protecting the environment is the goal of a sustainable economy.

## 8. Education

Because human development is the process of realizing spiritual unity, true education is the instruction of human beings toward this goal. Insofar as we are educated by the impressions of everything to which we are exposed, the educational process cannot be separated from the movement of society as a whole. Therefore, each individual shares responsibility for the spiritual development of others. The print, radio, film, TV media, and all forms of cultural and commercial expression also share the responsibility to promote human development. However the educational system, as the institutional representative of society, must take the lead in providing the social impetus for realizing the greatest human potential.  Along with teaching traditional academic studies, teachers who promote true human progress will provide the greatest service to society. Dogmatic thinking, which continues to divide humanity or which keeps us alienated from the rest of life, must be stopped.

## 9. Politics

The political arena is global in scope and is comprised of factions and forces that exist even down to the personal level. Political behavior to date has largely been the acting out of limited self-interests in which individual or group achievement comes at the expense of others. "Success" is predominately accomplished by imposing authority, interests, or simply by taking something that belongs to another. This type of behavior is antithetical to human progress on every level. It results in manipulation, greed and violence. The most aggressive and powerful human groups today control the Earth's resources and labor, and the "lion's share" of the production, distribution, and consumption of food, machinery, weapons, drugs, energy, money, etc. The motivating idea for benevolent politics, on the other hand, is to organize activities that are not at the expense of others, but are for the benefit of all. In order to maintain a balance of forces, humanity requires a global political institution based upon moral, universal human values. The formal expression of such an institution would be the establishment of global executive, judiciary, and legislative bodies to provide vision, planning, and the execution of those policies and procedures that empower and help humanity to grow while protecting the welfare of life. These global bodies would evolve from the ground up and would not be imposed top-down.

## 10. True Progress

Life is comprised of physical, mental, and spiritual attributes. Although there are improvements and advancements in the physical and mental realms, we recognize that every improvement or advancement in the physical and mental realms creates new sets of concerns and problems. As activity begets activity, the consequences of our actions forever "raise the stakes" forcing our hand to even greater levels of problem solving and conflict resolution. True progress is spiritual attainment and can be measured and recognized only by the increasing degree of love, devotion, and cooperative spirit that human beings realize for the care of themselves, each other, and all of life. The consequence of true progress is the overall advancement of humanity, thereby diminishing the condition of conflict and problems as a whole.

11. A New Vision - Spiritual and Social Synthesis

An entirely new vision for society is required that synthesizes spiritual and social values and integrates all aspects of individual and collective life. History demonstrates a largely unconscious attempt by individuals and groups to compensate for and fulfill the most fundamental human aspiration—to be happy and feel loved. We also recognize that human life is a weave of needs, desires, emotions, feelings, thoughts, and expressions most often complicated by fear. Fearing for survival, human beings desperately try to avoid pain, conflict, and death. Fear is the root of the problem that alienates and divides humanity into dogmatic, self-serving groups whose actions threaten the life of the planet. As human beings, we must accept total responsibility for creating the conditions of our reality and understand, therefore, there exists no problem greater than our capacity to solve. The most precious treasure that we possess is the capacity to love. Our vision needs to be centered on this treasure and displayed by the nurturing care of ourselves, each other, and all of life. It has been said that "the realization of spiritual unity (love) is the ultimate fulfillment of life." Spiritual unity (love) is the antidote to fear. Therefore, every aspect of society must support and be geared in this supreme direction. It is time to plan, implement, and maintain a complete spiritual-socio- economic system, a new way of living, which acknowledges humanity, protects the environment, cares for all life, and allows all to grow physically, mentally, and spiritually. This is the direction we must now take.

# Endnotes

1        Monika Kropej, *Supernatural Beings from Slovenian Myth and Folk Tales* (Ljubljana: Scientific Research Center of the Slovenian Academy of Sciences and Arts, 2012), 16, http://sms.zrc-sazu.si/pdf/Kropej_2012_Supp_06.pdf.

2        "Aborigine Creation Story," told by Aunty Beryl Carmichael, http://www.indigenouspeople.net/legend.htm.

3        "Comanche Creation Story," http://www.indigenouspeople.net/legend.htm.

4        Wikipedia, "Might Makes Right," last modified January 13, 2019, https://en.wikipedia.org/wiki/Might_makes_right.

5        Wikipedia, "Divine right of kings," last modified February 19, 2019, https://en.wikipedia.org/wiki/Divine_right_of_kings.

6        Here the word priest is used to refer to all the religious authorities, regardless of religion.

7        Wikipedia, "Classical liberalism," last modified February 21, 2019, http://en.wikipedia.org/wiki/Classical_liberalism.

8        Wikipedia, "Classical liberalism," last modified February 21, 2019.

9        P.R. Sarkar. "History and Superstition," *Prout in a Nutshell,* Volume 1 Part 4 (Ramnagar: Ananda Marga Publications, 1958), The Electronic Edition of the Works of P. R. Sarkar, Version 1.4.0.6., Ananda Marga Publications, 2009.

10       "United Nations Conference on Environment and Development (UNCED), Earth Summit," United Nations Sustainable Development Goals, https://sustainabledevelopment.un.org/milestones/unced.

11       See Appendix A for the "Eleven Principles of Progressive Development."

12       P. R. Sarkar, "The Significance of The Word 'Yuga," *Ánanda Vacanámrtam*, Part 9, (Kolkata: Ananda Marga Publications, 1979), The Electronic Edition of the Works of P.R. Sarkar, Version 1.4.0.6, Ananda Marga Publications, 2009.

13       P. R. Sarkar, "The Kśatriya Age." *Human Society Part 2* (Kolkata: Ananda Marga Publications, 1967), The Electronic Edition of

the Works of P.R. Sarkar, Version 1.4.0.6, Ananda Marga Publications, 2009.

14     P.R. Sarkar, "The Kśatriya Age." *Human Society Part 2.*

15     P.R. Sarkar, "The Kśatriya Age." *Human Society Part 2.*

16     P. R. Sarkar, "Nuclear Revolution," *Prout in a Nutshell,* Volume 4 Part 21 [a compilation] (Ranchi: Ananda Marga Publications, 1969), The Electronic Edition of the Works of P.R. Sarkar, Version 1.4.0.6, Ananda Marga Publications, 2009.

17     P. R. Sarkar, "Nuclear Revolution," *Prout in a Nutshell,* Volume 4 Part 21 [a compilation].

18     P.R. Sarkar, "The Kśatriya Age," *Human Society Part 2.*

19     P.R. Sarkar, "The Kśatriya Age," *Human Society Part 2.*

20     P.R. Sarkar, "The Kśatriya Age," *Human Society Part 2.*

21     P. R. Sarkar, "The Vipra Age," *Human Society Part 2* (Kolkata: Ananda Marga Publications, 1999), 180.

22     P. R. Sarkar, "The Vipra Age," *Human Society Part 2.*

23     P. R. Sarkar, "The Vipra Age," *Human Society Part 2,* 176.

24     P. R. Sarkar, "The Ksattriya Age," *Human Society Part 2,* 179.

25     P. R. Sarkar, "The Ksattriya Age," *Human Society Part 2,* 226-227.

26     P. R. Sarkar, "The Ksattriya Age," *Human Society Part 2,* 195-196.

27     P. R. Sarkar, "The Ksattriya Age," *Human Society Part 2,* 234.

28     "(Part Two) 5. Devadatta, the Buddha's Enemy," Life of the Buddha,     http://www.buddhanet.net/e-learning/buddhism/lifebuddha/2_5lbud.htm.

29     In 814, Louis the Pious upon his accession to the throne began to take very active measures against all sorcerers and necromancers, and it was owing to his influence and authority that the Council of Paris in 829 appealed to the secular courts to carry out any such sentences as the Bishops might pronounce. The consequence was that from this time forward the penalty of witchcraft was death, and there is evidence that if the constituted authority, either ecclesiastical or civil, seemed to slacken in their efforts the populace took the law into their own hands with far more fearful results. See http://en.wikipedia.org/wiki/European_witchcraft#Christianization_and_Early_Middle_Ages

30     P. R. Sarkar, "Women: The Wageless Slaves of the Vipras," *The Awakening of Women* [a compilation], (Kolkata: Ananda Marga Publications, 1967), The Electronic Edition of the Works of P.R. Sarkar, Version 1.4.0.6, Ananda Marga Publications, 2009.

31 P. R. Sarkar, "Women: The Wageless Slaves of the Vipras," *The Awakening of Women* [a compilation].

32 P. R. Sarkar, "The Vipra Age," *Human Society Part 2*, 203.

33 P. R. Sarkar, "The Vipra Age," *Human Society Part 2*, 183-184.

34 P. R. Sarkar, "The Vipran Age," *Human Society Part 2*, 188.

35 P. R. Sarkar, "The Vipran Age," *Human Society Part 2*, 213.

36 P.R. Sarkar, "The Vaeshya Age," *Human Society Part 2*, (Kolkata: Ananda Marga Publications, 1967), The Electronic Edition of the Works of P.R. Sarkar, Version 1.4.0.6, Ananda Marga Publications, 2009.

37 P. R. Sarkar, "The Vaeshya Age," *Human Society Part 2*.

38 "Brief history of the Frankfurt house, M A von Rothschild & Söhne," The Rothschild Archive, https://www.rothschildarchive.org/business/m_a_rothschild_sohne_frankfurt/.

39 See *The Untold Story of Western Civilization*, Volume 5, Chapter 2 regarding the capitalist description of intellectuals. Those who serve them, they call policy-oriented intellectuals, while those who criticize the capitalists are called value-oriented intellectuals.

40 Sirin Kale, "Two-Thirds of Young Women are Sexually Harassed at Work," VICE, August 10, 2016, https://broadly.vice.com/en_us/article/43gy39/two-thirds-of-young-women-are-sexually-harassed-at-work.

41 Jenavieve Hatch, "Watch a Man Call a Woman 'Hysterical' for Talking About Domestic Violence," Huffington Post, July 12, 2016, https://www.huffingtonpost.com/entry/watch-a-man-call-a-woman-hysterical-for-talking-about-domestic-violence_us_5784fecae4b0ed2111d78b05.

42 Alexandria Gomez, "Five Facts About Domestic Violence That May Surprise You," Women's Health, June 10, 1916, https://www.womenshealthmag.com/life/a19976721/domestic-violence-johnny-depp-amber-heard/.

43 See *The Untold Story of Western Civilization*, Volume 5, Chapter 2 for an in-depth look at this phenomenon.

44 See *The Untold Story of Western Civilization*, Volume 5, Chapter 1.

45 Examples include the Fukishima nuclear power plant, cigarettes, Bridgestone tires, Bopal, etc.

46 P. R. Sarkar, "The Vaeshya Age," *Human Society Part 2*, 269.

47 P. R. Sarkar, "The Vaeshya Age," *Human Society Part 2*, 199.

48      P. R. Sarkar, "The Vaeshya Age," *Human Society Part 2*, 199.

49      P. R. Sarkar, "The Vaeshya Age," *Human Society Part 2*, 255.

50      "The Enlightenment," Washington State University, March 11, 1998, https://brians.wsu.edu/?s=Enlightenment.

51      Wikipedia, "Classical liberalism," last modified February 21, 2019

52      Wikipedia, "Classical liberalism," last modified February 21, 2019

53      P. R. Sarkar, "Shúdra Revolution and Sadvipra Society," *Human Society Part 2*, (Kolkata: Ananda Marga Publications, 1999), 270-271.

54      P. R. Sarkar, "Shúdra Revolution and Sadvipra Society," *Human Society Part 2*, 272.

55      Michel Crozier, Samuel P. Huntington, and Joji Watanuki, T*he Crisis of Democracy: Report on the Governability of Democracies to the Trilateral Commission* (New York: New York University Press, 1975), 96-97, http://meteopolitique.com/fiches/democratie/oligarchie/Analyse/Claude Julien/crisis_of_democracy.pdf.

56      Kathleen Elkins, "9 charts that reveal how the American middle class has declined since 1970," Business Insider, Jan. 6, 2016, http://www.businessinsider.com/charts-decline-of-the-middle-class-2016-1.

57      P. R. Sarkar, "Shúdra Revolution and Sadvipra Society," *Human Society Part 2*, 276.

58      See Chapters 4 and 5 for a discourse on Prout Politics and Economics.

59      P. R. Sarkar, "Shúdra Revolution and Sadvipra Society," *Human Society Part 2*, 278.

60      P. R. Sarkar, "Shúdra Revolution and Sadvipra Society," *Human Society Part 2*, 279-280.

61      Shrii Shrii Anandamurti, "Dharma Sádhaná," *Ánanda Vacanámrtam*, Part 31, (Kolkata, Ananda Marga Publications, Date unknown), Discourse most likely given before 1978. The Electronic Edition of the Works of P.R. Sarkar, Version 1.4.0.6, Ananda Marga Publications, 2009.

62      Shrii Shrii Anandamurti, "Dharma Sádhaná," *Ánanda Vacanámrtam* Part 31.

63      Shrii Shrii Anandamurti, "Dharma Sádhaná," *Ánanda Vacanámrtam*, Part 31.

64      P. R. Sarkar, "Living Beings and Their Mentality (Discourse

5)," *The Liberation of Intellect: Neo-Humanism* (Kolkata, Ananda Marga Publications, 1982), The Electronic Edition of the Works of P.R. Sarkar, Version 1.4.0.6, Ananda Marga Publications, 2009.

65      "The Evolutionary Layers of the Human Brain," The Brain from Top to Bottom, April 28, 2020, http://thebrain.mcgill.ca/flash/d/d_05/d_05_cr/d_05_cr_her/d_05_cr_her.html.

66      "How the Brain Works," Brain Up!, April 28, 2020, http://www.brainupfl.org/2016/01/10/how-the-brain-works/.

67      "The Evolutionary Layers of the Human Brain," The Brain from Top to Bottom, April 28, 2020.

68      Marc Bekoff, "Do Animals Have Emotions?" Bark, February 2015, http://thebark.com/content/do-animals-have-emotions.

69      Regina Bailey, "The Amygdala's Location and Function in the Brain," ThoughtCo, January 20, 2019, http://biology.about.com/od/anatomy/p/Amygdala.htm.

70      "The Evolutionary Layers of the Human Brain," The Brain from Top to Bottom, April 28, 2020.

71      "Brain Structures and their Functions," Serendip Studio, https://serendipstudio.org/bb/kinser/Structure1.html, April 28, 2020.

72      David Robson, "A Brief History of the Brain," New Scientist, September 21, 2011, https://www.newscientist.com/article/mg21128311.800-a-brief-history-of-the-brain.

73      "The Evolutionary Layers of the Brain," The Brain from Top to Bottom, April 28, 2020.

74      Daniel Willingham, "Can I Learn to Think More Rationally?" Scientific American, March, 2017, https://www.scientificamerican.com/article/can-i-learn-to-think-more-rationally/.

75      P.R. Sarkar, *The Liberation of Intellect: Neo-Humanism*, (Kolkata, Ananda Marga Publications, 1982), 4.

76      P. R. Sarkar, "Devotional Sentiment and Neohumanism (Discourse 1)" *The Liberation of Intellect: Neohumanism*. (Kolkata: Ananda Marga Publications, 1982), The Electronic Edition of the Works of P.R. Sarkar, Version 1.4.0.6, Ananda Marga Publications, 2009.

77      P. R. Sarkar, "Geo-Sentiment (Discourse 3)," *The Liberation of Intellect: Neohumanism* (Kolkata: Ananda Marga Publications, 1982, The Electronic Edition of the Works of P.R. Sarkar, Version 1.4.0.6, Ananda Marga Publications, 2009.

78      P. R. Sarkar, "Geo-Sentiment (Discourse 3)," *The Liberation of*

*Intellect: Neohumanism.*

79      Warren J. Blumenfeld, "God and Natural Disasters: It's the Gays' Fault?" HuffPost, November 5, 2012, http://www.huffington-post.com/warren-j-blumenfeld/god-and-natural-disasters-its-the-gays-fault_b_2068817.html.

80      Jenna Johnson, "Donald Trump: They say I could 'shoot somebody' and still have support," The Washington Post, January 23, 2016, https://www.washingtonpost.com/news/post politics/wp/2016/01/23/donald-trump-i-could-shoot-somebody-and-still-have-support/?noredirect=on&utm_term=.1593b2582001.

81      P. R. Sarkar, "Exploitation and Pseudo-Culture (Discourse 7)," *The Liberation of Intellect: Neohumanism* (Kolkata: Ananda Marga Publications, 1982.

82      We use the term here to define a person who causes evil, harm, distress or ruin to others.

83      P. R. Sarkar, "Exploitation and Pseudo-Culture (Discourse 7)," *The Liberation of Intellect: Neohumanism.*

84      P. R. Sarkar. "Geo-Sentiment (Discourse 3)," *The Liberation of Intellect: Neohumanism* (Kolkata, Ananda Marga Publications, 1982), The Electronic Edition of the Works of P.R. Sarkar, Version 1.4.0.6, Ananda Marga Publications, 2009.

85      P. R. Sarkar, "Exploitation and Pseudo-Culture (Discourse 7)," *The Liberation of Intellect: Neohumanism.*

86      P. R. Sarkar, "Exploitation and Pseudo-Culture (Discourse 7)," *The Liberation of Intellect: Neohumanism.*

87      P. R. Sarkar, "Exploitation and Pseudo-Culture (Discourse 7)," *The Liberation of Intellect: Neohumanism.*

88      Valerie Tarico, "20 Vile Quotes Against Women By Religious Leaders From St. Augustine to Pat Robertson," AlterNet, June 30, 2013, http://www.alternet.org/gender/20-vile-quotes-against-women-religious-leaders-st-augustine-pat-robertson.

89      Wikipedia, "Liberation theology," last modified February 17, 2019, https://en.wikipedia.org/wiki/Liberation_theology.

90      Wikipedia, "Dakota Access Pipeline protests," last modified February 16, 2019, https://en.wikipedia.org/wiki/Dakota_Access_Pipeline_protests.

91      P. R. Sarkar, "Exploitation and Pseudo-Culture (Discourse 7)," *The Liberation of Intellect: Neohumanism.*

92      P. R. Sarkar, "Exploitation and Pseudo-Culture (Discourse 7),"
*The Liberation of Intellect: Neohumanism.*

93      P. R. Sarkar, "Pseudo-Humanism (Discourse 8)," The *Liberation of Intellect: Neohumanism* (Kolkata, Ananda Marga Publications,
1982, The Electronic Edition of the Works of P.R. Sarkar, Version
1.4.0.6, Ananda Marga Publications, 2009.

94      P. R. Sarkar, "Pseudo-Humanism (Discourse 8)," T*he Liberation of Intellect: Neohumanism.*

95      P. R. Sarkar, "Pseudo-Humanism (Discourse 8)," *The Liberation of Intellect: Neohumanism.*

96      P. R. Sarkar, "Sama-Samája Tattva (Discourse 6)," *The Liberation of Intellect: Neohumanism* (Kolkata,  Ananda Marga Publications,
1982), The Electronic Edition of the Works of P.R. Sarkar, Version
1.4.0.6, Ananda Marga Publications, 2009.

97      P. R. Sarkar. "Geo-Sentiment (Discourse 3)," *The Liberation of
Intellect: Neohumanism.*

98      P.R. Sarkar, "Living Beings and Their Mentality (Discourse 5),"
The Liberation of Intellect: Neohumanism.

99      P. R. Sarkar, "Awakened Conscience (Discourse 9)," *The Liberation of Intellect: Neohumanism* (Kolkata, Ananda Marga Publications, 1982, The Electronic Edition of the Works of P.R. Sarkar, Version
1.4.0.6, Ananda Marga Publications, 2009.

100     P. R. Sarkar, "Awakened Conscience (Discourse 9)," T*he Liberation of Intellect: Neohumanism.*

101     P. R. Sarkar, "The Four Types of Progress," *Ananda Vacanám-
rtam,* Part 31, (Kolkata, Ananda Marga Publications, date unknown),
The Electronic Edition of the Works of P.R. Sarkar, Version 1.4.0.6,
Ananda Marga Publications, 2009.

102     P. R. Sarkar, "Awakened Conscience (Discourse 9)," *The Liberation of Intellect: Neohumanism.*

103     P. R. Sarkar, "Exploitation and Pseudo-Culture (Discourse 7),"
*The Liberation of Intellect: Neohumanism.*

104     P. R. Sarkar, "Sama-Samája Tattva (Discourse 6)," *The Liberation of Intellect: Neohumanism.*

105     Matthew 22:37-40.

106     P. R. Sarkar, "Neohumanism Is the Ultimate Shelter (Discourse
11)," T*he Liberation of Intellect: Neohumanism* (Kolkata: Ananda Marga Publications, 1982), The Electronic Edition of the Works of P.R.

Sarkar, Version 1.4.0.6, Ananda Marga Publications, 2009.

107     P. R. Sarkar, "An Ideology for a New Generation (Discourse 10)," *The Liberation of Intellect: Neohumanism* (Kolkata: Ananda Marga Publications, 1982), The Electronic Edition of the Works of P.R. Sarkar, Version 1.4.0.6, Ananda Marga Publications, 2009.

108     P. R. Sarkar, "Bondages and Solutions (Discourse 2)," *The Liberation of Intellect: Neohumanism* (Kolkata: Ananda Marga Publications, 1982), The Electronic Edition of the Works of P.R. Sarkar, Version 1.4.0.6, Ananda Marga Publications, 2009.

109     P. R. Sarkar, "An Ideology for a New Generation (Discourse 10)," *The Liberation of Intellect: Neohumanism*.

110     P. R. Sarkar, "An Ideology for a New Generation (Discourse 10)," *The Liberation of Intellect: Neohumanism*.

111     P. R. Sarkar, "An Ideology for a New Generation (Discourse 10)," The Liberation of Intellect: Neohumanism.

112     P. R. Sarkar, "An Ideology for a New Generation (Discourse 10)," *The Liberation of Intellect: Neohumanism*.

113     P. R. Sarkar, "An Ideology for a New Generation (Discourse 10)," *The Liberation of Intellect: Neohumanism*.

114     P. R. Sarkar, "Bondages and Solutions (Discourse 2)," *The Liberation of Intellect: Neohumanism*.

115     P. R. Sarkar, "Bondages and Solutions (Discourse 2)," *The Liberation of Intellect: Neohumanism*.

116     P. R. Sarkar, "Bondages and Solutions (Discourse 2)," *The Liberation of Intellect: Neohumanism*.

117     P. R. Sarkar, "Neohumanism Is the Ultimate Shelter (Discourse 11)," The Liberation of Intellect: Neohumanism.

118     P. R. Sarkar, "Neohumanism Is the Ultimate Shelter (Discourse 11)," *The Liberation of Intellect: Neohumanism*.

119     See Julian Jaynes, T*he Origin of Consciousness in the Breakdown of the Bicameral Mind* (New York: Houghton Mifflin Harcourt Publishing Company, 2000.

120     See *The Untold Story of Western Civilization*, Volume I. pp 235-237.

121     See *The Untold Story of Western Civilization*, Volume I. pp 70-79.

122     Alfred North Whitehead, *Process and Reality* (New York: The Free Press, 1978), 344.

123     Wikipedia, "Origen," last modified April 26, 2020,   https://

en.wikipedia.org/wiki/Origen.

124     "Max Planck: 'Regard Consciousness as fundamental . . .'"http://bigthink.com/words-of-wisdom/max-planck-i-regard-conscious-ness-as-fundamental, originally from *The Observer*, January 25, 1931.

125     Quotetab, April 28, 2020, https://www.quotetab.com/quote/by-heraclitus/for-those-who-are-awake-the-cosmos-is-one.

126     P. R. Sarkar, *Elementary Philosophy*, p.1

127     Swami Krishnananda, "Everything About Spiritual Life, Chapter 5: The Nature and Control of the Senses" April 28, 2020, http://www.swami-krishnananda.org/everything/everything_05.html.

128     P. R. Sarkar, "What is Dharma," *Ananda Marga: Elementary Philosophy.*

129     "John Carew Eccles," New World Encyclopedia, April 28, 2020, http://www.newworldencyclopedia.org/entry/John_Carew_Eccles.

130     "John Carew Eccles," New World Encyclopedia, April 28, 2020131 http://www.spaceandmotion.com/Philosophy-Plato-Philosopher.htm.

132     J. R. Seydel "Cosmic Consciousness: Soul of the Soul," AbZu2, February 9, 2014, https://abzu2.wordpress.com/2014/02/09/cosmic-consciousness-soul-of-the-soul/.

133     R. Buckminster Fuller, *No More Second Hand God (Carbondale: Southern Illinois University Press,* May 1963), https://books.google.com/books?id=-p3gDQAAQBAJ&pg=PA30&lpg=PA30&dq=Bucky+Fuller+-+%22We+have+plenty;+we+have+the+means&source=bl&ots=oFm730PGag&sig=ACfU3U2oA4c61gORETA94aguoAxFrRybAg&hl=en&sa=X&ved=2ahUKEwjVnaXQ5IvpAhVuh-AKHbD0Bn0Q6AEwDHoECBUQAQ#v=onepage&q=Bucky%20Fuller%20-%20%22We%20have%20plenty%3B%20we%20have%20the%20means&f=false134.

135     Alexander Howard, "Paralyzed Man Can Feel Sense of Touch Through Mind-Controlled Robotic Arm," September 15, 2015, http://www.huffingtonpost.com/entry/robotic-arm-darpa-revolutionizing-prosthetics_us_55f740f8e4b09ecde1d971d9.

136     In his writings, Mr. Sarkar uses Sanskrit terms, which is the language of Tantra, to explain his ideology.  Although we will try to minimize the use of Sanskrit terms for the sake of clarity, they will appear frequently in quotes from Mr. Sarkar and at times we may also use these terms because their use may be more applicable than their

English equivalent.

137     P. R. Sarkar, "What is Dharma"? *Universal Humanism* (Jamal-pur, India: Ananda Marga Publications, 1955)

138     P. R. Sarkar, "What is Dharma"? p. 6

139     Peter Baska, "Can Our Brain Waves Affect Our Physical Re-alit/"? November 26, 2011, http://www.huffingtonpost.com/peter-bak-sa/-can-thoughts-manipulate-_b_971869.html.

140     Stephen Hawking, *The Grand Design* (New York: Bantam Books Trade Paperback Edition, 2012), 42-43.

141     Stephen Hawking, *The Grand Design,* 172.

142     Robert Lanza with Bob Berman, "'Biocentrism': How Life Cre-ates the Universe," http://www.nbcnews.com/id/31393080/ns/technol-ogy_and_science-science/t/biocentrism-how-life-creates-universe/#.Vu1bvccWVdl.

143     Amit Goswami, Richard E. Reed, Maggie Goswami, Fred Alan Wolf, *The Self-Aware Universe: How Consciousness Creates the Material World,* by http://www.goodreads.com/book/show/319015.The_Self_Aware_Universe.

144     P. R. Sarkar, *Elementary Philosophy*, p. 8.

145     Ralph Waldo Emerson, "The Over-Soul," April 28, 2020, http://www.emersoncentral.com/oversoul.htm.

146     Paul Davies, *God and the New Physics* (New York: Simon and Schuster, 1983), 69.

147     Raphael Demos, "Introduction to *Plato Selections*," 1927, http://www.ditext.com/demos/plato.html.

148     P. R. Sarkar, *Elementary Philosophy*, 10.

149     Duane Elgin, "We Live in a Living Universe," 2000, https://duaneelgin.com/wp-content/uploads/2010/11/we_live_in_a_living_universe.pdf.

150     David Pratt, "Consciousness, Causality, and Quantum Physics," 1997, https://www.bibliotecapleyades.net/esp_paradigmaholo06.htm.

151     Patrick Zeis, "20 Carl Jung Quotes That Spark Conscious Con-templation, July 16, 2018, Balanced Achievement, https://www.bal-ancedachievement.com/grow-more/carl-jung-quotes/.

152     Dr. Jay Lombard, *Mind of God* (New York: Harmony Books, 2017), 65.

153     P. R.Sarkar, "Concept of Guṅábhivyakti and Jadasphota," *Ánanda Vacanámrtam,* Part 33. (Jamalpur, India: Ananda Marga Pub-

lications, 1969).

154     Peter Russell, "Spirit of Now – Evolution of Consciousness," April 28, 2020, http://www.peterrussell.com/SCG/EoC.php.

155     P. R. Sarkar, *Elementary Philosophy*, p. 27.

156     Buckminster Fuller, *No More Second Hand God and Other Writings*, April 28, 2020, , https://archive.org/stream/NoMoreSecond-handGodAndOtherWritings/RBuckminsterFullerNoMoreSecond-handGodAndOtherWritings_djvu.txt.

157     Robert Lanza with Bob Berman, 'Biocentrism': How Life Creates the Universe, http://www.nbcnews.com/id/31393080/ns/technology_and_science-science/t/biocentrism-how-life-creates-universe/#.Vu1bvccWVdl.

158     Dr. Jay Lombard, *Mind of God*, 55.

159     Dr. Jay Lombard, *Mind of God*, 65.

160     Duane Elgin, "We Live in a Living Universe," 2000, https://duaneelgin.com/wp-content/uploads/2010/11/we_live_in_a_living_universe.pdf.

161     Dr. Jay Lombard, *Mind of God*, 119.

162     Bernard Haisch, "Is The Universe A Vast, Consciousness Created Virtual Reality Simulation?" 2014, http://www.thegodtheory.com/VRHaisch.pdf.

163     Bernard Haisch, Is The Universe A Vast, Consciousness Created Virtual Reality Simulation? 2014.

164     R. C. Henry, "The Mental Universe", *Nature* 436:29, 2005, http://www.collective-evolution.com/2015/11/11/physicists-say-consciousness-may-be-a-state-of-matter-the-non-physical-is-indeed-real/.

165     Wikipedia, "James Jean," last modified March 6, 2020, https://en.wikipedia.org/wiki/James_Jeans.

166     Bernard Haisch, Is the Universe a Vast, Consciousness Created Virtual Reality Simulation?, 2014, http://www.thegodtheory.com/VRHaisch.pdf.

167     Victoria Jaggard, "What is the Universe: Real Physics Has Some Mind-Bending Answers," Smithsonian.com, September 15, 2014, http://www.smithsonianmag.com/science/what-universe-real-physics-has-some-mind-bending-answers-180952699/?no-ist.

168     Gabriel Cohen, syndicated from spiritualhealth.com, May 6, 2013, http://www.dailygood.org/story/426/how-imagination-shapes-your-reality-gabriel-cohen/.

169    Duane Elgin, We Live in a Living Universe, 2000.

170    *The Untold Story of Western Civilization*, Book 1, Volume 2, 97.

171    P. R. Sarkar. *Elementary Philosophy*, 66.

172    Jerry Alatalo, "Peace On Earth: Where Nothing Ever Happens," The Oneness of Humanity, March 14, 2014, https://onenessofhumanity.wordpress.com/tag/wisdom-of-plato/.

173    P. R. Sarkar. "What Is My Relation with the Universe and the Cosmic Entity?" *Ananda Marga Elementary Philosophy*, (Kolkata: Ananda Marga publications, 1955).

174    P. R. Sarkar, "Psychic Assimilation in Psycho-Spiritual Practice" *Ananda Marga Ideology and Way of Life in a Nutshell* Part 9 [a compilation], (Bihar: Ananda Marga Publications, 1959).

175    P .R. Sarkar, "Shakti and Its Proper Application," *Ananda Marga Ideology and Way of Life in a Nutshell*, Part 9 [a compilation] (Jamalpur: Ananda Marga Publications, 1958).

176    For a discussion of the relationship between John the Baptist and Jesus see *The Untold Story of Western Civilization*, Book 1, Volume 2, Chapter 3, 180-187.

177    "The Church's Development of the Hell Myth," Yeshua before 30 CE, April 29,2020, http://30ce.com/developmentofhell.htm.

178    Vanamali Gita Yogashram, *The Complete Life of Krishna* (Rochester, VT: Inner Traditions, 2012), 379.

179    Dr. Jay Lombard, *Mind of God*, 98-99.

180    Dr. Jay Lombard, *Mind of God*, 48.

181    P. R. Sarkar, "Bondages and Solutions (Discourse 2)," *The Liberation of Intellect: Neohumanism* (Kolkata: Ananda Marga Publications, 1982).

182    Dr. Jay Lombard, *Mind of God*, 48.

183    See Sarkar's "Namah Shivaya Shantaya" for a description of Shiva's spiritual precepts and teachings.

184    Dr. Jay Lombard, *Mind of God*, 43.

185    Pagels, Kindle Book. Location 180 of 3931

186    Hippolytus, *Refutationis Omnium Haeresium 1*. cited in Pagels: 196 of 3931

187    Hippolytus, *Refutationis Omnium Haeresium 1*. cited in Pagels, 104-105

188    P. R. Sarkar. *Subhásita Samgraha*, Part 21. October 21, 1971 DMC, Ernakulam, (Kolkata: Ananda Marga Publications, October 21, 1971).

189     Irvin J. Boudreaux, "The Divine Window of Escape," A Pastor's Thoughts . . . monastics, mystics, and more. May 11, 2016, https://ijboudreaux.com/2016/05/11/the-divine-window-of-escape/.

190     Carlos Castaneda, *Tales of Power* (New York: Washington Square Press, 1991).

191     P. R. Sarkar. Intuitional Practice and Its Necessity, *Ananda Marga Elementary Philosophy* (Kolkata: Ananda Marga Publications, 1955).

192     "Spiritual Teacher Responsibility," Toltec, April 29, 2020, http://www.toltecspirit.com/four-agreements/spiritual-teacher/.

193     Joel and Michelle Levey, "The Dos and Don'ts of Picking a Spiritual Master," Huffpost, November 5, 2011, http://www.huffingtonpost.com/joel-michelle-levey/finding-a-spiritual-teach_1_b_949566.html.

194     P. R. Sarkar. *Elementary Philosophy*, 112-113

195     Wikipedia, "Desert Fathers, last modified April 24, 2020, https://en.wikipedia.org/wiki/Desert_Fathers.

196     "Paramahansa Yoganda Quotes on the Need for a Guru," Paramahansa Yogananda, April 29, 2020, http://www.yogananda.com.au/gurus/yoganandaquotes08.html.

197     Having said this, it is necessary to mention that the preservation of semen is necessary to nourish the nerve cells and nerve fibers, which allow one to develop firmness of mind and intellectual sharpness. This is why athletes do not like to have sex immediately before a sports event. They know that it temporarily drains their energy.

198     Dr. Alan Godlas, "Sufism's Many Paths," Sufism--Sufis--Sufi Orders, April 29, 2020, http://islam.uga.edu/Sufism.html. This site also has a very comprehensive link to websites that address all aspects of Sufism.

199     "Kabbalah Love; Quotes," L'AcademyOfLife.Org & KabbalaWisdom.org, April 29, 2020, https://kabbalahwisdom.org/kabbalah-love-quotes/.

200     If you live in the United States or Central America visit Ananda Marga - New York Sector, http://www.ampsnys.org/.

201     Duane Elgin and Coleen LeDew, "Global Consciousness Change: Indicators of an Emergin Paradigm," http://www.duaneelgin.com/wp-content/uploads/2010/11/global_consciousness.pdf.

202     Arjun Walia, "'Consciousness Creates Reality" – Physicists Admit The Universe is Immaterial, Mental & Spiritual," June 6, 2015, http://howtoexitthematrix.com/2015/06/01/consciousness-creates-reality-physicists-admit-the-universe-is-immaterial-mental-spiritual/.

203     Prabhat Rainjan Sarkar produced over 100 books on the subject of Intuitional Science.  See The Electronic Edition of The Works of P. R. Sarkar - V7.5, available at http://www.innersong.com/products/dharshan/ElectronicEdition.htm.

204     Wikipedia, "Politics," last modified March 1, 2019, https://en.wikipedia.org/wiki/Politics.

205     Wikipedia, "Code of Hammurabi," last modified February 27, 2019, https://en.wikipedia.org/wiki/Code_of_Hammurabi.

206     Wikipedia, "Politics," last modified March 1, 2019.

207     P. R. Sarkar, "The Human Search for Real Progress," *A Few Problems Solved* Part 6, (Allahbad: Ananda Marga Publications, 1967), The Electronic Edition of the Works of P. R. Sarkar, Version 1.4.0.6, Ananda Marga Publications, 2009.

208     P. R. Sarkar, "The Human Search for Real Progress," *A Few Problems Solved* Part 6.

209     P. R. Sarkar, "Virtue and Vice," *Human Society Part 1* (Kolkata: Ananda Marga Publications, 1959), The Electronic Edition of the Works of P. R. Sarkar, Version 1.4.0.6, Ananda Marga Publications 2009.

210     P. R. Sarkar, "Sin, Crime and Law," *Prout in a Nutshell* Volume 3, Part 12 [a compilation] (Kolkata: Ananda Marga Publications, 1986, The Electronic Edition of the Works of P. R. Sarkar, Version 1.4.0.6, Ananda Marga Publications, 2009.

211     Shrii Shrii Anandamurti, "Human Expressions and Human Movements," *Ánanda Vacanámrtam* Part 30 (Valencia: Ananda Marga Publications, 1979), The Electronic Edition of the Works of P. R. Sarkar, Version 1.4.0.6, Ananda Marga Publications, 2009.

212     P. R. Sarkar, "Talks on Prout," *Prout in a Nutshell* Volume 3, Part 15 [a compilation] (Ranchi: Ananda Marga Publications, 1961), The Electronic Edition of the Works of P. R. Sarkar, Version 1.4.0.6, Ananda Marga Publications, 2009.

213     P. R. Sarkar, "Talks on Prout," *Prout in a Nutshell* Volume 3 Part 15 [a compilation].

214     P. R. Sarkar, "The Three Causes of Sin." A Few Problems Solved Part 6.

215     P. R. Sarkar, "Social Discourses: Politicians," *The Thoughts of P. R. Sarkar* (a compilation) (Kolkata: Ananda Marga Publications, 1957 – 1981), The Electronic Edition of the Works of P. R. Sarkar, Version

1.4.0.6, Ananda Marga Publications, 2009.

216    P. R. Sarkar, "The Three Causes of Sin," *Prout in a Nutshell,* Volume 2  Part 8 [a compilation] (Muzaffarpur: Ananda Marga Publications, 1970), The Electronic Edition of the Works of P. R. Sarkar, Version 1.4.0.6, Ananda Marga Publications, 2009.

217    P. R. Sarkar, "The Three Causes of Sin," *Prout in a Nutshell,* Volume 2  Part 8 [a compilation].

218    P. R. Sarkar, "Democracy and Group Governed States," *Prout in a Nutshell,* Volume 3, Part 14 (a compilation), (Kolkata: Ananda Marga Publications, 1988), The Electronic Edition of the Works of P. R. Sarkar, Version 1.4.0.6, Ananda Marga Publications, 2009.

219    For a deeper understanding of this situation read *The Untold Story of Western Civilization,* Volume 5, Chapter 1.

220    P. R. Sarkar, "Economic Democracy," *Prout in a Nutshell,* Volume 4, Part 21 [a compilation] (Kolkata: Ananda Marga Publications, 1986), The Electronic Edition of the Works of P. R. Sarkar, Version 1.4.0.6, Ananda Marga Publications, 2009.

221    P. R. Sarkar, "The Importance of Society," *A Few Problems Solved* Part 3 (Kolkata: Ananda Marga Publications, 1978), The Electronic Edition of the Works of P. R. Sarkar, Version 1.4.0.6, Ananda Marga Publications, 2009.

222    P. R. Sarkar, *Problems of the Day* (Bhagalpur: Ananda Marga Publications, 1958), The Electronic Edition of the Works of P. R. Sarkar, Version 1.4.0.6, Ananda Marga Publications, 2009.

223    P. R. Sarkar, "The Future of Civilization," *A Few Problems Solved* Part 6.

224    P. R. Sarkar, "The Future of Civilization," *A Few Problems Solved* Part 6.

225    P. R. Sarkar, "The Significance of Language," *Prout in a Nutshell,* Volume 4, Part 17 [a compilation] (Kolkata: Ananda Marga Publications, 1989), The Electronic Edition of the Works of P. R. Sarkar, Version 1.4.0.6, Ananda Marga Publications, 2009.

226    P. R. Sarkar, "The Importance of Society," *A Few Problems Solved* Part 3.

227    P. R. Sarkar, "Dialectical Materialism and Democracy," *A Few Problems,* Solved Part 2 (Kolkata: Ananda Marga Publications, Date unknown), The Electronic Edition of the Works of P. R. Sarkar, Version 1.4.0.6, Ananda Marga Publications, 2009.

228    P. R. Sarkar, "Democracy and Group Governed States," *Prout in a Nutshell*, Volume 3, Part 14 [a compilation].

229    P. R. Sarkar, "Discourses on Prout," *Prout in a Nutshell*, Volume 1, Part 5 [a compilation] (Jamalpur: Ananda Marga Publications, 1959), The Electronic Edition of the Works of P. R. Sarkar, Version 1.4.0.6, Ananda Marga Publications, 2009.

230    P. R. Sarkar, "Discourses on Prout," *Prout in a Nutshell*, Volume 1, Part 5 [a compilation].

231    P. R. Sarkar, "Discourses on Prout," *Prout in a Nutshell*, Volume 1, Part 5 [a compilation].

232    P. R. Sarkar, "Social Values and Human Cardinal Principles," *A Few Problems Solved* Part 2 (Kolkata:  Ananda Marga Publications, 1970), The Electronic Edition of the Works of P. R. Sarkar, Version 1.4.0.6, Ananda Marga Publications, 2009.

233    P. R. Sarkar, "Form and Formlessness," *Ananda Marga Ideology and Way of Life in a Nutshell*, Part 7 [a compilation] (Bhagalpur: Ananda Marga Publications, 1957), The Electronic Edition of the Works of P. R. Sarkar, Version 1.4.0.6, Ananda Marga Publications, 2009.

234    P. R. Sarkar, *A Guide to Human Conduct* (Jamalpur: Ananda Marga Publications, 1957), The Electronic Edition of the Works of P. R. Sarkar, Version 1.4.0.6, Ananda Marga Publications, 2009.

235    P. R. Sarkar, *A Guide to Human Conduct*.

236    P. R. Sarkar, "You Are Not Helpless," *Ánanda Vacanámrtam*, Part 7 (Patna: Ananda Marga Publications, 1979), The Electronic Edition of the Works of P. R. Sarkar, Version 1.4.0.6, Ananda Marga Publications, 2009.

237    The above presentation of the moral tenets is largely taken from P. R. Sarkar's *A Guide to Human Conduct*.

238    P. R. Sarkar, "Problems of the Day," *Prout in a Nutshell*, Volume 1, Part 4 [a compilation].

239    P. R. Sarkar, "Sadvipra Boards," *Prout in a Nutshell*, Volume 4, Part 18 [a compilation] (Ranchi: Ananda Marga Publications, 1969), The Electronic Edition of the Works of P.R. Sarkar, Version 1.4.0.6, Ananda Marga Publications, 2009.

240    P. R. Sarkar, "Sadvipra Boards," *Prout in a Nutshell*, Volume 4, Part 18 [a compilation].

241    P. R. Sarkar, "Discourses on Prout," *Prout in a Nutshell*, Volume 1, Part 5 [a compilation].

242    P. R. Sarkar, "Discourses on Prout," *Prout in a Nutshell,* Volume 1, Part 5 [a compilation].

243    P. R. Sarkar, "Talks on Prout," *Prout in a Nutshell,* Volume 3, Part 15 [a compilation].

244    P. R. Sarkar, "Problems of the Day," *Prout in a Nutshell,* Volume 1, Part 4 [a compilation].

245    P. R. Sarkar, "Requirements of an Ideal Constitution," *Prout in a Nutshell,* Volume 3, Part 12 [a compilation] (Kolkata: Ananda Marga Publications, 1986), The Electronic Edition of the Works of P. R. Sarkar, Version 1.4.0.6, Ananda Marga Publications, 2009.

246    P. R. Sarkar, "Sin, Crime and Law," *Prout in a Nutshell,* Volume 3, Part 12 [a compilation].

247    P. R. Sarkar, "Justice," *Human Society Part 1* (Kolkata: Ananda Marga Publications, 1959), The Electronic Edition of the Works of P. R. Sarkar, Version 1.4.0.6, Ananda Marga Publications, 2009.

248    P. R. Sarkar, "Social Discourses: The Penal Code," T*he Thoughts of P. R. Sarkar* (a compilation).

249    P. R. Sarkar, "Justice," *Human Society Part 1.*

250    P. R. Sarkar, "Science and Population Control – Excerpt D," *The Awakening of Women* [a compilation] (Ranchi: Ananda Marga Publications, 1961). The Electronic Edition of the Works of P. R. Sarkar, Version 1.4.0.6, Ananda Marga Publications, 2009.

251    P. R. Sarkar, "Justice," *Human Society Part 1.*

252    P. R. Sarkar, "Justice," *Human Society Part 1.*

253    P. R. Sarkar, "Justice," *Human Society Part 1.*

254    Jeffrey J. Selingo, "Wanted: Factory Workers, Degree Required," The New York Times, January 30, 2017, https://mobile.nytimes.com/2017/01/30/education/edlife/factory-workers-college-degree-apprenticeships.html?utm_source=pocket&utm_medium=email&utm_campaign=pockethits&_r=0&referer=https://getpocket.com/.

255    Michael J. Hicks and Srikant Devaraj "The Myth and the Reality of Manufacturing in America," Ball State University, Center for Business and Economic Research, 2015, https://conexus.cberdata.org/files/MfgReality.pdf.

256    Heather Long, "U.S. has lost 5 million manufacturing jobs since 2000," CNN Business, March 29, 2016, http://money.cnn.com/2016/03/29/news/economy/us-manufacturing-jobs/.

257    See *The Untold Story of Western Civilization,* Volumes 4 and 5

for an in-depth analysis of capitalist objectives and their impact on the working class.

258     "Statistics About Diabetes," American Diabetes Association, 2020, http://www.diabetes.org/diabetes-basics/statistics/.

259     "Heart Disease," CDC National Center for Health Statistics, January 19, 2017, https://www.cdc.gov/nchs/fastats/heart-disease.htm.

260     "Obesity Statistics in the United States," National Conference of State Legislatures, September 4, 2014, https://www.niddk.nih.gov/health-information/health-statistics/Pages/overweight-obesity-statistics.aspx.

261     Dada Maheshvarananda, After Capitalism: Economic Democracy in Action (San German, Puerto Rico: InnerWorld Publications, 2012), 62-66.

262     P. R. Sarkar, "Talks on Prout: The Five Fundamental Principles of Prout," *Prout in a Nutshell*, Volume 3, Part 15 [a compilation].

263     "Groups and Projects," Transition Town Totnes, April 29, 2020, https://www.transitiontowntotnes.org/.

264     P. R. Sarkar, "Decentralized Economy – 1," *Prout in a Nutshell*, Volume 4, Part 21 [a compilation] (Kolkata: Ananda Marga Publications, 1982), The Electronic Edition of the Works of P. R. Sarkar, Version 1.4.0.6, Ananda Marga Publications, 2009.

265     P. R. Sarkar, "The Significance of Language," *Prout in a Nutshell*, Volume 4, Part 17 [a compilation] (Kolkata, Ananda Marga Publications, 1989), The Electronic Edition of the Works of P. R. Sarkar, Version 1.4.0.6, Ananda Marga Publications, 2009.

266     Amitai Etzioni, "Communitarianism," Communitarianism-Institute for Communitarian Policy Studies, 2015, 4, https://icps.gwu.edu/sites/g/fijles/zaxdzs1736/downloads/Communitarianism.Etizioni.pdf.

267     David DeGraw, "The Economics of Revolution," *Part I: Peak Inequality: The .01% and the Impoverishment of Society* (New York: David McGraw, 2014), http://daviddegraw.org/peak-inequality-the-01-and-the-impoverishment-of-society/#society.

268     David DeGraw, The Economics of Revolution, *Part I: Peak Inequality: The .01% and the Impoverishment of Society*.

269     Ivana Kottasova, "These 8 men are richer than 3.6 billion people combined," CNN Business, January 17, 2017, http://money.cnn.com/2017/01/15/news/economy/oxfam-income-inequality-men/.

270      P. R. Sarkar, "The Importance of Society," *A Few Problems Solved,* Part 3.

271      P. R. Sarkar, "Quadri-Dimensional Economy," *Prout in a Nutshell,* Volume 3 Part 12 [a compilation] (Kolkata: Ananda Marga Publications, 1986).

272      P. R. Sarkar, "Quadri-Dimensional Economy," *Prout in a Nutshell,* Volume 3, Part 12 [a compilation].

273      P. R. Sarkar, "The Transformation of Psychic Pabula into Psycho-spiritual Pabulum," *A Few Problems Solved,* Part 8, (Kolkata: Ananda Marga Publications, 1986), The Electronic Edition of the Works of P. R. Sarkar, Version 1.4.0.6, Ananda Marga Publications, 2009.

274      "Commercial Economy," Business Dictionary, April 29, 2020, http://www.businessdictionary.com/definition/commercial-economy. html.

275      . P. R. Sarkar, "Socio-Economic Groupifications," *Prout in a Nutshell,* Volume 3, Part 13 [a compilation] (Kolkata, Ananda Marga Publications, 1979), The Electronic Edition of the Works of P.R. Sarkar, Version 1.4.0.6, Ananda Marga Publications, 2009.

276      Wikipedia, "The Accursed Share," last modified July 12, 2017, https://en.wikipedia.org/wiki/The_Accursed_Share.

277      P. R. Sarkar, "Quadri-Dimensional Economy," *Prout in a Nutshell,* Volume 3, Part 12 [a compilation].

278      P. R. Sarkar, *The Awakening of Women* (a compilation). Available at http://anandamargabooks.com/portfolio/the-awakening-of-women/.

279      See *The Untold Story of Western Civilization,* Volume 5, Chapter 6.

280      P. R. Sarkar, "Developmental Planning," *Prout in a Nutshell,* Part 15 (Kolkata: Ananda Marga Publications, 1979), The Electronic Edition of the Works of P. R. Sarkar, Version 1.4.0.6, Ananda Marga Publications, 2009.

281      P. R. Sarkar, "Developmental Planning," *Prout in a Nutshell,* Part 15.

282      P. R. Sarkar, "Decentralized Economy – 1," *Prout in a Nutshell,* Volume 4, Part 21 [a compilation] (Kolkata: Ananda Marga Publications, 1982), The Electronic Edition of the Works of P. R. Sarkar, Version 1.4.0.6, Ananda Marga Publications, 2009.

283      P. R. Sarkar, "Decentralized Economy – 1," *Prout in a Nutshell,* Volume 4, Part 21 [a compilation].

284    P. R. Sarkar, "Cooperatives," *Prout in a Nutshell,* Volume 3, Part 14 [a compilation] (Kolkata: Ananda Marga Publications, 1988), The Electronic Edition of the Works of P. R. Sarkar, Version 1.4.0.6, Ananda Marga Publications, 2009.

285    P. R. Sarkar, "Cooperatives," *Prout in a Nutshell,* Volume 3, Part 14 [a compilation].

286    P. R. Sarkar, "Cooperatives," *Prout in a Nutshell,* Volume 3, Part 14 [a compilation].

287    P. R. Sarkar, "Some Specialities of Prout's Economic System," *A Few Problems Solved,* Part 9 (Kolkata, Ananda Marga Publications, 1979), The Electronic Edition of the Works of P. R. Sarkar, Version 1.4.0.6, Ananda Marga Publications, 2009.

288    P. R. Sarkar, "Socio-Economic Movements," *A Few Problems Solved,* Part 9.

289    P. R. Sarkar, "Talks on Prout," *Prout in a Nutshell,* Volume 3, Part 15 [a compilation].

290    P. R. Sarkar, "Talks on Prout," *Prout in a Nutshell,* Volume 3, Part 15 [a compilation].

291    P. R. Sarkar, "Some Specialities of Prout's Economic System," A *Few Problems Solved,* Part 9.

292    SHARE is a creation of Bob Swann of the BF Schumacher Center for a New Economics that also created a local currency and an agricultural trust as a means for making financial resources available to local people to develop their own economy. See SHARE, Microcredit Program, http://centerforneweconomics.org/content/share-microcredit-program

293    P. R. Sarkar, "Decentralized Economy – 1," *Prout in a Nutshell,* Volume 4, Part 21 [a compilation].

294    "Local Currencies Program," Schumacher Center, April 29, 2020, http://www.centerforneweconomics.org/content/local-currencies?gclid=CMaH5cuKyNICFYEYgQodWTEFHA.

295    P. R. Sarkar, "Decentralized Economy – 1," *Prout in a Nutshell,* Volume 4, Part 21 [a compilation].

296    P. R. Sarkar, "Decentralized Economy – 1," *Prout in a Nutshell,* Volume 4, Part 21 [a compilation].

297    "Groups and Projects," Transition Town Totnes, April 29, 2020, https://www.transitiontowntotnes.org/

298    P. R. Sarkar, "Prama – 1/Dynamic Equilibrium and Equipoise,"

*A Few Problems Solved*, Part 8 (Kolkata: Ananda Marga Publications, 1987), The Electronic Edition of the Works of P. R. Sarkar, Version 1.4.0.6, Ananda Marga Publications, 2009.

299     "LETS - Local Exchange Trading Systems," April 29, 2020, Transaction Net, http://www.transaction.net/money/lets/.

300     "ROCS - a Robust Complementary Community Currency System, Transaction Net, April 29, 2020, http://www.transaction.net/money/rocs/#issue.

301     Wikipedia, "Barter," last modified January 20, 2019, https://en.wikipedia.org/wiki/Barter.

302     See Berkshares Inc., Local Currency for the Berkshire Region, April 29, 2020, http://www.berkshares.org/ for a good example.

303     "SHARE Microcredit Program," Schumacher Center, April 29, 2020, http://www.centerforneweconomics.org/content/share-micro-credit-program.

304     Wikipedia, "Revolving Loan Fund," last modified November 19, 2018, https://en.wikipedia.org/wiki/Revolving_Loan_Fund.

305     Wikipedia, "Credit union," last modified February 22, 2019, https://en.wikipedia.org/wiki/Credit_union.

306     Wikipedia, "Rural economics," last modified February 23, 2019, https://en.wikipedia.org/wiki/Rural_economics.

307     See "The Totnes Food Link Project," Transition Town Totnes, April 29, 2020, https://www.transitiontowntotnes.org/groups/food-group/food-link-project/.

308     "Local Economic Blueprint," Totnes REconomy Project, April 29, 2020, https://reconomycentre.org/home/economic-blueprint/.

309     Wikipedia, "Totnes," last modified December 9, 2018, https://en.wikipedia.org/wiki/Totnes.

310     P. R. Sarkar, "Cooperatives," *Prout in a Nutshell*, Volume 3, Part 14 [a compilation].

311     P. R. Sarkar, "Multi-Purpose Development Schemes," *Prout in a Nutshell*, Volume 4, Part 18 [a compilation],(Kolkata: Ananda Marga Publications, 1989), The Electronic Edition of the Works of P.R. Sarkar, Version 1.4.0.6, Ananda Marga Publications, 2009.

312     P. R. Sarkar, "Multi-Purpose Development Schemes," *Prout in a Nutshell*, Volume 4, Part 18 [a compilation].

313     P. R. Sarkar, "Multi-Purpose Development Schemes," *Prout in a Nutshell*, Volume 4, Part 18 [a compilation].

314    P. R. Sarkar, "Multi-Purpose Development Schemes," *Prout in a Nutshell*, Volume 4, Part 18 [a compilation].

315    Wikipedia, "Millennials," last modified April 29, 2020, http://en.wikipedia.org/wiki/Millennials

316    P. R. Sarkar, "," *Prout in a Nutshell*, Volume 4, Part 19 (Kolkata: Ananda Marga Publications, 1989), The Electronic Edition of the Works of P. R. Sarkar, Version 1.4.0.6, Ananda Marga Publications, 2009.

317    "Ananda Nagar: An Integrated Rural Development Project," April 29, 2020, http://www.anandanagar.org/.

318    The level of specific details that Mr. Sarkar shared in his lectures and strategies was extraordinary. He made the following comment about growing fruits from seedlings: "The seedlings should be grown until they are one and a half feet tall. The plants should then be uprooted and their roots soaked in water for half an hour. Next, the main root of each plant should be cut off one inch below the base of the plant, and the remaining roots should again be soaked in water for ten minutes. The plants should then be planted in a field or packed for distribution. Plants which are prepared in this way will produce large, sweet fruits. The fruits will be better than those produced from seedlings, but not as good as those produced from grafted plants."

319    P. R. Sarkar, "Integrated Farming," *Ideal Farming*, Part 2 (Kolkata, Ananda Marga Publications, 1988), The Electronic Edition of the Works of P. R. Sarkar, Version 1.4.0.6, Ananda Marga Publications, 2009.

320    P. R. Sarkar, "Cooperative Production," *Prout in a Nutshell*, Volume 3, Part 14 [a compilation] (Kolkata, Ananda Marga Publications, 1988), The Electronic Edition of the Works of P. R. Sarkar, Version 1.4.0.6, Ananda Marga Publications, 2009.

321    P. R. Sarkar, "Agrarian Revolution," *A Few Problems Solved*, Part 2 (Kolkata, Ananda Marga Publications, date unknown), The Electronic Edition of the Works of P. R. Sarkar, Version 1.4.0.6, Ananda Marga Publications, 2009.

322    P. R. Sarkar, "Questions and Answers on Economics – Excerpt C," *Proutist Economics* [a compilation] (Kolkata, Ananda Marga Publications, Date unknown), The Electronic Edition of the Works of P. R. Sarkar, Version 1.4.0.6, Ananda Marga Publications, 2009.

323    P. R. Sarkar, "Cooperatives," *Prout in a Nutshell*, Volume 3, Part 14 [a compilation].

324     P. R. Sarkar, "Farmers Cooperatives," *Prout in a Nutshell*, Volume 4, Part 20 [a compilation] (Kolkata, Ananda Marga Publications, 1982), The Electronic Edition of the Works of P. R. Sarkar, Version 1.4.0.6, Ananda Marga Publications, 2009.

325     P. R. Sarkar, "Questions and Answers on Economics – Excerpt C," *Proutist Economics* [a compilation].

326     P. R. Sarkar, "Questions and Answers on Economics – Excerpt C," *Proutist Economics* [a compilation].

327     P. R. Sarkar, "Talks on Prout," *Prout in a Nutshell*, Volume 3, Part 15 [a compilation].

328     P. R. Sarkar, "Cooperatives," *Prout in a Nutshell* ,Volume 3, Part 14 [a compilation].

329     P. R. Sarkar, "Talks on Prout," *Prout in a Nutshell*, Volume 3, Part 15 [a compilation].

330     P. R. Sarkar, "Economic Dynamics," *A Few Problems Solved*, Part 9 (Kolkata: Ananda Marga Publications, 1987).

331     P. R. Sarkar, "Discourses on Prout." *Prout in a Nutshell*, Volume 1, Part 5 [a compilation].

332     P. R. Sarkar, "Socio-Economic Movements," *A Few Problems Solved*, Part 9 (Kolkata: Ananda Marga Publications, 1984).

# Index

# About the Authors

Charles Paprocki has spent many years working with troubled teenagers, prison inmates, welfare recipients, and migrant workers in the human services system. He also owned a graphics and advertising agency in New York City where he combined his skill and knowledge to create social marketing campaigns. He was one of the core leaders to create the Universal Pre-K program in New York State and the local food movement in Illinois. His last work was to manage an organic farm in southern Illinois. He has consulted with international NGO's on management strategies and participated in the Earth Summit in Brazil and the Social Summit in Denmark. He is now retired and living in Carbondale, Illinois.

Tom Paprocki has worked several years in social services, including starting a preschool and daycare center in rural southern Illinois and serving as an administrator for a drug education and crisis center. After receiving a Masters in Public Administration, he was hired by the NASA Goddard Space Flight Center as a Presidential Management Intern. He served thirty years at Goddard, which included positions as head of Personnel, Procurement, and Institutional Resources. He spent the next seven years as Director of Management Operations, which included facilities, acquisitions, environmental and health services, security, and logistics for the research and launch facilities at Greenbelt, Maryland and Wallops Island, Virginia. He is now retired living in Dunkirk Maryland.

www.ingramcontent.com/pod-product-compliance
Lightning Source LLC
Chambersburg PA
CBHW030234030426
42336CB00009B/91